TORMENT SAINT

Handbook of Psychobiography (2005; editor)

Tiny Terror: Why Truman Capote (Almost)
Wrote Answered Prayers
(Inner Lives series)

An Emergency in Slow Motion:
The Inner Life of Diane Arbus

TORMENT SAINT

THE LIFE OF
ELLIOTT SMITH

WILLIAM TODD SCHULTZ

B L O O M S B U R Y

NEW YORK · LONDON · NEW DELHI · SYDNEY

Published by Bloomsbury USA, New York

All papers used by Bloomsbury USA are natural, recyclable products made from wood grown in well-managed forests. The manufacturing processes conform to the environmental regulations of the country of origin.

LIBRARY OF CONGRESS CATALOGING-IN-PUBLICATION DATA

Schultz, William Todd.
    Torment saint : the life of Elliott Smith / William Todd Schultz. —First U.S. edition.
        pages cm
    Includes bibliographical references.
    ISBN 978-1-60819-973-0 (alk. paper)
    1. Smith, Elliott, 1969–2003.   2. Rock musicians—United States—Biography.   I. Title.
    ML420.S668S38 2013
    782.42166092—dc23
    [B]

                                                                2013014534

First U.S. Edition 2013

1 3 5 7 9 10 8 6 4 2

Typeset by Westchester Book Group
Printed and bound in the U.S.A. by Thomson-Shore Inc., Dexter, Michigan

For Adrienne

"For him, personally, his song is only a scream. Art for the artist is only suffering, through which he releases himself for further suffering. He is not a giant, but only a more or less brightly plumaged bird in the cage of his existence."

—KAFKA

"What is a poet? An unhappy man who hides deep anguish in his heart, but whose lips are so formed that when the sigh and cry pass through them, it sounds like lovely music . . . And people flock around the poet and say: 'Sing again soon'—that is, 'May new sufferings torment your soul but your lips be fashioned as before, for the cry would only frighten us, but the music, that is blissful.'"

—KIERKEGAARD

The intellect of man is forced to choose
Perfection of the life, or of the work
And if it take the second must refuse
A heavenly mansion, raging in the dark.

—YEATS

CONTENTS

INTRODUCTION **THE SMITH MYTH**

I was standing on the concrete floor of storage locker 2010, near the Silver Lake portion of Los Angeles, surrounded by songwriter Elliott Smith's things, and wondering where to turn to find him. He was here somewhere, but he was gone too, eight years gone, simultaneously present and absent, a strained melody. To the left was a plastic tub filled with T-shirts, many worn in performances. His personal vinyl records—*Elliott Smith*, *Either/Or*, *XO*—still in cellophane wrappers, were filed neatly in a cardboard box, five or six copies of each. Books piled up nearby, underlined and with notes in margins—*Physicians' Desk Reference*s spanning several years, various fiction titles, an analysis of the effects of abuse on young boys. A bag beside the books contained prescription bottles, medications still inside—Serzone (for depression), Klonopin (for anxiety and seizures), Strattera (for ADHD). An electric guitar leaned on a stand, amplifiers and mixing boards ran up the right wall. Then there were his writings, scribbled on the backs of legal documents, on napkins, on random torn-off sheets of paper and Pee-Chee folders. I sat down and read through a hastily written but still lucid treatise on existence and nothingness, another on the failure of language to capture experience ("Language is like Legos: fun to work with but less useful"). Songs were also included, handwritten, in nascent or variant versions, original drafts to "Say Yes," "King's Crossing," "Between the Bars," and "A Distorted Reality's Now a Necessity to be Free," the last on sketch paper with what looked to be a cigarette burn in the center. All these things reposed, the life's debris, its residue, the possessions of a person no longer around to animate them. Outside it rained hard; it would do so all day and night.

There are too many Elliott Smiths to count, too many anybodys to count, self a bulging multiplicity. There's Texas Elliott, Portland Elliott, New York Elliott, Silver Lake Elliott. There's Elliott in a basement on a hill, underground with a stellar view. There's Elliott between bars, Elliott in the studio, Elliott in his Prada suit, "dollared up in virgin white" at the Oscars. He's clean, he's wasted; he's paranoid, he's lucid; he's fragile, in search of some situation where he's better off than dead, or he's a butterfly, spending the day higher than high. He's drinking fortified green concoctions for his health, he's extinguishing lit cigarettes in his flesh. He's alive in the music and he's dead, finding no good reason not to do it.

Which of these Elliotts is true, and which false? Are some more real than others, closer to the core? Those who never knew him, or knew him slightly, or only heard his music, which is all that remains now, are left with one, inevitably final option. We are interpreters. We are pattern finders. That is biography. It's the connective tissue between facts. It's the plot inferred, spread over messy, desultory life. It's a true fiction. One approach was suggested by Elliott himself in the song "Stickman." Spin the world on its flipside, and "listen backwards for meaning." It may be the only path. It's not possible to listen forward anymore.

Elliott was disarmingly bright, according to everyone who knew him, an avid reader of Dostoevsky, Kafka, Beckett, Stendhal, Freud, the Buddha, all of whom destabilized notions of identity. I think he knew how little we know about who we are. The idea comes through in lyrics. "I don't know who I am," he says simply; at times he wishes he were no one. He's a stickman shooting blanks at emptiness, living with "one dimension dead." He's an invisible man with a see-through mind. He's a junkyard full of false starts. He's a ghostwriter, feeling hollow. "I lost my plot in a game of shells," he writes in an early draft of "King's Crossing." There's a sense, comforting and commonsensical, that if we want to know about someone, all we need to do is ask him. It's not that easy. Sometimes he doesn't know. Sometimes he doesn't want to know. As Elliott said summarily: "Confusion is King/It's the talk of my town."

In any case, Elliott Smith is gone, dead from two knife wounds to the heart in October 2003.[1] If he had any answers, in a spasm of insight, any light to shed on the origins of his art—the astonishingly accomplished music he left behind—we can't ask for them now. But that doesn't mean we can't know anything. We can. It's there in the art, the music, where he lived most freely, most fearlessly, most authentically. The music keeps telling us who he is.

And what the music elicits—in me, in most everyone who hears it and takes to it—is a strangely comforting, sensual melancholy, a gentle sadness, the kind that comes with soft rain. It's the same for all truly great dark art. There's a pleasure in seeing our shadows paraded beautifully. It's liberating to find them so prettily decked out, a sort of reverse Halloween. The repressed returns and it actually looks and sounds good. Like other shadow-driven artists—Sylvia Plath, for instance, or Diane Arbus—Elliott struggled with childhood traumas. He turned trauma into visionary aesthetic achievements—the art was trauma-fueled, trauma-determined. When Elliott died, he was hard at work recording songs for a double-album magnum opus on the order, he hoped, of the Beatles' *White Album*. This was to be a brand-new sound, full of unpretty noise, more corrosive and biting than anything he'd done before. If the songs seemed perfect he worked, according to David McConnell, who was there in the studio as Elliott assembled tracks, to fuck them up.[2] It was a kind of disfigurement. He was turning the pretty inside out, finding the ugly in it. He was turning himself inside out.

There are closer, more recent comparisons too (beyond Plath and Arbus), ones Elliott was asked about frequently while he was alive, as if, for interviewers, making sense of him required figuring out how he was not some simple, uninteresting duplication of what had gone before. By far the most obvious is Kurt Cobain, who died in 1994, when Elliott was 25 (Cobain was born in 1967, Smith in 1969). This was the year Elliott released his first solo album, *Roman Candle*, recorded on a four-track with a borrowed Le Domino guitar. Jennifer Chiba, Smith's girlfriend at the time of his death, says Elliott romanticized and envied Cobain's suicide. One night he actually dreamed of Courtney Love, according to a different friend. The context was sexual, but more too: Love signified fame. To have *her*, he realized later in thinking the dream over, was to have *it*. The Cobain obsession was less about Kurt, per se, than about what Kurt had managed to achieve, against pretty heavy odds. Plus, Cobain died at an apex. He built up a fabulous city, then blew it to hell—an atavistic impulse Elliott explored in the song "A Passing Feeling." He gets into the same subject in draft lyrics for "King's Crossing," where an unnamed judge, appointed for life, delivers the following verdict: everyone should die in their prime.

Cobain was a talented child, a gifted artist with a room full of carefully drawn cartoon characters (Aquaman, Donald Duck, Goofy). His parents divorced when he was eight, and it scarred him. He saw his mother and father as betrayers. The suicide option appeared early on; at age 15 he made a home movie titled "Kurt Cobain Commits Bloody Suicide."

Just like Elliott, Cobain was drawn to the Beatles. He started singing "Hey Jude" by age two. His posthumously published journals mention John Lennon as an idol. In the 1980s he moved on to punk. Buzz Osborne of the Melvins—also from Aberdeen, Washington, Cobain's hometown—turned him on to Black Flag and Bad Brains. The Pixies he connected with "so heavily that I should have been in that band"; he wrote "Smells Like Teen Spirit" in an attempt to "rip off" their singular alternating soft and loud dynamics, a musical form one finds in a number of Nirvana tracks.

It's uncanny, the points of intersect between Smith's and Cobain's biographies. Both lived in the rainy, dreary Pacific Northwest, a climate that virtually breeds depression. (In fact, in 2008 *Business Week* ranked "unhappiest cities" in the United States; Portland was number 1, Seattle number 20.) Both rejected the jock mentality of peers with whom they felt they had nothing in common. Daringly for high schoolers, Smith and Cobain befriended gay classmates. Cobain, in an interview with the *Advocate*, identified himself as "gay in spirit": "I started being really proud of the fact that I was gay even though I wasn't." He relished pissing off homophobes, or anything else vaguely connected to mainstream, censorious attitudes. Both endured early divorce, its resulting feelings of abandonment and loss of security showing up regularly in songs. The songs were sometimes self-denigrating. Jarring for its time, Lennon wrote "I'm a Loser"; Cobain declared "I think I'm dumb" over and over in "Lithium"; Smith called himself "damaged bad at best."

Kurt's parents remarried, like Elliott's did, and the new families occasioned resentment. The dark leitmotif of Elliott's early life was a prevailing sense of mistreatment. Same for Cobain, who witnessed domestic violence against his mother, once hospitalized with a broken arm. Then there's the most important parallel of all. Smith and Cobain transmogrified emotional trauma, twisted it into art. Anger and sadness were replaced by words and melodies. Music was a liminal space, a poultice, a confession made to millions. The way in became a way out; it worked, it had the potential to heal, for a time. But the darkness got darker, more devouring. And somehow, for some reason, along the way it overpowered any creative use that might be made of it. It was a killer. Drugs were a neutralizer, they delivered a comforting nothingness, but they too were more death, a way of not feeling—which Elliott equated to failure—a way of not being alive.

There are two broad avenues for making sense of these commonalities. Milieu is one, the prevailing mid-1980s zeitgeist. Smith and Cobain played and hung out in the same clubs and bars, they absorbed similar punk, indie, anything-goes aesthetics. Satyricon, for instance, named after the Fellini film, was opened in 1983 by former cab driver George Touhouliotis in Portland's Chinatown, a "real shithole" of a neighborhood with open drug dealing, fights, knives, guns.[3] "A mere attempt to walk the sidewalks . . . required a helmet and full body armor," recalls local historian SP Clarke.[4] Heroin dealers, addicts, sociopaths, homeless, the mentally ill—all manner of malcontents loitered about in an atmosphere of chaos and incipient violence. Venturing into the club was genuinely scary; the fear and risk made the music more legit, more authentically vanguard. Most important bands came through the place, including Nirvana, Pearl Jam, Mudhoney, the Wipers, Dead Moon, Everclear, and later, Elliott's Heatmiser—in short, "any group that was worth its weight in flannel, leather, or torn denim."[5] "It was the Reagan era," recalls booker Chris Monlux, "it was kind of a punk-rock time." Touhouliotis wasn't so much interested in the music. He was drawn, instead, to the culture, what the bands seemed to represent, which he characterized as freshness, realness. "God loves freshness," he said. "He hates repetition." Sam Coomes, who had come to Portland from San Francisco in the wake of The Donner Party, and who played with Elliott in Heatmiser after replacing original bassist Brandt Peterson, refers to the mid-80s as "the heroin days": "It was more outré or something . . . It was truly underground. The people who frequented places like Satyricon were real fanatics."[6] The goal, according to dancer Kitty Diggins, was mayhem. "We always had carte blanche to do whatever we wanted to do." Club regular Fernando Viciconte remembers one emblematic night when the theme happened to be porn. Twelve TV sets transmitted sex acts onstage; offstage mushroom tea circulated. In this atmosphere of ubiquitous hardcore, Viciconte picked up a guitar with three strings, connected to a "small, shitty

Peavey amp." He wasn't feeling it, so he pulled down his pants and toyed with his balls on a chair. "I played three songs naked in front of mushroomed folks. I'd been in town a week."[7]

The myth, or reality, is that Cobain met Courtney Love at Satyricon (relevant memories are hazy). Not particularly personable and introverted by nature, Cobain, says Touhouliotis, never said anything. He was "in the back with most of his face covered with hair." Nirvana bass player Krist Novoselic did all the talking; Touhouliotis in fact initially pegged Krist as the band's frontman. Locating the birth of the so-called grunge movement is tricky, to say the least, but many point to 1989, when then unheard-of Nirvana opened at Satyricon for the up-and-coming Dharma Bums (in time, the relative statuses of the bands would be reversed).[8] Another "local-locus" for grunge-minded units was Belmont's Inn on Portland's east side. The sound there was more acoustic-tinged, however, a style "borne out of bands practicing in basements across the area," necessitated also by strict club rules concerning volume levels in residential areas.[9]

Neither Elliott nor Cobain had the slightest interest in minimizing their punk roots. Elliott described his first successful band, Heatmiser, as "fist in the air, post-punk." He went on to say, "The thing I liked about punk in the first place is still alive in my head, that kind of angle on things, that you have to keep changing, and not get stuck in a little box. And not become, like, a connoisseur of yourself."[10] Punk's air of revolt and protest, its condemnation of conformity and mediocrity, also informed Elliott's earliest songwriting. He recalls, in an interview from 1998: "When I first started to make up lyrics, they were bad high school poetry about, you know, complaining about all the emphasis on money and power, and how people don't care about creativity, or all the guys on the bus in suits, and everybody's got the same overcoat, and everybody looks the same. I had green hair, and I just couldn't understand how everybody shopped in the same stores and worked in the bank. It just seemed totally boring."[11] In one sense, boredom *created* punk. Punk was an antidote, a DIY eruption, a sometimes only ostensibly musical version of Ginsberg's "Howl." Of course, once Elliott went solo, it wouldn't be long before his gently sad songs were categorized as folk, a comparison Elliott detested. Near the end of his life Cobain, too, was headed in an "ethereal, acoustic" direction. He'd been punk, he'd been a rock 'n' roll god. Both left him dissatisfied. He was particularly disturbed by fame, temperamentally unsuited for it. Plus, his music was an attack on the mind-set most of his fans embodied. They were the very people he excoriated in songs. This put him in a catch-22. "He talked a lot about what direction he was heading in," R.E.M. singer Michael Stipe said. "I know what the next Nirvana record was going to sound like. It was going to be very quiet, with lots of stringed instruments."[12] Cobain had a plane ticket and a car to pick him up. He and Stipe planned on recording a trial run. But at the last minute Kurt called to say he wasn't going to make it. Soon after, he was dead.

As for Satyricon's era, Coomes offers this summary: "People used to come to those shows to get loose and lose their shit. Now the motivations are different—they come to make YouTube videos on their iPhones. I don't know what the fuck is going on . . . The older people today are complaining that the kids are too well-behaved and clean and commercialized. It's a strange turn of events."[13] Kitty Diggins adds, "[We] weren't trying to be cool, [bands] didn't care about being signed or anything like that. They were just a bunch of fucking weirdos and dorks and geeks that were creating strange music and strange performances. I don't see that happening at this point."[14]

So there are sociological explanations for the similarities of style and attitude between Elliott and Cobain. But there are psychological factors at work, too. Early divorce, remarriage, abuse, a native shyness, a sensitivity and perceptiveness, emerging depression, anger—these elements required, for both, the construction of a specific sort of armor. The armor included thoughts of suicide, acts of self-harm, and the use of drugs as a means of dulling emotional pain. What saved Elliott and Cobain, what allowed them to stay alive as long as they did, was the gift. These were two exceptionally talented people. They put biography to use. It was a source of pain, but it was raw data. It was malleable, it could be reworked, it was at once actual and metaphorical. And it spoke powerfully to others with similar life histories who saw Elliott and Cobain as interpreters. The art was a revision of a damaged personal past, a release of pent-up feeling that fans vicariously shared. It almost made the suffering worth it.

There's one last shared detail. It has its own convoluted sociological and psychological derivations. Elliott and Cobain both died violently. For ardent fans, or even mild ones, the shock was brutal, yet also, in the weeks and months following, untenable. Either because they didn't believe it, or didn't want to believe it, they constructed, with extraordinary zeal and industriousness, alternate scenarios. These weren't suicides, fans claimed, but murders. Chiba killed Elliott, Love killed Cobain, according to subsets of followers. Heroes don't die, especially not shamefully, weakly. They are called to adventure, which they accept humbly, reluctantly; some magical helper, in this case genius, propels them into dangerous, unknown worlds; there they are tested, transformed; they resurface, finally, to share wisdom with the world, reborn, made whole, stronger, visionary. In most formulations of the hero journey, a particularly apposite obstacle presents itself: female temptation. A seductress must be pushed aside. This is where hurt and angry fans bore down. With remarkably durable hatred, expressed daily on message boards, blogs, and websites, the evil harpy is made to pay. She did it. She's the destroyer. The hero is a blameless victim of wrongdoing. The hero stays pure. The hero is martyred.

Cobain's one approximate doppelganger. But another name comes up too, a more oblique referent, the English singer-songwriter Nick Drake, who died in November 1974, when Elliott was just five. Elliott recalled hearing a little of Drake and liking him, but he felt Drake was softer lyrically, less focused on hard, painful realities, despite the fact that, on most days, Drake's life was exactly that—frequently hard, frequently painful. With a phrase some have applied to Elliott, who was routinely asked about his "depressing" songs or what it felt like to be such a "sad sack," one of Drake's orchestral arrangers, Robert Kirby, calls Drake "the patron saint of the depressed." Others say he came to represent a certain type of "doomed romantic" musician in the U.K. music press, a "shadowy tragic figure who nobody ever knew." He was an enigma, not so much by choice, but by necessity.

Performing was traumatic for Drake (as it was for Smith, who would sometimes throw up before going on stage). There were occasions when he simply walked off in the middle of gigs, unable to overcome feelings of vulnerability. "The folkies did not take to him," a friend says. "They wanted songs with choruses. They completely missed the point. He didn't say a word the entire evening. It was actually quite painful to watch. They must have known they weren't going to get sea-chanties and sing-alongs at a Nick Drake gig!"

By the time of *Pink Moon*, his final album, Drake was smoking massive amounts of marijuana. Soft signs of psychosis appeared, connected either to the drug use, his depression (which can sometimes include psychotic features), or, according to some, an incipient schizophrenia. Drake wanted the record to be "him more than anything." Producer John Wood says it is "probably more like Nick than the other two records. He was very determined to make this very stark, bare record."

The release was a disappointment, sales poor. By this time Drake had grown markedly asocial. Out of necessity he returned to his parents' home, and life there revolved around his moods and needs. He rarely slept; his parents would wake to hear him shuffling around the house at all hours of the night. Then in 1972 he broke down completely and had to be hospitalized for five weeks.

Anger emerged shortly thereafter, a somehow liberated demon. "I had told him he was a genius, he said," Wood wrote in an autobiography. "[Then] why wasn't he famous or rich? The rage must have festered beneath this inexpressive exterior for years." Either because of an inability to form and keep them or a sexuality many have wondered about, Drake's relationships with women were tentative, few, and entirely chaste. A week before his death a woman who identifies herself as a "best (girl) friend" tried ending the relationship. "I couldn't cope with it," she says. "And I never saw him again." Drake died, according to a coroner's inquest, of "acute amitriptyline poisoning—self-administered." The drug is a so-called tricyclic antidepressant, dangerous in overdose because of its cardiac-related side effects. As with Elliott, it's not entirely clear what happened. The parents were asleep at the time. In light of the serious, ongoing psychological difficulties and the loss of relationship, suicide seemed likely. On the other hand, some believe the overdose was unintentional, an attempt to defeat a ferocious, depression-related insomnia. "I'd rather he died because he wanted to end it," his sister says, "[rather] than it [being] the result of a tragic mistake . . . a plea for help that nobody hears."

Just as Cobain's did, Drake's life and art links up with Elliott's. There's the music—unadorned, melancholic, personal, not folk by any means, but not exactly rock 'n' roll either, a difficult-to-categorize, idiosyncratic self-expression.[15] Then there's the life, beset by emotional difficulties and relationship unsuccess. Drugs were a way out; they worked for short periods. The music worked too. It was a way of saying in art what was unsayable in life, a truth that was almost too true, a declaration the life wasn't always strong enough to absorb. At the end, no one knows for sure what actually happened. Drake was alone in a sleeping house.

By now it is a ready-made cliché—the rock star dying young, whether by excess, by accident, or by suicide. For some, it's part of the act, macabre performance art, a final song. This last mode, suicide, can be elusive. In fact, it almost always is. It might masquerade as excess—reckless, immoderate drug use. There is subintentioned suicide too. The person may simultaneously wish to live and die. No special effort is made to stay alive, but none is made to keep living, either outcome perfectly acceptable.[16] In July 2011 another name was added to the ledger: Amy Winehouse. She was found dead in her London apartment, at the dreadful age of 27—just like Jim Morrison, Brian Jones, Janis Joplin, Jimi Hendrix, Kurt Cobain. Commentators now speak of a "27 Club," as if these losses obey some hidden or avoidable calculus. They don't. No one or no thing is reaching out from the beyond to pluck megastars. The commonality is youth, combined with talent, creativity, experimentation, and a gradually evolving tendency to numb emotional pain and vulnerability, of the sort many artists confront chronically, with drugs and alcohol. If there is any calculus at all, the formula describes addiction, a monstrous taskmaster. Elliott sang, in one song, of waiting for sedation to disconnect his head. The head to be disconnected was too turned on. Art has its relentless elements. It is an unending draw.

But whatever its proximate causes, the loss list is long and sad and hard to accept. There's an impulse to start adding up all the masterpieces never recorded, works deleted by death. What would they all have become, how would the work have grown and changed, to what degree might they have overcome early conflicts, early weaknesses and insecurities, the baggage they'd been dragging uphill, had they managed, somehow, by effort or by chance, to live? We don't know. Imagining possible futures only deepens the sadness, the sense of what could have been. Also, what they left behind is finite. New songs turn up now and then, recordings thought lost or bootlegs of live performances, but what remains is exhaustible. It can't be mined forever. At some future date the process of discovery will end, then it's all rediscovery, which brings its own thrill and excitement, but not the sort that comes from freshness, newness, the next album.

Drake, Cobain, and Elliott Smith are part of the saddest of sad confederacies. All young, all shy, all fragile, all enormously gifted, all dead by apparent suicide, although Smith's case is officially unresolved, and in Drake's uncertainty remains about whether he intended to end his life. They were also in frequent emotional pain, and that reality, a baseline state, found its way into the music. Drugs equaled forgetting, but the art equaled remembering, so the cycle repeated itself. One other affinity is this—there was a feeling, shared by family, friends, and loved ones, that Cobain and Elliott, in particular, needed to be rescued from themselves. Death left a residue of guilt and failure among survivors. They share the blame. They could have done more. They let it happen. Or so they believe.

So affinities were plentiful and sometimes startling in their specificity. But this is a book about Elliott Smith. The question is, What set him apart? What's different about him? In what ways was he *not* like anyone else?

An immediate impulse, one countless critics have a hard time setting aside tactfully, is to say he was just plain good, his songs different and ineffably *more than* those written and recorded by most others—more realized, more composed, more finely structured. It's the same thing many of his friends, most of them extraordinarily gifted themselves—people like Tony Lash, for instance, and Sean Croghan—also say. Elliott was, in their estimation, the very best musician, the best songwriter, they ever knew. It is possible, though not easy, to identify the next Kurt Cobain, perhaps even the next Nick Drake, or for that matter the next Jim Morrison or Janis Joplin. There really is no next Elliott Smith.[17] Elliott adored the Beatles from an early age. A quality he sometimes seemed to share with them was this: he could not write a bad song.[18] It's an overused phrase, but Elliott was the total package. He had an incredible melodic sensibility, a sophisticated musical sense—a taste—that is instantly arresting. Even when his subjects are ugly—drug use, suicide, worthlessness—they sound disarmingly gorgeous. An example is the song "Abused," which tackles a topic obviously taboo in pop, but cloaks it in pretty higher-register phrasings. Somehow a delicacy comes through; one sings along almost nervously, given the lyrics' hideousness. But the impulse is irresistible. Smith was aware of his talent for beautiful sounds. It came too easy. It was unstoppable. So there were occasions when he undermined it. As noted before, he tried, especially in his later years, "fucking songs up."[19] The instinct at work was most likely boredom. The urge was to do something new, something different, to make sounds that did not come naturally or easily. Photographer Diane Arbus had a similarly gory aesthetic. To her, art had to be difficult to get, even physically. She had made up her mind about an almost naively simple equation: easy was bad art, difficult was good art. When it came easily, she found ways to muck it up.[20]

That Elliott wrote beautiful songs about painful or heinous experiences is a tendency he shares with Cobain, who often did the same (as in "Rape Me" or "Lithium"). Part of the appeal *is* the incongruity, the mismatch between words and melody. But the beauty in Elliott is more pronounced, more reliable. In some mysterious way it also seems more ingrained, part of a broader mode of being in the world. Again, it was easy because it was natural.

The music was extraordinarily accomplished. But the other part of the package was the words adorning it. Elliott was a brilliant thinker, a bona fide intellectual. He read widely and studied philosophy and modern systems of thought at Hampshire College, including poststructuralism, feminism, and feminist legal theory. He was interested in language, how words captured or failed to capture experience, their uses and limits. His sensitivity to and awareness of these matters lent his lyrics a complexity, an originality hard to categorize or compare. Songwriters like Bob Dylan—whose work Smith admired, especially the album *Blood on the Tracks*—or Joni Mitchell come to mind. But something about Elliott is *sui generis*. Parts of Dylan are nonsense. Riveting, imagistic nonsense—as in *Highway 61 Revisited*—but nonsense all the same, wordplay for the sake of wordplay, not always or principally in the service of meaning. And Mitchell could be fey, pretentiously poetical, a quality Elliott avoided entirely.[21]

Elliott certainly could be Dylanesque—abstract, symbolic, image driven. Songs like "Junk Bond Trader" and "Strung Out Again" conjure *High-*

way 61–style apocalypses, with skinny Santas, evil emperors, and parliaments of owls. He could also be Mitchellesque—delicate, attuned to subtler emotions. Yet in his core Elliott was a realist. The words have a sharp, hard edge. Most of the time he's looking at particulars, describing something actual. It is always imbued with shades of feeling, but it's tied to the world—situations, people, relationships. Punk-folk is one way to describe the aesthetic. There is an element of protest, of contempt, and the cultivation of an outsider viewpoint. Apocalyptic folk might be another. Never does one get the sense in Elliott's songs that anything is going to turn out right in the long run. He was no Pollyanna. He was sadder, but he was also wiser.

Like most good art, and all great art, Elliott's words combine directness and clarity with essential obscurity. They are simple and incomprehensible. They make immediate sense and then, on second listen, make no sense at all. They leave listeners wanting to know more. A line like "Her momma called me a thief/and her dad called himself commander in chief" appears to reference actual sets of relationships, but it does so at one remove. The context is personal, maybe autobiographical, but the vehicle is allusion, abstraction, metaphor. The critical consensus is that Smith was exceptionally open in his songs, self-disclosing. He also hides in them. He's there to be known, but he's also not there. He was a realist—tied to a world of fact—and he was a magical realist, especially later in his career, concocting incredible settings and imagery in which the personal achieved exaggerated representation. This was intentional. Elliott feared cliché. He feared being labeled, stuck in a box. So what he did, purposely, was confuse. In some instances the songs amounted to "sonic fuck you's," as he put it once—grenades tossed at simplifiers and pigeonholers.[22]

The other thing unique about Elliott, at least in relation to other rock stars, was his personality. Brandt Peterson, who played with Elliott in Heatmiser, warned me against hagiography. He suggested I resist all idealizing depictions. This is sound advice. Hagiography is unsustainable (and worse yet, boring). Still, it's hard not to be impressed by the single-mindedness of interviewees. Most people who knew Elliott—well or just slightly—say roughly the same thing. He was a "super sweet," "incredibly generous," "gentle," and "well-intended" person. Scott Wagner interviewed Elliott for

The Rocket in 1997. He also worked at 1201, a bar Elliott frequented on SW 12th Street in Portland (it's no longer there). The interview occurred at My Father's Place, a different bar still in operation across the river on the east side of town, where Elliott played video poker and drank "whiskey with a beer back." "He was super fidgety," Wagner recalls. "That was just his way." The article's focus was music—Elliott's Heatmiser days and his newer solo work—but also up for analysis was what Wagner and co-writer John Chandler called, in a nifty turn of phrase, the "Smith myth." To Wagner, who had followed Elliott for many years, he was a "can't miss, amazingly gifted talent." "We'd hear a record and say, 'Yeah, he's a genius!'" But there was also something else, an unassuming gentleness. "He was never putting on an air," Wagner says. "He was, if anything, distracted by the circus around him. His smile was always sheepish. He could never trust his happiness. He was just one of those guys—a flawed character you root for," sort of "beat-up looking." "Everyone wondered what his secret was. It seemed like he needed to mask something."[23] John Chandler, who interviewed Elliott on three occasions across his career, and ran into him in Portland frequently, zeroed in on the same attributes. "He was one of those people who lived with his filters open," Chandler says. "He had a very low bullshit level. He's the good part of Portland hipsterdom. He was never silly, loud, dumb, or buffoonish."[24] There were times, too, when the Smith myth got tough for Elliott himself. He was all too aware of the image fans foisted on him. It was him, in some ineffable fashion, but he also mocked it, fled from it. In a final interview with Elliott in 2000, which took place in late October, Chandler asked him what he planned to be for Halloween. "Oh, a morose, gloomy, sorrowful songwriter," Elliott deadpanned, "who always dresses in black and all these people want to know about him and who he really is."

To Jennifer Chiba, Elliott was a "weird mixture of confident and shy"; "more unsure than nervous," in Wagner's estimation. Always hoping the world was as well-intended as he tried to be, he displayed vulnerability openly. Even with total strangers he could be jarringly candid. In fact, according to another close friend, Smith was obsessed with telling the truth. It was virtually a family trait. Somehow truth always needed to come out, even when half-truths would have been a lot less discomforting. This candor was one of the major elements of the myth—more real than legendary. Elliott spoke for the underdog. He was the outsider commenting lucidly from a distance, making fans feel less alone, their underdog pain beautiful. Always hyperaware of anyone being mistreated, Elliott was closely attuned to injustice and rejection. He spoke up, and he turned the other cheek. Even when he got shit on, according to another intimate, "he never shit on people back." It was a matter of dignity. It was also simply the right thing to do, the kind thing. What Smith did not have, at least so far as I have been able to discover, was enemies. He was hard to dislike, impossible to hate, even though, like anyone, he could be judgmental, petty, or condescending at times, even downright mean. The strongest impulse anyone felt around him was protection, chiefly because he wasn't very good at protecting himself.

An incident from winter 2003 is revealing. It illustrates several elements of Elliott's personality simultaneously—his vulnerability, his openness, his self-consciousness, even his need to tell the truth. Elliott was performing at the Henry Fonda Theater for two nights, January 31 and February 1. At the end of the song "Pretty (Ugly Before)," someone in the audience called out, "Get a backbone." It was a very strange moment, a rare expression of distaste, especially in the setting of a concert filled with fervid fans. According to two different people I spoke with who were at the gig and deeply in the know, the person delivering the insult was Valerie Deerin, they allege, a recent ex-girlfriend. These same two people do not believe Elliott himself was aware Deerin made the comment; it came amid the usual between-song crowd noise. At any rate, what's interesting is Elliott's reaction, which is complex and multidimensional. "Get a what?" he asks. "A backbone?" He goes on, "Get a backbone, what the fuck? . . . I could tell you a dream I had last night, otherwise I can't be more fucking for real. I mean, honestly. Get a backbone? Okay. I'll try."

Shock and anger turn to obligingness. He says he'll try. Then he apologizes: "I'm not trying to pick on you. Maybe I didn't understand what you were saying. Whatever. I've been playing a lot of dark songs tonight, so I'm sorry . . . Don't get bummed out. They're just songs."[25]

The next night, at the conclusion of "Stickman," another self-denigrating number implying some amount of spinelessness, Elliott—this time aware of the fact that Deerin had probably shouted the remark—revisits the incident. "Someone bringing up my backbone tonight? It's here, behind me." Several crowd members shout, "What?"

"I don't know. Last night someone said to get a backbone . . . I'm pretty odd playing as it is. I don't know. My answer was, I'll try." Not in any way singling out Deerin, which would have been uncharacteristic, Elliott says, "It's like, people think . . . *some* people . . . they need to take you down because they think you think you're better, like that you're some kind of hot shit, to take you down, and that's just bullshit. Fair enough? That was my little tirade tonight."[26]

Not a very major tirade, as it happens. It's remarkable—Elliott does not tell the person to fuck off. He doesn't ignore the person either, the easiest response of all. Instead he confirms his honesty. He can't possibly get any more real, any more vulnerable. He vows to try, to grow one, to get stronger, in effect agreeing with the insult's sentiment. Then he says he's sorry, and the next night makes a point of announcing that he does not think he's hot shit, he does not think he's any better than anyone else.

All this was in a peculiar musical context; Elliott was performing, in a position of vulnerability, and the catcall arrived out of the blue, utterly unexpectedly. But it would be a mistake to imagine Elliott as timid, unable to access anger. Over the years he did get into a number of fights, even during middle school in Texas. He never initiated these scenes. In every case he was standing up for a person who was being insulted or mistreated. One such episode occurred in a bar in Brooklyn. A friend or girl was involved; a group of guys were trash-talking. Elliott took a stand and, as a friend describes it, "got the shit beat out of him."[27] At one point during the tumult a bottle was broken; Elliott was dragged across the glass, which cut his back badly.

On a different occasion Elliott, his sister Ashley Welch, and Jennifer Chiba had gone to hear friends Beck and the Flaming Lips at Universal City Walk in fall 2002. Flaming Lips was the opening act, in what some called "the coolest marketing ploy of all time." The buzz, apparently, was that Beck's "brilliantly somber" *Sea Change* album was a "snoozer," so "hiring a psychotic carnival like the Flaming Lips to back him up would not only liven up the gigs, but open ticket sales to an entirely different audience."[28] At intermission Elliott and Chiba wandered backstage for a drink and to say hello to people. In line ahead of them was a young couple they did not know, engaged in a verbal argument, some run-of-the-mill domestic dispute. Cops were summoned; they began roughing the couple up, pounding their heads against the pavement. At first, Elliott stood close by, alerting the officers to the fact that he was watching what they were doing. The officers demanded he move aside; he refused. The standoff escalated, and after several seconds Elliott was pepper sprayed. He reacted strongly by waving his arms and reaching out, at one point, according to police, making physical contact, albeit unintentionally. The officers then took him down, drove their knees into his back, cuffed him, and carted him off to the facility's jail. While doing so, they slammed him into walls, causing his ears to bleed. Afterward Chiba and others took him to an emergency room. Charges were filed and never dropped. In fact, they were active at the time of Elliott's death. He hired an attorney to contest the allegations, but a scheduled court date was postponed. In any case, the incident had long-term effects. Elliott was intensely worried about the prospect of going to jail. He also came to fear police retaliation of some sort, all during a time when his drug use was causing high amounts of paranoia anyway.

Lips front man Wayne Coyne, whose performances sometimes begin with him descending from an alien mother ship in a bubble and floating across the audience, wasn't pleased with Smith's backstage behavior. "It really was nothing but sad," he told *Billboard* in the days following Elliott's death. "You just sort of saw a guy who had lost control of himself . . . He was everything you wouldn't want in a person . . . It was horrible . . . It was ugly."[29] Steven Drozd, the Lips' drummer, added: "There's an undercurrent of fucking real sadness in a lot of his music that just fucking crushes me. And that's just really the way he was. I hate to sound that way, but he really was. And I can hear it in his music. That's totally him."[30]

In the end, what Elliott left behind, what he lived, amid the sadness, the struggle to get past his particular form of psychache, was compassion, more than anything else, compassion and genius. Compassion made him uniquely lovable. Tales of his sensitivity to others' pain are legion—he didn't judge, he didn't lecture. He moved quietly, invisibly, as on the occasion when, seeing a homeless man sleeping on the street, he tucked a hundred-dollar bill in his boot, a small gift for the person to be surprised by and grateful for later. The genius is just as stunning. That he was able to make his art while fighting off addictions, holding suicide at arm's length, is astonishing. It's a testament to the power of his gift, which was irrepressible. There was no self-extinction drive in the gift, only the gift-maker. To live for one's art is a cliché, but for a time the music did seem to keep Elliott alive, until the pain of living eclipsed the pleasure of the sounds and lyrics. As he put it once in a song, he was high on the sound, but there's no power in the air. The battle's on the ground.

Elliott was very deeply loved, by many, many people. The largest mystery of all is why he so often could not believe that. He knew it, it was obvious, he heard what people told him about how much they cared, but there was also a gnawing sense of worthlessness he never quite managed to rise above. Others valued his life with enormous displays of affection. He didn't.

CHAPTER ONE HEY MISTER, THAT'S ME UP ON THE JUKEBOX

Surreal **was the** word Elliott Smith used more than any other to describe his deeply improbable, man-out-of-nowhere appearance at the 70th Academy Awards, about which no subsequent interviewer failed to ask him, to the point where the interviews themselves must have seemed just as surreal as that 1998 night. The feeling was the opposite of schadenfreude, more an instance of enjoying the success of a person (also richly deserving) never pegged to be quite so successful. Elliott stood for the overlooked under-rated, the loser plucked out and suddenly winning, and those talking with him, many of whom identified strongly, took obvious delight in the anoma-lousness of the outsized recognition. It was slightly absurd, slightly comical, but also slightly thrilling. Surreal, like its woollier cousin Kafkaesque, is a hackneyed trope, pulled out nowadays to describe a traffic jam in L.A. or a line at the DMV. But Elliott had it right. Surrealism equals incongruous juxtaposition, which captures the night's original song category ideally. Here was Elliott Smith, looking barely adolescent, singing about faking it through the day with Johnny Walker Red, maybe the most un-Oscars-like opening line ever. And here, right beside him, was titanic Celine Dion, her heart forever going on, with a mawkish side of Michael Bolton thrown in for measure. It does not get more Kafkaesque. The *poète maudit* versus the anti-poets, the hero and the clowns.

Elliott's shortened performance of the nominated song "Miss Misery" from Gus Van Sant's *Good Will Hunting* might have been, in a closed uni-verse, a career high point, a peak experience, an apex leading to more fame, more money, more opportunities. A complete game-changer all around, in other words. In some ways it was that, in some ways not. To Elliott, success was complicated, artistically and psychologically. Although it may have held momentary appeal, it wasn't especially desirable. The year before, Elliott was on a big pop kick, listening to *Magical Mystery Tour* every day. On that album's penultimate song, "Baby You're a Rich Man," John Lennon (whom Elliott adored and often covered) asks two pointed questions: "How does it feel to be one of the beautiful people?" and "What do you want to be?" Elliott was set to find out, one way or another. As he told John Chandler years later, "[The Oscars] was a dream come true. But it wasn't my dream."[1]

Pre-Oscars, Elliott was nowhere near a nobody, but he was just as far from a major somebody poised for widespread commercial recognition. Outside of Portland and pockets of the West Coast, almost no one had any idea who he was. His whispery, withheld, homemade sensibilities fit badly with "big-time" aspirations; he was comfortably, satisfyingly unknown, playing mainly in tiny, intimate venues where adoring fans shout out songs and sing along to lyrics. There had been three individual albums on two different labels, Cavity Search's *Roman Candle* (1994), with a long list of unnamed songs, Kill Rock Stars's *Elliott Smith* (1995), and the *Magical Mystery Tour*–inspired *Either/Or* (1997). The last effort was unusually poppy, even upbeat in spots. As Elliott told John Chandler and Scott Wagner in April of 1997, "I'm feeling pretty good about songwriting right now. I feel pretty positive . . . I already did my time where I felt everything I did was a big piece of crap, and that the music business was going to grind me into dirt. Now I just feel good about it. I want to do it."[2] A portion of this attitude change had to do with the nature of the music itself, which was less "idea-driven," according to Elliott, less about catching feelings. But he'd also recently started taking antidepressants. He told Wagner he was on Paxil; he guessed it was helping.[3] "I spent a whole year with my head spinning around . . . What little notoriety that I've gotten bummed me out bad . . . It was extremely easy for me not to care what people thought about me when no one knew who I was."[4] Once they did know, it was harder for Elliott to separate out what people saw him as—the lugubrious singer-songwriter, an appellation he disliked—from what he hoped he was. Preconceived notions were, as he put it, infecting everything. Yet with *Either/Or* in the can, skies cleared—or so it seemed—and inner dissonance faded.

The record was released in February 1997, a little more than a year before the March 1998 Academy Awards. By summer and fall, whatever Paxil-abetted good feeling Elliott had manufactured was gone. He was more and more depressed, suicidal, drinking heavily. There were blackouts, incidents of alcohol poisoning. At one point Elliott remembered "waking up on the street covered in cuts and bruises."[5] At the Crocodile Club in Seattle he pulled friends aside to make various ominous-sounding pronouncements. Speaking in frightening past tense, he told them there was nothing any of them could have said. They had done nothing wrong. If I'm not around much longer, he warned, remember I love you. It was a clear, terrifying goodbye. By this time there had already been at least one suicide gesture, a jump from a car and a fall down a cliff. Now the fear was magnified; friends were concerned he was an imminent danger to himself. Various calls were placed, one to manager Margaret Mittleman, who had worked with Elliott since 1994. Roughly two weeks later an intervention occurred, organized by Slim Moon, the founder of Kill Rock Stars. In Chicago, and with the help of a counselor, Smith was blindsided, pressured to check into an Arizona facility that he promptly walked out of, fearing long-term confinement. "Some beautiful songs try to make you think that, for a moment, there's no crap in the world," Moon said. "But Elliott's songs admit the world's fucked up . . . He appeared really fragile, and he internalized everything. He would go on and on in his songs about how nothing was going to relieve his pain. But at the same time he was searching hard for something to relieve it."[6]

"It got kind of weird," Smith allowed vaguely. "I started drinking too much and I was taking antidepressants, and they don't mix." On the other hand, he says he got a strange sort of optimism going, "even though the way I was living wasn't showing it." Mentally, he pushed for productivity and positivity. He told himself things were going to improve. "I'm never going to stop insisting," he said, "that things are going to work out."[7]

But this internal pep talk came long after the fact. It sounded good, but it didn't stick. In the moment, the intervention was infuriating—a humiliating, frightening ordeal—and it more or less ended Elliott's relationship with Moon. For Elliott, suicide signaled a sort of freedom. It was an option the removal of which he could not abide, confinement nullifying a coveted escape clause. "Dying people should have that right," he believed. Lacking it while locked up and under constant observation made him feel "even crazier." His image of hospitalization was almost comically grotesque, yet another Kafkaesque nightmare of panoptical conformity and fear. "Let's just say I didn't want to go there," Smith told *New Musical Express* in 2000. "If you took TV culture and then focused it through a magnifying glass onto a blade of grass and burned it up—that's what it was like in there, this concentrated version of the same kind of pressure that people feel all the time. You know, 'Get ahead! Get ahead! Be like everybody else!' It's ridiculous. It made things worse. A lot of that seemed to be based on fear: maybe if we scare these people enough they'll act like they don't feel like they do."

As he often did when dealing with residues of various types of negative emotion, Elliott shaped the experience into art, of a sort less indecipherable than usual. In what might be his angriest song, the acid "Everybody Cares, Everybody Understands," a broadside against synthetic sympathy, the "chemical embrace that kicks you in the head," he warns do-gooders they "fucking ought to stay the hell away from things" they know nothing about. "Memory Lane," first performed just after the intervention, tracks the same line of thought. The title references Serenity Lane, a collection of Oregon drug and alcohol treatment centers, most located in Portland, where Elliott had lived. These are the places you go when you "lose the chase," Elliott writes, when you are "dragged against your will." All anyone knows is "you're not like them." So they "kick you in the head"—as in "Everybody Cares, Everybody Understands"—"and send you back to bed." The solution is separation, which makes for a place to stay. He's comfortable apart, he says. He'll keep his doors and windows shut; he swears he'll never tell a soul again.

Intervention backfired, it seems, or so say the songs. Elliott's response was fury, a lingering sense of helper-hypocrisy and betrayal (a few of the interveners, after all, were also drug and alcohol users). So he closed down. All future openness would be limited to the songwriting, which itself grew increasingly, deliberately abstract, or to carefully selected intimates who might be trusted not to use confessions against him. Elliott was always very careful about what he revealed; there were subjects he refused to elaborate on. Intervention solidified that attitude. He resolved not to repeat any inpatient experience, even when it might have saved his life.

But as 1997 dragged painfully on, something unexpected altered the mood. Through a mutual friend, Smith met filmmaker Gus Van Sant in

Portland. They hung out a little, discussed home recording—something Van Sant was also interested in—questions about different microphones and cameras. Van Sant came to see Elliott perform, although as Elliott clarifies, "He didn't discover me playing in a coffee shop or anything, like I heard somebody wrote. In fact, I've never played in a coffee shop."[8] One of Van Sant's old boyfriends knew Smith; he introduced Van Sant to the first album, *Roman Candle*, which he listened to while shooting *Good Will Hunting.* "When we edited the movie," Van Sant told *LA Weekly* in November 2003, "we put all of the [Smith] songs into it, so the spirit and sound of the movie is largely Elliott Smith." Editing took place in Portland, and at some point in the process Van Sant called Elliott up. They had coffee, talked, and then Van Sant showed Elliott the movie in his home, on a VHS tape. He told Elliott, "Now, don't be shocked too much, because we've put a lot of your songs in there. And normally I wouldn't show you the movie with your songs in it, but they work so well that I want to."[9] Elliott "really liked" the film, he said, "which was great, since I don't like a lot of movies." He found he related to some of the characters "to a certain extent where I could get into the vibe of the movie."[10]

As Elliott explained, Van Sant also wanted him "to write a song for the movie because he thought it would be nice." Miramax, too, preferred a new number, since "you can't be nominated for an Oscar if the song came out on a record before."[11] The result of this gentle pressuring was "Miss Misery," which was not, as it happens, an entirely new song, although that's the story Elliott was urged to tell. In fact, in an early version there is no mention of the title character, no Miss Misery at all. Instead of "Do you miss me, Miss Misery, like you say you do?" Elliott writes, "But it's all right, some enchanted night, I'll be with you," a line including a modicum of hopefulness. In the former, the Oscars version, Elliott hopes he's missed, but he isn't quite sure; he distrusts what he's being told. He guesses the imagined woman would rather see him gone. She might prefer he vanish "into oblivion." It's a portrait of a jangled ambivalent relationship. The alternate take suggests resilience. Elliott can't hold his liquor, he writes, but he does all he can to keep his attitude buoyant, he tries staying positive.[12]

Who is this Miss Misery? Some suggest she's girlfriend Joanna Bolme, who accompanied Elliott to the Oscars (he was provided with one extra ticket). Around that time, Bolme says, things were changing. "We had an on-and-off relationship by then. Drug use on his part was the main culprit. Drugs, and his lack of interest in his own life."[13] That last detail—indifference to life, a passive wish simply to die—suggests another inspiration. Miss Misery might be depression itself, Elliott's muse of melancholy. He was a major fan of Kierkegaard, whom he read at different points throughout his life. The Danish philosopher himself suffered from lifelong depression. No reductionist, he saw the affliction as an absence of faith, a failure to expect joy, happiness, goodness, purely the fault of the person in torment, who could, if he worked at it, will himself into a different state. "My depression," Kierkegaard writes, "is the most faithful mistress I have known—no wonder, then, that I return the love."

In the *Good Will Hunting* version of the song Elliott's narrator barely manages to get by, with alcohol's help. He pours poison down the drain, but it puts "bad thoughts" in his head. A stranger in the park tells him he's strong, hardly ever wrong, but he shrugs these sentiments off. He doubts Miss Misery really wants him around. One of Elliott's themes is oblivion, its lure and solace; here he imagines vanishing into it. He says he tries to *be*—to keep existing "in the life"—but comes back to Misery when she wants him to; he's under her thumb, he's at her mercy. A constant in Elliott's life, as in Kierkegaard's, was suffering. Torment was his faithful mistress too. He returned to it because it was what he knew—the "gentle sadness" of melancholy. Yet as he did when faced with most clichés, easy labels tossed his way, he nuanced around simplification. Discussing suicide, whether it's courageous or cowardly, he calls it "ugly and cruel," and says he needs his friends to stick around. Then he adds: "I prefer not to appear as some kind of disturbed person. I think a lot of people get mileage out of it, like 'I'm a tortured artist' or something. I'm not a tortured artist, and there's nothing really wrong with me. I just had a bad time for a while."[14] In fact, he was pretty consistently tortured, but he wasn't only that. He wanted badly to get healed, he tried assorted treatments, including Paxil and other nontraditional remedies, but they only partially or temporarily sufficed. Miss Misery kept reappearing, literally and metaphorically.

For a time the Oscars was a remedy of sorts, or at least a powerful distraction. Early on, people at Miramax predicted he'd be playing the song on TV some day, but when the nomination actually came, it was, Elliott felt, a "totally freakish accident."[15] So much so that initially he decided not to perform. The exposure was just too weird, he said, too ridiculous, and also, according to several of his friends, terrifying. The specter of success, its trappings and creativity-crushing responsibilities, unnerved him. But also, the event itself was *not him*. It didn't square with who he thought he was, what he was all about. He belonged on the outside; he never bought in. His songs were dissections, dismantlings of "pompous . . . self-congratulatory ventures."[16] He compared his appearance to riding in the space shuttle or walking on the moon. It would be, he figured beforehand, fake and worthless. Plus, "There's such a pressure to be happy and successful and a winner in America," Elliott explained. "That's such a joke. And you're meant to project that image at all times, otherwise you're a loser. Then if you complain about the cult of the winner, people assume you are espousing the cult of the outsider." The fact is, Elliott did not want to espouse anything. His songs were simply, essentially about what it meant to be a person. They weren't manifestos. They also weren't finger-pointing didacticisms, a feature of early folk Elliott found repellent.

In the weeks leading up to the big night, he was freaked out, according to friends. He didn't want to perform; he didn't want *not to* either. No move made sense. But if he elected to bow out, event organizers told him, someone else would take his place. The song had to be done, after all. At some point in these back-and-forth negotiations the name Richard Marx was slyly floated. The ruse worked, although Elliott seemed to know it was a bluff. He would perform, he decided. Not for himself, but for his friends and mother. It would make it easier for her to tell acquaintances what he did, he reasoned ("There's a silver lining in the corporate cloud," Elliott declares in the *Figure 8* song "Wouldn't Mama be Proud"). He asked to arrange the strings parts; producers agreed. He also planned a secret mockery, a bit of implied mischief most would likely not even get. The idea was to wear a white sport coat with a pink carnation, in homage to the 1957 rock 'n' roll tune by Marty Robbins, who wrote the song after driving past a high school and finding students dressed for prom. "I'm dressed up for the dance," Robbins sings, "I'm all alone in romance . . . A white sport coat and a pink carnation/I'm in a blue blue mood." The sentiment fit: a sad, dateless loser dressed up to no purpose. But in the end the carnation got dropped. The tacky white sport coat also disappeared, in favor of Prada.

The ceremony took place at L.A.'s Shrine Auditorium, just across the street from where Elliott's sister Ashley Welch lived at the time. Billy Crystal hosted, as he had the year before. Curtains opened grandly to reveal him on the bow of a slowly sinking *Titanic* replica, an overbaked nod to the famous Leonardo DiCaprio shot. Titanic was the film that year, a forbidding favorite with fourteen nominations and eleven eventual Oscars. While Crystal mugs, the camera swings to Jack Nicholson and Dustin Hoffman smiling approvingly. "Welcome to the *Titanic*," Crystal announces foreshadowingly. "We are just like that great ship. We are huge, we are expensive, and everybody would like us to go a lot faster." More laughter and applause follow. Crystal then launches into a song-and-dance collage aimed at best picture nominees. *Titanic* gets the *Gilligan's Island* treatment. As for *Good Will Hunting*, Crystal sings to audience members Matt Damon and Ben Affleck, "Your script was tight and, dammit, so are your buns!" You're a hit, he continues, and it's clear to see, "and you haven't yet hit puberty." "Dropping your pants is a lot of fun, just like they do in Washington," Crystal observes in reference to the next film, *Boogie Nights*.

Elliott was, of course, anything but A-list material. Organizers actually tried suggesting he go in through the back door. "The Oscars people didn't treat [Elliott] with respect," says Joanna Bolme. "They looked at him like, 'We gotta get this guy on and off as quickly as possible.'"[17] Elliott and Bolme did in fact walk the red carpet, everybody snapping photos, Elliott at one point crushed by industry throng, all of whom pushed past him toward superstars. Winding his way, he found himself directly behind Madonna, that night's Best Original Song presenter. His chief concern was to not step on the train of her dress—long, black, and billowing, cut revealingly down the middle. Finally he managed to squeeze past her. (There is a brief pan of Smith online, standing behind Madonna as she's being interviewed, with Joan Rivers riffing in the background.)[18]

Bolme is right. Although Elliott was the only nominee who wrote and performed his own song, the only one who actually played an instrument, "Miss Misery" was by far the most truncated tune. The song came in at a scant 2 minutes, 14 seconds. Dion was given 3:39, Bolton 3:22, and Aaliyah, 3:12.

First to appear were Aaliyah and Michael Bolton, followed by Trisha Yearwood, Elliott, and Dion. In short, four bombastic vocals, emotionally overripe, and one fragile dose of absolute discontinuity, fresh out of inpatient treatment for alcohol and suicide. As Sam Coomes put it, "Pretty much the worst music on earth . . . and then Elliott comes out. Very similar to the sort of extreme mental shift you get on an acid trip."[19] Bolton's hair was cut short—no mullet. He wore what looked like a trench coat over a white-collared, open shirt. Before going on he was introduced gushingly as "the exciting Michael Bolton." The song was "Go the Distance." He vows, "I will search the world; I will face its harms." A case of full-frontal courage against all odds. In a tightly fitting black dress, Aaliyah takes a similar line in "Journey to the Past": heart don't fail me now, she pleads, courage don't desert me. Dion, the last to perform, stands before rolling mist in a turtle-neck gown and a "heart of the sea" necklace. "My Heart Will Go On," she predicts. In Elliott's songs, hearts do the opposite. They waver, they get rained on.

In later interviews Elliott said he was too bewildered to get nervous, but most friends saw it differently. They describe him as "scared shitless." He stepped out to a strings intro in his white Prada suit, hair customarily disarranged, guitar slung around his back. There had been talk of him sitting on a chair, but the Oscar people nixed the idea; it wouldn't look good, they figured. Plus, the chair would need to be gotten rid of before Dion took the stage moments later. Dion disarmed Elliott. Backstage she asked if he was nervous; he said he was, and she reassured him, suggesting he use the adrenaline to make his song better. It is a beautiful song, she added. "Then she gave me a big hug," Elliott recalled. "It was too much . . . She was really sweet, which has made it impossible for me to dislike [her] anymore . . . It was too human to be dismissed."[20]

As he begins, Elliott's voice, never especially powerful, seems to tremble slightly. Everywhere friends were watching, in bars or houses on Hawthorne in Portland, literally holding their breath. Jennifer Chiba remembers the night clearly. Her first response? "Who the fuck is that?!" She says, "I didn't know that that's what he was about. It was breathtaking."[21] A close friend said it was like, for a moment, your favorite thing in the world was everybody else's favorite thing. From a far distance, friends and family held

Elliott's fear. They hung on each tremulous line. They rooted for him to power through. And he did. He bowed twice. Once by himself, then later sandwiched between Yearwood and Dion.

Presenter Madonna, who had just released *Ray of Light*, her long black train pooling and dragging like an animate oil slick, called the songs "a contrast in styles," a clear reference to Elliott, the single contrasting example. A bit of hostile posturing occurs. As Madonna reads Dion's name—the *Titanic* theme a forbidding favorite—she turns to the side and rolls her eyes. Then, seconds before she crowns "My Heart Will Go On" as winner, she winces, "What a shocker." The crowd murmurs; the songwriters hop to the stage, collecting their statues. Everybody knew who was going to win, Elliott said later. "If I won it," he adds, "I would have put it in my closet. But Celine will put it on her mantelpiece."[22]

This was to become, in terms of assorted reverberations, the longest two minutes of Elliott Smith's life. The show was over, but it went on eternally, a snatch of time Elliott was forever taken back to. There's a tendency to see discontinuous events like these as turning points, moments of upheaval leading to transformation, lasting change. Elliott, ever the enemy of simple formulations, resisted that idea. "I don't feel like things are very changed," he said afterward. "I do the same things I did before. I think about the same things . . . It was really weird. It was pretty fun. For a day."[23] The picture of him as fragile stuck. He hated it, found it too personal and dismissive, but there was nothing he could do about it. "People were saying all this stuff simply because I didn't come out and command the stage like Celine Dion does."[24] He decided, then, to stop reading his press. He tired of questions constantly redirected back to who he was, as opposed to focusing on the music, which he liked talking about more. Plus it interfered with attempts to get out of his own "weird headspace." He practiced a self-erasure. "I don't think it's important who I am," he said. "I really like playing music, but I don't really want to be anything in particular."[25]

What the Oscars crystallized for Elliott most powerfully was the problem of ambivalence, and of fame—how much to want, how much to run away from. At least with regard to material circumstance, things had changed. Now he was known. And he would be signed shortly to behemoth DreamWorks, a far cry from the Cavity Search and Kill Rock Stars labels.

There was money, too, and with it opportunities for self-destruction. Success, in other words, made drugs possible, as one friend put it. The numbers vary, but in years to follow, from 2000 to 2002, Elliott would come to spend upward of one thousand dollars per week on illicit substances. Suddenly he was in the spotlight. Suddenly he lost privacy—he got recognized, he was asked for autographs. Before he drank, sometimes heavily, but he wasn't drunk all the time, and not every night. Drugs were different, though; they became all-consuming. They were like a career to which he would dedicate himself single-mindedly. He wasn't a drug addict when he wasn't known, a friend explained.[26]

The most forbidding challenge was emotional. Music was one thing, by far the most natural, uncomplicated aspect of Elliott's life. It couldn't and wouldn't stop coming. The drugs slowed but never kinked the flow. Yet post-Oscars, Elliott was increasingly uncomfortable in his own skin. The accolades embarrassed him. There was guilt too, a need to diminish his own self-importance, a feeling of "what I do is no better than anyone else." His belief, one he recognized at a very deep level, was that he was the wrong kind of person to be big and famous. The poorness of fit was obvious. The world of Madonnas and Hoffmans and Nicholsons was not one he wished to live in or even really visit. "It was all these famous singers," he recalled, "and then it was like, 'Who's that guy? In the white suit? With the dirty hair? Who hasn't sold millions of records? What in the world is he doing there?'" The question was a good one: "I was wondering the same thing," he said.[27]

To Jennifer Chiba, the conflict had mainly to do with an incongruence between warranted attention on the songs—praise the songs deserved—and Elliott's inner feeling that "he was crap." He got enough of a taste of fame, John Chandler says, then decided, "Why would I want this?" "I don't want to sell me. I'm not a product," he said. He "tried on the fame hat, then said, 'No. Not for me.'"[28] Even "Miss Misery" itself became tiresome, an aural reminder of all those things he wished to move past, to forget. "I'll play it when I don't have to be the weird Oscar guy anymore," he said. "I don't think it's a crowd pleaser. No one really calls that out . . . I'm really tired of it."[29] He didn't get the prize, of course, but he wouldn't have wanted it anyway. As he told Jonathan Valania, "If there's one thing I can't stand, it's winners."[30]

Elliott returned to the Oscars in songs, the night's packed, complicated meaning an ongoing source of curiosity. On one hand, he was dismissive, he deflated the event's importance, laughing off its empty bombast.
At the same time, there seems to be an ongoing attempt at making sense
of things, of figuring his final attitude toward the whole ordeal, which remained, in different ways, emotionally unfinished. He tired of the interviews, the subject was grating and almost depressing; but on his own, in the
music, he kept bringing it up.

One song friends say has Oscar connotations is "Stupidity Tries," off
the album *Figure 8*. It's a paean to fecklessness, absurdity, and self-doubt.
At its root is a brilliantly dense commentary, more comical than confused
or anguished (although some of the latter managed to leak in too). Elliott
recorded versions of the tune at Abbey Road studios, a location of deep
meaning to him, yet even that fact he mostly minimized. As it begins Elliott's got a foot in the door but he's not sure why, it makes no sense; he'll be
cut down to size, he figures. They found some "privateer," he sings, "to sail
across the sea of trash" ("sea of trash" was lifted from a Sluggo song on a
Hullabaloo release). This might be the single instance of "privateer" appearing in a rock song, but the word choice is deft. These were independent
renegade attack vessels, of benefit to smaller naval powers, sometimes made
up of pirates and convicts. They disrupted commerce, attacked and captured foreign ships. So, on Oscar night, it was Elliott in his humble craft,
taking aim at the moneyed *Titanics* of the world, the big ships. Nautical
references continue. He looks from floor to floor for a port of call, a place to
unload, a storm-protecting harbor, as if he just wants to get out. In early
versions of the song he refers to himself as a Spanish lord; the recorded
version adds specificity. He's a "drunk conquistador conquering the Gover-
nor's Ball"—his abilities, in other words, as professional warrior diminished
comically by drink. The tune ends on a note of meaninglessness: Elliott
can't think of a thing he hopes tomorrow brings. "Oh, what a surprise" he
adds. Nothing new comes. He's back where he started. The enemy's still
within; he's not exactly Elliott, but he's there nonetheless, to be dealt with
somehow.

"Wouldn't Mama Be Proud?", also off *Figure 8*, reads like another
Oscars-related number, although it's hard to say for sure. Here Elliott's a

great pretender, his mother a pretty NCO, or noncommissioned officer.[31] He said she'd have something to tell her friends about what he did in light of the Academy Awards, so her pride in him is a source of satisfaction. Though the sky has gone black, he's told he's on the right track; his mother knows he can keep it together.

Even much later tunes like "A Distorted Reality's Now a Necessity to Be Free" contain, in some versions, surprising Oscar references. Draft lyrics picture Elliott fit poorly "in my Prada white" (crossed out) with the additional line, "didn't have a chance," also crossed out, replaced by "dollared up in virgin white." "Go By" repeats the reference, although it's not clear when he wrote the lyrics. It's therefore either prescient in a weird way or retrospective, the first possibility most uncanny of all. He is wound up tightly, "dressed all in white," some "torn main sail"—another sea allusion.[32] He blows out to drift.

Fame is always a surprise. One doesn't know what it means until it arrives. Before that, it's an abstract, a possible future, nothing to contend with except intellectually. When it comes, though, it's a problem. It fits or it doesn't. It feels good or it feels bad. Elliott was always insistent that he wanted to make music *for himself*; if others happened to like it, that was fine, a pleasant surprise, but in some essential way unintended. Barry Manilow said the following about Judy Garland; it captures Elliott's situation perfectly: "Everything she did was filled with the truth. I think that's the big difference between her and everybody else. Everyone else, oh yeah, they're great singers—they do verbal acrobatics. But they don't tell the truth. This woman always told the truth." Faking it is protection; it's the faker on display. Openness is vulnerability. It is you up there, only you. Be careful, Elliott said, if you decide to be open. It's your life you're talking about. And in Elliott's case, that life held secrets. No wonder he wanted the hype to decline. He was now a Somebody. But he preferred being a Nobody.

CHAPTER TWO CENTER CIRCLE

There are artists who begin vaguely, aware of a gift but not sure what to do with it, how to make it tangible. This is perhaps the more average scenario. Then there are artists, like Elliott, who discover their medium immediately. One feels they were "born with it," whether they truly were or not. Elliott was writing songs in seventh grade. They came in the wind. He found a voice and he never stopped making music, even after it was nearly impossible to do so. It only stopped when he stopped. The Best Original Song nomination, then, was hardly a fluke. From the sixth grade on, if not earlier, Elliott was writing an original song almost every day.

It all started prosaically in the suburbs of Dallas, Texas—first Duncanville and then Cedar Hill. Elliott spent the first fourteen years of his life there, a fact he later memorialized with a tattoo of the state on his upper left arm, a permanent visual reminder of a complex period, one he returned to frequently, in his head, in different types of therapy, and in the music itself. There was turmoil from the very beginning, almost from before the beginning. Smith's father, Gary Mac Smith, left his mother, Bunny Kay Berryman, when Elliott was zero, as he liked to say. Reasons for the parting are impossible to describe. Neither Gary nor Bunny have spoken about it on record, nor have they said much at all about Elliott officially, electing to keep their memories to themselves. On record, Elliott also had little specific to say about his father's departure. If the subject came up in interviews, which it did on occasion, he turned elliptical, politely signaled it out of bounds. No amount of coaxing ever succeeded in drawing the facts out of him. Friends of his, from the time and from later in his life, recall a mainly amicable separation. Some refer to possible infidelities. One recalls Elliott saying that his father, a Vietnam vet and psychiatrist (still practicing in Portland, Oregon, as of 2012), "ran off with a young nurse." This may or may not be true. But a conjecture is that the line from the song "King's Crossing"—"dead men talk to all the pretty nurses"—obliquely references the event. Whatever really happened, Gary, his biological father, was gone, and with him the possibility of an ideal intact family. Elliott literally was zero, and he felt like a zero, he often said. His birth name was Steven Paul Smith, an appellation he never felt fit, one he'd eventually erase (although not legally).[1] Had he been a girl, Chiba says, the intention was to call him "Monday." For his first four years, life was Elliott and Bunny. It wasn't easy, it wasn't always perfect, but it was hardly a particularly painful time either. Pain came later, as it often does, a sort of deferred trauma. His father's leaving was a prototypical first abandonment that left him wondering when the next one might occur.

Bunny taught school in the Dallas area, a career lasting thirty years. First grade was her passion, but she covered all levels, mostly elementary, at a number of different schools, serving a variety of populations. The kids loved her, and she loved them back. Her family included many amateur musicians; playing and singing was a regular occurrence. Elliott always expressed insecurity about his voice. He wasn't the sort of person, he said, who could wake up in the morning and immediately sing perfectly on key. He had to work at it, find his style, his truest tone. Bunny and her mother were naturals. It all came easily to them. Margaret Berryman, Elliott's grandmother, sang in a Sweet Adeline choral group; she also played piano. Bill Berryman, Bunny's father, joined the Musician's Union when he was just a teenager so he could play at dances. At that time he specialized in drums (an instrument Elliott took up too). Bill Berryman's real talent, however, was the "vibes"—sometimes called the vibraharp or vibraphone, visually similar to the xylophone or glockenspiel but with aluminum rather than wooden bars. Berryman's gift for the instrument was nationally recognized; he was always in several bands at once, even well into his 70s and 80s. An online flyer from December 2006 describes him—then 87 years old—as a "musician, mason, and minister who shares his love of music by playing his vibraphone at local nursing homes and assisted living facilities."[2]

Berryman didn't choose music as a primary profession; it was simply too difficult to earn a living. Instead he made and installed signs. For a time he owned a motel; he welded; he built barges; and he worked for the

Titche-Goettinger Department Store in Dallas, managing the store's commercial division. But music was the constant, his true joy and passion.

There were occasions when Berryman and his wife Margaret babysat Elliott in the Oak Cliff area, and music always featured. One grandparent might sit at piano—Bill Berryman played it too—as the other sang, or both sang, in harmony. These babysitting afternoons would have been among Elliott's first exposures to music, played by genuine and abiding lovers of the art. Bunny had a younger brother, Price, also in bands as a guitar player. Occasionally he sat in as well.

Like her parents, Bunny played piano some. She was also in a number of choirs at Graceland College (no connection to Elvis). The school, currently, is a private liberal arts university with campuses in Iowa and Missouri, changed from the days when Bunny attended. Founded in 1895 as Lamoni College, it was established by, and affiliated with, the Community of Christ, formerly known as The Reorganized Church of Jesus Christ of Latter Day Saints (or RLDS). Graceland was not exactly Mormon when Bunny was there. Some describe it as more Protestant-like, with all the "weird aspects" of Mormonism excluded. Its mission was to proclaim Jesus Christ and to promote communities of joy, hope, love, and peace. Its members adopted no official religious creed, believing instead that the perception of truth is always qualified by human nature and experience. In other words, the so-called "faith journey" was held to be highly individualized and heterogeneous.

Elliott's grandfather Bill was ordained as a minister, working as pastor for the Dallas Restoration Branch of the RLDS, which proclaimed the church's "original doctrines," including the "privilege of worshipping Almighty God according to the dictates of conscience, and allowing all men the same privilege, to worship how, where, or what they may." In a short summary of what he stood for, and how his faith directed his life and actions, Berryman said simply, "I try to teach about how to live and get along with your fellow man."

Growing up with religion all around him did not turn Elliott into any sort of official believer. The family actually only went to church "sometimes." He did, however, refer to an "idiosyncratic version" of spirituality, a church "of which I'm the only member." "I see no reason," he said, "not to believe in whatever I want to. I almost don't care if I'm correct in what I believe. If there's nothing more than what you can see happening, that would make the world seem small." As for what happens when you die, Elliott was agnostic. He didn't much like the idea of being buried or "burned up." As he put it, probably more than half-jokingly, "I would prefer to walk out in the desert and be eaten by birds."[3] Elliott never quite warmed to the idea of God, never embraced it personally or intellectually. Hell was a different matter. The idea fascinated him, unnerved him. In later years he'd sometimes sign his name "Helliott," as if declaring some invisible affinity.

From day one Elliott, born August 6, 1969, was a happy, creative, artistic, well-adjusted boy. There were no signs of any sort of mood problem, any emotional or behavioral difficulty at all. Family and friends called him Stevie. The switch to Elliott—a high school girlfriend's nickname for him that finally just stuck, deriving, some believe, from the film E.T., whose alien-loving main character was also named Elliott—came years later, after the trying out of several pseudonyms. On certain early high school song credits he signed off as Johnny Panic, a name, according to friend Garrick Duckler, he never seriously considered being called in public. Later he contemplated Elliott Stillwater-Rotter, which Duckler felt was too "big and clunky . . . it didn't suit his style."[4] Whatever the case, over time "Steve" rankled. "He would often say things like, 'Steve Smith. Yep. That's the name they gave me. Good job, mom and dad. Real original,'" according to Duckler. "Yep, pretty flashy."

His father's leaving was a blow, but not one he had the ability to feel acutely or comprehend at the time. But a change he would register, one with fixed repercussions in his life and art, arrived when Elliott was four. Bunny remarried. The man, Elliott's stepfather, was Charlie Welch.

Welch was a self-employed businessman who liked to move around. He wasn't exactly nomadic, but he had the wandering mentality. He sold insurance for Farmers over several decades. For a time he owned an art gallery. He fished—catch-and-release fly and Texas bass. He played bridge, golf, and later in life, around 2004, was a contestant in the World Series of Poker at Binion's Horseshoe in Las Vegas, where he shared a table with Johnny Chan.[5] In a photo taken in 2006, Welch wears a baseball cap and sunglasses. His beard and mustache are gray. Bunny stands beside him, smiling, her resemblance to Elliott striking.

As childhood friends of Elliott's recall, Charlie grew up in East Texas. His father was honorable, pragmatic, strict, hardworking, never effusive or loving. He worked the oil fields, and lost some fingers in a job-related accident. The focus was on raising tough kids, on finding success the hard way, being your own person, paying your own way. In his stepfather role, Charlie, like his own father, was anything but easy to please. Any imperfection, trivial or not, was noticed and commented on, so the household atmosphere was tense. (In one version of the song "Junk Bond Trader," Elliott describes a need to "execute every day with precision.")

Information on Welch is hard to come by. Just like Elliott's biological parents, he's never spoken publicly about Elliott, and there is a sense that, even in private, his thoughts are closely guarded. In one of his last and by far most revealing interviews, Elliott says, in an odd turn of phrase, "I lived with my mom's second marriage."[6] "The domestic situation just wasn't good," he adds charitably, "but it's not something I want to dredge up because that's been worked out between me and the person and they don't need to feel bad about it forever." To a different interviewer in 2001 he treads a similar line: "Most of my recollections from that time I really wouldn't want to share on the record."[7] The obvious question is what, exactly, *did* happen? What was there for Charlie Welch to feel bad about?

On this subject Elliott's friends are just as careful with their words as he was, partly because he usually discussed his personal history only when he'd been drinking, they say, so it was difficult to separate fact from boozy fabrications. Some refer to abuse outside the family. Some confide, reluctantly, that they know things they won't ever tell (though it is impossible to say to what, exactly, they may be referring). In the documentary film *Searching for Elliott Smith*, released in 2011, close friend Sean Croghan fights off tears when the topic of Charlie is broached, and deflects direct questions. Tony Lash, Elliott's high school friend and bandmate, refers obliquely to Smith's discomfort around his stepfather, but stops short of supplying additional details.[8] Yet another bandmate, Shon Sullivan of Goldenboy, describes an encounter at Denver's Orpheum, where Elliott was playing. It was a cold, snowy night. Charlie and Bunny met Elliott in a tiny backstage room. "It was definitely a moment," Sullivan recalls. "I got the sense he didn't want me to leave. They came with a birthday gift, the Beatles *Anthology* book.

He was definitely upset that night. His mom was really sweet, the total mom—'Elliott, make sure you wear a jacket, honey it might get cold out there.' It was trippy. Elliott was suddenly seven years old."[9]

Suggesting a more than average need to atone for remembered sins, on at least two occasions Welch wrote Elliott letters to offer explanations for his behavior, and to apologize, it seems, although he never quite says he's sorry, at least not explicitly. He admits, however, that he realizes Elliott wasn't happy in his early life in Texas. He's unsparing in his self-appraisals, but there are moments when he retracts ever so slightly. He calls himself inexperienced, hot-tempered. He figures he must have come across as mean, and admits that in many ways he was. But he assures Elliott he's changed, he's a different person now. He laments the fact that Elliott won't let him into his life more, give him the chance to show how he is not any longer who he used to be. He suggests the two of them sit down to talk at some point. He calls the letter important and very significant. It is signed with a flowing "Charlie."

What Welch describes in the letters, undoubtedly wrenching to compose, and therefore praiseworthy, is emotional abuse. He never mentions any physical beating of any kind. More likely than not, most of these hurtful episodes occurred when he and Elliott were alone, out of earshot of Elliott's mother, who wasn't fully aware of the pain Charlie's behavior engendered. But because of its intangibility, the fact that it never leaves bruises, emotional abuse can be particularly damaging. There's the nagging possibility it didn't even happen, at least not in the way one recalls. There's retrospective doubt. It seems to be "all in the mind." What results is a sort of self-undermining uncertainty, a sense Elliott was all too familiar with. As he says in the song "Abused," recorded but never officially released by the family—the title alone was considered distasteful—the closer you come to the fact of the matter, the more confused you get. Childhood realities are memory; memory is distortion, at best reconstruction, part fact, part fiction. Early drafts of "Abused" show Elliott trying on different scenarios, being beaten, broken, raped, hated. Kids are pictured sleeping in their clothes so nothing shows. His soul might be bruised, he says, but it still contains love and care; he was thirty-two before he knew it was there, before he felt it at all, he writes. On one hand, he's learned to defend himself; on the other, he's taken to attacking himself too. Whatever the outcome—he declares, wishfully—he is through reenacting a past that paints him black and blue. I feel I'm well, he adds, I dropped defenses at last.

It's not known how Smith reacted to the letters. They did not bring about any sort of reconciliation, however. He never did let Charlie into his life, although the art was a different matter. He let him in there, constantly, both directly and indirectly. It's possible to take any one Smith song, bend it ever so slightly, and point it in the direction of a presumed emotionally damaging childhood. When Elliott writes, in "Roman Candle," "I want to hurt him, I want to give him pain," the impulse is to link this "him" to Charlie. Sometimes Charlie even appears in name. "Flowers for Charlie" imagines a stoppage of the war. "I'm not a good G.I. Joe," Elliott sings, "and I won't fight you." (Remarkably, the song's melody recapitulates John Lennon's "War is Over," the popular Christmas-time tune, a fact Elliott was most likely aware of.) In life, too, Elliott's tendency, according to friends, was to vacillate. Some days he'd espouse forgiveness, deciding he was done battling a long lost cause, working to reduce Charlie to just somebody whom he used to know; then he'd revert to calling him a "fucking asshole," a "murderer."[10] In a kind of summary judgment, he once told Jennifer Chiba, "My childhood made me feel like I didn't exist. I was nothing."[11] The two of them had regular conversations about the problem of "unpacked rage and the fear that goes along with it." Victims of rage, they decided, "associate those feelings with violence—to express anger means 'I am like the tormenter,'" so the anger got denied or rechanneled.[12] Elliott is thoughtful, as always, on the subject of anger dynamics. In songs he refers to needing an enemy in order to focus rage's confusing pathways, as in "Easy Way Out."

In the last year of his life Elliott was besieged by all sorts of memories, as well as countless very frightening thoughts, some set in reality, some not, as he struggled to get off heroin and crack. As quickly as the material came, Elliott disowned it, sometimes in the same sentence. But once he did tell Chiba about a beating (although, here again, it is impossible to say whether any beating truly occurred). It took place, he seemed to feel, on the day Bunny and Charlie married (Elliott would have been four). It was the first beating, he said. And he didn't tell his mother about it. He'd "witnessed her being sad all the time, and when she met Charlie she was happy"—so he refused to ruin the very big day by risking destructive disclosures.[13]

In time Elliott would receive exceptionally adoring allies to help diffuse the psychological blows. Half-brother Darren Welch, Bunny and Charlie's son, was born on July 15, 1975, and Ashley Welch on October 23, 1976, when Elliott was seven. There were several different family homes in total—two in Duncanville, Texas, one in Cedar Hill, a Dallas suburb. Elliott's sixth-grade Duncanville home was on a U-shaped street called Parkside Circle, steps away from Lakeside Park. Town lines were sharp. When the Welches later moved to Cedar Hill—the home sat at the top of a steep street—the property just next door had a Duncanville address. Elliott's Cedar Hill home featured four and one half acres, its prior owner keeping cows and horses. There were woods, a barn, stables, a corral. The kids built treehouses, played baseball in the front yard.

A friend with whom Elliott grew especially close was Steve Pickering, nicknamed "Pickle." A skinny kid not usually found on ballfields, who wore braces and then-trendy Aviator-style glasses with Coke-bottle lenses that lent his eyes an owlishness, Pickle first met Elliott (whom Pickle calls Steve) in sixth grade at Byrd Junior High. They were in the same English class taught by a Mr. Brewer in Room 301, located along what was called "yellow hall" (the school hallways were color-coded). Elliott was the new kid; Pickering and others had not known him in elementary school. Eventually Elliott was seated directly in front of Pickle, and the two visited when Elliott passed back assignments and tests. "We unofficially competed for class smart-ass," Pickering recalls, the two trading droll quips and insults.[14] It was typical junior high–type stuff. Elliott was an excellent mimic; he could "do" just about anyone or anything, with changing voices and body postures. At one point he instigated a fake tough-guy routine lasting most of a week (one of Elliott's favorite things to do, a habit lasting all his life, was run jokes into the ground until they became almost absurdly comical). "Meet me at the flagpole after class," Elliott told Pickle in mock-bully mode. "Meet me at Lakeside Park this Saturday if you want an ass-whooping!" The conceit went on so long that Pickle took the silliness for a true invitation—not for a fight, exactly, but for a kind of play-date. So one weekend he rode his ten-speed to the park near Elliott's home. Elliott didn't show, but Pickle managed to pinpoint his home after inquiring about him with neighbor kids. As it turned out, "Steve" had strep throat. But Pickle returned later, and the friendship blossomed.

The two boys shared a name, and they nearly shared a birthday (Pickle was born August 3). Both were also in band, a massively popular, very serious extracurricular. Pickle played sax, Elliott clarinet. In 1982 Elliott was elected Byrd Symphonic Band president, beating out Pickering, in fact, who wound up serving as treasurer. A yearbook photo shows the two posing with bright smiles in front of a brick wall; Pickering wears a tie, Elliott's shirt is open at the collar. (There was, as it happens, another Steve Smith in band at the time; Elliott went by Steve P., the other boy was Steve E. Both played clarinet, Elliott first chair).

In the farm-style Cedar Hill house Elliott's room was at the very back, the rest of the family situated on the other side of the home. Elliott and Pickle spent a lot of time in that room, doing what 1980s-era 12-year-olds tended to do. They were deep into Dungeons & Dragons, although they weren't terribly advanced players. As a gift Elliott bought Pickle a "Dungeon Master's Guide," a sort of instruction manual for the game. Mainly it was just Elliott and Pickle, although once they invited a different boy to take part, only to discover he was at level 15—too good, too intense. They also spent hours riding their ten-speeds around aimlessly, bored and looking for stuff to do. Virtually every home had a basketball hoop where various Steves, Scotts, Marks, Mikes, or Davids—the likely boys' names of the era—congregated. They would shoot around, play HORSE or 21. "Elliott was really good," Pickering remembers. "I got beat by him all the time but we just kept playing anyway." Elliott was on the junior high team. For kicks Pickle thought of trying out too, but the opportunity never materialized. Chess was another pastime; here again, according to Pickering, Elliott "always won."[15]

Darren and Ashley were a constant oblique presence in the house, "two little kids just running around," Pickering says. But one detail struck Pickle forcefully, even at the time. The three siblings were unusually close. There was zero rivalry, zero stepsibling pathos. Elliott was "surprisingly positive" toward his brother and sister, with none of the customary "get out of my room stuff." He was always "very willing to include the younger kids in whatever he was doing. It was obvious," Pickering says, "that he liked being around them and vice versa. He had a great deal of affection for them." Another friend, Kevin Denbow—a long-haired "dude" who wore Ozzie T-shirts and whom most people fancied a sort of metalhead, reached the same conclusion: "He was real parental toward Darren and Ashley. He had a real tight bond with both those kids. He was very protective. He'd always stop what he was doing and take care of them. He was very inclusive."[16] One particular night Elliott scheduled a "sleepover" in his room, with Darren and Ashley spending the night on the floor in sleeping bags.

Around this time Elliott also made the acquaintance of Mark Merritt, another band student. Merritt remembers his junior high years as "the worst of my life. Elliott and I met at a lunch table. Music came up, naturally. I played guitar, and found out 'Steve' did too. Our personalities just kind of matched." At one point Elliott lent Merritt sheet music for Rush's "La Villa Strangiato," from the *Hemispheres* album. "Listen carefully to the bass line," he told him gravely. From then on Merritt was a Rush-head; he even started experimenting on bass with an old guitar. "I discovered that bass players weren't just some kind of third wheel," he says.[17]

Merritt names Elliott "one of the reasons I survived junior high." Once the two were sitting on a bench just after gym class, minding their own business. An "asshole jock" sauntered up and, with no warning, threw a basketball in Merritt's face, shattering his glasses. Stunned, and not in the habit of aggressively sticking up for himself, Merritt understandably drew back, reaching for what was left of his frames. But Elliott went after the bully. "Fuck off," he said. "That's my friend." There were no blows, as it turns out, but Elliott's response, his courage and support, left an enduring impression. "He took my bullets," Merritt explains. "He always stuck up for his friends. I was a dork, and he wasn't. But still I knew he had my back." Innocent victims of abuse elicited feelings of identification, it seems, and Elliott, rather than ignoring the violence, took strong action. His impulse was to sympathize; compassion came easily.

With its massive yard the Cedar Hill home needed a lot of tending to. It was on the subject of this tending that Elliott and Charlie clashed, the latter "always coming up with stuff for Elliott to do," Pickering says. "When are you going to mow the lawn?" was a more or less constant refrain. Bunny,

Pickering says, was always "real friendly," "positive and upbeat." Charlie usually less so, in comparison. "There were raised voices. More than I would have tried with my dad," according to Pickering. The sense was that Elliott was "more willing to engage in confrontation and talking back than most other boys." Pickering does not recall any fights with Charlie, no physical violence of any kind. But tension was visible, an accepted norm. Denbow's impression was the same. "Elliott always had chores to do. He didn't take much to authority, period. He was rebellious against authority figures at school too." As Denbow remembers, even back then "Charlie was not Elliott's favorite person. I never saw anything that would lead me to think Charlie was abusive. But he was real strict. Charlie's rules were Charlie's rules. Elliott was far more of a freethinker than Charlie was."[18] Still, as Pickering is quick to acknowledge, he never had any problems himself with Charlie. Charlie never yelled or "said anything bad." He was always real welcoming when Pickering stopped by, "and I was over there all the time." To Pickering, the arguments were typical adolescent boy stuff. "I'm sure there was some stepchild dynamic too," Pickering figures. "As in, 'You are not my dad.' But at the same time I didn't see anything unusual." When Merritt came by Bunny was almost always around—"an absolute sweetheart. She put up with a lot. She was what we'd call a cool mom." Charlie, on the other hand, was typically out and about, working or "doing his own thing." On occasions when Charlie entered the house, "I would have to be on guard," Merritt says. "Be on my best behavior. We tried to do what little we could with that whole situation." Charlie's presence, in other words, fomented an aura of apprehensiveness. Everyone walked on eggshells, careful not to make too much noise.

Charlie was an athlete, so he pressed Elliott in a similar direction, to the point where he actually became, to some degree willingly, a bit of a jock. Pickering recalls Charlie "all the time pushing Elliott to go on weekend runs"—10Ks at seven A.M.., Saturday morning. Grudgingly Elliott complied, sometimes enjoying it more than he'd expected to. There was basketball, and Elliott actually made the team; there was also soccer and football. More than either Elliott or Darren, Ashley was especially athletic, a fast runner on the track team. She played softball all through her life, her position centerfield for a softball club team at University of Southern Cali-

7th grade yearbook photo with Elliott wearing a T-shirt from a 5K/10K run in Cleburne. (Photograph courtesy of Steve Pickering.)

fornia, where she went to college. Elliott liked soccer, but the competition proved to be short lived. Charlie ultimately pulled him off the team in favor of Boy Scouts. He reasoned, Elliott later observed dryly, that it would be good for him to "wear a uniform and march around and learn how to tie knots."

Elliott told a comic tale about football in particular (he wore jersey number 64). He was "a little on the small side in height and weight," so coaches started him out at wide receiver, despite the fact that "in junior high nobody can throw the football." Every play he'd run about ten yards or so, then collide into his defender. "You hit kind of hard for about the first ten plays then the rest of the game you're just kind of running out there and bumping up against the guy. He doesn't want to hit you very hard either." Unlike other kids on the team, he caught with his hands instead of his chest, but still nobody passed to him. So he was moved to defensive line. "You're down there like inches away from somebody's head," he recalls, "and some guy is going, 'I'm going to fuck you up!'" Looking back, he can't quite believe he played so many sports. "I can tell you it doesn't build character," he informed an interviewer in 2003. "Except maybe the character to not play sports because you were forced to."[19] Pickering had a different take. "The concept, to me, of 'I play football and I don't like it,' didn't make sense to my twelve-year-old brain." He figures Elliott liked the sport more than he ever let on. After all, it's not as if he ever had a problem resisting Charlie's demands, Pickle says. If he truly didn't want to play, likely he could have opted out.

It was as if, in his imagination at least, if not in reality, these defensive linemen roamed Elliott's neighborhood in face-masked packs, hungry for more contact, looking to fuck him up again, as he suggested at times to interviewers. There was a feeling he had of spreading menace, mostly internal, but engulfing the outside world as well. In Cedar Hill, except for stalwart friends like Pickle, Merritt, and Denbow, Elliott as a sixth grader rarely met anyone at all like him, anyone he felt simpatico with. Plus he was just plain bored. But he also had to do all he could to sidestep confrontations: he kept quiet, he sometimes avoided the outdoors, an arena of fear. Some of this was overworked imagination, no doubt, excess sensitivity. But fights weren't uncommon; certain kids around at the time lived for fisticuffs, needing little excuse for action. When a new family moved in next door, one with an older fourteen-year-old boy from the football team, Elliott looked up to the new kid, mainly because he feared he'd kick his ass, he told a journalist years later. They had a pool table, so Elliott was over there all the time. On occasion there were sleepovers too. Yet the overall family strategy, according to Elliott, was to not make waves. So long as you weren't black or gay, so long as you kept a nice, low profile, "they left you in peace."[20] The fact that the Berrymans were amateur musicians also caused trouble. They were thought of as a "family of freaks" and looked down on accordingly. Why, the thinking apparently ran, would anyone spend so much time doing anything as useless as music? Especially when it didn't bring in any money?

Pickering recalls just one full-fledged fight, Elliott versus a much bigger kid. "I don't think I'd have fought the guy," says Pickering. Both wound up in the principal's office, where, while waiting to be seen, they shook hands and resolved their differences.

"Interviewers write about Elliott being completely miserable in Dallas," Pickering notes. "I thought we were having a great time." Denbow agrees, figuring that childhood misery made for "a better backstory" than goofy escapades and suburban Texas boredom.

* * *

As sixth grade faded, so did all interest in ten-speeds, basketball, movies at the Red Bird Mall, and games of Dungeons & Dragons. Seventh grade brought with it an intense focus on music—any kind of music, any time, from "Carry on My Wayward Son" to Hank Williams. And it was the beginning, the origin, of Elliott's obsession with recording in whatever way he could, with whatever technology happened to be available. Pickle played keyboards, and Denbow was learning guitar. Merritt had started on guitar, but bass slowly grew on him. At first it was all about listening, and the big crush, one all Elliott's friends shared, was the ornate, prog-rock Rush. "We were heavy-duty Rush freaks," Denbow says. "We slept and breathed Rush from sunup to sundown." Elliott got his hands on a Rush music book, and according to Denbow, he was "very meticulous" about analyzing the music— he was "*into it* into it." "Broon's Bane," from the album *Exit Stage Left*, was a song with extra-special fascinations. As a means of challenging himself musically, something he did often, Elliott worked to learn the song's intro, sounding it out by ear. "He had that drive," Merritt says. "He was by far the best musician of all of us. He wanted to see where it would take him." For months he would "veg out," Denbow recalls, on one particular album, just as he had many years later with *Magical Mystery Tour.* It was U2's *October,* then the Clash's *London Calling* or the Police's *Synchronicity.* AC/DC was in the mix, along with Led Zeppelin, Kiss's *Kiss Alive,* Pink Floyd's *Animals,* Kansas, and the Who's *Who's Next,* which Elliott gave to Pickering. Pickering always saw Elliott's tastes as exceptionally "advanced and diverse for a thirteen-year-old." There was nothing unusual, of course, about liking Kiss and U2, but Elliott always searched out a group's "more obscure material," the tunes no one knew about or listened to. One birthday Elliott asked for R.E.M.'s *Fables of the Reconstruction,* and Pickering got it for him as a gift. Quirky, new-wave stuff struck his fancy too, for instance the band Madness, whose video was getting heavy play. Occasionally Elliott would do the "Madness walk," preceded by the shout out "One step beyond!"

Like countless sensitive, introspective teenagers with tinges of melancholy and an ear for poetry, Elliott was also a Jackson Browne fan. He owned the album *Late for the Sky,* which Bruce Springsteen called Browne's masterpiece, with its Magritte-inspired cover of a car on a street at twilight. The songs dealt with love loss, apocalypse, and death, which Browne compares to a song he can't sing but also can't stop hearing. Once while Pickering and Elliott were hanging out the song "The Pretender" came on the radio. That set Elliott off on a long analysis of Browne's lyrical content. In Pickering's view, Browne was a "big early influence."

Far more than anything else, however, it was the Beatles that Elliott looked to for inspiration. Countless evenings and weekends he and Pickle talked, played chess, and listened to *The White Album* and *Abbey Road*. But they liked the older stuff too. Pickering owned *Beatles '65*, so when the boys were over there instead of at Elliott's home, they would put it on—that or *Sgt. Pepper's Lonely Hearts Club Band*, which Pickle also owned. Denbow recalls a deep exchange on the subject of singing and singing style. Elliott had played John Lennon's surrealistic anti-lullaby "Cry Baby Cry" from *The White Album*, one of Lennon's nonsense songs, as he liked to call them (others include "I Am the Walrus" and "Lucy in the Sky with Diamonds"). Most rock singers they listened to were screamers—a problem for Elliott, who never felt comfortable barking out vocals. At this point in his musical development he agreed to sing only under duress, after every other alternative had been excluded. "Cry Baby Cry" features a softly lilting melody, sung by Lennon, with a falsetto finish, sung by McCartney. "I told Elliott that he ought to just whisper when he sang," Denbow remembers. "That way no one even knows if you're not in tune. I also said it was easier to hit high notes if you had that airier, whispery sound." Elliott tried it out, and lo and behold it worked. In later years a hushed fragile tone became Elliott's signature vocal delivery. It may have originated in his back bedroom in Cedar Hill, Texas, at Denbow's instigation.

But more than just listening to songs, the boys worked hard to learn them as flawlessly as possible, no matter how long it took or how many repetitions. Here again, Elliott was "way ahead of most people," Denbow says. If you ever wanted to know how to play a particular tune, Elliott was the guy you went to for help. "If it was musical and he was involved, he would rise to the top," says Denbow. In Elliott's room sat an old upright piano. He and Merritt had pushed it there painfully across heavy carpet, after getting Elliott's parents' permission to relocate it. He played it endlessly, as Denbow recalls. The Lennon album *Shaved Fish* was a fixation then, with its compilation of singles including "Imagine," "Mother," "Mind Games," and others.

Elliott learned these songs on piano, playing the same piece over and over till he got it exactly right, his innate perfectionism urging him on. Around the same time he perfected the rapidly fingered synthesizer solo from Led Zeppelin's "All of My Love," plus the solo from George Harrison's "Old Brown Shoe," another song Elliott especially loved.

Pickle has a similar memory, from around the time he and Smith first met. They were in the Cedar Hill home discussing piano. Elliott had one year of lessons under his belt, Pickering six. Even so, in Pickering's estimation "he was still way better than I was." Elliott casually offered to play something that struck Pickle as a bit surprising: Dan Fogelberg's "Auld Lang Syne" tune, the Christmastime staple. "He just knocked it out of the park. All arpeggios. All over the keyboard. Hitting it with a lot of flourish. I was stunned and flabbergasted." Pickering humbly reciprocated, trying out the '70s instrumental "Music Box Dancer," or perhaps, as he remembers it, the theme from *Chariots of Fire*. The feeling even then was that nothing measured up to what Elliott did, what he was capable of. His talent, the effortless way he learned and played, set him miles apart from all other practicing young musicians, even a trio as capable in their own right as Pickle, Denbow, and Merritt.

In the short span of a year or two, music grew utterly self-defining. Nothing else came close to comparing. It was most of what Elliott wanted to talk about, most of what he wanted to do. So, inevitably, a band was formed. Denbow, one year older, played guitar, Pickering keyboards (a Lowrey Micro Genie with sixteen different preprogrammed sounds and twelve drum rhythms), Elliott guitar and piano, and Merritt, guitar and bass. In the Red Bird Mall there was a hybrid record and instrument store called the Melody Shop, where Elliott bought his picks and strings. A drummer from Lancaster had tacked up a note saying he was looking for a band, and the boys piled into Pickering's dad's gray work van to audition the kid. It didn't go anywhere. Pickering's not sure why. But later a different prospect named Tim Hunt was found. Hunt possessed the one transcendent prerequisite for teen band drummer work: he owned his own kit.

This makeshift unit was never officially christened, although for a short time Elliott thought about proposing Deviation. Occasionally the group discussed other "deadly serious names," as Pickle recalls, but more often they tossed around potential joke names like The Used Carburetors. Yet, although fated to remain nameless, the band put on one public performance, likely the first of Elliott's musical career (he would have been around thirteen). The occasion was a talent show at Trinity Methodist on Clark Road in Duncanville, a church Elliott's and Merritt's families attended semi-regularly (Merritt places Elliott's family's religiosity at 4 on a scale of 1 to 10). "This was a big deal for us," Pickle emphasizes, the preparation and lead-up heavy with several practice sessions devoted to getting as ready as possible. In all, wearing suits and clip-on ties, the band performed two numbers: the goofy "Tequila" and, next, the mischievously pagan "Stairway to Heaven," with Pickering handling Stairway's flute sounds on his Lowrey. It would be Elliott, however, tearing into the song's long concluding guitar solo which, per usual, he worked at and worked at until it was note perfect. Miraculously, a rehearsal tape exists in which Elliott, Merritt, and Pickering go over the two tunes. Elliott sings "Stairway" atop the musical accompaniment. The sound is faint because his voice was not amplified. He manages the guitar intro flawlessly, Pickle tackling the synth. "Tequila" features Elliott on guitar, Merritt on bass. It ends haphazardly in the practice tape, with a stray bass note. Merritt exclaims, "I can't hear!" then Elliott answers, "You have to watch!" for cues signaling the song's end. Merritt recalls the performance being greeted warmly, despite the fact that the song choices clashed comically with church ideology. The attitude of all involved was, Did we really just play "Stairway" and "Tequila" at Trinity Methodist!?

All along, the question of singers for the band was a vexation. The very last thing any of the boys wanted to do, Elliott included, was sing "Stairway," or anything else, for that matter. Vocals were therefore usually handled by a pretty girl named Kim, one year younger than Elliott, a band officer whose mom was a sixth-grade math teacher at Byrd Junior High, and who lived four houses down the street from Denbow.[21] In the middle of the night Elliott snuck out to deliver a set of handwritten "Stairway" lyrics so Kim could work at learning them by heart (although she never quite did, setting the lyrics in front of her on a music stand for the real performance). Her father was awakened by a rapping at the window—"What's going on?" he thundered. Then he swung open the front door and took off after Elliott down the street. He never did corral the prowler. When Kim's dad returned home he said, jokingly, "Whoever that kid was, he sure can run fast!"

Like Elliott, Kim played clarinet. She'd also taught herself guitar, and "always chose to learn popular songs with lyrics I liked." She got to the point where she could manage almost any Eagles song, and others by Linda Ronstadt and Willie Nelson. She played and sang in talent shows between fourth and seventh grades, and spent a lot of time more or less "singing in the shower." Elliott she got to know during band rehearsals. "It was a huge deal," she says. "Band was bigger than football, even. The concerts were huge. The class was around seventy students, in junior high." By high school, that number reached upwards of three hundred.

To Kim, Elliott was always happy, always cracking jokes—"witty, funny, smart, charming." "He was just always so entertaining," says Kim. "He wasn't just book smart, but commonsense smart too. And if he made a joke, he'd do things like throw in some obscure algebraic term to make it even funnier."

In school, Elliott was a "hot commodity." Everyone liked him, everyone wanted to be around him. Kim recalls, "He was a Leo. A sort of bigger than life personality." Slowly the two discovered the different things they had in common. Both were long-distance runners—Elliott always wore his cherished runner's wristband. Both also went to the same church—where the performance took place—along with Merritt. It was small, in relative terms, fewer than a hundred in the congregation, nothing close to a megachurch, far more modest and humble. During sermons kids sat in back pews, doing their best to keep quiet. Sunday school classes formed part of the curriculum too, and Kim recalls Elliott attending, yet not regularly. It wasn't a matter of serious religiosity or devotion; church was just something you did in suburban Dallas. It was taken for granted, a form of socializing, a means of creating community.

At long last, in November 1982, love came knocking, in the fragile, suddenly fervid way it does for preadolescents, replete with drama and whispers, as well as abject terror. Kim, a self-described "typical 80s cheerleader type," noticed another popular girl giving Elliott threateningly close attention—flipping her hair, flirting. As fate would have it, this was the same girl who had stolen Kim's boyfriend back in fourth grade. She vowed,

"Oh no! Not this time. Not again!" And in fact, there was no repeat, no second theft. It would be Kim and Elliott who got together. In the delicate argot of Junior High, they became officially "boyfriend–girlfriend." Soon enough they were holding hands on their way to class, in effect proclaiming their exclusivity. "All the other girls kept asking me, 'Has he kissed you yet? When is he going to do it?'" Kim recalls. The decisive moment arrived on the way home one day, as they strolled together after school. "Suddenly he just stopped," Kim says, "and planted one on me." They had a necklace made. She wore one half, he wore the other. It symbolized their "steady" union.

Kim noticed Elliott's basic difference, how he stood out from others in the class. He was more mature, deeper when discussing his inner life, reflective and sometimes strangely calm. He also simply looked different. He liked to wear black parachute pants with "a million zippers and pockets." He rarely washed his hair, and he always wore tight T-shirts. Then, most conspicuously of all, there was his virtuosic musicality, so obvious to everyone. He could play "piano like nobody's business," and he'd taught himself guitar virtually overnight. "He loved playing fast, so fast, over and over, like classic Van Halen–type stuff. It was chord-slide, chord-slide. And then when the riffs came, he really tore into them, never a wrong note."

They didn't exactly date; they were too young for that at twelve and thirteen. Their contacts occurred primarily in band or at church. Youth activities were often on the agenda. Sometimes the kids went on overnights, staying in motels with chaperones. On one such occasion, either Elliott or his friend brought along a small bottle of Black Velvet. Kids rendezvoused in a room and traded nasty-tasting swigs. But leaders busted them. Many got grounded "for months" in the aftermath. At times Elliott and Kim met up at night too. They sat on the trampoline in Elliott's large backyard and talked for hours. "One night he was very distraught," Kim remembers. "Very upset about Charlie. He never got into what the problems were, exactly. He talked in generalities. But it was beyond anything I could comprehend. He wasn't just worried about himself; he was concerned for Ashley too." Kim had noticed Bunny and Charlie at church. To her, Bunny was sweet, Charlie a "big, quiet, ominous man"—ominous not in the sense of frightening, but more because he was a dad and difficult to know or feel entirely comfortable with. He was tall, with dark hair, and "he didn't smile a lot." "In my opinion—and I was just twelve, you know—it was an absolute disconnect. I did not see how they were a couple at all."

But it wasn't all hard, all ominous feeling. Kim sometimes headed over to Elliott's house to hang out or listen to music. One Christmas they snuggled under the tree for hours until Bunny gently suggested she had to go. There were also mini holiday concerts. It was the Welch family custom to open presents on Christmas Eve. But first, the kids were expected to put on a program. They wrapped towels around their heads—Elliott, Ashley, and Darren—and made like the Three Wise Men. Music featured too, as always—Elliott on piano or clarinet, Ashley on trombone, Darren on guitar. They wrote alternate lyrics to popular songs, recasting them in goofy musical formats. Bunny made personalized stockings with apples and oranges inside and chocolate-covered cherries.

"Kim was Elliott's big crush," Denbow says. Merritt remembers her as a very sweet kid, "definitely attractive," and "very kind-hearted." "Even with geeks like me," Merritt says, "she was still 'part of the family,' if you will." Just like Elliott, in other words, Kim had a native kindness and compassion. Denbow owned a motorized scooter, just barely secure enough to hold two people. Some nights during seventh and eighth grade, and even into the beginning of freshman year, he'd sneak out after midnight, then sputter over to Elliott's. Elliott stealthily crept out the back door of his home, and the boys rode to the Byrd bleachers to "make out with our respective girls" (Kim had a friend named Nicole whom Denbow was involved with). Essentially the same routine was followed on different nights with Merritt, and sometimes marijuana got thrown into the mix, though neither Elliott nor Merritt felt comfortable confessing the fact that they smoked it. For a long time they kept the naughty secret to themselves. There were more hook-ups too, one with a girl named Michelle Schwartzott—a clarinet player, like Elliott, whom everybody called Zott. She and Smith scandalously "made out" in the back of a bus during a band road trip (Kim never got wind of this, and it may have occurred after she and Elliott had broken up). Zott was a senior with a cool muscle car, Elliott (by this time) a freshman. She was a big-sister type, as it turned out, not girlfriend material. Elliott used to mention her to Kim, and though she wondered whether the two had ever hooked up, it never came out in conversation.

No more gigs materialized, but it didn't really matter. The band was far less interested in performing than they were in recording, although occasionally they jammed in Elliott's oversized backyard, running extension cords from outlets in a nearby shed. Pickle's father was an amateur musician himself—an incredible guitar player, according to Merritt—and he owned a four-track reel-to-reel with Radio Shack tapes. In his room Elliott kept a boom box and used a mic to record from it; he also, in time, picked up a Gibson SG solid-body electric guitar—his first, according to Denbow—plus a Sigma Japanese version of a Martin acoustic (given to him by his father, Gary, and which Denbow inherited and owns to this day), a yellow DOD overdrive valve for distortion, and a blue DOD stereo chorus supplying a sort of deep purple reverb sound. Most of the actual recording took place at Pickle's home, since that is where the four-track lived. Mainly it was rock, late at night—arpeggio guitar, heavy metal, distortion. Elliott progressed quickly—"really quickly," Pickle recalls—from merely learning his instruments to writing his own songs, the first of his life. Pickle says, "To me, that was out there, man. It was revolutionary. Not only figuring out other people's songs but writing his own." He goes on: "Elliott had a sense of possibility that made you excited to be there. It was like, 'Of course I'm going to write a song.' It opened the world to a lot of new things. He could envision and execute things totally out of the ordinary and make them seem perfectly natural. It just seemed like a lot of things were possible when you were around him . . . I got a lot of courage from him."

A very early recording session, Elliott's virginal effort, occurred in fall r winter of 1983, when he was thirteen or fourteen. He used his Gibson G, although at times he also borrowed Pickering's dad's Gibson Les Paul, guitar Elliott later bought from Pickering senior. "For most of the tracks," ckering says, "we recorded the guitar by simply running the cord directly m the guitar to the tape recorder"—with no amp or effects. For optimum ibility Pickle checked out a Maxi-Korg synthesizer from school, also ed a Korg 800DV. It was the property of the Duncanville High School d program. Two songs were Rush covers—"Closer to the Heart" and)divisions"—with Pickle on synth and Elliott on guitar. There were finger-picking tunes, mellow and happy and often quite beautiful, such e folk song "Soul Cake," later recorded by Peter, Paul, and Mary as

"A Soalin." But the remaining five numbers were original compositions by Elliott, each exclusively instrumental. One of these, a tune the boys played a lot, was a heavy-metal exercise christened "#37." Others were delicate, pretty, minor-key guitar phrasings that Elliott sometimes concluded with "happy" major chords, as Pickering recalls.

Merritt was present for one unexpected songwriting session that took place during a summer trip to South Padre Island, and which set a sort of standard for Elliott's deceptively haphazard creative process. Merritt's family was on vacation and Elliott had been invited to tag along. The two sat around strumming in the motel room, wasting time as the rest of the Merritt clan wandered off exploring. At one point Elliott simply said, "Let's write a song." He kept picking, trying out different chords and variations, waiting to hear something interesting or fresh pop out. Bit by bit a structure came together—bridge and chorus—and now and then Elliott paused to scratch out lyrics. Merritt, like Pickle, was in a minor state of shock. It was one thing to learn songs others had written—the Rush tunes, Kansas tunes—but something else entirely to try composing an original piece. But "I'll be damned if the kid didn't do it," Merritt says. And to his astonishment, "it didn't suck! It completely blew me away. He'd just lean back and play." The tune was in G, and to this day Merritt recalls one particular line: "See the poor man as he walks while the rich man takes the train."

Virtually anyone who played with Elliott—Denbow, eventual high school and Heatmiser bandmate Tony Lash—notes his fascination with leading tones and passing chords, transitioning moments between major notes in a measure, movements from verse to chorus and back to verse. To Elliott, every moment in every song had potential; the subtleties often made the tune, amounting to an idiosyncratic signature. Part of this interest came from the Beatles, passing chord geniuses. Even their toss-off songs, such as "Your Mother Should Know," feature gorgeous travelings from chorus to verse, or vice versa.

In a fascinating interview from 2000 Elliott talks in detail about his songwriting process. As he did frequently, he begins by saying he simply imagines things, makes things up "just during the day."[22] He calls imagination "the divine force"—"if you don't block it up it will come out and surprise you." It's not about language, he says, but more about shapes, an interesting fact to talk about but hard to describe usefully with words. "I'm really into chord changes, and that's the thing I liked when I was a kid. I don't make up a riff, really. It's usually a sequence instead, that has some implied melody in it." He says he's drawn to chords in which the bass note is a fifth—a C with a G in the bass, for instance. He also used half chords—chords in which you don't want all the strings to sound. His advice to would-be songwriters is to "just relax and stop thinking about what people want to hear. Put it in the blender and see what comes out."

That's what Pickle, Merritt, and Elliott were doing most of the time in Pickle's home in Duncanville, Texas: throwing things in the blender and seeing how they came out. That Elliott was meticulously, diligently working on and trying out tonal and chordal variations in seventh and eighth grade describes an obvious musical gift. As Denbow said, he rose to the top. It came ridiculously easily and naturally. "He was the guy everything was centered around," says Denbow.[23] And just as revealingly, Elliott shared his oversized talent. He wasn't stingy with it. All the boys took stabs at writing songs, but the band was basically Elliott. Everyone knew that. As Pickle put it, "Elliott was John, Paul, and George, and we were all Ringo." But Elliott never made anyone *feel* like Ringo. What he gave Pickle, Merritt, and Denbow was an identity, an exciting one, and they have never forgotten that. Their gratitude, expressed with deep emotion, is palpable.

It wasn't Elliott's habit at this stage to name songs (in fact, even many of the songs on his first solo album are unnamed). The majority were repeat exercises, such as "#37," with its driving electric guitar solo in the middle. Yet most were still enormously challenging for the teenagers to play, legitimate songs with characteristic ABABC pop structure. And Elliott pushed himself. He was aiming for "more advanced songs," Pickle says (advanced, that is, in relation to peers). "He didn't like to write songs with fewer than five chords."

Over time lyrics entered the mix, straightforward scene-setting reflections, not open to interpretation, according to Pickle, in which Elliott simply described a visual picture. A song called "Ocean" amounted to a three-verse meditation on the sea at night, a kind of literal snapshot, "not distant or impressionistic," Pickle says, "but more like a photo." It's a solemn, creamy, arpeggio-laced melody, sleepy and hypnotic. In recordings Elliott sometimes sings it, but Kim does too in alternate takes. The tide is pictured coming in and out along a lonely, moonlit shore. In its solitary way it falls to rest on the beach as Elliott peers out at "the endless moon." He's struck by the water's serenity, magic, and mystery. It floods his house and "takes control of me."

From here there followed a metamorphosis into first-person narrative that Pickle traces to a Jackson Browne influence, the songs just a bit more introspective, a bit more confessional and searching. Elliott kept a poster in his bedroom of a halcyon nature scene from the flipside of a brochure advertising the Outward Bound program (which Pickle is quick to point out Elliott did not himself endorse; he just liked the image). The poster inspired a tune Elliott titled "Outward Bound," recorded in the summer of 1984.[24] Along with the slightly less fully realized "Ocean," this qualifies as Elliott's very first fully complete song with both music and lyrics. At least four distinct iterations exist, first with piano accompaniment, later with guitar, some sung by Elliott, some by Kim. Each iteration includes slight lyrical variations. It's irrepressibly catchy, impossible to hear and not sing. It's also positive, hopeful, bright, and future oriented, a definite outlier in the Elliott canon. The vibe is country, Kim's vocal especially sweet and twangy (Pickle notes, "We ran a lot of reverb on it. *A lot*"). The story focuses on moving to a new life in the Northwest, "under a cloudy sky." The singer, tired of running under the gun, abandons "the business life" to "write down my favorite sounds." He sees the beauty in the trees, feels the cool and autumn breeze. "I'm outward bound" he declares, leaving the cities and the towns. "My life has just begun."

"Basically," Pickle recalls, "it was 'This is what I like about the Northwest.' He'd been there a few times to visit his father Gary in Portland. Not exactly a 'fuck you' to Texas, really. Objective observer-type stuff about the feelings he got when he spent time with his dad. So he's in the song too."

Strikingly, the time signature is ¾. The song, in some ways Elliott's most complete, is a waltz, in other words, like many of the country/western tunes he could not help but absorb in those days, and also like several Beatles numbers, such as "You've Got to Hide Your Love Away" and "Norwegian Wood" (whose time signature is a waltzy 6/8 rather than the more common ¾). "We had done plenty of ¾ in band class too," Pickle explains, so although the form itself wasn't unprecedented, its effect on Elliott was. From the very beginning, waltzes had resonance. Later Elliott made use of ¾ again and again, returning to it either unconsciously or with deliberate intent, it's hard to say. Something about its jaunty timings jibed ideally with his rhythmic sensibilities even back in eighth and ninth grade.

Beyond that, the waltz form seemed also to summon ancient feelings, acting as emotional trigger (or vice versa). It signified childhood mysteriously. So often, when Elliott turns to those days in his more mature songs, he drops into the same evocative time signature. "Flowers for Charlie" is a waltz. So is "No Confidence Man," yet another Charlie-themed number. The list of Elliott waltzes is long. He even noticed it now and then in interviews. Not every one centers on childhood or Charlie, but enough do that the link comes to seem less than accidental. Waltz is the dream, childhood the dream's latent content, its emotional subtext, one aligned with the other in symbiosis.

"Waltz #2 (XO)," for instance, the third song on Elliott's 1998 XO album—there is also a "Waltz #1"—is his certain masterpiece. It's got a roadhouse, Wild West, player-piano feel to it. And yet again, the tune, with its staccato ¾ beat, takes him back to Cedar Hill, the suburbs of Texas with Bunny and Charlie. Waltz "Outward Bound" was no Texas fuck you, more a love letter to wet, green Oregon, and to father Gary Smith and the promise of a new life he'd been getting tastes of during those semi-regular trips up north. There's love in "Waltz #2 (XO)" as well—qualified—but a deeper impulse is anger, aimed squarely at Charlie. Brilliantly laid out in metaphorical cloakings, the song's a secret life history, summarizing Elliott's feelings about the Cedar Hill atmosphere and the intricacies of his relationship with mother and stepfather. He was always exceptionally worried about the possible hurtfulness of his lyrics. The thought that they might cause harm pained him. So a habit was established according to which he'd begin songs directly, explicitly autobiographically, then revise away from fact toward vagueness and abstraction. Choice specifics grounded the song, but meanings trailed off into obscurity. Emotionally, it was an elision of the personal—there but camouflaged—a self-erasure. He was in the songs, they were him, it was his personal past reconsidered, the sum total of who he was, but they were more too, a mix of voices, first, second, and third person, all getting a word in, all with something crucial to say. "XO," as Smith told an interviewer in 1998, means "hugs and kisses," the sort of thing people throw in at the end of letters. A more arcane, connotative meaning was "fuck off." "But that's a really rare meaning I didn't know about," Elliott explains, apparently sincerely.

"Waltz #2 (XO)" kicks off with a hard, blunt beat, followed by vaguely ominous-sounding, A-minor guitar chords. Piano enters—that saloon vibe Elliott always enjoyed, even from the Cedar Hill days ("It almost sounds out of tune," as Denbow said, "but still it works somehow"). The setting is a karaoke bar. Bunny sings the Everly Brothers tune "Cathy's Clown" ("He's not a man at all . . . Dontcha think it's kinda sad/that you're treating me so bad/or don't you even care?"), a possible allusion to Charlie, whom Elliott had seemed to link with clowns in other songs too. He can't read her expression. She just stares off into space. What Elliott notices—the Charlie subcurrent—she does not. But his feelings for her are obviously positive. He vows, "I'm never going to know you now/but I'm going to love you anyhow." (An earlier song, "Dirt," foreshadows the China doll reference: "You're a China doll/You don't feel nothing at all . . . You can't get over him/Because you know what's in there.")

Then the next singer's name is announced. To Elliott it's remote, but somehow familiar. He's doing fine now, he says, the forgotten name some sort of painful stimulus; he's glad it fails to register. The implication is that the second singer is Charlie, and his message—the song he covers—is "You're No Good," made popular by Linda Ronstadt. Elliott characterizes "You're No Good" as an act of revenge for the message of the first tune. It's also the reaction Elliott often got from his stepfather—a habitually fault-finding perfectionist, a fact Charlie refers to in the letter he sent.

The third verse revisits the "You're No Good" theme. Elliott asks "Mr. Man" to leave him alone: "In the place where I make no mistakes/In the place where I have what it takes." If living with Charlie could sometimes be toxic, an atmosphere of never-ending close scrutiny and summary judgments resulting in feelings of worthlessness, then the mistake-free place Elliott imagines is one emptied of Charlies, a place he can just be who he is without fear and anger. Live, Elliott sometimes heightened the song's contrast between Bunny and Charlie. Instead of "XO Mom," which he sings in the recorded version, he said, plainly, "I love you, mom." It's the kind of bald declaration Elliott was not usually inclined to make, preferring instead to keep the autobiography a lot more scrambled. On one hand, he seems to be telling Bunny he does not blame her for Charlie, and what he did; on the other, he allows himself a small amount of disappointment, finding her emotionlessness (in the first verse), neglectful, as if he wanted more feeling from her, as if he wanted her to stand up for him more than she did (a fact confirmed to me by several of Elliott's very close friends).

On balance, it's hard to arrive at any certain position about what, exactly, happened with Charlie. What presents itself is the usual clotted, messy biographical chaos of competing vectors. Judging from the letters he wrote, Charlie regretted his parenting. It was too strict, too unforgiving. He acknowledged that, and he tried apologizing. But friends like Pickle and Denbow, both of whom spent large amounts of time in the Welch household, noticed nothing conspicuously harmful. The sense, however, shared by Merritt, for one, and by later friends to whom Elliott had confided, supplying varying degrees of detail, is that he had lived through several damaging scenes, events that went beyond insults and other personal attacks. Some friends, after all, can't talk about Charlie without becoming visibly emotional. They had heard too much; they had seen the effects of Elliott's time in Texas, through Elliott's eyes, at least. As later bandmate Brandt Peterson said, "The basic understanding was that he had been physically hit," despite the fact that Elliott never provided (to Peterson) any details. "But he wasn't trotting it out there like 'poor me.'" Peterson recalls arriving at Elliott's house one morning, just after he had awakened from a dream "that troops were storming up the stairs, coming to get him. He was in a state of panic. It was genuinely terrifying. He wasn't making the shit up."[25] The dream, Peterson believed, had some connection to a fearful history, if not, in specifics, to Charlie particularly. And as other friends confessed, there were things they knew about Elliott's time in Texas that they will never tell; it would not do anyone any good, they say. At the same time, Elliott's memories of mistreatment tended to enlarge themselves, his disclosures growing more and more extreme, more unguarded. Even he expressed doubt on occasion—Was he recalling accurately? Was he reconstructing more than remembering veridically? Depression has a way of pushing memories around, like a blindfolded person gets steered when struggling to pin the tail on the donkey. It is impossible to say. Maybe Elliott had it right; maybe he was, in some form and to some degree, abused. Or it may be that he elaborated on a past in order to make it more effectively explanatory. It had to be bad, he figured unconsciously, because that's what the present was, and that's what the future promised to be.

The songs treat Charlie as an irritant, like an obscure, dissonant sound one intermittently hears and tries tracking to its origin. He always seems to be there, in name or in effigy. Poet Sylvia Plath had her "bee sequence," a set of poems devoted to the subject of her long-dead father Otto (a bee expert), her own restive poltergeist. Elliott has his Charlie sequence, equally urgent, equally drenched in pain and loss. Charlie is not by any means the lyrics' preeminent theme, he's not ubiquitous. But he also refuses to sit still. And Elliott's attitude vacillates; he's not sure how to dispatch the Charlie haunter, or how, exactly, Bunny figures in the equation. As noted in one song—yet another waltz—he brings him a flower, declares the war over; he's got enough trouble, he figures, just trying to stay alive in the present. (As he told one probing interviewer, he didn't see much point in putting his thoughts about Texas out in print because "the person" has apologized.) Elliott wants to move on, to forget—something he talked about often—to put it all behind him. Yet Charlie modulates into nameless, spreading menace, always trying to get Elliott alone, the cause of "sick confusion headaches." Elliott's a "bastard," a "little boy in blue" in the song "Plainclothes Man." "Someone's going to get to you," he says, "and fuck up everything you do." Even his feelings for Bunny start qualifying themselves. People tell him he'll rediscover his love for her, "But I don't know/I don't think so . . ."

Another of Elliott's least disguised songs, one that never made it on to an album, probably with good reason, is titled, with apparently intentional obscurity, "Some Song." Here both Charlie and Dallas are named outright, Charlie a one-note symphony—of denigration, one guesses—who beats Elliott up over and over, turning him into a freak who pines for a violent girl, someone who's unafraid, who might exact a surrogate revenge. Elliott pictures himself heading to Dallas with murder on his mind, TV having taught him how to kill. Notorious murderer John Wayne Gacy even comes to mind—the so-called "Killer Clown" targeting young boys. It's a striking reference. If Charlie is "Cathy's Clown," then a clown killer seems especially poetic. (Gacy was beaten by his father, who repeatedly verbally assaulted him.) The song includes no murder, but it ends with the realization "I'll never be fine."

"2:45 AM" is still another Charlie/Bunny number. Like "Some Song," it's unusually direct; friends see it as almost anomalous in its open expressions of feeling and attitude. It starts with Elliott sleepwalking, his memories no longer muted, but talking. Almost sympathetically, Charlie is described as the boss who "couldn't help but hurt you"; and he turns Bunny into a deserter. Pain of abuse is coupled with love loss. It may not always show, but Elliott is cracking up, he says, and looking for someone—some hard, tough ally—to erase past harm. The song ends with him walking out on "Center Circle"—a place, one assumes, of isolation, and also danger. "Both of you can just fade to black," he sings. "Been pushed away and I'll never come back." Drums kick in as the song fades, blunt snare runs that sound like gunshots.

So the music, the many waltzes, took Elliott toward a difficult childhood, but it also took him away, recording on Pickle's dad's four-track, or listening to Beatles records in his back bedroom. It was reminder and escape at once, as art so often is. But there was a different dad, a real dad, too. Far from the vantage point of Texas, Elliott at first found Gary Mac Smith an "enigma." He had taken off, he was a concept, a mental structure—part deserter, part potential solution. As Elliott recalls, his father had come back from Vietnam a hippie, living in Los Angeles initially, writing songs "about the things he knew—horse racing, drug dealers." He was, maybe more than anything else, a contrast, an antidote. To Elliott, Dallas was religious, constipated, essentially "white-trash," a place where ambitions stopped at earning more money than your neighbors, buying bigger cars. At age five Elliott stayed with Gary for the first time, he says, and did so for a week or two on subsequent summers. That was the regular routine, the set-up for visitations. The impression was of his oddness—"I even thought he looked kind of weird." There was some anxiety as well, not so much about how he and his father would get along, or about being disappointed with what he saw in his father's world, but about Bunny, leaving her alone with Charlie, believing, rightly or wrongly, that something might happen to her. Gary collected records, Elliott recalls, and while on one of these early trips he fell in love with the Beatles's *White Album*, a crush he'd never get over. "On my mother's side of the family," he notes, "nobody was listening to that kind of music." Instead it was "Gershwin, jazzy ballads, old stuff like 'Moon River.'" Gary taught Elliott guitar, showing him chords for Dylan tunes, Beatles too. Everywhere Elliott turned there was music, it seems—the kind his mother's family played, and the kind, far more exciting, that his father made available. It was in his blood, and it was a fundamental aspect of whichever family he happened to be with, in Texas or anywhere else.

As Elliott got older and more aware, more antiauthoritarian, more cognizant, also, of the alternative Gary Smith embodied, the clash with Charlie intensified. In Pickle's words, Charlie's attitude was "You'll do it because I said so; I'm the adult, you're the kid." It was typical strong arm parenting stuff. My way or the highway. But by twelve, thirteen, and fourteen Elliott was feeling less like the kid, and more independent, more assertive. Everyone who knew the two of them offers the same observation about Elliott and Gary. Friends saw them as weirdly similar souls; they could see the two loved each other immensely. Pickle says, "They looked alike, talked alike, had the exact same mannerisms . . . He was clearly his father's son." Jennifer Chiba recalls breaking down in tears when she first met Gary. "He looked just like Elliott. It was haunting how similar they were. He was very careful in the words he chose, just like Elliott was."[26]

So Elliott made what must have felt like a bit of a jailbreak, after months of discussion and deliberation, no doubt, about which he kept secret, withholding details from Pickle and others up to the last possible moment. It was decided he'd move to the place he'd written about so gushingly in "Outward Bound," the Northwest he loved best; he cast his lot with a mirror, an adult version of what he might one day become, an approximate future self Gary embodied. It was a tough spot to be in. He wanted to stick around for his mother. He knew he'd deeply miss his siblings, toward whom he'd always felt very protective. Yet he also understood he and Charlie could not coexist. By the day it got worse. The conflict was constant, no end in sight. He had to stay and keep silently taking it, or he had to disappear. Years later he filled Chiba in on the circumstances of this winter 1983 departure. What he said and how he said it amounts to a chilling testimony.

"He called his dad and asked if he could live with him full-time," Chiba recalled being told. "His dad said he had a new family now (a wife, Marta, and one small girl, another coming along soon). He had to talk it over with them first. Then Elliott said, 'Dad, if I can't make the move, someone is going to die. And I'm going to die too.'" The threat, extreme and desperate, summed up years of feeling, years of fear and anger. The situation in Cedar Hill was dire, at least so far as Elliott described it. It could not last. Elliott would not allow it to last. One way or another, it was going to be over. He'd made up his mind and he'd let his father know about it in frighteningly clear terms.

For Pickle and others, the news came as a shock, like a late arriving, month's dead letter. Elliott dropped it on them casually, almost as an afterthought. And he never went into the reasons behind the decision. As Pickle put it, "in divorce, the family you are not with always seems to be more desirable," so in that respect the change of scenery made immediate sense. Instantly everyone wanted to spend as much time with Elliott as possible; his leaving was a tremendous blow, to Darren and Ashley especially, who loved him enormously. But "center circle" was an untenable permanent home, some sort of dangerous blow-up likelier by the day. Therefore halfway through his freshman year of high school, after what must have been scores of anguished conversations between the two sets of parents, Elliott traveled north to Portland, Gary's new home. The idea of it would have been immensely appealing, a relief from inner and outer torment. Whether reality matched expectation or not, Portland altered Elliott completely.

Denny Swofford, who with Christopher Cooper brought out Elliott's first solo album, put it plainly: "Portland was the foundation that allowed Elliott to become the person he was."[27]

CHAPTER THREE **RAINING VIOLINS**

Portland in the early and mid-1980s was a very small big city, with one upscale shop, Nordstrom's, featuring personal shoppers, long glass perfume counters, and "tasteful" classical piano to buy to, and down the street a more affordable, low-key Meier and Frank's with eight or nine floors reached by escalator, and that staged, at Christmastime, a Santa's Village on the top level. Bug-eyed toddlers rode a monorail along the ceiling. In display cases mechanical elves shifted slowly in winter scenes. One could easily walk most of downtown via Broadway or 10th, starting at Portland State University, to the south—near Hot Lips Pizza, where Elliott first met good friend Sean Croghan of the band Crackerbash—and ending at the famous Powell's Books on 10th and West Burnside.

There wasn't a lot to do if the goal was to kill time. Adventures had to be fabricated. Cable TV was new; only the rare home had it, or the MTV that came with it. And video stores were hard to locate—one had to rent not only the movie, but the machine to play it on. The chief way kids got around, before acquiring licenses to drive, was the bus system, called Tri-Met. One bought a ticket, good for several hours, then transferred from line to line. Malls were the main hangout. There was Eastport Plaza, with Tower Records, Lloyd Center, in northeast Portland; Washington Square, in the southwest; and Clackamas Town Center, which Elliott and his dad sometimes jokingly called Tackamas Clown Center, with its second floor food court and ice rink below (later made famous by Tonya Harding, who practiced there). Kids took buses to all these destinations, then simply wandered around, out of the rain, chasing girls or boys or eating free food samples at Hickory Farms, or going to movie matinees. There was another semi-mall downtown, the Galleria, with its central escalator one took to the second or third floors, and an "alt" place called the Metro, a circular set of restaurants with a piano just inside the front door, played by a tall, self-taught African American named Dehner Franks. The Metro was where street kids gathered, new-wave/punk devotees with Mohawks and chains and nose rings, some of whom were homeless, some of whom hailed from rich Portland Heights families. They stood around in clusters and smoked, or wandered across the street to the Pioneer Courthouse Square, which boasted, for several years, one of the city's first Starbucks. People traveled some distance just to buy the bitter brew. It was like a destination resort.

Still, in the early 1980s coffee shops had yet to dominate the downtown landscape, as they do today; instead there were bookstores, all independent, like the Green Dolphin or Holland's Books, selling mainly used hardbacks at good prices. And of course there was Powell's, the mother lode, to some the very best used bookstore in the world. In it one could easily burn hours, trolling for first editions, leafing through magazines, shuffling among the color-coded sections.

Rain was a constant sidekick; it fell in relentless and thorough drizzles, and no local carried an umbrella. One got used to it. It came with the territory. Portland was almost never not wet. The saying was: If it isn't raining now, just wait 15 minutes. Sun came reliably in August and September. Between those months the day typically dawned gray, even for much of July. Parades on the Fourth were just as likely to be rainy as not.

For kids into records like Elliott was, Django's downtown on a corner at 11th Street was a source of endless amazement. It sold hard-to-find used vinyl in room after labyrinthine room—rock, folk, punk, everything imaginable. There were T-shirts and posters too, the latter all over the walls, of Marx, Freud, Einstein, Jim Morrison, Bowie, Pink Floyd, Sid and Nancy. Elliott spent a lot of time at Django's. In fact, it was where he sold some of the first cassettes he'd later make with friends Garrick Duckler and Jason Hornick. And to his utter astonishment and, in some measure, terror, people actually bought them. He checked the supply and watched it dwindle, not quite certain he wanted the tunes in circulation. Part of him thought they sucked, part thought they were cool.

Like most other cities, Portland was class segregated, a fact kids recognized implicitly, if not with full awareness. No average white teenager traveled with any degree of regularity to North Portland, a kind of mythical shadow land inhabited by mostly poor African Americans, and decades away from the hip gentrification of today. The southeast, between 52nd and 82nd, from Division to Duke, was the land of poorer, working-class whites who smoked and wore "wife-beaters" and listened to Van Halen, Def Leppard, and AC/DC, and who bought and sold bad dope most high schoolers referred to as "ragweed." One never knew how much to smoke in order to get high. It was a sort of guessing game. The West Hills, where rich kids lived, was almost unknown to kids from the other side of the river, who never went there, except for sports. To a southeast teenager, kids from private schools like Jesuit, Catlin Gabel, or Oregon Episcopal School secreted a bewildering, hard-to-name mystique. They dressed differently, talked differently, and moved in an atmosphere of prideful assumption. They weren't you, and they wanted nothing to do with you. They played effete sports like tennis or golf, took spring break in France, spoke foreign languages, and got ferried from one enrichment class to another by moms who didn't work, in cars that did work, unlike cars in the southeast.

Elliott started at Lincoln High School (the Cardinals) in the middle of his freshman year. As he did in Texas, he joined band, again on clarinet. Evidently too late for the class picture, band is the one photo he appears in 1984's yearbook. The class was taught by Mr. Glen Fernley, a young sideburned man with glasses. Also in band that year was Tony Lash, who played flute. Lash was one year ahead of Elliott, a tall kid with brown hair parted in the middle. The two didn't meet immediately. A mutual friend made introductions, knowing both were "huge Rush fans."[1] There wasn't a lot of talk about Texas, or the subject of why Elliott had moved to Portland, such lines of conversation "not the sort of stuff you talk about when you're fifteen," according to Lash. What they did talk about, and eventually make together, for more than a decade, was music. There was also a fair amount of goofing off, Elliott's absurdist sense of humor on immediate display. Lash and Smith "got a big kick out of driving everyone crazy by playing 'Hot Tamales' in a very dissonant fashion."[2] During band they'd break into it at various inopportune moments, to the point where drummers threatened to beat them up if they didn't stop.

Lincoln was (and still is) a downtown west-side public high school, bordered by Jefferson and Salmon streets, not far from Burnside, with a view of the West Hills above and the Jim Fisher Volvo sign to the north. Just up the street stands the exclusive MAC club, which wealthy west-siders some-times waited years to join, with its athletic courts and bars, its aura of clois-tered privilege. If you belonged, as many of the families of Lincoln kids did, then you *belonged*. It was a clear mark of social standing, it denoted wealth. Lincoln students were a dignified cohort, a confederacy of white kids from the southwest hills, who for whatever reason opted not to attend one of the town's private high schools, like Catlin or OES (although some did spend time at those schools in elementary or junior high years). In the minds of other kids scattered around the city, Lincoln equaled "rich"—the kids were soft, you could beat them in sports. Jefferson was the black school; Franklin, Cleveland, and Marshall were home to middle-class and poorer whites.

Despite the fact that he'd occasionally visited over the years, to Elliott, the Texas freshman, Portland and LHS in particular provided jarring atmo-spherics. There were fewer boys named Scott, Mark, Mike, and David—all Texas generics in the 80s. Now, in quixotic contrast, boys announced them-selves as Garrick, Flemming, Dawson, and Jubil. And the families owned second homes—at Gearhart or Cannon, on the coast, or at Black Butte or Sun River, to the east, which was hot in summer and snowy in winter. The world was damp, hilly, with rivers, and beaches one and a half hours away, and mountains to ski. Classmates drove not trucks but BMWs. The aspira-tions were Ivy League, kids had parents who had gone to Columbia, Yale, Dartmouth, Harvard, and they were aggressively groomed for the same outcomes. The aura of Republicanism and Christianity, of regular church-going was replaced by high-minded agnosticism, and politics that ran to the liberal. It was a better fit for Elliott, no doubt, but it also took some getting used to. No one wanted to beat him up anymore, which he felt as a big relief. And maybe most fundamentally, he was simply less bored. "I realized there were other people living differently, that the world was more interest-ing and more wealthy than the south suburbia of Dallas," where you "live and die in a few square miles without ever going outside, and meet [only] people who look like you."[3]

Perhaps to smooth the transition and prolong a friendship that was pivotal and deep, Pickle came to visit over spring break in March 1984, just a few months after Elliott started at Lincoln. Both sets of parents arranged things, the two breaks—in Texas and Oregon—overlapping. For Pickle there was instant culture shock. The greenness was neon. All the kids had a nasal accent. And their relative freedom, busing around town on Tri-Met, was a revelation. "We went all over the place," Pickle exclaims.

It was a busy household Pickle discovered. There was Gary, Elliott's older facsimile, and Marta, Gary's wife, trained as a clinical social worker. But there were also two very young girls, new sisters, Rachel first, followed by Sophie. It couldn't have been an ideal time to add an introspective and emotionally complex fourteen-year-old into the mix, one coming from a home he had felt to be oppressive. It's not clear whether any overt or covert resentment came Elliott's way—he never spoke (on record, at least) about feeling unwanted, and most outward signs were encouraging. Elliott was quickly making friends at Lincoln, like Tony Lash and others. "He had obviously adapted," Pickle recalls thinking. "He wasn't the outsider at school or anything like that." But there were signs of unease, some even large. "It wasn't like I moved out into nowhere," Elliott says, "but it was a difficult move. It took some getting used to. I didn't sleep at all for about the first six months I lived there." The situation back in Texas with Bunny—Charlie's temper, that is—was fresh in his mind; he remembers—with just cause or not—feeling "very worried" about his mother, imagining something might happen to her. But in the end "everything turned out okay."[4]

A more unusual reaction, which Elliott later described to several friends, including Jennifer Chiba, was selective mutism, a kind of wordless living up in his head, not making a sound. He might have wanted, under the tense circumstances, to minimize the impact of his presence there, to be as inconspicuous and unimposing as possible, especially at first. It was also in his nature to be shy and quiet—he was never one for chit-chat, and when small talk was called for he burrowed inward. But there was more at work too. Elliott went notably silent in the presence of Marta. He did not let her in, he would not engage, there was an absence of social nicety. At the dinner table in this home people speak, Marta once exploded, according to Chiba. Marta apparently came to believe Elliott was more than slightly crazy—rather than merely opaque or passive-aggressive—a true pain to deal with, although in an interview on January 28, 2010, with *Oregonian* columnist Margie Boule (with the overweening title "The Truth About

Elliott Smith"), she emphasizes the fact that "Elliott had a very middle-class upbringing," adding, "Once you get to a certain level of fame, it's incredible the things people say that aren't true." She may not have actively disliked him at the time—she was distracted by the girls, no doubt, preoccupied by caring for them—but she clearly did not adore him either. The feeling was mutual (and in later years, this disconnect only deepened, to the point where Elliott told friends he "hated" his stepmother). In certain respects, then, Portland reestablished the dynamics of Texas. There was, on one hand—and in Elliott's subjective framing—the loved biological parent, a person Elliott could feel close to and care for and rely on, and on the other a fraudulent, nemesis stepparent, a source of tension, anxiety, and fear. It's not exactly a novel scenario, but the fact that Elliott experienced it twice, with two different families, obviously ups the emotional ante. He wouldn't feel comfortable in his own skin until he moved out entirely, made his own world, one he could possibly live in and manage, but that was several years down the road. And as Pickle noticed, Elliott was just plain gone a lot: "He had a level of freedom and independence that surprised me, and he was able to handle it well, especially for a high school freshman." A solution to turbulence at home was to not be at home, it seems. Elliott may have been too young to pursue that remedy in Texas—at least for most of his years there—but in Portland he was up for it, and it appeared to work.

That first spring break with Pickle in tow there was skiing in active snow at Mt. Hood, which Elliott enjoyed—he'd apparently received instruction during January and February—and a large amount of aimless wandering around, to places like Pioneer Square. On the first night of Pickle's visit Elliott took him to meet a few of his new friends. In the car on the way over he proposed a ruse he figured might be amusing. Pickle was to talk with a "big, huge, ridiculous Texas accent." "He fed me phrases," Pickle says. "He wanted me to refer constantly to jumper cables and pickup trucks." Then there would occur, at the end of the evening, a theoretically hysterical reveal. The Texas act would abruptly stop. But even though his throat hurt from all the strenuous voice work, Pickle says no one noticed. The joke was a dud, and therefore even funnier. Texas wasn't so out of place in Oregon after all.

Another day the two were downtown again—the thrill of public transport an ongoing, pleasant surprise for Pickle ("You would not want to ride the bus system in Dallas!")—walking the streets and blowing whistles issuing a goofy sound. They passed a number of street dealers with lexicons of drug lingo—"Hey kid, you want to buy some used furniture?" Out of nowhere a car pulled up packed with older boys intent on hassling them. "We were not having it," Pickle says. "They were stuck at the light. We told them to screw themselves." Later that evening, at Clackamas Town Center, the same boys miraculously rematerialized near the food court. "It was four versus two. It scared the hell out of us. Pure panic, pure adrenaline." The confrontation escalated; Elliott and Pickle got backed up against a railing, the ice rink one floor below, its Muzak filling the mall air, skaters executing endless figure-eights. Pickle just started talking. He launched into a nonstop, free-form monologue fueled by fear and desperation, and before long the older boys were "in stitches." They wandered off shaking their heads. Disaster successfully averted.

But by far the main activity, the one that never stopped making perfect sense, was music. For Elliott, an early, transient, adolescent fireman dream was out—there was some sort of physical impediment having to do with height or weight. Being around his father now, he also imagined becoming a psychiatrist. He says he would have liked to have "done the same job." And he'd read a lot on the subject, especially Freud. But he figured he wasn't the type. Plus, as he put it, "I don't have enough to offer other people."[5] Back in Texas he'd considered training as a mathematician even, but he wasn't sure how independent he could be—whether he'd need to work in a business or an organization or university. So the subject "what to do" always came back around to what Elliott was actually already doing. Writing songs, learning instruments, figuring out how to record, and with whom.

Pickle had brought along his electronic keyboard, the Lowrey, which he set up in Elliott's room. Elliott pulled out a flyer advertising a legitimate recording studio, and what he wanted to do was find a way to get over there. The rate was hourly—fifteen dollars per—and Pickle can't recall where the money came from, but the two boys made their way, hauling equipment up a skinny stairway to a converted office upstairs, with professional-grade microphones and sound foam all over the walls and ceiling, and an eight-track reel-to-reel setup, with the possibility of various effects. In the end four songs were recorded over four hours—all instrumental, no singing, mainly keyboards and Elliott's Gibson SG guitar. Most of these tunes were carryovers from the Dallas days, but there was one new number in the batch, written by Elliott in Portland. Elliott was clearly into the process, the details of getting the sound just right. "He was very interested in recording and recording technology even then," Pickle remembers.

The new number, "Inspector Detector," he had written in the spring, just before Pickle's arrival. Pickle watched Elliott finish it and work out the arrangement. This time, Elliott had worked on the keyboard, which was different, Pickle recalls, "since most of his songs at the time were guitar compositions." The verse begins in a minor chord. When it comes back around, Elliott throws in a half-beat major chord. "That's from a wrong note he hit when working it out. He decided he liked the major chord anyway, as an accent, but decided not to use it every time." Inspector Detector was the name of a large, bearded, suit-and-tie-wearing police officer in the *Speed Racer* cartoon series. Pickle says, "At the time, I thought the riff/guitar solo in the middle conjured up images of a guy in a trench coat sneaking down a dark hallway looking through windows, on some secret mission." Elliott's guitar playing on the song was minimalist: "He doesn't throw in a lot of flashy licks but hits some good notes to create an effect. He was already working out the 'less is more' concept that some musicians never quite get."

The boys rerecorded "#37" during this studio jaunt too. It was in fact the chief reason the two booked the time—to get the song down on tape. One year before, they'd talked over the possibility of adding lyrics. Pickle came up with some but "I didn't think they were that great and neither of us wanted to sing." Why 37? Pickle guesses it was a take-off from the number 42 in *Hitchhiker's Guide to the Galaxy*—humorously selecting a random number and assigning mysterious significance to it. "I know I read that book in junior high and I'm pretty sure he did too."

Spring break over, Pickle headed back to Texas. Several months later, in July 1984, his first year of high school at Lincoln now finished, Elliott did the same. His life situation had reversed itself. Now it was Bunny he visited for weeks at a time—and Ashley and Darren—whereas before it had been Gary. The occasion, and this would repeat itself one year later, was his August 6 birthday. He'd spend it with his mother and his two half-siblings, and with Charlie too, of course.

By this time Elliott and Kim had broken up, although he would spend quite a bit of time with her, as it turns out. They phoned over the year he was away, and sent letters back and forth, but the "long-distance" relationship challenge proved to be too much. They were thirteen and fourteen, and it was largely "out of sight, out of mind." They stayed friends all the same. To Kim, he was always a "dedicated" boyfriend. Very sweet, very attentive. In fact, she says, he was the type of boy a girl could take advantage of if she wanted to—but Kim never did. She recalls the breakup happening over the phone one night, prior to his return. One thing she noticed immediately was that "he was much calmer when he came back from Portland," as if the time away from Texas, in particular, had done him a world of good.

Back in Cedar Hill, there was more music to make—as always—but Elliott also wanted to get high. This was new. Before it had been a rarity; now it was something more than that. It wasn't a daily thing, the pot smoking, but Elliott told Denbow he'd been buying dope in the back of Tri-Met buses in Portland. Sketchy guys concocted elaborate shell games that kids picked up on; slowly they figured out what to say and do in order to get what they wanted. It wasn't cheap, but it did the trick. Pickle almost never drank and he abstained completely from smoking. Denbow, however, was game. He and Elliott were accustomed to sneaking out—they'd done it many times before—so the basic plan was predetermined. Denbow would roll up at night in his pickup (he no longer relied on the rickety scooter), and the two would meander into South Oak Cliff, a rougher part of Dallas. "We were basically buying Mexican dirt weed," Denbow recalls. It was terrible, but cheap—one-quarter ounce for ten dollars. A real bargain compared to what Elliott was used to paying in Portland. The effect dope had on his state of mind intrigued Elliott. Pickle, for instance, recalls a very long description by Elliott of how smoking marijuana appeared to affect his perception of time. He was into the phenomenology of the altered states experience. He approached it almost philosophically.

When not scheming to get high the boys reverted to the usual ways of passing time. They shot hoops. They went to the Red Bird Mall. They also snuck into R-rated movies. Denbow recalls seeing *Johnny Dangerously* with Elliott, also *The Outsiders*.

But this was all down time. The true mania was for getting the band back together, rehearsing and recording. They ran through "Ocean" and "Outward Bound" again, sometimes with small lyrical revisions. Another tune was "Barriers," a Rush-inspired number for which Elliott played electric lead guitar, rhythm guitar, and acoustic piano. The last two verses are "pretty heavy," according to Pickle, with intimations of mortality. *Life goes on and on,* Elliott sings, *and mine may soon be gone; who knows how long before I sing my swan song.* As usual, one version features Kim singing, another Elliott, who typically had to be pushed into recording vocal tracks. "He's not yet a great singer," Pickle suggests. "He's aware of that himself and fairly unsure when it comes to singing, even when it's his own work. Kim was definitely more confident, though there are spots when the melody is out of her range—and out of Elliott's too. The idea of moving the songs to a different key to make things easier for the singer didn't really occur to us. Even if we had thought of it, I don't know if we could have pulled it off."

These rehearsals paved the way for the most exciting prospect by far— heading into a genuine, truly high-level studio. In the back of a free publication called *Buddy Magazine*, Pickle's dad found an ad for "Pla-Back Recording" ("hear the quality," the ad trumpeted), run by a Lew Blackburn. Pickle made calls to set up a time and get directions. The studio itself turned out to be a converted garage in Blackburn's home in South Dallas. He held a degree in music education and figured he'd try to make a go of it in the music business. (It did not pan out, and later he became president of the school board for the Dallas Independent School District.) The space boasted an eight-track reel-to-reel, a large professional mixing board, effects, quality microphones, acoustical treatment, and a piano. "We were all pretty impressed," says Pickle, garage setting notwithstanding.

In all there were two trips to Pla-Back, one week apart. Summer band was on, and everyone—with the exception of Elliott—spent several hours per day on the parking lot at Duncanville High marching and learning music for fall. Drill activities were par for the course for freshmen—marching, counting, shouting. As a result Kim was actually too hoarse to sing on the night the group first booked the time. So they did a quick mix-down of the instrumental tracks, then had to pay Blackburn to keep the half-inch master for another week, when they planned to return and add vocals.

The set-up was crowded. Elliott and Pickle wedged in to supervise mixes, along with Blackburn—who engineered—and Pickle's father. They were hurried for the first instrumental mixes, so these wound up lacking studio effects such as reverb. Still, "we were happy with the final product and considered it a success," Pickle says. No copies were printed up or distributed. Instead, each player got his own individual tape, "and that was about it." Pickle also left with a quarter-inch reel-to-reel master he could play on his dad's home four-track.

The songs—"Barriers," "Ocean," "Inspector Detector," "Mayan," and "Outward Bound"—were a mix of old and new. "Mayan" was a Pickle tune, the sole outlier, all others Elliott's compositions. Pickle had been to Mexico with his family and found the ruins "cool," so the name struck him as suitably evocative. Elliott suggested throwing in some heavy-metal hammer-ons, but Pickle talked him out of it. He did, however, at the last minute toss-off a forty-two-second classical-style acoustic guitar intro they kept. As the opening concludes power electric guitar chords crunch down, supplying a happy, upbeat melody, punctuated by Pickle's synthesizer. "Inspector Detector" was played about thirty beats per minute faster than it was in Portland back in March. Elliott's guitar solo pans back and forth from left to right—to all a pretty sweet effect. "Ocean" got a hefty dose of reverb, creating a sort of wave sensation from the effects pedal of Elliott's guitar, the DOD Stereo Chorus.

In the end the feeling was of prideful accomplishment, an outrageously productive way to spend a vacation/reunion. Although unnamed, this was a real band, Elliott's first. They sealed the deal in a real studio, and left with a tape of original compositions, played with genuine skill and undeniable musicality. And the songs revealed range. They weren't carbon copies. The waltzy ¾ "Outward Bound" with its catchy country/western twang sounded nothing like "Barriers" or "Inspector Detector." "It shows," Pickle adds, "just how versatile Elliott was as a songwriter, even at a very young age." He also worked individual songs over and over, creating different versions in an attempt to maximize the overall effect. Lyrics would be tinkered with, new solos would get thrown in. Some songs might begin as piano compositions, then transform into guitar-driven pieces. And bits from one tune, sections that never quite worked out, would show up elsewhere. The tendency was dynamism, not stasis. Writing songs was about rewriting, getting them into the best shape possible under the circumstances. In any case, the group left richly satisfied, with a sense of mission accomplished. The receipt for the studio time plus tapes shows a cost of $93.88, and to everyone involved, it was worth the money.

This irrepressible impulse to write and record, which originated in Texas with Pickle, Denbow, Kim, and Merritt, instantly reestablished itself back at Lincoln, when Elliott returned. It was what he knew, what he was good at, what gave him the most pleasure, so he just kept at it, constantly working to craft better and better, more ambitious and complex, more realized songs, and finding people to do it with. Through Elliott, Tony Lash (who a few years later would end up at the Berklee School of Music) met Garrick Duckler and Jason Hornick, both musical as well, and the drive to write songs and, more important, record them, absolutely exploded. Duckler, a clever, arty, startlingly intelligent kid with a sly smile in yearbook photos, was president of the Russian Club, which devoted itself to "learning the Russian culture and having fun." There were potlucks, games of Russian Scrabble, attempts to tie-dye Russian T-shirts (whatever that amounted to, exactly). Hornick was co–vice president and treasurer. Both were academically accomplished, as was Elliott. Hornick in particular stood out. A bona fide superstar, he was an athletic scholar, class marshal, and Oregonian All-Star. He won the TJ Davis Scholarship, the Bausch and Lomb Award, the Reusselaer Award, and he was a member of the Math Club at Lincoln, Mu Alpha Theta, along with Adam Koval, who later joined the group as drummer after Lash, one year older, had graduated. Elliott and Hornick were two of six National Merit Scholar finalists at Lincoln, the selections based on PSAT and SAT scores, along with a submitted essay. A yearbook photo shows the boys side by side, Elliott in a Led Zeppelin T-shirt (a reproduction of the *Houses of the Holy* album cover), sporting an earring on his left lobe and a mildly embarrassed smile, his arm around Hornick, who peers off to the left. Hornick had a head of thick, curly black hair and sometimes wore a beard, surprisingly heavy for a high schooler (in certain pictures he looks about thirty, obviously an "early maturer"). These

Elliott, Jason Hornick, and Alice Vosmek (L–R), National Merit Scholars, 1987. (Lincoln High School Yearbook.)

were kids of clear accomplishment, outstandingly bright, creative, with pro-liferating intellects and droll, ridiculous senses of humor. The music was driven by Elliott—whom Lash called the most gifted musician he had ever known, who played with "incredible feel and insight"—but everyone wrote songs, and everyone contributed ideas.

A school article, with the hopeful title "A Dream Coming True," de-scribed the band in one of its early iterations, having formed, officially, in 1985. The name, at this point, was Stranger Than Fiction. Elliott played guitar and piano, and sang "many of the songs," his voice still a work in progress, a necessary evil. Hornick, who had taken five years of classical and jazz piano, also sang occasionally, and played piano and synthesizer. Garrick Duckler contributed stand-up acoustic bass; he'd had two years of lessons. Tony Lash joined six months after the band's formation, some time in 1986. "Although the band has not had many opportunities to play live," the article explains, "they have worked diligently to produce a tape that they hope to sell to a recording studio"—more likely, a recording company, and in short order there would be made, not one, but numerous cassettes of material. In 1985 it was Hornick and Elliott who crafted the "musical scores"; Duckler and Hornick wrote lyrics, as did Elliott on occasion. Lash recalls Duckler, especially, serving as the band's wordsmith. When Elliott turned his attention to words, it was Duckler he consulted and worked with. A picture shows the group sprawled out on a lawn, Elliott in sunglasses and tennis shoes lying with his back to the camera, Lash on the right, also wearing sunglasses. The effect is Beatlesesque, *Magical Mystery Tour* era.

Practices were haphazard affairs; they got fit in, somehow, some way. Mr. Fernley's band class met second period, and the group tried rehearsing however usefully they could in the fifteen minutes before or after class. A daunting prospect, to say the least, but it got to be a regular affair. "It was amazing we could figure the songs out in so little time," Lash notes. "These were actually pretty complex arrangements," tunes with almost no conventional pop structure, mostly sets of "discontinuous sections"—songs within songs, connected by passing chords of the kind Elliott first became fascinated with in Texas. The passing chords flirtation is interesting—and durable, for better or worse. To Lash, they weren't always musically satisfying. It was as if "they never really landed" on any solid melodic anchor. Especially later, on Smith albums such as *Figure 8*, Lash's belief is that the songs' preoccupation with transitions, with getting from one section to another, "seemed to reflect Elliott's more emotionally disengaged state," as if the music described a psychological reality. For now, though, in Stranger Than Fiction, the stakes were considerably lower. Elliott was only just beginning to settle on the semblance of a style, a musical signature. The work was transitional, its aesthetic short lived. The idea was to see what came up, what worked and what didn't. And unlike a lot of high school groups, bands devoted to clichéd, simplistic rock covers of the "Taking Care of Business" variety, scheming desultory house parties and possible far-flung bar gigs, there was scant interest in performing live. Recording was the thing; that was where the energy got directed. The tracks had to be laid down, they had to be cemented. It was a kind of obsession—creating cassettes, producing a body of original work. So most days after school, relying on whatever four-track they managed to get their hands on, the group headed to someone's basement—often classmate Eric Hedford's just off Scholls Ferry Road—to compose, refine, and lay down tracks. The practice was to record live, then add vocals later. Looking back, Lash feels Elliott's talent was essentially taken for granted, not fully grasped. "He could play all the stuff himself, with such depth of songwriting. He just had a lot of music in him, it was obvious. Music and ability."

In an exceptionally smart, subtle, tasteful, and in many ways beautiful short account of those years at Lincoln and his friendship with Elliott, Garrick Duckler describes what the two were up to in Stranger Than Fiction, and how the songwriting and recording process tended to play out. One fact is that Elliott took the task extremely seriously; it was not some kind of toss-off hobby, the sort of thing teenagers do "for the fun of it." "I was not a musician," Duckler writes, "or, at least, a very good musician, and I think in some ways this is what made writing songs together fairly easy—that it was something that two friends did together because they were comfortable and free around each other rather than something that came from shared musical proficiency . . . I think we trusted each other not to be too cheesy or too cold or too intrusive or too meddlesome, but to be helpfully analytic."[6]

Duckler (a psychotherapist now in San Francisco) finds some "adolescent grandiosity" in this, but only partly; he and Elliott shared a very specific, private way of talking and thinking about their internal lives, to the point where it felt as if they existed on a deserted island, cut off from the experiences of others, who spoke in ways incomprehensible to them. It was a long inside joke when they were together, and sometimes it was funny, sometimes not particularly so. But they found it made no difference so long as what they created together was surprising or at least entertaining in some way. They knew what they were up to but then, on the other hand, they didn't. It was all very intuitive.

Duckler could not and did not try to compete with Elliott on the level of musicianship—few people did—so most of the time he sent along lyrics that Elliott put to music, although other times Elliott would play something of a melody Duckler would try fitting words into, always a poetic and rhythmic challenge. At times Duckler and Hornick also collaborated, and other

Elliott backstage with Jason Hornick, several years post–high school. (Photograph by JJ Gonson.)

lyric writers were sometimes brought in as well. Whatever the case, as-sembling words was not, initially, a task Elliott instinctively took to. His chief role, as it had been in Texas, when the vast majority of songs were instrumental, was to create sound. Between Duckler and Elliott there was that almost uncanny, somewhat mysterious, wordless symbiosis, an ability to share ideas that were iffy and nascent. Although everything revolved around the fixation on making tapes (the process of craft), inevitably or even necessarily—this was a band, after all, not a set of studio musicians—performances did occur. One took place in fall of 1986, at Lincoln's home-coming dance. Duckler, standing behind his upright bass, wore an off-white oversized suit resembling David Byrne's from the Talking Heads' 1984 *Stop Making Sense* tour, while Elliott, his hair short, sported a white T-shirt and psychedelic shorts. In a yearbook picture he plays electric guitar left-handed, the image reversed.

One of the band's initial efforts was 1985's "The Machine," employing, as Elliott remembers, "this drum machine called Dr. Rhythm, which was not slick in any way at all. It didn't even sound remotely like real drums. The cymbal went 'chhhhhhh.' So we'd program that and something else at the same time onto a track. We did a lot of bouncing or ping-ponging, whatever you want to call it. We'd try not to put more than a couple things on the same track. Everything was totally dead. We didn't have any effect at all."[7] The description does the song little justice. It sounds joylessly mechanical, the effect of a bunch of fifteen-year-olds messing around with apparatuses. In fact, "The Machine" is an ambitious, ornate number, kicking off with smoothly repetitive, looping piano that also provides transitions between verses, hopped up by pouncing synthesizer. Elliott's John Lennon affection is sweet and obvious; at times he adopts an obliquely English accent. And the song is a social critique, also along Lennonesque lines, an attack on racial, sexual, and religious prejudice; although much quicker paced, it owes a debt to Pink Floyd's "Welcome to the Machine," which describes a similarly deadening indoctrination. At one point near the end Elliott tears into a slightly gratuitous, over-the-top guitar solo before it all sweeps to a close, the kind Pickle talked him out of during the recording of "Mayan."

The tapes, from here, just kept coming, the songs almost embarrassingly easy to come by. It is the beginning of a trend all his musician friends came to recognize in Elliott—he was alarmingly productive, alarmingly fecund, "high on the sound," as he once put it. He could write tunes in a single sitting, and they were actually stunningly good. There was this impression of effortlessness, and for others it was impossible to keep up, so they just stopped trying. Duckler notes six different albums over two or three years, almost all of which were recorded, not in studios, but basements or kitchens. Some of these were sold to friends, or given away, some got bought at Django's, a fact that took the two friends out of the more comfortable, risk-free realm of "misunderstood geniuses." In the event a real person purchased the music—a true stranger—then it wasn't a secret society anymore. The word was out, on the street; people were listening to what they made. News of sales always left the band in a "blurry daze." They'd imagine possible reactions—"I can't believe they went to that banal chord progression after the minor third. I'm going to throw myself out the window!" One purchase was made by a girl who worked at Django's, who seemed, to Elliott and Duckler, way too cool to be listening to Stranger Than Fiction. They resolved never to go back. It was simply too stressful.

"Any Kind of Mudhen," spelled out in lower-case on the cassette sleeve, and including thanks to, among others, Karl Marx, Ronald Reagan, and GOD, was the band's first complete effort, recorded from June 26 to July 18 in 1985, when Elliott was fifteen years old.[8] Duckler plays double bass, Elliott guitar and piano, and Hornick piano, electronic keyboard, and synthesizer. There are thirteen distinct songs, for a total of no less than fifty-five minutes of music.[9] Some are political (Reagan-era diatribes), some are jokes, some are romantic (and achingly adolescent) meditations center-ing on lost relationships and questions of identity. In most cases—and this was the norm for the time—lyrics were written not by Elliott, but by Duck-ler. For now, in these very early stages of song making, Elliott remained, as Duckler saw it, "fiercely dismissive" of the words he managed to string to-gether. Nothing was close to good enough. Nothing ever sounded, to him, acceptably original. He detested cliché, and the effort to get beyond it wore him out. His feeling was that Duckler, however, possessed a gift, a natural talent, so it was a relief to focus only on putting his words to music. Just four songs on the cassette are Elliott's through and through: "The Ma-chine," "Joy to the World," "Reeba" (spelled out "pbida," Russian for "fish"), and "To Build a Home," although Elliott is usually credited for the music. In one funky, James Brown–ish tune Duckler imagines America afloat in the sea, "ignoring all morals or reality." Reagan puts quarters in the CIA ma-chine; even John Lennon is conveniently forgotten, his name replaced with "a date." A joke song—Duckler's "It Was a Sunny Day"—begins side two, introduced by synthesized harpsichord. There's talking and laughing in the background. At one point someone says, "Stop the tape." A deep baritone voice—Duckler's—altered to sound even deeper, describes a sunny day on which a couple walks down the street, "her hair like the frog on an all beef patty." He looks at her, she looks at him—"boy, did we look good." The speaker declares, "We don't have to be any kind of mudhens." He reaches into his pocket and pulls out some meatloaf, then shoves the girl's face into it. The deliberately goofy song ends prettily, with Elliott singing harmonies over a funky bass line. "Joy to the World," one of Elliott's contributions, be-gins acoustically as "The Machine" trails off, with no actual separation between the two tunes. Descending notes from the yuletide staple shift to minor tones as Elliott asks what will come "when the lights go down on everyone." Along his street he gets wind of a party going on. At some point it will blow them all away, he says, but "if we try we can get this wheel turning." In the party people's eyes he sees a light burning. There's hope there, even if the Lord does not come, in contrast to the Christmas song; things can somehow turn around, through learning, not by trying to measure up, make the grade, or jump to the sound of the whistle blowing. The song subtly calls for independence, nonconformity, rising above a mob mentality. It recalls "Outward Bound," which decried the business life and "running under the gun," and found meaning in nature and writing down sounds.

Violin (played by Sara Harris) introduces the last song on the cassette, Elliott's "To Build a Home." It's just piano and Elliott singing in clear, authentic tones that don't sound at all unlike any of his later solo records. The lyrics, Elliott's, seem to reference the plight of Native Americans—another political sentiment. They move out to nowhere and live off the land, build a home without government aid, in the place where the buffalo roam, devoid, interestingly, of people. But America catches up with them, and they pack up again, heading someplace new. Isn't it sad, Elliott writes, "to find out what is and what should never be are the very same thing."

In all, the songs are guitar and piano driven—as usual—with numerous experimental Elliott-supplied transitions of the sort he liked to put together, creating songs within songs, as Lash described, each section its own discrete world. One thinks of John Lennon, who often did the same with his "bits," in mash-ups like "Happiness is a Warm Gun" from the *White Album*. It's hard to call any of the tunes catchy or hooky, but there's an ambitiousness and a scope suggesting utter seriousness of purpose. The blend of piano and guitar—how one gives way to the other, how they overlap smoothly—points most directly to Jackson Browne, especially the *Late for the Sky* album Elliott so admired. The lyrics are dense and clever, and at times sweetly sincere, but they don't always pop; they lack the specificity and originality of Elliott's mature work, but then that's hardly shocking—they were written at age fifteen. In poetical terms, they'd be labeled "juvenilia." There are also occasions on which words don't fit easily into the musical line; the singer, sometimes Elliott, sometimes Duckler, rushes to get them out in time, unloading hefty mouthfuls of verbiage. It's clear, as well, that Elliott's working out his vocal style. Later with Heatmiser he would channel Joe Strummer or Elvis Costello, affecting a breathy bark. Here he's withheld, more natural. Often there's that hint of an English accent, a residue of listening to Lennon and the Beatles.

If there's an overriding theme in mudhen, it's self-definition and relationship failure, sometimes in combination. Other guys get in the way of connections. Love is given then thrown away. Forever "is a temporary instability and never is a permanent possibility."

When not holed up with four-tracks painstakingly crafting these complicated compositions, the three friends simply did a lot of goofing off. They were high schoolers, after all, and they shared—obviously delightfully—a taut, abjectly sarcastic sense of the world. This was another form of art they worked at perfecting, and every drawn-out joke came with a hidden, inside back story. Hours were spent listening to music and discussing, usually playfully, what they heard—sounds and lyrics. As Duckler puts it, we "were all (in very different ways) very nerdy. Jason and I, for instance, actually got in trouble for using complete sentences when we worked at Baskin-Robbins."[10] Elliott (and Duckler) passed time reading Freud's lectures—as well as existentialists, Dostoevski, and volumes on renaissance painters or the history of weapons—and Elliott "was so surprised," Duckler says, "when I got him Gifford and Seidman's book on *Ulysses* for his birthday that he started to read it right there on the spot."[11] Most weekend nights featured rolling aimlessly in Hornick's car, because "either we had no real life and had no place to go or because we couldn't really think of anything that would be as enjoyable (or both)." They'd finally settle on some destination— "two for one dozen donuts or something absurd"—while playing, in the car, one complete album after another. R.E.M.'s *Murmur* was out, and at the time no one had heard of the band. "We still felt," Duckler jokes, "that Michael Stipe's lyrics could actually mean something someday." Conversations about the music were of a particular sort, specific to their way of talking generally, about anything. "There was no academic minutiae that bores me to tears," explains Duckler, "but there wasn't a lot of vague 'that's awesome's.'" Nor was there any tally aimed at identifying "who was great and who sucked." "Jason was a great mimic and Elliott would give kind of an emotional rendering of what was literally being played and I would throw in a metaphor (on the band Yes, 'It's like they're fishing for whales instead of salmon with these lyrics here')." It was all playful, all slapstick, and the true goal was just to make the other person crack up.

Sometimes mild disagreements emerged, never lasting or significant, yet there was little of the typical "one-upmanship" one meets with in movie versions of male bonding. Being exceptionally smart and inventive, the boys turned every drive around into a night at the improv. "Elliott would hunch over and make his arms into claws and try to grab one of us as we tried to flee from his clutches. I made a scary devil face," says Duckler, "that Elliott would try to get me to do and Jason would plead for me to stop doing it. And Jason would run like a Tauntaun, one of the creatures from the planet Hoth." To Duckler, Hornick's Tauntaun captured the humor's flavor perfectly—"stunning, crazy, but also based on astute observation." Other evenings they might arrive at 7-Eleven, feeling "terribly awkward" around other people. While waiting in line Hornick mumbled, sotto voce, "Bats. Them iz some crazy-ass blind motherfuckers." Then they'd suddenly stand erect to make it as hard as possible not to laugh.

Duckler remembers one episode at earnestly alt Reed College (where he later went to school). The occasion was an experimental jazz band performance of some esoteric variety, as deliberately recondite as possible. One terribly sincere guy played a hammer and whisk, another struck a fire extinguisher with a shot glass. Every ounce of irony was "sucked out of the room"; it was "a moment of great solemnity as if we were at the funeral of melody or something," nobody speaking, everybody hanging on each note. "Elliott and I could not handle it. We literally ran outside bursting out over the gravity of everyone's expressions. My girlfriend at the time came running after us, saying, 'I can't take you guys anywhere. You're like little boys.'"[12]

As for deeper, less comical affinities, Duckler and Elliott shared interests in psychology, a certain slant on internal life. These attitudes were, in Duckler's estimation, "the basis of our friendship, and after . . . working on all these songs together and doing all the things we did, there was a long time when neither one of us really trusted anyone else with this type of communication. Among everything else, Elliott was an intuitive person and he was (until the fame machine got him) able to hold the complexities of other people with insight and compassion . . . I wouldn't say we were innocent and everything was great but we certainly weren't burdened by anyone else's opinion . . . The three of us were intensely critical people but not particularly judgmental people. We were slightly depressed people who enjoyed each other and appreciated anything that made us feel genuinely astonished." And when they needed it, they created their own astonishment. High school at Lincoln was, in short, a genuinely fruitful time, marked by more or less nonstop artistry, generativity, and galloping inventiveness. As Elliott told Duckler many years later, "Those were the most creative years of [my] life." The Stranger Than Fiction cassettes on their own go a long way toward proving the sentiment. They set a bar that, with every next effort, got higher and higher.

"Mudhen" was followed by "Still Waters More or Less," recorded from November 1985 to March 1986, at The Hedhoues (presumably a friend's house) and Woofbark Sound (according to liner notes), near 140th and SE Holgate. The drum machine—given the name Ed Luther Kassier before—was replaced by Tony Lash, and the difference is striking. The songs, with lyrics by Duckler again, but also by Glynnis Fawkes and Susan Pagani, and in three instances by Elliott, take on added gravity and resonance.[13] They sound, in other words, more like real songs; the album improves measurably on its more erratic predecessor. There is pith and polish to spare. When Elliott sent him the tape, Pickle's first thought was: "A lot of these songs sound like they were written by the smartest kids in class—for each other." It's true, there's a conversation going on, with "Strawberry Fields"–like allusions Duckler and Elliott understood, if naive listeners didn't. And these *were* the smartest kids in class—no one failed to recognize that—grafting their thoughts on politics, relationships, and family life onto increasingly complicated musical arrangements, some lasting ten minutes, most made up of the same discontinuous sections that somehow, in the best of cases, managed to cohere.

The cassette is a smorgasbord of sound once more showcasing Elliott's astonishing range. There's boogie-woogie, psychedelia, ragtime, straight blues, lengthy ornate piano intros and interludes (beautifully played), endless electric guitar stingers and leads. In their strange, defiant heterogeneity, these songs—except in small patches—are glaringly unlike the kind of tunes characterizing Elliott's later solo work. That sort of quiet, internal, focused succinctness is mostly missing. Nor do they sound at all like Elliott's next band, the far louder, harder Heatmiser. The influences, in fact, cover the map—a little R.E.M., a bit of Pink Floyd—Roger Waters's *The Final Cut*—some Yes, some early Peter Gabriel Genesis, and as always, a healthy dose of Rush. There's even some James Taylor guitar ("You Can Close Your Eyes") and Carole King piano ("It's Too Late") thrown in. One song, "The Crystal Ball," lyrics by Susan Pagani, models itself on Lennon's "Lucy in the Sky With Diamonds." A mysterious dark-eyed girl appears and disappears, tempts and abandons. There are castles, deserts full of purple camels; kangaroos "grab your mother." As butterflies hover and balloons fall, she's there "by your side"—in the same second-person as "Lucy"—near "looking glass windows and marmalade shades." Another song, "Vatican Rock," samples "Johnny B. Goode," with alternate politicized lyrics by Duckler; the Chuck Berry tune Elliott jammed on with his bandmates back in Texas.

This time there are three songs with lyrics and music by Elliott, and all three appear on side two. The first, which starts the second side, is "Jump Across the Mountain." It's an indictment of the rich, their easy, clueless hypocrisy, most likely a response to the wealth Elliott encountered for the first time at Lincoln. A marquis and his wife prepare for a "quiet wedding," with a thousand guests. The homes are stately; ladies have a "jet-set reputation to protect" although, as Elliott points out, "we're all animals, you know." No one ever brings up the state of the nation; it's a topic carefully avoided. Deserted people choke in the sand, victims of "wrong moralities." "Look at what has happened in the streets of Cape Town," Elliott concludes. The repeating chorus he sings softly with no irony, coming back, he says, to "claim the hand of my families." The lilting melody and sharp finger-picking make the song the cassette's catchiest. It sticks in the ear.

"Tunnel Vision" is a funkier groove with heavy bass, staccato piano chords, and runs that pounce and ramble as in the much later song from Elliott's *Figure 8* album, "Honky Bach." Vocals appear to be traded off with Duckler. At one point crowd noise voice-over gets interjected, a melange of chatting conversation. Although it's all a state of mind, Elliott sings, he still can't quite get over his tunnel vision. In fact, everyone's got their own tunnel vision. Some can kill and find it "intrinsically wonderful"; or feel like "they had a right to."

The song "Sound to Me" is Elliott's most personal. It starts with arpeggiated acoustic guitar, the kind of chord/slide pattern Kim always noticed in Elliott's playing. This acoustic solo goes on at length, jazz style, with touches of flamenco added at intervals. Eventually a soft melody takes hold, interrupted by the chorus—"Summon me as one who cares/speak to me as one who dares/fight with me against a sterile death." Talk with me, not at me, Elliott implores, and although it's not certain whom he might be addressing, the autobiography seems obvious. He asks to be understood, not dismissed. He wants to be really listened to. Like with a lot of these songs, whether by Duckler or Elliott, politics enter in, driven chiefly by distaste at the policies of the Reagan years. The President sings lullabies to the "dozing nation." Churches are the "morgue of the living." Corporations back segregation, and *Let's Make a Deal* is more than a game show. How can one be so dead yet somehow, at the same time, alive, Elliott wonders. It's worth noting again just how political so many of these early songs are. That kind of lexicon came most easily, it seems. It was something to write about, a ready subject. It was also possibly safer, a way of cloaking the personal in generalized conceptual and ethical critique. Not that Duckler's and Elliott's grievances were entirely tendentious. Oregon was one of the vanishingly few states Mondale carried. Reagan-bashing was status quo for Portland. It would have been impossible to miss. All the same, these political leanings are absent from Elliott's mature work, at least explicitly. The fiasco of George W. Bush, for instance, receives no mention, except very briefly and sans attribution. In later years Elliott finally braved the personal, he crossed that border, although never without hesitation, a fear that his words might sting.

The cassette concludes with the nearly ten-minute tune "Laughter," another restless offering with discontinuous movement, unexpected stops and starts, a mixture of electric and acoustic guitar, and more blending of the political—"the porcelain President doesn't want to think"—with words suggesting personal origins. Lyrics are credited to Duckler, but this time authorship seems possibly mixed. When Elliott sings "I see myself in my father's mistakes," and describes guilt bleeding out like something no one ever sees—calling it "our form of laughter," then adding "you can't put us back together"—it's difficult not to place the words in biographical context, especially because they resurface in altered forms later on. The mother figure appears too; she's described as left-handed, worrying passively in a style suggestive, perhaps, of Bunny. The singer laments being born into a "fixed deck," the cards doubting him. It's a line reused in Elliott's tune "Alameda," where he shuffles a "deck of trick cards" like some "precious only son."

Over the next few years, and with occasional minor personnel changes, these first two cassettes were followed by four more, two of which did not include Hornick: *Menagerie, Waiting for the Second Hand, The Greenhouse* (under the band name Murder of Crows), and *Trick of Paris Season* (under the band name Harum Scarum). *Menagerie* was recorded in three days in 1987, again at Woofbark Sound.[14] On the way over to the studio—actually a converted garage run by a skinny guy with a big moustache who explained, ambiguously, that he "was only there for free rides"—Hornick slid *Sgt. Pepper* into the car deck. "Elliott was happily surprised by this," Duckler recalls. "I think the message was: On this day something strange and new is happening. That meant (without us even knowing it) that we were inviting in the idea that someone else would care about what we were doing. The mixture of this blessing of letting other people hear what we were doing had a particular excitement and worry about it." The "letting in" wasn't total, however. On the credits Elliott signed off pseudonymously as Johnny Panic, as he did later when he recorded other songs alone, for instance a playful a cappella version of the *Rocky* theme. Tony Lash was away at college, so drums were handled by Adam Koval from Lincoln, another National Honor Society member. Lash would return to play for *Trick of Paris Season*, which appears to send up an old *Life* magazine piece on a Paris nightclub maneuver in which a man wraps his mouth around another man's head, as if to swallow it whole.

Elliott had very strong opinions about all these songs and cassettes. They made him proud and happy, and he found it easy to work with, and be around, his bandmates and friends, but at the same time the feelings expressed sometimes struck him as embarrassing. His perfectionism and self-criticism got in the way of simple pleasures. Once he went over to Duckler's and actually took many of the tapes, only to give them back in the end. As

Duckler put it, "Finding any room for him to accept (let alone enjoy) his own talents was almost completely impossible," even though, of course, he was acutely aware of them. Although he didn't devote inordinate amounts of time to moping around, his depression, according to Duckler, "was a fundamental part of who he was." It helped him relate to others; it also allowed him to better understand suffering. And "when he was depressed he felt, as he would often say, more like himself than when he was not depressed."[15] It was beginning to become, even in these adolescent years, a major aspect of his self-definition, a core posture. For now, its agonies were slight. Later they'd grow to be anything but.

When asked in 2003 about the Stranger Than Fiction recordings, Elliott was evasive (albeit jokingly), for the sorts of reasons Duckler cites. "I don't want to say what [the name of the band was] because I don't want anyone to dredge it up," he laughs. Interviewer Marcus Kagler mentions the possibility of the songs coming to light. "No, no, no," Elliott says. "Of course not. Otherwise why would I be so secretive about it? No, never. There were maybe a couple hundred copies of [albums] on cassette. I really promised myself a long time ago I would keep [them] from ever seeing the light of day. They're not songs so much as a lot of transitions because that was my favorite part of the song. You know, when it goes into the chorus and comes out into the verse. They weren't very linear songs, but they didn't repeat much. I think repetition in rock music or any music at all really kind of got to me when I first started to write. I wondered why every part of the song wasn't the most exciting part of the song."[16]

Despite this prevarication and dismissiveness, the reluctance to see much continuity between his juvenilia and his mature songwriting, the six cassettes are in fact precocious wonders, the kinds of compositions few fifteen-to-seventeen-year-olds could even dream of arranging or playing, let alone record in a fashion that was anything but totally amateurish. And it's not true that the songs never saw the light of day. *Waiting for the Second Hand*, from 1986, with a picture of the four band members superimposed over a clock face on the front cover, features all lyrics by Duckler—on this occasion Elliott wrote no words at all—and music by Smith and Hornick. Credits include a running joke centered, for whatever reason, on fish. Hornick is listed as playing barracuda, Elliott as playing trout and long-nosed pike. One particular song, the next to last on side two, leaps out from the rest like a hooked salmon (to continue the fish metaphor). The title is "Fast Food," and the reason the track instantly pops is because it's the first version of Elliott's "Junk Bond Trader" from the 2000 album *Figure 8*. So fourteen years later, it did resurface. The melody remains perfectly intact; the lyrics—Duckler's—get a major rewrite for *Figure 8*, although small sections of those persist as well.

"Fast Food" starts with a recitation of weaknesses, delivered comically over Elliott's electric piano and a synthesized trumpet riff (later replaced by electric guitar lead). He's a masochist, didactic, infantile, an egotist, "plus a few synonyms which I could not list." Several lines made it on to early *Figure 8* cuts—references to rhetoric, to a policeman directing traffic ("keeping everything moving, everything static"), to people being paranoid, to the need to make some sort of decision and a desire simply to be accepted— "Can you hear me as I am?" But whatever the version—1986's or 2000's—it's a crowded, complex song, lyrically convoluted and musically obscure, lacking any discernible hook or even a bona fide chorus. It is a bit like Dylan— verse heavy, catchy, yet difficult to pin down. In a penultimate take that didn't translate to *Figure 8* (where the song got dressed up and partly effaced in respect to meaning), Elliott expresses himself unusually clearly. He finds he's living in a small reality, boring as a drug he's tired of taking, reeling from the loss of a "first dream love" that failed "because you felt too much." All he ever got, he says, was rhetoric, no sympathy, which turned him into a "sad symphony." In the end he figures no one will ever quite connect "this broken heart together." It was a form of broken that wasn't fixable. His heart, shattered by tough love and bad love, was going to stay that way.

Before high school ended Elliott took one more trip to Texas. This time his Portland persona blared. He wore Birkenstocks and a Nike T-shirt, a perfect combination of new-age hippie and *Runner's World*. His hair now was mainly blond, from sun that manages to infiltrate Portland around the middle of July or so. With the help of Tony Lash he'd been picking up drums, so at the tail end of an August birthday celebration for Pickle—his sixteenth, just days before Elliott's own—he banged away with surprising panache as the rest of the boys tore into "Johnny B. Goode" and Kansas's

In Texas again for Pickle's 16th birthday. (Standing, L–R, Kevin Denbow, Elliott, Mark Merritt. Steve Pickering in the foreground.) (Photograph by Dan Pickering.)

"Carry On Wayward Son." Denbow, in particular, was a big Kansas fan, "Dust in the Wind" on everyone's radar. The boys set up in Pickle's living room "to crank things up to eleven." At one point Pickle's dad shouts to turn off the guitar effects pedal: "Can't you hear that thing?! Y'all have torn your ears up!"[17] Two mics were positioned carefully, the jam recorded on Pickle's sister's boom box. Elliott adored the drum set, though it wasn't particularly high quality. "He just loved to play," Pickle says. "He's not worried about it sounding perfect, not worried about the fact that he's playing someone else's song, not worried about jumping into a rock 'n' roll standard . . . There's no sarcasm, no irony—just pure enjoyment of the music." In the middle of things the drum kit actually falls apart—the bass beater shifting all the way off the bass drum—but no matter, Elliott keeps at it. "It was loud, fast, and sloppy," says Pickle. "In short, everything that rock 'n' roll

The birthday jam session, "cranking things up to eleven!" (L–R, Denbow, with back to camera, Pickering, and Elliott on drums.) (Photograph by Dan Pickering.)

played by teenagers should be." In the moment, Elliott set his clawing perfectionism aside. He simply let rip.

Meanwhile back at Lincoln, high school wound down with the usual avalanche of festivities. Kids danced with dads at the Dad's Club Barbecue. There was formal day and masquerade day, the latter including a tug-of-war at lunch on the back field. Band and choir held three different performances, one with boys in black and red tuxedos. The annual winter semi-formal featured Nine Days Wonder playing '60s and '70s rock, Grateful Dead and the Beatles. The school play was *Grease*, which "fried the stage." And in June the annual Rose Festival arrived, complete with a so-called Fun Center along the waterfront, its Ferris wheel rising above the platform of the Morrison Bridge. This typically several-weeks-long event included a Starlight Parade, and a larger, more lavish Rose Parade that years later Elliott made the subject of a song by the same title. From floats people threw out candy "that looked like money"—milk chocolate coins wrapped in tin foil. That year's theme was "When I was a Kid . . ." Princesses from every

Steven Smith

Lincoln High School senior photo, 1987. (Lincoln High School Yearbook.)

high school in town finished the prompt with lines like "To me, being a kid means keeping dreams and wishes alive," or "One of the best things about being a kid was that it was limitless." Lincoln's representative on the court was Mara Linville; although the school was "very supportive" of Mara, she did not win the "Queen of Rosaria" title.

In yearbook sidebars kids described their highlights of the year. Most listed snow days, finding five-dollar bills, or "extreme party violence." Elliott's offering was, as usual, amusingly outside the mainstream: "During lunch I was downtown with some friends. We were singing and joking around when a man across the street shouted over to us, 'It's raining violins!'" Seniors also penned "final words." Tony Lash (from the year before) had proclaimed "One down, one to go; another town, and one more show." Duckler quoted Winston Churchill: "God's not dead, he's alive and working on a less ambitious project." Elliott recycled a Tom Waits line, "Just let me fall out the window with confetti in my hair."

The now pressing question was what to do next. Duckler was off to Reed College, Hornick to Amherst; Lash had already started at Berklee. Dispersal was inevitable. For Elliott, the situation was complicated. There was a girl in the picture—pretty, freckled, auburn-haired Shannon Wight. Wight was politically involved, part of the club "SPLAT," run by the talented Mr. Sweeney, who in free evenings took classes in classical Greek at Portland State University, taught by Dick Schultz. The club promised "a new perspective on Latin America," focusing not just on politics, but cultural aspects. Students dealt with real life issues, "instead of just consuming ethnic food," according to that year's yearbook. They also raised funds to host a Nicaraguan student.

Wight initiated crew along with Alice Vosmek (who later dated Brandt Peterson around the time Heatmiser was formed). The rowing team, coached by Tom Leonardi, practiced on the Willamette River, which divides east and west Portland. Wight and Vosmek worked with *Polyglot* too, Lincoln's art and literary magazine. In a group shot she playfully throws her arm around a fellow *Polyglot* board member.

The highlight of Wight's senior year was a two-month stay in Paraguay arranged through Amigos de las Americanas, an organization that sent students to Latin America for public health–related work. Wight taught women health and sanitary practices, even helping to build latrines. For part of the time she lived with a family in Contera Boca, enjoying the contrasting simplicity of the lifestyle. And although her Spanish wasn't very good, she and her family acted out a lot of what they needed to say to one another. A picture shows her sitting and eating, surrounded by her Paraguayan hosts, wearing a braided ponytail and blue tennis shoes.

For a sizable number of Lincoln kids—or at least for their clasping parents, sometimes micromanaging every academic move—life had always been about scheming admission to prestigious colleges with names that bestowed instant status. Even the 1987 Lincoln yearbook was called "Gettin' In," and page 225 printed senior "destinations"—Stanford, Smith, Amherst, UC Berkeley, Reed, Scripps, Duke, Northwestern, Cornell, Columbia. Other Portland public schools had no such illustrious listing to trumpet. At Franklin on the east side, for instance, senior "information" was unostentatiously shared, and by far the most frequent plan described was "work," or else attendance at Portland Community College on SE 82 Avenue, a long strip dominated by cheap Chinese restaurants, car dealerships, massage parlors, and meandering prostitutes. Yet by middle school in the Lincoln cluster, and on through the high school years, prepubescent aspirants racked up extracurriculars, internships, and splashy volunteer credits helping out the less fortunate. They worked with tutors, avidly tracked down enrichment opportunities, learned exotic languages, brown-nosed teachers to boost grades from B to A. It was a sort of career—puffing up the résumé, massaging GPA, practicing the SAT to the point of nausea. It was life or death. For Elliott, however, there was very little buy-in. He was exceptionally smart and his grades were excellent, but when it came to choosing a school, the decision was a passive one. He followed Wight to nontraditional Hampshire College, in Amherst, Massachusetts. As it happens, the two broke up before classes even started, but Elliott attended regardless, and made it through in four years.

Given his lack of genuine enthusiasm for college generally and Hampshire particularly, it's not surprising that Elliott's feelings about the school were mixed. He was not alone. Other kids had misgivings too, understandable in light of the nature of the school's "invention" (as most phrased it) from scratch. When Elliott arrived in the late 1980s, Hampshire was almost exactly the same age as he was. It was an idea in constant revision, in a state of never-ending evolution, the deliberate creation of nearby colleges Amherst, Smith, Mount Holyoke, and University of Massachusetts. The idea was to reinvent higher education from the top down, to design an utterly new sort of undergraduate experience in which the "favorite tradition [was] lack of tradition."[19] Doors officially opened in 1970, when two thousand applicants competed for two hundred seventy spaces by sending in "anything that told about themselves," from homemade bread to light shows. Admission posters proclaimed "1,200 students, 1,200 majors"—a sound bite capturing the self-paced, self-created ethos the school championed. Founders believed that "the best learning is that in which a student progressively acquires the ability to teach himself" and in so doing comes to "terms with his culture without being its creature." Because it was never preordained how long the average student might stick around, kids identified themselves in relation to date of entry rather than date of graduation. Certain students managed to get through in the standard four years, as Elliott did, while others wound up on what was sardonically referred to as the "nine-year plan." Attrition was a problem. The less focused, less effectively independent scholar might drift, paying the then-expensive tuition of twenty thousand dollars, before simply dropping out. There was no preset menu of required courses, no core curriculum. Instead students recruited faculty to work with them, then essentially wrote a learning contract stipulating agreed-on paths of study focusing on anything from "Faulkner to folk music, mole-cules to microwaves."[20] As alum Chip Brown explained in a 1990 *New York Times* article ("What's New at Frisbee U?") that many at the school re-garded as heresy, "what emerged was a kind of graduate school for eighteen-year-olds." Students got written evaluations rather than grades. Progress was assessed by way of a series of exams in three "divisions." For Division I, where "to know facts is not enough," students investigated "modes of in-quiry" embodied within the college's four schools—Humanities and Arts, Social Sciences, Natural Sciences, and Communications and Cognitive Science. Division II constituted what most other universities designated as a major, although it also stipulated Community Service and Third-World Exploration. Coursework and research were organized around a theme. As Brown put it, "Someone interested in weaving, for example, might jump off into an exploration of the chemistry of dyes; write a paper about the impli-cations of weaving in aboriginal societies; work up a computer-based ex-periment in pattern recognition; or perhaps compose a sonnet sequence about the joys of being a Luddite." Division III amounted to what is now called a capstone or senior thesis. A committee of faculty was assembled, followed by a thesis defense. "Undivs" were also recommended to students. These were "useful and thought-provoking" experiences such as managing a co-op. Sometimes they led to Divs, sometimes not.

As all incoming freshmen were required to do, Elliott first lived in the dorms. There were two—the smaller Merrill House (with its "clothing op-tional" floor) and the larger Dakin House. Students might say, by way of introduction, "I live in Merrill C, floor two" or "Dakin F, floor three." But as Elliott less than charitably confided in a 2003 interview for *Under the Radar*, most members of his cohort he came to see as "annoying" (he could not "stand the atmosphere") so as soon as possible he moved out to one of the college apartments called MODS—Greenwich House, Prescott, and En-field. Each pod in one of these MODS might accommodate anywhere from six to eight people, and each had a totally different feel depending on the group of students who had petitioned to live together. Those in MODS gen-erally cooked for themselves; they did not eat in the dining hall. Some MODS were studious non-imbibers; others consisted of relatively hard-core partiers.

Elliott in his first year at Hampshire. (Courtesy Jimi Jones, Hampshire archives.)

Yet apart from the absence of clear, uniform requirements, the belief that students were responsible, like inchoate PhD candidates, for independent self-definition and the articulation of an original line of inquiry, despite the fact that most lacked any solid sense of foundational disciplinary knowledge, what really set the school apart was its hyperactivated culture, which Brown summarizes as "antisexist, antiracist, antihomophobic, and antispecist." Around 1990 the professors in the five-college consortium were queried as to political identity, and apparently 100% of those at Hampshire rated themselves either radical or liberal. What students got, in some ways oppressively and sanctimoniously, was a total, unrelenting dose of culture war indoctrination. By Thanksgiving of freshman year the word "girl" had been banished from the lexicon. One could not be anything but a feminist of, ideally, the most extreme stripe. During orientation incoming classes attended tutorials with titles like "The Dangers of Casual Racism and Privilege." It was a process of very determined unlearning geared to expose false consciousness. In courses students fell into the habit of prefacing each and every comment with "As a lesbian, I believe . . ." or "As a member of an underrepresented class, my sense is . . ." One typical student told Chip Brown for his *Times* piece, "Sometimes it's hard to be a heterosexual male here," a feeling Elliott likewise failed to escape. Another felt as if "students are trying so hard to be open-minded they're close-minded." Yet another said, "I consider myself a feminist, but people on campus don't think I am."

For all the adhesively politically correct groupthink, most students still felt a sense of pride in the place. It was cool, politically progressive, avant garde. If you went to Hampshire, you were different, part of an experiment, part of a new, bold way of doing things in higher education. And for Elliott in particular, a major perk was the ubiquity of music all around Amherst and Northampton, clubs that were justifiably famous. On Pearl Street there were live venues galore—grunge, folk, singer-songwriter stuff, even tribute bands, including an excellent Rush outfit, all accessible for very little money. One of Bob Dylan's sons attended the school around the time Elliott did, helping to start up a band of sorts called The Supreme Dicks. It was one part music, one part performance art, one part deliberate irritation. At some point, possessed by the prevailing spirit of adventurousness, a student started a baseball team, and on that one roster alone there were no fewer than nine people in different bands, some in several at once.[21] All around campus there were places to play, and the music department housed what was then a more or less state-of-the-art recording studio with a multitracking setup. Concerts were staged in the dining hall. Nirvana played there in the early years, as did Phish. Usually local bands served as opening acts.

In his first week at school Elliott managed by chance to make his next important and lasting musical contact, one that would persist for at least the ensuing six or seven years. "We started recording almost immediately," said new friend Neil Gust, who like Elliott adored Elvis Costello, and as Elliott noticed, "listened to decent music." But what most thrilled Elliott about Gust, and it would not have been an assessment he'd make at the time about too many other people, was that "he played the guitar better than me." He could "make his instrument sound really good; [he could] make it sing." Gust's feelings for Elliott were equally expansive. He found him incredibly prolific, a true craftsman when it came to songwriting, and outrageously skilled at the subtleties of recording. For the latter their habit was to rent a four-track from the music department that they kept for the weekend. The two fell in with a "Southern Californian stoner-photographer guy" sporting a cartoonish L.A. drawl, who liked music and "wanted to jam." They'd get together with acoustic guitars—neither had access then to an electric—and although Gust found it occasionally "stupid and really embarrassing," at least in retrospect, the stoner kid recited poetry on top of the music. It was, all things considered, pretty classic Hampshire stuff.

Once Gust and Elliott stumbled upon a sort of natural echo chamber in a dorm stairwell, of all places. Experimentally, they blasted what they were recording through speakers. In the space the sound ricocheted, and they would re-record the echo through mics set up at different levels. "We got this amazing stereo reverb," Gust recalls. But it was an "obnoxious thing to do," loud and irritating, even by capacious Hampshire standards. In response three of what must have been a rather scant number of "jocks" at the school stole the mics, which Elliott and Gust later recovered, to great relief—given that they were rented—in some remote closet.

In no time the two friends did what so many at Hampshire also took a stab at. They formed an acoustic duo, called, with Dada-esque panache, Swimming Jesus (apparently the savior had yet to perfect walking on water). They covered Tom Waits, Elvis Costello, the Beatles, and threw in whatever originals they managed to assemble, some written by Gust, some by Elliott. There was a different outfit too, featuring Gust, Elliott, a friend named Dylan, and two others. But most promisingly of all, during breaks from school over holidays and summers when Elliott returned to Portland, the old Stranger Than Fiction reassembled, this time with the fresh moniker Harum Scarum. They even performed. The venue was Satyricon, their name was on the marquee, Tony Lash recalls, and they appeared on the night of a mysterious explosion at Sav-Mor grocery, that ultra-famous event in the history of Portland rock. Yet per usual, performing was not atop the list of priorities. Again the intent was to record, Elliott's abiding monomania. This time they assembled in the studio of Chicago transplant Neil Karras at a place called The Palace at NW 12th and Glisan. All serious or semiserious bands of the time hung out there or rented practice space in variously sized cubbies, from virtual closets to twelve-by-ten-foot "living rooms." In essence the building amounted to a partitioned warehouse with fifty units total and very little insulation between walls. To effect some sort of organization for what was in fact abject chaos, the heavy-metal outfits got sent to the basement, where they plugged power strips into antique outlets on the ceiling, the rooms illuminated by a single hanging bulb. From there it was all feedback and barre chords and anguished screechy solos; you heard yourself by playing louder and more uninterruptedly than the band next door. Pond rehearsed there—initially calling themselves Moodpaint—as did Beauty Stab (later The Dandy Warhols) and Tony Lash's other band Nero's Rome.

The place was run by icon Bill Fisher, whose presence was fierce and unforgettable. Red haired, flip-flop-wearing, sprouting huge mutton-chop sideburns, he stood about six foot three and weighed somewhere in the neighborhood of two hundred fifty pounds. Karras says he "considered himself an alpha male" and never let you forget that fact. He was endlessly in your face, his legs "whiter than plain yogurt," an enormous joint rolling around his overactive mouth.[22] It was from Fisher that Karras rented his recording space, which came to be called, a little vaingloriously, Palace Recording. Karras paid him five hundred dollars per month, then tried recouping that sum with bookings. It was never easy. But he had a solid setup, plus an eight-track and sixteen-track. Fisher made of the location a gestalt of musical entrepreneurship. He had a booking agency, a music store inside; he even put out a magazine called *The Insider*. For a glorious span of years he managed a living off the aspirants circulating enthusiastically, as did Karras, barely.

Lash made the connection with Karras, who knew him from Nero's Rome. *Trick of Paris Season* (1989) was the cassette that came of the week-long session, the one featuring a crazed-looking man shoving his head into another man's pried-apart mouth, which he spreads with both hands on the black-and-white cover.[23] In all there were ten songs on two sides, most melodic rock numbers with Elliott on guitar, tearing off his occasional trademark Van Halen-ish solos. Karras recalls being impressed with his playing, which was obviously accomplished. All the songs were sung by Elliott, with, this time, Elvis Costello/Joe Strummer bark and bite. Garrick Duckler appears as "himself," with Hornick on bass and Lash on drums. All songwriting is credited to Duckler and Elliott, with the exception of "Small Talk"—with its "monster voice" narration—which is credited to the band as a whole. The sound is a bit Cheap Trick, in Karras's estimation, and compared to earlier Stranger Than Fiction efforts, especially the first two, it is simpler, more direct, and lacking in long-drawn-out digressions and abrupt changes of time and mood. What is maybe most notable about *Trick of the Paris Season* is that it includes two songs—"Catholic" and "Key Biscayne"—that Elliott resurrected later, with rewritten lyrics. So again, he did not always abandon these early efforts, set them aside as markedly inferior; they were part of his stock. He reused them when so inclined, if something about them struck him as worthy. Then he remade them to suit current preoccupations. "Catholic" became *XO's* "Everybody Cares, Everybody Understands," Elliott's attack on "synthetic sympathies." "Key Biscayne" became one of his two "Mr. Goodmorning" songs, with its repeated line, taken from the original, "don't sleep, don't go to sleep, don't go to sleep tonight." The re-recording features a deft, arresting acoustic guitar intro, immediately engaging, one of Elliott's most charmingly upbeat, toe-tapping melodies.

Back at Hampshire the relationship with Gust deepened, taking on unexpected complexities, as did Elliott's PC indoctrination as he moved to Division II and Division III requirements, the latter including a thesis. Gust and Elliott shared a close friend, a roommate, who happened to be gay and who, at some point in the process of what Gust described as a sort of "love triangle," made it clear he had feelings for Neil that Neil did not reciprocate (Gust does not name this person). That possibility fading, Elliott and the roommate became particularly close, and as Gust says, "I sometimes thought they were friends at my expense, and as a result I would sometimes act like an asshole to Elliott." Laughingly Gust adds: "We were like nineteen, twenty years old. We were not fully developed emotionally."[24] Whether it was this same roommate or somebody else, according to close friends of Elliott's someone at Hampshire, a young man, confessed a serious crush on him. In response, not sure exactly how to react, and feeling genuine confusion, he spent several weeks investigating, imagining internally the possibility that he might be, or could be, gay. In other words, he tried on a gay identity, almost to the point of attempting to talk himself into it. He thought it might be easier somehow; he wished, at least in the moment, that he might actually be gay. But in the end he found he could not do it. It wasn't him. In any case, this may be the "love triangle" Gust had in mind, though he never does spell out details. As weeks dragged on, Elliott grew more confused with Neil's feelings. He asked him why there were times he acted like he wasn't his friend. He could not understand the capriciousness of Gust's affections. Gust, for his part, "knew exactly what he was talking about . . . Sometimes I would be friendly with him, and sometimes I wouldn't." And this was not a matter that could be blithely shrugged off, since over time the two had decided to form yet another band after graduation. They first thought about moving to Chicago, but finally decided on Portland, where Tony Lash lived, and both Neil and Elliott "loved" Lash's drumming, which reminded them of the drummer from the Pixies. So at last, at a Fourth of July party in the summer prior to senior year, Elliott opened up. He said to Gust, "If we are going to do this together I need to know . . . I want to talk to you about something." As the two took a walk together Gust realized: "Okay, if we are going to live together, then I have to tell him." It was a freighted moment. What came out, for the very first time ever, was Gust. He let Elliott know he was gay. Gust says, "I just blurted it out." At first he couldn't believe he'd said it. He was frozen, terrified, he found he couldn't speak, and impulsively he started to cry.

It's telling that Gust chose to come out to Elliott. No doubt he sensed what friends in Texas and in Portland already knew for certain: that he would not judge, that his compassion was guaranteed. Faced with any sort of vulnerability, Elliot sympathized. He knew what it felt like. At this point in his life, it was one of the things he did best. As Gust recalls, "He was completely . . . amazing." The two took a short walk, sat on a curb together, and talked for hours. Elliott was "totally nonjudgmental and sympathetic," Gust says. He was the only person who knew for another six months, "so he helped me come out." "One of the things I loved most about Elliott was that he was a deeply compassionate person. He even took me to task when I was being judgmental with others."[25] Being in a band meant being accepted "by these cool people," self-created indie rockers whom Gust occasionally found "pretty gross," but even here, in competitive context, "[Elliott] was totally unwilling to do it at the expense of someone's feelings." It wasn't worth it, overriding one's impulse to avoid belittling judgments. "He knew all that stuff instinctively," Gust adds. "He was always like that." It was an admirable, extraordinary posture. And although he would not always stick to it—like anyone, Elliott had his weaker moments—his commitment to making it on his terms was clear from the start.

All this was who Elliott naturally was, but it was also swirling in the thick Hampshire "anti" atmosphere. Financial aid, grants, and work-study were set up for Elliott, and he worked a number of campus jobs, at a farm, caring for sheep, and at a dog kennel—the "Livestock Guarding Dog Project"—where he helped with research on "Scandinavian attack dogs" thought to be peculiarly well-suited to protecting sheep and goats. He liked what he was studying, a hybrid concoction of philosophy and pre-law focused on "how to think" and "thinking about how you think and other people think," a very meta sort of curriculum in which one spent a lot of time in one's own head, reflectively introspecting about introspection, critiquing facile categorical bifurcations. In the late 1980s in academia this kind of dismantling of Kantian structures was *de rigeur* and painfully inescapable. As it did so many undergrad and graduate students, it took Elliott in a post-structuralist direction, into the clotted, sometimes annoyingly wheel-spinning fulminations of Foucault, Barthes, and most of all, Derrida, as well as their assorted epigones. Division III required a mentor, someone to supervise thesis work, and to that end Elliott made the acquaintance of one of Hampshire's most ardent founders, Lester Mazor, who according to one of his research assistants, "did not do superficial." When anyone complained about Hampshire's then-hefty price tag, Mazor's standard response was "You can drive a Chevy or you can drive a Mercedes, and we are a Mercedes." Mazor hosted law lunches anyone might attend, for which he often brought in speakers. He was demanding, he pushed students hard, but usually in a fun, friendly fashion. Like others at Hampshire, Mazor was a student of the culture wars, an outspoken participant in the "PC" debate. A large man with strong forearms and a thick white beard—at least later in his career—Mazor looked a bit like Santa Claus (although in basketball scrimmages, he was apparently famous for his "rough" un-Santa-like play, which earned him the nickname "Lester the molester"). He'd served as a law clerk to Warren E. Burger and taught law at University of Utah before taking a job at Hampshire at its inception, as Henry R. Luce Professor of Law. His courses included hyperspecialized offerings such as "From Potsdam to Perestroika: East Central Europe Since 1945," as well as smaller independent study seminars, one with the acronym D.W.E.M, a.k.a. "Dead White European Male Seminar."

Elliott's thesis was no doubt right up Mazor's alley. Its title was "Toward a Poststructuralist–Feminist Critique of Law," and it zeroed in on procedural changes in the way rape cases got tried in the courts. These were the Foucauldian, Derrida days of the death of the author, according to which all interpretations were equal, every reading a "misreading," and the self a "paper I." Students dutifully memorized the relativistic, deconstructionist mantra, "All meaning is context-bound and context is boundless." In Wittgensteinian fashion people spoke of the end of philosophy, or of its transformation into analyses of language games. Declarations of sincere, unironic belief came for a time to seem passé, the new goal a dismantling into a virtual meaninglessness that was celebrated as some sort of release from dogma and received wisdom. At any rate, this is the intellectual context in which Elliott would have been doing his reading, thinking, and writing. Rape and legal theory was an altogether different matter. Anti-sex feminism was in marginal vogue, leading to antipornography law creation of the sort articulated by Catharine MacKinnon and Andrea Dworkin. "Pornography is the theory," said Robin Morgan, "and rape is the practice." In 1983, four years before Elliott started at Hampshire, Dworkin and MacKinnon drafted ordinances sidestepping obscenity law and labeling pornography a violation of women's *civil* rights, by virtue of which pornographers might be sued for harm in civil courts. Versions of these ordinances were passed in select cities—for instance, Bellingham, Washington, in 1988—although later found to violate freedom of speech protections.

In all, adding up to an examination of undecidability and indecipherability (on the poststructuralist side) and sexist, male-dominated, patriarchal hegemony (on the feminist side), it was more than enough to keep a smart twenty-year-old's head spinning. That it did and more to Elliott, as some of his later comments made plain. But he got it done, and he went "straight through" the school, leaving with debt to repay. Retrospectively, he felt he hadn't proved much. The most he showed himself and others, he said, was that he "could do something I didn't really want to do for four years." His studies he did find interesting, but they "had no practical application in the world." He had a BA in philosophy and legal theory; what this allowed him to look forward to were jobs in bakeries or in the spreading of gravel. It wasn't about the academics anyway. To him they were just that—academic. As ever, it was the music that mattered. And Hampshire supplied that, most notably in the person of Neil Gust. Now Gust and Elliott were about to do something remarkable, at first together, then later intractably separately.

CHAPTER FOUR SOME REVERSE PYROMANIAC

The obligatory grind of college now over, Elliot headed back home to Portland, to the kind of existence—or at least living arrangement—he'd always wanted. As he said to an interviewer in early 2001, he started feeling "untwisted up" as soon as he "didn't live with anybody." No more lawn mowing, as in Cedar Hill. No more stepparents, except very occasionally, when necessary. No more attack dogs, loud summertime townies (who enjoyed calling Elliott a faggot), dorms, or half-assed hemming and hawing about what to do with his life. All the adolescent fireman talk evaporated (although other hesitations surfaced temporarily). It was time, at last, to commit to the idea of making a band. Stranger Than Fiction, Murder of Crows, Harum Scarum, the dabblings when on vacation in Texas—all juvenilia, very promising but overripe. It was time to get serious. And as Denny Swofford, co-owner of Cavity Search Records, put it, "Things were popping in Portland in 1991."

The decade was ushered in less than auspiciously, with a legendary, literal bang, the cause of which remains a mystery to this day. Right next to Satyricon sat the abject, shabby Sav-Mor Grub grocery, pit stop for undesirables—alcoholics, junkies, transients, "the displaced, distracted, and dysfunctional."[1] It was where Satyricon patrons, many of them local college students from places like Reed and Lewis and Clark, commingled with an "entirely different series of social strata altogether."[2] Late one night the place was mysteriously—all too conveniently—blown to bits. Some said gangs were behind the evildoing, others pointed to the police, still others to city administrators, who viewed the erasure as a public service. The disappearance of Sav-Mor Grub, so went the basic sentiment, might lead to the disappearance of the people who frequented it, a magical, inexplicable sucking of chaos into a crater. (Didn't happen, needless to say.)

A building was one thing; loss of life another. Larry Hurwitz ran Starry Night, a stone's throw from Sav-Mor Grub. "Elliptical on the subject of gate receipts," "ruthlessly competitive for his share of the local music market," and rarely beneath assorted acts of intimidation, Hurwitz was a "slippery" impresario with a "consortium of underlings at the ready to do his perfidious biddings."[3] He generally covered his tracks; he generally kept his hands clean. But on January 20, 1990, more than one hundred eighty tickets to a John Lee Hooker show were discovered at the Starry Night door by Chris Monlux, one of the event's promoters. Cheated fans were incensed. Who printed the bogus ducats, they demanded to know? Hurwitz promptly denied involvement, then dished out blame on a kid named Tim Moreau, his employee, whom he ostentatiously fired. Moreau disappeared, never to be seen again. Detectives scoured his apartment, finding credit cards, a checkbook, and one hundred fifty dollars in cash. There was little sense the kid had any plan of vanishing. All the more interesting was apparent evidence of counterfeit ticket conspiracies. Hurwitz hightailed it for Southeast Asia, where the law finally caught up with him. He was arrested for Moreau's murder in 1998.

Then, finally, there was a near miss. Elliott's Stranger Than Fiction bandmate Tony Lash was hanging out late one night at a friend's house in North Portland. At the time, February 1990, he was drumming for Nero's Rome. A stray bullet fired from the street ripped through a house wall, penetrated the back of a couch on which Lash was lying, then lodged in his lung, barely missing his spine and heart.[4] The lung collapsed, and Lash spent several weeks in recovery, grateful for what was, in retrospect, a very close call, a random brush with death. The bullet is still in him.

In effect, as Portland rock historian S.P. Clarke explains, "vital layers of innocence and naiveté" were peeling away from the Portland scene, replaced by assorted seedy miasmas. Some kind of metamorphosis seemed near. Change was percolating. Physical structures and bit players formed part of the master narrative, but the real story, the one on which the physical structures and bit players depended, was the music, the art, the sounds getting made and played.

Portland was no average destination, more a second-rung rest stop between far sexier Seattle and San Francisco where bands *most* wanted to gig. To Pete Krebs of the band Hazel, Seattle was nebulously "a little more rough, just a rougher scene overall." The "guys were even bigger up there—big dudes, with long hair, all six foot three, like Soundgarden." Portland was "rain saturated," full of "wet brick" people. There was "a great deal of darkness to it. Not at all a very lighthearted place. We were a backwater," Krebs says, the scene "gloomy, somber" and heroin drenched. Even the venues, like Satyricon, were toilets. The Wipers, a late-1980s Portland band, supplied the basic soundtrack in songs like "Doom Town"—according to which life was "incomplete," replete with "blank stares" and a feeling of nonstop losing. In a word, depressing, the mood leaking out between downpours like dysthymic drizzle. There was also a sense of smallness of scale, with everybody once removed at most from everybody else. "It got to the point," Krebs says, "where you could tell who was at a party by the bikes out front." Hookups and dramas were commonplace, fueled by "drugs, alcohol, punk, rain, and violence."[5]

Seattle, the nominal grunge capital of the world, was corporate, full of bands looking to get signed, hungry for mid- or major-label recognition, willing to do what it took to make it big. Portland was different, getting signed anathema, the kiss of death. "People were making music *for the sake of it*, for the sake of creativity alone," says Jason Mitchell, Elliott's close friend (and later, tour manager/merch man). "We thought it was like that everywhere. We didn't know any better. It was just phenomenal music all the time." The attitude was "Screw labels, we do what we want."[6] And of course, as always, this was part, maybe large part, braggadocio. No serious band works hard performing and writing original music to go nowhere. No serious band aspires to cashless anonymity. But that was the tacit aesthetic. And it was liberating. There was a freedom, originality, creativity, and patent level of bizarreness in Portland that defied easy categorization. It was anything goes. And the results were intoxicating.

Fifteen to twenty bands played the circuit in mixed bills, at Satyricon, the X-Ray, La Luna, EJ's, with roughly one thousand loyal followers packing the houses, weekend after weekend. The trend in names was for single staccato monikers, sharp punches to the solar plexus: Hazel, Sprinkler, Pond, Lungfish, Crackerbash, Joybuzzer, Sugarboom, Bedspins, Iceburn, Antenna

A poster for a mixed show at La Luna. (Photograph by Henry Love.)

("We'd joke," says Krebs, "'Hey! Want to go see Table? They're playing with Chair this weekend.'"). It was "power pop at its finest," says Denny Swofford, "some strange combination of brilliant and uncomfortable. Just like a circus act. But upbeat and positive." Neil Gust recalls a feeling on arrival of "enormous energy and enthusiasm to rock out. It was a competitive and energetic scene." Krebs, for his part, recalls "no competition at all. We used to actually draw straws to see who would play first and who would head-

Pete Krebs (left), Elliott, and Hazel's Brady Smith. (Photograph by JJ Gonson.)

line." Even posters were made with the express intent of making it difficult to tell who was at the top of the bill.

In some ways Hazel's Krebs epitomized the zeitgeist. Born in Orange County, he ended up at Oregon State University in Corvallis, a talented, artistic kid who didn't "apply myself" in high school and who wound up spending time in a military school in Pennsylvania. His dad was a boxer and war hero, his finger blown off at Pearl Harbor, his face slanting sideways from angled blows he took in the ring. Just like Elliott once he got to Portland, Krebs was raised by his biological father, along with a new mom—a stepmother—who herself had two girls from a prior marriage. OSU was cut short when Krebs got diagnosed with Hodgkins Lymphoma, for which he received radiation treatment in Portland at St. Vincent's Hospital. It did the trick; there was no chemo. He'd mostly taught himself guitar at age ten, with short-lived lessons from an angry classical guitarist in a wheelchair. For the first few years of his early adolescence "all I listened to was the Beatles"—a habit Elliott knew well. Then he came across various journalistic accounts of the punk phenomenon and bought up all the Sex Pistols, Clash, and X records he could get his hands on. "X was *the* band," he says.

Needing cash, Krebs found work in a warehouse in what is now called the "Pearl District" but which, then, was anything but tony. There he met Reed College grad Brady Smith, a bassist who turned him on to the Pixies and Shocking Blue, a band Kurt Cobain had also admired. The two wrote an album in "a couple nights," and "cobbled together some bass lines." Jody Bleyle, who later helped form Team Dresch, a serious all-girl band, signed on to play drums. A Reedie like Brady Smith, she was small, short-haired, deliriously happy on stage, ferociously feminist off—an "out of control Muppet," according to Denny Swofford. At the time, Krebs shot pool with a dancer and self-described "spirit man" named Fred Nemo. They talked casually about adding some sort of performance art element to the group. There was little esoteric or highfalutin about it; they simply thought it might be cool. And so, in a task "critical to the success of the band," Nemo supplied psychedelic inflections. Slightly balding with a long, stringy ponytail, he convulsed around the stage. One typical shtick put him in a pink tutu firing plastic heart-shaped arrows into the audience. In a YouTube video of "Joe Louis Punchout" performed live at the X-Ray he ricochets wildly in a calico dress, buffeted by invisible obstacles, in front of a pair of boys, almost jockish, in backward baseball caps banging their heads to Bleyle's complex, disjointed rhythms. The song is hard but infinitely subtle, intelligent pop, short and sweet. Krebs, in a genius of understatement, plays it totally straight in round glasses, white T-shirt, and blond hair (he looks, in fact, very much like Cobain). Nemo's "whack shit onstage"—swinging a rotary phone by its cord, standing on stepstool ladders while balancing a pitcher of water on his head, stripping down to bikini briefs and sliding into a women's one-piece—made for its own contrapuntal adornment. The music paid scant notice. Deliberately, it wasn't in on the joke. "I had no idea what he was doing most of the time," Krebs says. "I didn't want to get fucked with while I was playing. But I never thought of him as anything but a bandmate." "J Hell," a Hazel seven-inch vinyl record, named for Krebs's college girlfriend Janel (who later sang in the band Trailer Queen), sold fifteen hundred copies at a rapid pace.[7] Kids picked them up at shows, or at independent record stores like The Ooze or Ozone (which Janel ran and

Hazel (L–R, Brady Smith, Bleyle, Krebs.) (Photograph by JJ Gonson.)

co-owned along with Bruce Grief, and which some considered the nucleus of the Portland music scene at the time). Clearly something exciting and potentially profitable was taking root amid the mayhem and chaos. And in the middle of it all, in some ways fomenting it, were two avuncular entrepreneurs, a pair of deeply committed music madmen (and Dylan devotees), Christopher Cooper and Denny Swofford.

Swofford made the scene in Portland in 1990, drifting south from Seattle where he worked for bands like Mother Love Bone. At that time he was in thrall to the haunted addict musician Andrew Wood, who like Elliott occasionally recorded alone with a four-track. To Swofford, Wood—the subject of a DVD titled *Malfunction: The Andy Wood Story*—was genius in ongoing process. Heartbreakingly, he died of a heroin overdose in March 1990. Swofford split town, not sure of his next move. Needing to make money, he got a job at Coffee People on NW 23rd and Burnside, a ritzy street getting ritzier, with shoe shops and upscale salons, and a fabulous, cheap pizza joint called Escape From New York, run by a comically cranky, blunt East Coast transplant named Phil (Elliott's dear friend Sean Croghan would work there). The coffee job was joyless; every day Swofford gathered up his measly tips and beat a path to the record store Music Millennium, a few paces south, where he spent all he had on seven-inches. In the '90s the chief way to learn about new, obscure bands, apart from seeing them live, was through these typically two-track vinyl records. They had an A-side and

Blue-haired Elliott with Coffee People coffee, the shop in which Swofford worked for a time. (Photograph by JJ Gonson.)

Chris Cooper at Satyricon. (Photograph by JJ Gonson.)

a B-side. Bands chose the songs extremely carefully, because the seven-inch constituted a calling card. It was an aural handshake. Many had inserts, with lyric sheets, pictures, or other band-related content, and the covers were artfully designed. Even the vinyl came in different colors— white, dark blue, red. As Swofford's collection grew, each new acquisition slid into protective plastic sleeves, he drew the attention of Christopher Cooper, who worked the store at the time for five bucks per hour.

Cooper had his own story. He'd attended the Parsons School for Design, then moved to Portland in 1991, looking for the "cohesive dream job," some means of combining his design sensibilities, very refined, with his adamant love for music. New York was, for him, "a lot of experimentation." He calls himself a "loose cannon." He decided to get out, and very deliberately, with planful intention, he sought a fresh start. For a brief period he worked as a carpenter on San Juan Island, in Friday Harbor. Believing what he needed was a semi-Spartan existence, he set himself up in a cabin with no electricity or running water. It was back to nature. It was the anti-NYC. The money was very good, so he built up a nice nest egg. The shift to working at Music Millennium was a love choice—music was what he lived for. The pay wasn't an issue, for the time being.

Swofford and Cooper hit it off instantly. "We were cut from the same cloth," Cooper says. "We bonded on the love of music." A band they both adored was The Jesus Lizard, whom Cooper calls "powerful and amazing" live. He checked them out locally at Satyricon, then traveled to see them in places like Seattle, Olympia, and Vancouver, British Columbia. After one such show, Swofford gave Cooper a lift back to town, and as Cooper recalls, "during that two-hour car ride from Olympia to Portland we essentially laid the groundwork for starting a label." They needed a logo, for starters, and a PO Box. The name was Cavity Search—a clever reference to the hiding of special valuables in dark, unexpected places.

Like no one before or since, Swofford and Cooper embarked on an impassioned, indefatigable crusade to absorb the Portland music scene. They saw everything; they knew everyone. It was, in Cooper's terms, "like a self-taught grad program in building a label. I knew nothing about it. I just told myself I needed to learn how music is presented and sold and distributed." The idea they hatched was simple. It was clear to both of them that Portland was special, exploding with talent and inventiveness, a hive of creativity. So five to seven nights per week they lived in the venues—sometimes at bars like the X-Ray, sometimes in basements or house parties. "We approached bands live. That's how we did it. We were committed to finding the very best bands and putting out their two best songs." It was exactly this mind-set that led to Hazel. Cooper had planned to check out Jakob Dylan, but Dylan canceled. So, opposed to wasting an evening, Cooper made his way to a Hazel show instead. What he realized was that, first, these were "amazing, creative, diverse people"—incredibly catchy musically, with a "crazy dancer." The next response was fated, preordained: "This is the first band I want to work with. What I saw, I realized almost immediately, was mind-blowing." The date was February 1992. It's seared into Cooper's memory. He and Swofford had CSR #1: Hazel's "J Hell."[8]

Initially the label was run out of the pair's bedrooms. It was a less than ideal arrangement, very DIY but limiting. In large part the challenges were simply a matter of space. So as things got going Swofford and Cooper rented rooms above Ozone that became, vaingloriously, "our first office." The precise location was 11th and W. Burnside, directly across the street from Powell's Books. Upstairs windows overlooked Django Records to the south, where Elliott and Garrick Duckler had breathlessly sold their Stranger Than Fiction cassettes back in the high school days. This single room slowly became three rooms. It was here that Cavity Search lived, up to the late '90s, when they moved to an East Side building just across from the Hawthorne Bridge.

Soon Elliott would meet Swofford and Cooper, and the event would change the direction of his life and art forever. He was, at the time, and like nearly everyone in a band or into music, an Ozone regular. Matt Schulte, who worked at the record shop from the start, recalls Elliott spending "three hours or more in Ozone once, thumbing through records one by one, saying three or four words the entire time." He "felt comfortable there," Swofford adds, "it was a safe place in which he could just hang out." To Swofford, "Portland was the foundation that allowed Elliott to become the person he was and to blossom." It was the scene, the bands, the politics, the personalities, and it was also the presence of Cavity Search. It's difficult to believe, given his adamantine interests, the way songs easily formed themselves in his head, but for a short period post-college Elliott had "almost completely" talked himself out of playing music. In his head he was, as Gust used to call it, all "bunched up." Part of the cause of this mental log-jam was, funnily enough, college. Reading Kant and other major philosophers wasn't a problem; Elliott liked learning about how people think, about categories of understanding and so on. But radical feminist philosophy, a major portion of his program at Hampshire, left him "demoralized." Jason Mitchell always felt Elliott "was just too sensitive, too emotionally sensitive. He internalized everything, even stuff that wasn't directly about him as a person. He never could shrug off or gloss over anything." And it was the same for feminism. "I just took everything to heart in a big way," Elliott says.[9] To be a straight white man, at the top of the Marxist mountain, fomenting hierarchical and patriarchal power structures, was a problem. To his list of woes, and it was always uncommonly long, sex and color became the latest additions. The best one could do—and this was the attitude pushed by fringe, hetero-sex-averse feminists he had spent so much time studying for his thesis—was to identify as a "nonsexist white male." Men, by definition, could not be feminists. The most they could do was sympathize, stick up for the sisters. "It got to a point," Elliott recalls, "where I couldn't look at a girl objectively without thinking of all these questions." He was, in his own mind, unworthy, illegitimate, innately flawed, worthless.

Jason Mitchell. (Photograph by JJ Gonson.)

He wasn't the solution, he was the problem. And this was an assigned position he recoiled from; the worst thing he could do was embody it, in whatever form it might take. He began by searching about for something "useful" he might pursue in the world—jobs that were necessary yet not coveted by anyone else. The very last thing he felt comfortable with—ironically, what he would one day become—was to be "the straight white guy on the stage going on and on about my feelings." Straight white-guy feelings were bullshit; they were what feminism aimed to expose, a power structure implicitly embedded in language itself. "Neil Gust was like, 'You're just talking yourself out of everything you want to do.' He just kept insisting that we were going to start a band and I kept being like, 'No.'" But no other option rushed into the breach. And Portland being what it was—music taking off, bands living together in apartments and houses all over town, writing original songs—Elliott was thrown back to a reality far more powerful than abstract theory. Music was who he was. It was what he did and what he made. It was the language he spoke.

So Neil won out. Portland, too, in its ambient way. The first step was easiest, a semi-foregone conclusion. Neil had heard Tony Lash's drumming in Harum Scarum, on songs like "Catholic" and "Bald Faced Lie," so one half of the rhythm section was set. Tony, as it turned out, was down for starting something new. Surprisingly, he never actually "aspired to be a drummer," but he did enjoy "rocking out." All three were heavily into the D.C. Dischord bands picking up steam in the late 1980s—Nation of Ulysses, Fugazi. "Basically," Elliott says, "we kind of wanted to be Fugazi." Another inspiration was Chicago's Urge Overkill, a double singer-songwriter attack led by King Roeser and Nash Kato, who met at Northwestern. Butch Vig produced their 1990 record *Americruiser*; it was a sound that inspired bands from Smashing Pumpkins to Nirvana, who used Vig for the paradigmatic album *Nevermind*; Urge Overkill later opened for Nirvana on the *Nevermind* tour.

The next step, far more difficult, and more freighted, was settling on a bassist. Several auditions were held, quite a few in fact, but nothing clicked. Alice Vosmek, whom Elliott knew from Lincoln High School, had dated Oberlin grad Brandt Peterson; she told Elliott Brandt was a bass player. Brandt knew Sean Croghan before leaving for college; Croghan was part of "the Gresham scene," a group of musicians from a small town in East County, Oregon, about twenty minutes from Portland. So a meeting was arranged. Peterson caught up with Elliott at a café or coffee shop, the two sitting at an outside table. There was instant affinity, some of which had to do with the fact that Peterson wore a button proclaiming "Another Citizen for Gay Rights." At the time the so-called Oregon Citizens Alliance, led by short, balding hatemonger Lon Mabon, was calling homosexuality a crime, leading initiatives to put the question on the ballot. Elliott told Peterson, "I like the button." The attitude hurdle was instantly cleared.

Brandt was an Oregon Episcopal School, Catlin brat, each private, expensive schools on the west side of town full of kids Lincoln students sometimes mixed with and knew from grade school at Ainsworth on Vista. Like Tony Lash, he was raised by a single mom, the manager of a travel agency. There was no abundance of money, private school aside, so Peterson took Tri-Met to classes. He hung out with "disaffected kids" downtown, got heavily into the B-52s, Napalm Beach, the Rats (the Wipers' *Is This Real?* especially blew his mind) and although he grew up playing sax in high school bands—soul/jazz configurations—and even spent time in a "horrible" Devo facsimile (just as Elliott did, named the Spudboys), he bought his

Sitting in with the Spudboys, Elliott on right. (Photograph by JJ Gonson.)

first bass in 1983, entranced by the possibility of "marking out the rhythmic feel of the tune, doing contrapuntal harmonic work." The way the bass "sits underneath everything and drives the music" seemed to capture his interest, suggesting a new direction. Before college Peterson lived in a house on SE Ankeny with junkie roommates who stole his stuff; for money he washed dishes. Oberlin got him out of this hopeless grind; it was a complete immersion in music, an "intense musical experience" all around. He played with Orestes Delatore of Bitch Magnet, learned from an endless list of brilliant drummers. Then, in 1989, his "elite college liberal arts degrees in government and political science" behind him, he came back to Portland to live with Oberlin friends and found a job sweeping up for a cabinet installation crew, on a shift starting at three A.M. "I was a pretty committed drinker by then," Peterson says, "and just as the bars were closing my shift would start." The drinking was part of a larger gestalt, one Brandt shared with Elliott. As he says, unsparingly and with admirable candor, "I was chronically, clinically, severely depressed. Just very sarcastic and negative. Dysthymic is the official name for it. I was the average drunk with no self-awareness."

He joined up with Red Vines in fall of 1989, playing jangly rock, a kind of country punk. They gigged at Blue Gallery and Satyricon, Teddy Miller on drums, Rob McNaulty of Saint's Pilgrims singing. Rehearsals were held in a warehouse around NW Davis Street. You could not smoke—the place was a fire trap—so everyone chewed tobacco. Largely because of his drinking and the depression it softened, Peterson, as he says, "shit the nest in that band." "I made it stop being fun. I just had this overweening anxiety for the bass to be loud enough." There was ongoing internal confusion, Peterson feels, looking back. In his view, playing in a band equaled being in a family. The prospect of playing for more than one band at a time, the sort of thing lots of players managed, was unthinkable. "I felt like every band I was in had to crystallize my identity totally. I felt like 'This is the place I'll be safe and where I'll be valued.'" A brief flirtation with Sprinkler followed—Peterson says he suggested the name—but he wound up in M99, a band Elliott knew and saw, as did everyone. They were a punk version of a bar band. The idea, then, for Brandt, was to "play every weekend and drink a lot." Heidi Hellbender sang, with James Mahone from Gresham on drums—"he could make rock tunes feel like swing." M99 brought out a seven-inch through Tim/Kerr records. "Seizure" was side A, "Black Eye" side B. Peterson played only on "Black Eye," for a reason he was growing sadly accustomed to. There was a blow-out in Vancouver. Brandt made the innocent mistake of talking to an interviewer; guitarist Rob Landoll objected, and there was an altercation, with pushing and shoving. Peterson is six foot two, an imposingly fit man. When he lost it, people paid attention; they also feared getting beat up. So M99 was over for Brandt. (They later brought out two albums, *Too Cool for Satan* and *Medicine*.)

The day Brandt met Elliott he told him, bluntly and in clear attunement to his history of conflict: "You don't want me in your band. It just gets fucked up. Everyone hates me and I get kicked out." But Elliott answered, "That won't happen this time." And with that simple rejoinder, the "star search" was over. Elliott and Neil would sing and write songs, Lash would drum, and Brandt would handle the bass.

The name? Heatmiser, yet another single-word slap in the face, this one with a twist. Fictional demon Heat Miser had appeared in Rankin/Bass's stop-motion animated Christmas special *The Year Without a Santa Claus* (1974). He's described as a vaguely ogre-like being, a blustery, quick-tempered hothead; his head's exactly that—hot—orange/red hair aflame, with a bulbous red nose in the center of his fat, angry face. He eats fire; he "never wants to know a day that's under sixty degrees"; everything he touches melts in his clutches. "He's Mr. Green Christmas, he's Mr. Sun," goes the song. No friend of Santa's, no friend of snow, no friend of cozy yuletide spirit. But a decent band name all the same, one part meaningful, one part random.

Songwriting was never an issue, Elliott's fecundity already semi-legendary. Like Chicago's Urge Overkill, Heatmiser was a two-pronged singer/songwriter set up. Neil and Elliott lived together in southwest, and "they'd sit around a lot and play guitar together and arrange together." The basic ideas were individual inventions, "but stylistically they'd blend to-gether."[10] Early on, rehearsal space was an issue. But Brandt knew Jason Mitchell, whom he introduced to Elliott. Mitchell was living with Moira Doogan, Trailer Queen's drummer. Before they took it over, the house—at 210 NE Morris—was rented by Bikini Kill's Kathleen Hanna and various members of Calamity Jane (directly across the street there were occasional gang-related shootings, eventually prompting Mitchell to move). Heatmiser first practiced and rehearsed in this home's basement, meeting once or twice per week. Slowly Mitchell and Elliott got close. They "palled around," went to shows, dive bars like the Space Room ("in orbit since 1959"), Club 21 on Sandy Boulevard, My Father's Place, and Patty's Retreat on SW Stark, a "mix of bad drag queens, rock 'n' roll kids, transients." Mitchell's tacit, unofficial job was "shoulder to cry on." "I was sort of the band's psy-chiatrist," he says. They didn't always go to one another with their prob-lems; they went, instead, to him. Mitchell and Gust also bonded—"Neil was actually my closest friend during most of these years." The two eventually wound up living together. Neil, says Mitchell, was "hilarious, fun, very driven, talented."

It was, at first, a democratic process. Neil and Elliott brought songs to the band, and ideas got floated, arrangements tweaked. "It was very col-laborative," Peterson says. "More or less built that way. One guy came with a tune, partly finished or not at all, guitar parts working together in complex ways, but not busy. It was like, 'This is what I'm working on, what do you think?'" Somehow, astonishingly to Peterson, "the tunes came together fast." Most were 4/4. Peterson wrote a little too. One of his tunes, "Glamourine," a "bass line with lyrics," was recorded but never put out. Elliott, Brandt says, "didn't want to sing lyrics other people had written." "Just a Little Prick" was another Peterson song, on which his E-string was tuned to D. That song eventually appeared, as did Elliott's "Mightier Than You," on Heatmiser's first cassette—in a sense, their first album—which they titled simply *The Music of Heatmiser*. "Elliott hated "Mightier Than You," Pete Krebs recalls. "It was catchy and bouncy and all, but he thought the lyrics were really dumb."

The Brandt compositions were anomalies. Really the band was Elliott's and Neil's; they were the dominant voices. They churned out the raw material—the subjects, the tone, the group aesthetic. And as always, from Texas, to Lincoln, seemingly from infancy, Elliott wrote "a ton of songs," Gust recalled. "He was so prolific, effortless. His process was advancing much quicker than any songwriter around him."[11] As Mitchell saw it, Elliott's moods had "the most profound impact on the band by far." We "followed his lead," Gust adds. "He was a great craftsman. I was learning how to write songs from him." And it was rarely easy, Neil's process a lot less effortless. According to Mitchell, "he was working really hard to keep up, to contribute 50 percent of the songwriting, to maintain an equilibrium in the band." There was no feeling of tension, nor resentment, nor competition— since the Texas days, no one felt equipped to compete with Elliott musically. It was more about balance and equity. Plus from its inception the band was a joint effort, with Lash and Peterson, although very gifted musically and trained at Berklee and Oberlin, playing essentially subsidiary roles. Peterson, by nature, was pricklier about it. He didn't automatically defer. "They always had ideas for bass lines," he says, "but I wasn't going to listen necessarily. I had my own ideas too." Still, even to Peterson, it was clear that Elliott's "writing process was exploding. He was phenomenally creative."

The Morris Street practices ended when Elliott and Neil found a larger house on SE 16th, just south of Division, where they lived with two female roommates and met as a band in the basement. At this critical juncture a new force entered the equation, a small, beneficent tornado from the East Coast named JJ Gonson. In no time, Gonson would transform the future of Heatmiser, and more important, Elliott's own life and music. Just as Pete Krebs and Elliott shared aspects of life history that served to strengthen their bond, that wordlessly drew them closer together, so did Elliott and JJ. The day after Gonson graduated from high school, she found herself locked up. "I was a junkie, a garbage head," she says, heroin the one drug she managed somehow to avoid, although it always loomed tantalizingly. She lived with prostitutes—"I was on the edge but I did not whore"—and sold acid to skinheads, a batch of which accidentally ran through the washer. Skinheads were looking for her; they weren't happy about the buy. Her mother flew her to Eden Prairie, Minnesota, for a seven-week treatment program. On the plane the first thing Gonson did was order a drink; her mother canceled it. "I got clean," she says. "I was actually eighteen so I could have legally signed myself out but I knew I was in trouble and I couldn't stop. I believed I had a disease. Addiction came easily." In the lockup she learned to blow smoke rings. She also got turned on to the Replacements and punk outfits like Big Black from Chicago.

Inpatient time over, Gonson took a degree from the School of the Museum of Fine Arts, Boston, that turned out to be useless. Her plan was to teach darkroom photography in either elementary or high school classrooms, but a recent measure annihilated art in public education. "They took their red marker and basically crossed it out," she recalls. But a better fate came calling. Gonson had latched on emotionally and personally to a number of Sub Pop bands whom she photographed for fanzines like *Rip, Cream, Spin, XXX,* and *Suburban Noise*. She even shot Nirvana when they played shows for "crowds" of 15 or so at MIT frat parties. Band members took to sleeping on her floor when they came through town; she cooked their meals, made sure they were taken care of. Her life was spent in clubs, shooting away, a kind of punk Weegee. Inevitably, at one point she joined a band herself, called Feeding Frenzy. Still, Gonson felt at loose ends, unsure where the ideal future lay. "I went walkabout a little bit," she says. "I ended up driving across the country," with no special destination in mind. Back in Boston she'd met quite a few Northwest bands, and in one of life's random good luck/bad luck throwdowns her car conveniently gave out in Portland, where she stayed with the Hellcows and landed a job at La Patisserie, the same place Jason Mitchell worked as a waiter. Mitchell quickly became her closest friend—as he seemed to do with everyone he came in contact with—and he introduced Gonson to Neil and Elliott "almost immediately." Heatmiser was not playing live yet; they were honing their craft, recording sporadically in the fashion Elliott and Tony Lash had by now perfected.

Even before heading west Gonson had done some band managing, mostly by necessity. She'd dated Sluggo, one of the members of Hullabaloo, and because the band was "clueless" when it came to bookings and other necessary evils such as putting together press releases, Gonson assumed that role for them, even going out on tour and working as a merch girl (selling T-shirts, etc.). "I've always been somebody who decides they want to do something then learns how," says Gonson. (There had even been, earlier, a stint as a self-taught electrician for a circus.) By trial and error, then, she learned band management, gradually accumulating a notebook "full of names of pretty much all the important promoters in the country." Firsthand, she also got intimately acquainted with venues. She knew which were solid, and which sucked.

So when Jason Mitchell took Gonson to see Heatmiser, at what was one of their virginal performances at the X-Ray between 2nd and 3rd and Burnside downtown (it's no longer there), she was no average spectator. She'd been around the block more than once. She knew music, she knew bands, and she knew what it meant to sell and promote. "Heatmiser wasn't like anything else," Gonson recalls thinking. "It was so much better. Just mesmerizing, phenomenal music. So organic. They were just channeling these songs. I know when I hear good music. I realized it when I first heard Elliott's voice." In a shot by Gonson of a slightly later X-Ray show, from May 1992, Elliott wears a Red Sox baseball cap, hoop earrings in both ears, and a cartoon T-shirt. Peterson stands to his right in a Madonna T-shirt and thick, black-rimmed "geek" glasses, cigarette eternally listing from his lips, as slender, blond Neil Gust sings. Behind them, seemingly tossed against brick walls, hang assorted velvet paintings of dogs and celebrities (e.g., Hulk Hogan) positioned at haphazard angles. Swofford's response to the music was just like JJ's. For him the sound was "raw, aggressive, and crushing." Later, when he came to know the band members personally, he was struck by something else just as unusual: "Heatmiser had manners. They understood a little about tact. They could be adult men. They were real people, not dumb kids. Properly reared. A smart band, smart individuals."

Second Heatmiser show at the X-Ray in May 1992. (L–R, Gust, Peterson, Elliott, Lash.) (Photograph by JJ Gonson.)

Hazel's "J. Hell" seven-inch had been so thrillingly successful, sales driven hard by a massive high school and college following, that the obvious question, a semi-urgent one, was what Cavity Search might bring out next. Hazel and Heatmiser played together almost once per month. There was an October 30, 1992, show at Satyricon, including Trailer Queen and Pond, a show on November 11 at Belmont's, then several more in 1993, at LaLuna and Clinton Street. Cooper and Swofford made up their minds swiftly. Somehow, no matter what it took, CSR2 was going to be Heatmiser. A summit was arranged in the Division house basement. By this time Cooper and Swofford knew the material exceptionally well; they'd been hearing it live for months. The band ran through several songs they figured might have vinyl potential, and instantly Swofford had his A side, a decision he'd really made beforehand. The song was Elliott's "Stray." Next was the matter of the B side, and here things got dicier. Completely naively, Swofford suggested another Elliott number. Instantly he picked up on the band's reluctance. These were dual singer-songwriters, after all, a hypothetical 50/50 split, Neil and Elliott. For a moment no one knew what to say. The minor faux pas lingered. Then Elliott spoke up. Tactfully, sensitively, but also with obvious force, he simply declared "no." The other song would be Neil's. The

The band Pond. (Photograph by JJ Gonson.)

suggestion was made deftly, belying its implications; Elliott emphasized how he liked Neil's song more than any of the other possibilities, and that was that. Swofford came away impressed; he acceded, naturally, to Elliott's wishes. The B side would be "Can't Be Touched." And the deal was struck. But the episode underscored what was, for most observers, an open secret. This was Elliott's band. To Swofford, "there was ongoing tension from the very beginning." Elliott didn't enjoy leading the charge, but his talents threw him into that role. It was inescapable. Still, his choice was to share the glory, at least for now.

The record's black-and-white cover shows a group of suited men in gas masks, the backside reproducing a Bomb Incident Plan including fourteen tips, such as "designate a chain of command." Production is attributed to Heatmiser, engineering to Tony Lash. Mixing occurred at "Dead Aunt Thelma's." The vinyl itself is white with a blue center label. And band contact, the person to reach for bookings, press, and other matters, is JJ Gonson. Prior to this moment, Gonson had spent three months in Europe looking at religious iconography, contemplating a project of an anthropological nature. For a time she figured on staying out of band management altogether, but when she returned to Portland, Heatmiser "sort of pro-

CSR2 7-inch "Stray," in white vinyl and sky-blue label. (Photograph William Todd Schultz.)

posed." She asked them what they wanted exactly, what they had in mind, what their goals were. "To make a living," they all replied. A path, in other words, out of dead-end, dispiriting jobs like framing or scraping paint off ceilings or making copies at Kinko's. "So that's what we set out to do," Gonson says. "Try figuring a way to get them free of their shit jobs, how to make money as a band."

A self-described obsessive worker, Gonson, once firmly committed, "worked her ass off for the band." She was tireless and utterly "dedicated."[12] She had the contacts, she had a wealth of experience, and she made effective use of both. The inaugural gig, which Gonson missed, was actually Valentine's Day 1992, at the X-Ray. Heatmiser opened for Nervous Christians, fronted by Dan Eklov, Gust's co-worker at TIS, a digital printing and graphics resource. From there they played almost every weekend, still practicing twice per week. They got, over time, incredibly fast and tight, Peterson recalls. Shows were "never poorly attended, always packed" with growing and avid followers. Although *The Rocket* characterized Heatmiser songs as "personal rather than political," and Elliott himself suggested Neil's numbers, in particular, "don't carry political diatribes that would be better off in a speech," the political still got strangely personal in the early 1990s, thanks to the efforts of Mabon's Oregon Citizen's Alliance. First there was Measure 8, the group's only statewide victory. It repealed an executive order banning discrimination based on sexual orientation; the measure passed 53 to 47 percent (it was later overturned). Next came the infamous Measure 9 in 1992, which aimed to amend the Oregon Constitution, preventing what the OCA called "special" rights for homosexuals and bisexuals. In the incendiary words of the measure itself, the state would officially affirm how "homosexuality, pedophilia, sadism, and masochism" were "abnormal, wrong, unnatural, and perverse." Throwing homosexuality in with pedophilia was an obviously vicious, ridiculous move, not to mention the labeling of homosexuality as immoral, a kind of living affront to the OCA's imaginarily decent—and virtually sexless—citizens. In the world of Mabon—porcine and pusillanimous—there were normal people, and there were perverts, any borderline depraved. Measure 9 failed, but homophobia earned official sanction. Peterson recalls a lot of "hateful discourse" circulating at the time; Jason Mitchell remembers attitudes being somewhat more subdued, but Gust, especially, was "very out"—although not more than he was comfortable being. For Neil, Peterson says, "It was like, 'I'm going to be in Portland and I'm going to be out.'" His sexuality was "an important part of his identity." And it was also, in the lyrical content, an important part of Heatmiser.

These Portland bands consisted of unusually well-educated, smart, thoughtful twenty-somethings, from colleges like Reed, Oberlin, Hampshire, the Berklee School, steeped in gender politics, keenly attuned to the superstructural ideological dynamics of sexism, homophobia, patriarchy. For Elliott, as noted, such cultural critiques could become paralyzingly shame-inducing. In Hazel there were intermittent clashes between Krebs and Bleyle, the latter a "genius," according to Gonson, adept at fomenting jarring but helpful chaos that fueled songwriting and performances, a sort of deliberate shit stirrer. Once she refused to record Krebs's songs unless he changed their pronouns. Krebs found the idea absurd, but he understood its meaning. Says Brandt Peterson, "I saw Heatmiser as a band, not on a mission to be a queer band, but more attuned to the complexities of trying to make relationships of any kind work in your twenties without homospecific or heterospecific baggage . . . We all shared a sense of gender politics . . . Although, really, it would be just as accurate, technically, to call Heatmiser a gay band as it would be to call it a heterosexual band. Any of us would have been happy keeping the ambiguity of whether we were gay or straight intact."

And there was ambiguity. Early reviewers pegged the band as a cliched "loud macho" outfit obsessed with chicks.[13] The misunderstanding chafed ("I guess they listened close," Elliott joked). Gust noted how the pronoun "she" was virtually absent from the tunes.[14] The idea, then, that his songs focused on girls was preposterous; lyric sheets were created to counteract possible confusion. Now it was clear boys were the subject, and the band, predictably, got labeled queercore or homocore. As he always did when he felt friends were being bullied or targeted for mindless abuse, Elliott stuck up for his bandmates. He wasn't down with any kind of victimization. He knew how it felt. "Hopefully it will come up more," he said of the subject. "And we're all gay in the band if someone's going to be homophobic."[15] Gust added: "Most magazines tiptoe around the subject, even though I tell everyone in interviews that I'm gay. It's all over the records."[16] There were moments when the issue was more than theoretical. At one show outside Portland, "fag this, fag that" comments could be heard as the band took the stage. "We were just nauseated," Peterson recalls.[17] Croghan's Crackerbash took on the OCA explicitly, writing "A Song for Lon Mabon." Apparently, according to press, Gust's "Can't Be Touched"—the B side for CSR2—also was OCA inspired. "I feel like a criminal," Gust writes, "don't crush me." He asks, "will you judge me?" then declares "I thought I couldn't be touched until they tagged me out."

In Stranger Than Fiction a large number of songs tracked political angles, offering up various social critiques. In Heatmiser, as Elliott once put it, the personal was political—the message there, but refracted. Neil, he explained, "writes about life, like me, like anybody. He just happens to be gay."[18] Whether he tired of explicitness or simply grew more internally preoccupied over time, Elliott's later, more realized work dropped politics altogether, save for very occasional and, one senses, reluctant forays into political themes, as in "A Distorted Reality's Now a Necessity to Be Free," where he wonders why his country "don't give a fuck" (a line he arrived at only after thinking over several apolitical alternatives).

Undaunted and definitely undeterred—in fact, enjoying the pseudo-controversy more than they liked to admit—the band played on as the OCA retooled, turning its warped attentions to county and municipal politics, where it passed two dozen local initiatives before the Oregon Legislative

Assembly authored a bill prohibiting governments from even considering LGBT rights measures, stripping all prior ordinances of lawful force. Anti-gay attitudes did not die, but Mabon and his OCA grew less strident, slowly degrading into irrelevance. Meanwhile, Cavity Search kept releasing Heatmiser seven-inches—for instance, 1993's "Sleeping Pill" and "Temper" (CSR7, on blue vinyl), with a sleeve design by Neil Gust and photos by JJ Gonson, mixed by Tony Lash. Momentum was building, and ambitions rose beyond the hoped-for escape from crappy day jobs. There was a feeling that something big could be happening. Other feelings were taking off too, suppressed at first, but finally openly acknowledged. Elliott and JJ were falling in love.

No one thought it was a wise move. The first person they told—the excellent listener, de facto psychologist everyone told everything to—was Jason Mitchell. "This is a really bad idea," he said. Bunny also weighed in. JJ had gotten to know her, they'd become "really close" and "liked each other a lot." She advised, "Don't get together; it's a bad idea." As JJ herself put it: "We both thought it was a bad idea." Yet this unanimously bad idea just seemed, day by day, anything but bad, and irrepressible anyway. It wasn't so much about the idea; it was about feelings. It came together quickly; it was always there potentially, just waiting for some sort of action that the two kept putting off. Yet, according to JJ, "it was impossible not to fall in love with Elliott." She didn't expect to, but she also could not help it. Though the two of them realized, without the slightest doubt, that they were creating the worst scenario imaginable—manager dating band member—they were helpless against the inevitable. "I was addicted to chaos at the time," Gonson says, and as she was beginning to learn, Elliott was "addicted to depression." Expressing a trend that would hold true for much of Elliott's romantic life, the bond was forged through trauma, personal histories of pain and emotional struggle.

Even so, initially it was "very fairytale." Elliott was sweet and wonderful, very tender, "super romantic." He was compassionate and supportive as JJ extricated herself from a prior ruined relationship that left her reeling. He'd sing to her, or they'd play guitar together and harmonize, sitting on a mattress on the floor, the one piece of furniture a lamp with a beautiful gold dome—Peter, Paul, and Mary songs, Carpenters covers like "Close to You" (Elliott also liked the Burt Bacharach tune "Walk on By," which he

JJ Gonson and Elliott at Satyricon in 1992. Gonson says, "Whatever that little thing on a stick was, Elliott doesn't seem impressed." (Courtesy of JJ Gonson Photography.)

called the saddest song ever written), the infinitely mournful "500 Miles" ("If you miss the train I'm on/You will know that I am gone"). They cuddled a lot, Elliott picked her flowers. He called JJ "Pitseleh"—her father's nickname for her, and the title of a later solo Elliott song about Gonson—and she called him "little bird," her way of reminding him to fly. "Pitseleh," which appeared after the relationship ended, revisits a feeling of doomed fate, with lyrics like "I'm not half what I wish I was" and "I was bad news for you . . . I knew it would never last." All the same, in it Elliott's apologetic: "I never meant to hurt you." Gonson made Elliott various gifts—a silver bracelet, a ceramic cow with a note inside reading, "More than you ever knew, more than you ever know, I love you little bird." Besides "Pitseleh," the Heatmiser song "Blackout" was also JJ-inspired. Again, this time more contemporaneously, there's a fear things won't work out, an expectation he'll be letting her down somehow, or worse, that she'll be disappointed in what she discovers. The feeling was that good things turned bad. It was a constant lament, a self-fulfilled prophecy. As one close friend explained it: "He would make these bad things happen to him so he could do it by his own hand," then tear himself up later. He was "obsessed" by an idea that his fate had been predestined when in fact, far more often than not, he was scripting it. Still, in the words of Pete Krebs, although Elliott made himself "out of reach," he "liked being reached for."

For the band, the JJ situation was worrisome. No one doubted she was a "massive go-getter," organizing all the "shit" they didn't want to concern themselves with.[19] For them, it was the music; for her, virtually everything else, from photographs to press clippings to questions of sleeve design. But her transformation into girlfriend was not met with "universal excitement." It seemed "like a problem," Peterson said. Gust was especially disturbed by the development. Because he and Elliott were exceptionally tight and had been for several years, Gonson threatened that feeling of exclusivity. The closer Elliott got to her, the less time he spent with Neil. To JJ the reaction felt like jealousy. Gust was possessive. "He thought, I guess, I was interrupting something." And although Neil made a mighty effort to "be okay with me all the time," inside he felt otherwise, Gonson intuited. It really wasn't okay. It wasn't what anyone had signed up for.

None of this was lost on Elliott. On the other hand, he was in love, and by virtue of a formula he had begun to perfect, the tumult brought inspirations. Gonson called it "emotional plagiarism." In songs he told stories he could connect with because he had created the chaos, the chaos was the story, the subject matter. Way back in high school there was the frustration, maybe more self-doubt, more an inner sense than a true problem, about not knowing what to say in his lyrics. For that reason Duckler was a godsend. Now Elliott solved the difficulty by creating the situations the songs would explore, often in minute detail, yet always opaquely rendered. Part of the engine was the depression that fringed Portland's chronic rain, the wet-brick reality that Krebs described. The bands were saturated with it. It was inescapable. According to friends the prevailing attitude, the local zeitgeist, was more or less "I'm a loser. Life is shit. I am shit." During darker intervals Elliott "viewed all his life as a waste. He had his bouts," one friend said. At the same time he was a deeply spiritual person, always interested in forms of religion, such as Buddhism, which he sometimes discussed with Gary Smith, or with Sean Croghan's father. Part of him knew "this was not how he was supposed to be living his life"—mired, that is, in dead-end, internal suffering and self-generated despair. But the biography fit the persona. It was hard not to latch on, however clichéd the tortured artist stereotype. Elliott saw through it, at times he dismissed it, but he also bought in, just as everyone else seemed to be doing. It was cool to be depressed. It was expected.

A subject Gonson and Elliott discussed with frequency was early trauma, what to do about it, how to deal with it. Can one forgive? Should one forgive? Pursuit of these questions was a constant, urgent theme in the relationship; they bonded emotionally through hurtful memories. Chaos begat depression, depression begat chaos. And everywhere Elliott looked, he found more of it. "Elliott suffered," Peterson says, "but everybody suffers. Neil suffered. Tony suffered. We all suffered." He goes on: "Abuse, though, is a kind of suffering that's really freighted with victimhood. On the other hand, Elliott was sometimes obviously horrified." Mainly it was implicit, assumed, the basic understanding being that Elliott's childhood had scarred him. He shared some details with JJ, but not with most others. It wasn't a topic he talked about openly until much later in his life.

And by necessity more than anything else, from the pain Elliott gathered artistic value. Pain was the muse. It had to be; it made the most of what was inside, what emerged when looking inward. On occasion the subject of antidepressants came up. His father, Gary, was a psychiatrist, after all, and in the late 1980s Prozac was all the rage, its effectiveness greatly oversold, with other SSRIs like Zoloft and Paxil quickly flooding the marketplace as well. But according to Gonson, Elliott was "literally in love with depression." They talked about it all the time. Yet like other creative types, "he didn't want meds because he thought they would damage his ability to write." To be happy was anathema. Drugs might deaden the suffering, and what that might mean or how it might alter creative process was not something he felt like exploring at the time. "Happiness writes white," the English poet Philip Larkin once declared. At this point in his life Elliott would have agreed instantly.

Depression and anxiety correlate. The former usually leads to the latter, and vice versa. Peterson really "cared deeply" about Elliott, Gonson says; there was a time during which they were "really tight," in Peterson's words, and hanging out a lot. Brandt recalls a beach trip to the Arch Cape area on the Oregon coast. In his memory high school girlfriend and Hampshire classmate Shannon Wight was along too, back in Portland and hang-ing out. The three of them decided to climb up a steep dune, applying copious amounts of sunscreen beforehand. It was all perfectly prosaic, an apparently tensionless little escapade, a respite from band demands. But once he reached the top Elliott experienced a major panic attack. Although Wight and Peterson tried to help him, talk him out of it, he could not move. He *would* not move. He was frozen in place. He was "scared and angry"— angry about being scared—and it took some doing to get him down. So there were occasions on which the inner turmoil proved beneficial, an at-mosphere conducive to making music; but there were others when it was simply a pain, a wracking, self-limiting embarrassment that went nowhere good.

As one possible cause or, just as likely, a side effect of the building at-tachment to depression, Elliott developed an intense intellectual interest in Hell. He read about it, he talked about it, he even had nightmares about going there. What had begun in abstraction, a fascination with the concept, evolved into abject fear—of the prospect of eternal burning. As Gonson recalls, "He did not believe in God, the God of organized religion. But he believed in Hell. He had this fear of the devil popping up and grabbing him at any moment," a kind of personification of anything evil, including thoughts of suicide. Even as late as *Figure 8*, recorded only a few years be-fore his death, he described dreams of being an "army man," and "dead en-emies" springing in his face. It got to the point, in the early '90s, where misery trumped everything else. He started to believe it was kinder to re-move himself from people's lives. Gonson tried reassuring him, saying "You don't have to run away to save people from you." At times this worked, but more often than not, it made no impact. When he went dark, he went darker than anyone else, to places where he seemed unreachable.

Of course, on the fringes of ubiquitous doom and gloom, there were good times too, hilarious times, most propelled by bottles of brandy or Elliott's personal favorite, Jameson Irish whiskey, which both deepened the depression and made it somehow laughably self-collapsing. As everyone got drunker, tears diluting the alcohol, the darkness took on a slapstick quality. In terms of drug use, Heatmiser was a clean band. But like all Portland outfits of the time, they drank, occasionally heavily. It was "a Portland thing," one friend says, a virtual depression party that left people listing off bar stools at all the usual places, "bawling our heads off" between bouts of video poker, which Elliott played avidly. At the moment they were the "rock illuminati," local rock gods, and they partied accordingly. One favored hang-out was the impossibly beat Club 21 on prostitute-perfused Sandy Boulevard, just diagonal from EJ's, a popular venue (now a jewelry/pawn shop). The evening might start with Elliott sitting around playing guitar, noodling with chord structures, listening for what might pop up, just like back in Texas with Merritt, and watching Univision on TV (with the sound off), or another favorite, *Xena the Warrior Princess*. Elliott loved cable TV; he loved bad comedies too, of the John Candy, Dana Carvey sort, the goofier the better. "You aren't really going to watch this shit are you?" was a constant re-frain. Also, as in Texas, there was a lot of simple listening to music, not of the sort one might imagine. Elliott adored sappy '70s rock, the same bands he first thrilled to in Cedar Hill—Scorpions, Kiss, even certain Ted Nugent riffs. He was never precious. And all this aimless killing of time eventually led to organized hilarity. Jason Mitchell recalls one evening when everyone descended on Club 21 in cheap tacky thrift-store suits, proceeding to get absurdly hammered, smoking endless amounts of cigarettes (Camel was Elliott's brand, later replaced by American Spirits). Karaoke was also a sur-prisingly intense, regular form of amusement, at Chopsticks Express or the Galaxy. Writer Scott Wagner—known as "Wags"—remembers one night when he and Elliott covered "Mammas Don't Let Your Babies Grow Up to Be Cowboys."

Another obsession, irresistible enough to interfere with band meetings and rehearsals, was Sega's "Sonic the Hedgehog" game, which hit the mar-ket in June 1991. The blue anthropomorphic character with an angry mien and shoes inspired by Michael Jackson's boots, ran at supersonic speeds and curled himself into a ball before attacking assorted enemies. Originally he was to be a band member of some kind with a human girlfriend named Madonna, but that idea got scrapped. At the house just off Division every-one played the game compulsively, or else watched while waiting his or her turn. This went on for hours. Gonson occasionally tried interrupting the mania, usually to no avail. When finally Sonic was made to prevail, every-one fell out to one or another nearby bar to debrief the imaginary victory.

One such evening Elliott was outrageously drunk but kept ordering Jamesons anyway, and kept getting served. He'd cart his drinks back to the table, and friends took turns "accidentally" knocking them over. "What the fuck?" he'd exclaim, "Are you people wasted?" According to Mitchell, booze never made Elliott angry. In fact, he says, "I never saw Elliott mad." Depressed, yes; sobbing, yes. Or, as Pete Krebs captured it in a 2003 interview, "I can't say that I've met anybody quite as fragile and almost comically freaked-out as Elliott."[20] All the same, his memories of Smith are of a "really funny, really super-smart, caring person," not a crazy person or drug addict. Mitchell agrees: "He was too smart. Very funny. Sensitive. Generous . . . He would spend hours listening to fans who identified strongly with his music." It was impossible to miss his "delicate nature," Mitchell explains, "and a lot of people around him were very protective of him. But though he could be easily crushed at times, he could also be a total rock." It sometimes got to be confusing, these alternating extremes. The root feeling, the sense Elliott elicited from anyone who knew him even slightly, was that he was "too emotionally sensitive. He internalized a lot more. You could never get to the bottom of the suffering. He could not explain it."[21] Except in the songs; the songs were the dissertation.

And as Denny Swofford realized early on, Portland itself sharpened the songs; it was the perfect rainy foundation for Elliott's brilliance. The college name change set the stage for self-redefinition, songs dropping from the skies like so many extraterrestrials, an endless supply of Elliott pet E.T.'s. All the brilliant, quirky, creative people around the scene—from Krebs to Bleyle to Gonson to Gust—just added to an already heightened feeling of possibility. Ideas kept coming, ambitions caught fire. Gonson steered Heatmiser's fortunes ably, they were free to concentrate on music and performance, and she was there for Elliott when he needed her, a sympathizer who could identify with the sorts of traumas he'd endured, the Old Testament visions of Hell. She'd been there too; he wasn't alone. Around this same time Elliott happened upon still another opportunity for self-definition, a visual representation of a contradictory identity. He'd already gotten a Texas tattoo, with a "sun that looked like a saw blade," as Gonson recalls it; Elliott says it resembled the sun in the KC and the Sunshine Band insignia. Actually, the state was originally meant to *be* a sun. A muscle man, giant tattooist asked Elliott, "What do you want a sol blade on your arm for?" He didn't, actually, so the sun turned into a map of Texas. Texas, in other words, was an act of revision, a later incorporation.

But the next tattoo, drawn coincidentally by the wife of the muscle man, speaks of deeper interior realities even than Texas. Gonson recalls Elliott being oddly taken with the idea of bullfighting, the man versus beast mythos, the concept of primordial struggle that he tended to romanticize. They argued about the subject, at times almost comically. JJ had been to bullfights in Portugal, and she emphasized the brutal, gruesome nature of what she'd seen firsthand—the bull being tortured, then taken out back and shot. It wasn't pretty; it wasn't romantic. Even so, to Elliott it "represented this cool thing," and he was not dissuaded. He decided he wanted a bull on his arm, "maybe because they're stubborn." The Schlitz Malt Liquor bull was a first option. But it was promptly rejected. What he got, in the end, was almost farcically removed from notions of a powerful, beastly bovine. The bull transmogrified into Ferdinand, from the children's story by Munro Leaf. That modest little tale, which Elliott grew up on, is a pacifism manifesto, an allegory of role refusal. Most of the little bulls in the piece run and jump and butt their heads. Not Ferdinand. He prefers to sit quietly under a cork tree and smell the flowers. One day five men arrive in funny hats to pick the fiercest bull for fights in Madrid. Ferdinand retreats to his cork tree. But a bee stings him, and he leaps up with a grunt, butting and pawing the ground as if crazy. The five men shout with joy. Here, they figure, is the fiercest bull of all. So they take Ferdinand away in a cart. But in the ring in Madrid "Ferdinand the Fierce" will not fight. "He saw the flowers in all the lovely ladies' hair and he just sat down quietly and smelled." The men take Ferdinand home. "And for all I know," Leaf writes, "he is sitting there still, smelling the flowers just quietly. He is very happy."

Elliott obviously enjoyed the story's—and the tattoo's—subtext. In 1997 he told an interviewer how the bull's "too gentle and content to attain fame," the "powerful beast doesn't want to use his powers." He adds, "it's about someone who lives in his own interior world and doesn't understand what's going on around him, but he's happy in it anyway. I like it." Ferdinand's the either/or dichotomy theme all over again, this time in static visual form. He's a bull who doesn't behave like a bull; he's also an anomaly.

He doesn't fit in, nor does he want to. He's an effete bull, his horns point-less appendages. Just like Elliott most of the time, he will not get angry, or when he does, it is almost by accident. "Between is all you've ever seen or been" Elliott wrote in a later song, and the line captures him and Ferdinand equally. He wanted to be in a chugga-chugga boy band, but on the other hand, he really didn't. He wanted intimacy, but he didn't. He desired fame intensely, envied those, like Cobain, who had gotten it, complained when radio shut him out, fretted about having to tour when his records didn't sell enough to make touring unnecessary, but fame also disgusted him, its pho-niness revolting. And maybe most basically, he wanted to live, but at the same time, and in a way that sometimes seemed almost impossibly relent-less, he truly wanted to die. Ferdinand turned out okay in the end. He sat and smelled the flowers. He was happy. Elliott was denied this positive outcome. I always feel like shit, he wrote. I don't know why, I just do. The fight, in other words, was not always in him. Or if it was, it was usually di-rected at himself, the one person he fought with regularly.

Heatmiser's self-released six-song cassette *The Music of Heatmiser* was re-corded at Sound Impressions in Milwaukie, Oregon, over just two days in late April 1992, engineered by Bob Stark and mixed by Tony Lash. Gonson was not yet officially in the fold. She had spent time in Europe hanging out with Nirvana prior to the Reading Festival. That show, played with "un-flinching ferocity," in the words of the BBC, quickly became legendary. At the time *Nevermind* was selling 400,000 copies per week. Amid this mood of spectacular possibility, Gonson had her epiphany—rock 'n' roll was where she belonged; bands were her business; it was all too simple, clear, unmis-takable. The songs on the Heatmiser cassette included, in the following order, "Lowlife," "Bottle Rocket," "Buick," Peterson's "Just a Little Prick," "Dirt," and the tune "Mightier Than You," featuring rare vocal harmonies. In red ink in front of a sunburst backdrop a sunglasses-wearing Peterson holds a bass; he sports a foam-billed trucker hat onto which a friend had sewed fake leopard fur.

The concept, the vision, was very organized and almost conservative in its basic nature: two guitars, bass, and drum, with no room left for even a

Elliott and Neil goofing off with Peterson and Lash in background on couch. (Photograph by JJ Gonson.)

tambourine. It was basic, sharp, and direct, no fuss, nothing extra or unnecessary—zero prog-rock noodling, in the words of one review—in many ways the antithesis of the kinds of songs Elliott had arranged in Stranger Than Fiction. The long guitar solos Elliott had always waited for and looked forward to bringing off, from back in the Texas days, were gone. Two guitars chugged ahead with nonstop distorted growl punctuated by occasional staccato barks of dazzling friction. Melody was in short supply; the songs were anything but sing-alongs. In comparison, Hazel comes across as almost poppy, or at least far more melodically organized. "Mightier Than You," the song Elliott did not especially like, was the one exception (much later it appeared on a Puddle Stomp compilation). Gonson recalls the tune as "very beautiful." Her sense is that it might have taken the band in "an interesting direction," one that never materialized, chiefly because Heatmiser lacked two mics when practicing, so harmony possibilities never got thoroughly explored. It simply wasn't practical. It also wasn't in the immediate game plan. At this point it was all about the pushing, roiling guitar back and forth, rumbling like a night train just beyond city limits, with scratchy vocals not always favored in the mix. The band was deliberately symmetri-

Neil's birthday party, thrown by Frontier Records, November 1993. (Elliott, left, and Neil Gust.) (Photograph by JJ Gonson.)

cal, going back to the days of the first seven-inch. There were the Elliott songs, and the Neil songs, lined up one after another. If Elliott privately recognized any songwriting disparity, he downplayed it, denied it, even as others occasionally broached the subject. It would be two more years before he struck out in his own direction, one now buried in layers of hard-driving noise and guttural throat-clearing. Meanwhile guitars bore in on the nucleus of the tune. "It was poetry how Neil played the guitar," says Gonson. "He was a truly gifted guitar player, maybe better than Elliott. Those two guys playing together was just stunning."

The first real album, *Dead Air*, appeared in 1993 through Frontier Records. (At this point Cavity Search was still a "start-up label," and so, according to Swofford, "it made more sense for Heatmiser to go with an already established label at the time.") It was an exceedingly long negotiation, one that dragged on and on and left everyone, including Gonson, exhausted. In fact, *Dead Air* was recorded before any contract at all had been signed; although despite all that, or because of it, Gonson says "it was probably the happiest recording experience they ever had."[22] Frontier was founded in 1980 by Lisa Fancher, a Southern Californian with two sisters who grew up

listening to British Invasion bands. Originally she planned on calling it
Frontierland, after her favorite section of Disneyland, but a lawyer discour-
aged that idea. Like Swofford and Cooper of Cavity Search, she had "zero
experience" in the music business apart from record collecting and writing
for fanzines (she reviewed the first Ramones album in 1976). Her inspiration, she says, was "feeling like I was directionless."[23] "I don't know what
made me think I could run a label," she says. "I have no business acumen
but at least I had pretty decent taste."[24] Her first release turned out to be a
Flyboys EP (she calls the band "Day-Glo pop punk," a "male Go-Gos"), but
she struck it big with the Circle Jerks' *Group Sex*, which appeared in November 1980, and which proved almost impossible to keep in stock or in
print. Later Frontier brought out Suicidal Tendencies and the Adolescents
(and almost signed the Pixies) before branching out some time in 1984, after
the punk scene had peaked, Fancher felt, in L.A. and Orange County. In
the '90s, which Fancher terms a "mean decade," she signed another Portland-
based outfit, Dharma Bums, fronted by Jeremy Wilson.

Sub Pop, a label founded in 1986 in Seattle, had also checked out
Heatmiser, although according to Elliott, "I don't know how interested they
were, to tell you the truth." Plus, Frontier actually returned phone calls,
despite having kept a staff "too few to play a full-court game of hoops."[25]
"We can have attention whenever we need it," Elliott explained at the
time.[26] "It's not like we're getting the short end of the stick," said Gust in
1993. "They do a great job. I love everyone at Frontier, all four of them!"

At this time, and for most of the band's tenure, in fact, Gust was "kind
of the business guy—super sweet and real communicative," according to
Leslie Uppinghouse, who mixed and toured with numerous Portland bands,
including Crackerbash, Hazel, Pond, and the Spinanes, as well as Heatmiser
(and later, the solo Elliott). There were three leaders, in Uppinghouse's view,
Lash, Elliott, and Gust, although as usual Elliott was disinclined to stand
apart in any way, whereas "Gust wanted to be the front man." Gust and Elliott
were always giggly, like "thirteen-year-old girls"—goofing off, joking—but
"there was a real love there too." Generally Elliott was very nervous, especially in performance, although Gust "never was." "Neil would be perplexed
most of the time by any drama circling around things."[27] Gust did the "pre-
work," Uppinghouse says, although as far as sound at shows went, everyone

Elliott in L. A., during Heatmiser tour, checking out the Frampton star.
(Photograph by JJ Gonson.)

in the band seemed to want different things. They settled for a sharpness with delay and reverb, a basically muddy kind of mix. None of this ever seemed to stress Gust out; he was on an even keel most of the time, yet if Brandt started acting the hooligan, which came naturally, or Elliott's equipment blew up—as it seemed to do a lot—"Neil would glare."

According to a review in local music paper *The Rocket* in 1994, *Dead Air* made hardly a media ripple when it was released (although it spent months on the paper's Northwest Top 20). Still, solid word of mouth assured decent sales and sent critics scrambling to catch up.[28] Part of the problem was an entrenched, genuine attitude of esprit de corps with other Portland bands, of non-competition. "None of us like to grandstand a lot," Elliott said. "None of us are super into having all the attention diverted to us, even for a little while when we're playing." Perhaps because of this basic reluctance to get out and demand attention or to fabricate some sort of strategic edge of anomalousness (which Hazel, for instance, possessed in spades with Fred Nemo), reaction ran the gamut. Comparisons were to Fugazi, Hüsker Dü, Helmet, the Replacements, Mission of Burma, grunge, punk-metal, alterno-metal, Quicksand, Seaweed—the list was long. Some called the album ho-hum, pretty straightforward, powerful power pop, the tunes, though, "sweeter than a mouthful of Dolly Madison Zingers." Others called it a textbook example of the strengths and weaknesses of early-'90s indie hard rock by "angry/sensitive young men," just barely distinctive enough "to rescue the music from the merely generic." Ned Raggett at Allmusic.com made the surprising, and probably not entirely supportable, assertion that Gust was the band's "true creative touchstone," with a knack for anthemic, empowering choruses "infused with emotional passion."

The record clocked in at thirty-seven minutes, fourteen songs fired off in total, two of them—"Lowlife" and "Bottle Rocket"—straight from *The Music of Heatmiser* cassette. "Stray" was re-recorded from the Cavity Search seven-inch, as were the remaining tunes. Heatmiser produced, along with Steve "Thee Slayer Hippy" Hanford, onetime drummer for Poison Idea, a punk band formed in Portland in 1980. Swofford felt the record was "perfectly raw," the best representation of the band's live power (and his favorite Heatmiser album by far). The coughed-out lyrics, too, with Elliott again in serious Joe Strummer mode, are raw and incredibly harsh, more angry and hurt than sensitive. It would require monumental interpretive panache to locate the slightest connection between the ethereal sentiments in Stranger Than Fiction and those of *Dead Air*. It is as if, in Heatmiser, Elliott yanked out by the hair some heretofore buried poltergeist and let it wail blistering truth. What made this return of the repressed possible is hard to say. Maybe intentionally, the record came sans lyric sheet, so the words could only be guessed at, and most head-banging listeners missed obvious themes. The loud attack, a pummeling by noise, also simultaneously released and

Nemo with cinder block.
(Photograph by
JJ Gonson.)

obscured all the feral self-deracination going on. "Still" starts things off with buzzing guitar and monotone verses. The theme is fear, denial, and deception, which together make for intensely physicalized emotional pain. "Don't open my body up," Elliott shouts, "I don't want to be in my body," as he turns his face up to an overhead light and keeps his eyes closed shut. It's as if some surgery is being performed, the idea of which makes him "ill," but he takes it because he figures that if he just shuts up, it will all be over soon. A possible subtext is abuse, but another is the need to keep secrets inside, protected against invasions.

"Mock-up" imagines a possible secondary self, an alter-ego representing someone or something demonic. Again the verses are monotone, as if to underscore a basic malaise or sense of nonentity. Love appears but it's a "wicked friend." So the singer—Elliott—decides to get well on his own, but the sad truth is he's "shot to hell" and all "fucking holes." He even rails against his own self-pity, calling it melodrama—too much whiny complaining about sick pride and dead hearts and the fear that he's dying. "Dirt" appears to be an angry letter of sorts to Bunny; she's that "china doll" feeling nothing at all—the same metaphor employed in *XO*'s "Waltz #2 (XO)." This doll is hopelessly in thrall to a man whom she can't get over. Some lyrics prove hard to decipher, but according to online sources he's compared to a "black ball" leaving hell in his wake. The stain rubs off, you become the same thing you adore, Elliott sings. And he ends with a declaration that he, too, feels nothing at all. He's adopted the same defensive vacuity. It passes on, and then it's constant. "I feel this way all the time," Elliott writes in the song's final line.

As she did in "Pitseleh," Gonson (with whom Elliott was still together) serves as "Blackout's" subject, the latter essentially an early draft, in wildly different musical terms, of the former. This time Elliott is the one rejected, whereas in "Pitseleh" he seems to do the rejecting, albeit reluctantly, because of who he is. He believes she's disappointed in him, that he's let her down somehow, falling apart right in front of her, self-medicating, even though "leaving you alone wasn't my decision," the implication being that he did it for the sake of the band. In the song the two sit on the sofa with a record playing, just as they often did in life, singing along or playing together. The same solution to pain emerges as it did in "Dirt" and as it did in many ways throughout Elliott's life, taking different forms from time to time and being arrived at through different means. "I won't feel a thing," he promises, lack of feeling being more manageable, although hardly more satisfying, than feeling rejected or denied.

"Stray" once more has Elliott in a deep sleep, empty, shaken and angry. He imagines someone coming to take his place, to assume his disgrace, when he finally wakes up "in the Lone Star State." Texas as symbol of trauma, the pain's origin, is always readily available. As idea, it was a black that crackled and dragged. The notion of actually being there again, even despite what seemed to be partly good times with Pickle and Kim and friends, was a looming, anxiety-drenched proposition. In "Cannibal" Elliott's head's about to explode "like the Fourth of July," but he still listens when his "mama calls me"; in "Lowlife" he's a landfill "waiting on lies"; "Dead Air" has him suffocating all night, running around brooding and tight "when you've got no reason for brooding." He keeps trying to speak out loud yet finds nothing but "dead air between you and me."

The broken, skipping-record quality of the tunes wasn't lost on Elliott;

Heatmiser outside the Sands. A Gust tune on Dead Air *was titled "Sands Hotel." (L–R, Elliott, Gust, Lash, Peterson.) (Photograph by JJ Gonson.)*

it is a line he uses in "Dead Air," in fact. But self-disgust, misanthropy, and incipient violence were in the ether. Nirvana made that fact clear with tunes full of guns, blowtorches, and dazed self-loathing. The armor now cracked, it was no longer possible to avoid looking inside to find what was there, no matter how scabrous. What with the relentless liberation of feeling that the album unpacked, it ought to have given Elliott some pleasure or pride. He certainly got a lot out and spread it thickly. Instead, according to Brandt Peterson, he "got sick of *Dead Air* really fast." He wasn't happy with

Somewhere in the Midwest with Heatmiser. (Photograph by JJ Gonson.)

the lack of dynamics (a Nirvana signature, one they perfected); he also disliked the narrow mix and tempo. There was tension around recording too, although the experience was mostly positive. Beforehand Peterson had taken off for El Salvador with his sister, giving no explicit return date. When he resurfaced he stayed for a night or two in the Division house basement before finding a place of his own not far away. But the band attitude had been "What the fuck?" Elliott and Neil were committed, very serious. "This is what we moved here to do, this is who we are," they told Peterson. And for a time Elliott was standoffish, the Central America venture threatening the band's very future. Even now, Peterson honestly felt, in relative terms, less on board than the others. At twenty-six years old, he kept asking himself "how much longer do I want to get kicked out of people's bands?" The possibility of alternative futures was hard to set aside. In retrospect Peterson saw his trip with his sister as a "very important turning point." The ill will it engendered was a harbinger of things to come.

For now, though, the next step was obvious: touring. Time had arrived to take things beyond the already-conquered Portland. A West Coast run was cobbled together, with dates in places like Vancouver, Eugene, and Seattle. Gonson also booked bigger stuff. At first Heatmiser opened for Pond. There was a surreal gig in a hotel ballroom in Bakersfield. In L.A. the band

Elliott in bear suit for Heatmiser promo. (Photograph by JJ Gonson.)

camped out at Lisa Fancher's place. Depending on the city, the shows were fairly well attended. One photo by Gonson puts blue-haired Mitchell at his customary "merch perch" in front of an array of hanging Pond and Heatmiser T-shirts, Elliott giving him a chaste peck on the cheek. Promo shots included a dyed-blond Elliott in a bear suit surrounded by smiling bandmates, his arms joined high in the air. Others made use of "heat"-related props—candles and glowing orbs, and another in which Peterson set his hand on fire with rubbing alcohol. He sticks it, ablaze, toward the camera lens as Tony Lash looks on in profile, Elliott in a white stocking cap with two stripes around the front. A few gigs were practically comical and more than a little dispiriting. One show was scheduled at a sports bar that didn't serve alcohol, TVs encircling the room, patrons glued to the action. The band decided to bail. Another had Heatmiser playing to Jason Mitchell, the sound guy, and Neil's brother, no one else in attendance. Travel was usually by rented minivan, which sometimes got broken into; a stereo was stolen in San Francisco. They all took turns driving and stayed with friends or fans along the road, or else rented rooms with two beds, each shared by two people. "One poor motherfucker slept in the van," Mitchell recalls, an outcome they rotated. It was, surprisingly, mainly business. Mitchell had

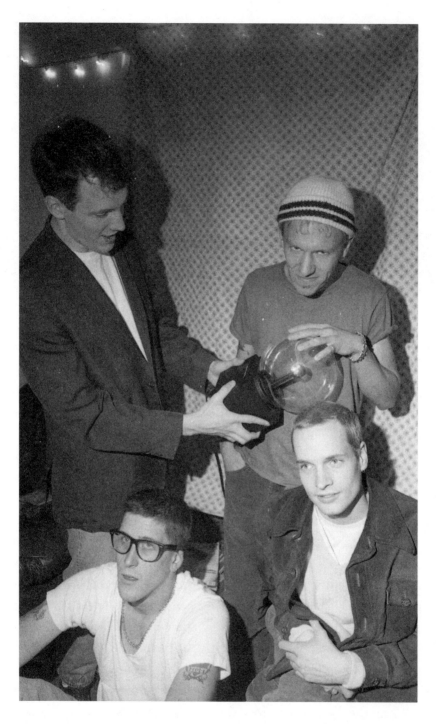

Heatmiser promo shot, Elliott with hand around glowing orb held by Tony Lash.
(Photograph by JJ Gonson.)

Another Heatmiser promo, with Peterson setting hand on fire with rubbing alcohol. (Photograph by JJ Gonson.)

anticipated a party every night, "but I was disappointed." By show's end everyone was too exhausted from the combination of driving and playing to get any sort of buzz on.

But there was a lot more than only travel torpor at work, or disappointment over gigs inadequately promoted. Almost from the instant *Dead Air* was in the can, Elliott began developing—mostly silently—an alternative narrative. His feeling, according to Peterson, was that he couldn't make "grown-up music in the context of this rock group."[29] This feeling no doubt came as a surprise even to Elliott himself. After all, he was the one who had returned to Portland to start this band. He was the one who got Tony Lash to drum for it. Also, Elliott was writing half the songs; it was in his basement that the band rehearsed; it was his then-girlfriend, Gonson, who managed. So, all that being true, if Elliott wasn't making the kind of music he wanted to, it was his own doing. Consequently, the frustration came with a fair amount of guilt and self-doubt. Letting down the people whom he'd worked to get so ardently on board was a possibility that gnawed at him endlessly. Yet, on the other hand, it was becoming increasingly clear that keeping the enterprise going, maintaining the status quo—writing, recording, touring, giving interviews—would require, to a degree he was also disinclined to accept, a hefty amount of self-denial. It was, all things considered, a bit of a no-win. He could keep not being himself, or he could start imagining the grown-up sound he was after. Neither option came without cost.

And all along, to one side, the grown-up songs were forming. In his head massive back catalogs of sound piled up one after the other, but in shapes and structures not suitable for Heatmiser. In certain obvious respects, the feeling of mismatch was expected. Here was a person precociously skilled melodically, who had grown up on the Beatles and Jackson Browne and the very prog-rock, Rush-besotted noodlings Heatmiser avoided, yet finding himself now in the difficult position of having to fit such sensibilities into formats that couldn't have been less hospitable. He could do it, he was doing it, it had all taken off promisingly, but the sacrifice grew harder to abide. So quietly, mostly surreptitiously, in a move that would alter the course of his life forever, Elliott decided to sublet his room at the Division house—he was leaving, but not really, since the spot was still his—and move in with Gonson, where he more or less lived, although never officially, for a year or a year and a half.[30] It wasn't just Gonson, actually. There were three other roommates, all connected with bands—Orphan's Reason, Jack, Bedspins. In no time at all Elliott was "there more or less nonstop," according to James Ewing, who now and then loaned Elliott equipment. "He had his issues," Ewing recalls, and his art was clearly unusually "solemn." At the same time, Ewing found him "sweet and funny." Once they both got the flu, suffering through it while watching Ken Burns's Civil War documentary. Another time Elliott wandered in with a Duran Duran single he'd bought, "Ordinary World." He heard something in it, something he wanted to study. He played it "four hours straight," despite its "cheesiness." In terms of partying, Elliott did not smoke dope, says Ewing, although everyone else did. To Ewing it seemed he drank no more than anyone else. "Once or twice only did I see him drunk," he recalls.[31]

In this house on 29th and SE Taylor, what Gonson calls "note-taking" began. He'd always done it, but now the effort came with special care. "He was documenting songs he couldn't use with Heatmiser," Gonson says. "He recorded them without the band because he couldn't record them with the band." In some cases these were tunes he'd been carrying around

Elliott and James Ewing in the Taylor Street house where Roman Candle *was recorded. (Photograph by JJ Gonson.)*

in his head for years (such as "Condor Avenue"); in others, they came together on the spot. As Gust put it later, "He generated way more music than I ever did, and his process was way more developed. So he found a different outlet for it, and when he really started to get it right, it was obvious: *oh, that's a lot better.* And I couldn't be mad at him for it."[32]

It was all totally low-key and casual, almost ridiculously lo-fi. Gonson owned a learning guitar, essentially a toy with a short neck and small body by the name of "Le Domino"—there were dominos on the frets and around

Elliott with Le Domino. (Photograph by JJ Gonson.)

the sound hole. The strings were nylon, and Elliott slid bits of paper underneath to prevent buzzing. He adored the goofy little instrument and played
it all the time around the house. Somehow it sounded bewilderingly good to
him. At the time Gonson owned a vintage Schwinn bike weighing "about a
million pounds" that she'd purchased in Boston. Elliott needed monitors in
order to hear himself; Gonson therefore rode the bike over to Artichoke
Records, where a collector worked, and swapped it for speakers. After buying a "Realistic" mic from Radio Shack they had what they needed, and
Elliott, for the very first time, started writing and recording the songs that
came to define him eternally, songs that, in their directness and softness,
could not have been any more different than the songs he made with the
band. He sat on a stool in Gonson's basement, set up the monitors in the
corners of the room, and got busy. It was all, as Gonson remembers, "as
minimal as it could possibly be." Looking for the best acoustics achievable
under the limiting circumstances, he also occasionally recorded in the corner of the stairs on the ground level, or sat on the bed. He was all over the
house, working track by track.

Thematically, judged by an index of suffering, the songs were similar
to the Elliott tunes on *Dead Air*—blistering examinations of a traumatized

inner life, now rendered gorgeously and inimitably, not drowned in miasmas of sound. Feeding the aesthetic was a surprisingly diverse set of inspirations. Gonson had been playing a lot of George Jones and Carter Family records, even the Carpenters, who covered several brilliant Bacharach compositions. Elliott had gotten very interested in how Joni Mitchell made records—he was listening to her, to Dylan, and to early Bruce Springsteen, his operatic, wordy, Dylan-obsessed albums such as *Greetings From Asbury Park, N.J.* and *The Wild, the Innocent, and the E Street Shuffle.*[33] Gonson recalls Elliott watching a Dylan performance on TV, "really carefully checking it out, speechless, dialed in, really studying it." Emotionally, he was on a thin wire, everything roiling and rising up. Gonson says, "He was so fucking angry and flipped out and furious," and as he wrote in "Pitseleh," he didn't think it would ever pass. "I knew the backstory," Gonson explains, "I was living it day to day. We bonded over it. In all these songs he was confronting abuse, really, for the first time ever." And that particular connotation generated intense fear, if not terror. As usual, he brooded a lot about the songs' possible impact. He was especially worried about hurting Ashley or Darren, Bunny too, or her family. So he rearranged early drafts, rewrote to such a degree that Gonson, who had heard all the original versions of the tunes, knew the recorded product by largely different lyrics. The sting was still there, just muted, more camouflaged. Symbolism softened directness.

Then one perfectly average day Elliott gave the cassette to Gonson with the simple words, "Okay. It's done." Not exactly sure, at the moment, what to do with it, she carried it around forever. Now and then Elliott played it for friends. Pete Krebs, for instance, recalls listening to the songs as he and Elliott worked their crap job scraping lead paint from a warehouse ceiling in the Pearl District. What was crystal clear, to all concerned, was that the songs were a new direction, an ideal avenue of musical self-expression. Once created, their stark potency was undeniable. But Heatmiser was still in operation, and for the time being, it too was unstoppable. The five-song EP *Yellow No. 5* had come out, accompanied by, in the words of Frontier Records, "ceaseless praise," with subtle hooks as welcome as "free beer." There was a feeling of maturation in the newer material, a sense of sea change, the record tauter, more hook-filled than *Dead Air*—which Elliott had taken to calling, in interviews, not a very good record—but with the same conversational guitar interplay between Gust and Elliott. The title was arrived at in one hour, according to Gust. "We had to come up with a name for the EP before it was going to some list that gets advanced to show that we have something new coming out," he told *The Rocket* in 1994. Peterson had worked up an inventive cover design (he also did the cover for *Dead Air*), a painting with van Gogh overtones, of a kid in a field with a jersey sporting a yellow number five. That got nixed, although what remained—a male face with a car in the background—retains intimations of Vincent, the visage slipping and sliding in distorted half-profile.

Elliott was thus split, in a spot he often wrote about, "in between" two different destinies, not likely to remain parallel forever. Heatmiser was either going to become more Elliott or Elliott was going to become more Elliott. In the end, the songs did the deciding.

CHAPTER FIVE YESTERYEAR SOON

Sensing what she had—a batch of songs that turned out to be the first serious solo work by a person who would later be called a "master" and a "genius" and "the best songwriter on earth," but one that just as easily might not have been made at all had Elliott felt satisfied with the creative outlet that was Heatmiser—and having seen and heard it all take shape so organically, Gonson carried Elliott's version of a basement tape, what she called "the least complicated record ever," over to Cavity Search's Chris Cooper at record store Music Millenium, his day job on NW 23rd in Portland.[1] "I just gave it to him," Gonson says succinctly. That's what she did. She brought people together, she creatively made things happen. But it was a dicey spot for JJ to be in. She was managing Heatmiser, not Elliott (nor did she ever, out of a sense of duty to Heatmiser, manage Elliott as a solo act). She was not exactly pushing the cassette; it was more low-key than that. She just told Cooper he ought to give it a listen, then form his own opinion about what he heard. She knew it was good, but she had no clue whether Cooper or Swofford would feel the same.

At the time tension kept growing around Gonson's involvement with Elliott, another reason to be circumspect. Brandt Peterson appreciated all she had done for the band—her organizational prowess, her work ethic, which was legendary—but as he said, diplomatically, "It seemed like a problem potentially." Jason Mitchell had already called the relationship "a bit of a faux pas perhaps. But totally understandable too." And Gust was nursing his own irritations. Plus, by now Elliott had essentially moved out, however unofficially, and that intensified feelings of confusion or even betrayal. He was not around much. He spent all his time at Gonson's to the point where additional roommate James Ewing wondered what was up. Elliott hadn't been paying any rent, but letters arrived for him at the house, student loan bills made out to Steven Smith. Again, none of this was lost on Gonson. She and Elliott knew what a bad idea it was to become romantic. But they did. All they could do was minimize the resulting weirdness.

Now with tape in hand, Cooper settled in to study what Gonson had passed along. During breaks from his Music Millenium job he punched the cassette into the deck of his VW bus. He waited for it to say what it would. He opened up to let it sink in. Slowly, as he listened over and over across the span of days, alone in the front seat, parked on a side street, he found himself beguiled, seduced by the music's simple majesty. He phoned Swofford: "You gotta get over here." "I knew Elliott was making music on his own," Swofford recalls, "not necessarily to put out. Just doing what he does and always did." So Swofford also gave the cassette a listen. His first response, which didn't last long, was that the songs "needed technical work." He adored hardcore Heatmiser—which this was anything but—and the absence of production values bugged him. "It sounded like shit," Swofford says, his perfectionist label-owner aesthetic driving his first impression. Yet after living with the cassette for twenty days straight, listening any chance he could, "I didn't want anyone to touch it. It was *perfectly bad*," he realized, the homely sound quality a large part of the charm and power of the total package.

In words others would claim as well, notably Lisa Fancher of Frontier Records, Cooper expressed his sense of the moment, a feeling of something large about to happen, something rare and unexpected, although not entirely shocking, given Elliott's talents: "The thought was that we had discovered Elliott Smith. We recognized and saw in him something nobody else did. He was, like, our guy. He embodied why we got into the business. He was our Bob Dylan."[2] No mean comparison, this, given Dylan's leonine status in the minds of Cooper and Swofford. To them Dylan was the apex. There was no one better.

Yet at this point it isn't clear Elliott wanted to go it alone. In his mind, the songs weren't a record. He just wanted to record them, to get them down before they scattered and faded. Plus, maybe the songs weren't even *his*; maybe they were Heatmiser's, rough, adaptable sketches capable of somehow fitting into the chugga-chugga format. On the other hand, that sort of integration seemed like a stretch. "The thing about a band that can get kinda boring," Elliott said, "is like . . . there's lots of rock bands and I get tired of turning everything into a rock song. I mean, I totally love playing the ones that ought to be like that but not everything I make ought to."[3] Not that he didn't try, to his credit. Elliott, at some point in 1993, actually played one of the tunes for Heatmiser. This was "Saintlike," later titled "No Name #1," for which Gonson wrote the music. But his bandmates laughed, Gust in particular, finding the sound almost corny and ultra soft. And according to Gonson, "that was the beginning of the end of the band. If they had not laughed, that could have been a Heatmiser song, and the band could have gone in a completely different direction." They could have gotten softer, in other words. But getting softer wasn't in the cards. It wasn't what they were in it for.

Instead it was Elliott taking the new direction, solo. Swofford had ditched his coffee shop job and rented that corner suite, studio apartment above Ozone. After Swofford made his intentions clear to Elliott, and Elliott expressed no strong opposition, he picked up a magnum of red wine, something decent to toast with. "Elliott knew we had the cassette," Swofford says. "He knew we wanted to put it out. We'd been friends for a while. He trusted us. He knew how it was going to go. He knew what he would get. He knew what the program was going to be." For reasons that likely had to do with sensitivity to his bandmates, a reluctance to turn the event into anything decisive or exceptional, Elliott asked for no paper, no official signed contract. It was to be a handshake deal, nothing more. "We were going to split everything 50/50," Swofford recalls. "In Elliott's mind, it was like 'It's just Denny and Chris. No big deal.'" Keeping it casual maintained the illusion that nothing meaningful was happening. A short, humble, inconsequential record was going to be released. No big push. No expectations. As Elliott explained self-consolingly, "They're a really small label. They try to do national distribution but it doesn't turn out to be that many places. It's fine with me . . . And if it helps them out then that's cool."[4]

What excited Swofford most of all was a fact others might have seen as a drawback: the songs were, as he liked to see it, never intended for release. They were pure, unaltered. The music "didn't get to be fucked with. He never went in and tweaked it out, unlike a lot of his later records." Cooper felt the same way. He called the record a "diary that went public." It was, in that framing, Elliott at his most intimate. "He was making the songs only for himself, not for anyone else. He had no idea, even, that it would be heard," Cooper believed.

This idea—that Elliott never had any intention of releasing the songs—proved hard to resist, easy to imagine. There has always been uncertainty about whether Elliott did or did not know what Gonson had done with the tape, how involved he was in getting it to Cooper. The more romantic narrative would render him unaware, innocently making up songs with no foreknowledge, no future-orientation, no expectation at all that anyone would actually listen to what he was cooking up in Gonson's house. But like most legends, it fits and it doesn't, it's true and it's false. "He didn't *not* know," Gonson clarifies. "But on the other hand it wasn't like a meeting or anything. I was just hanging out and constantly promoting, so I passed on the tape and from that point it was between Elliott and Chris and Denny. I just turned them on." "Nothing made me start doing it," Elliott explains, "because I'd been doing it for years. But it didn't occur to me to put anything out. In fact, it occurred to me *not* to put anything out." It was Gonson, he says, who suggested he make the songs available, and as they hashed it out she won him over. Friend Matt Schulte recalls Cooper telling him Elliott first shyly suggested the possibility of a single. Maybe, he said, one song, and one only, could be plucked from the mix and put out unpretentiously.

As for the diary notion, the belief that the lyrics were plucked from private writings and turned into songs, Elliott rejected that, most likely because it undervalued the work the writing required, the hours spent, often in bars, scribbling and revising and rethinking and sharpening, the effort required to get past hackneyed folksinger or singer-songwriter constructions, his long-standing remorseless war against cliché. "They're songs," Elliott said. "It's not like a diary, and they're not intended to be any sort of super-intimate singer-songwriterish thing. I like the Beatles. Dylan. All the good things about what they do or did is probably the same things that I'm trying to do."[5] Diary aside, part of him knew what it all could mean, how it might be interpreted. Still, "I was totally shocked," he says, when Cavity Search wanted to release the record. "I thought my head would be chopped off immediately . . . because it was so opposite to the grunge thing that was popular . . . [But] it immediately eclipsed my band unfortunately."[6]

Pre-show in L.A. (Photograph by JJ Gonson.)

It was the band then, and not a lot else, that gave Elliott pause. The band was the reason he contemplated holding off. But his unhappiness with how things were going kept intensifying. "I was depressing myself," he says. "It started to get to be a drag." For a time he convinced himself he needed to do it for Neil—Heatmiser was their idea, what they had set out to do. It wasn't that Gust told him to stick with it, or even implied that he do so—"it was just my own trip." The entire situation was a mess, the exact sort of thing Elliott hated to get himself into. For their part, Heatmiser expressed no misgivings. Tony Lash is clear on this point: "No one was put off by the fact he was doing it. No one was feeling insecure about it." In fact, Lash helped with the mixing in his own basement.[7] "He always looked to Tony," Swofford says. "Tony was a master. He always sought out Tony for support and guidance. They worked together to master it," even deciding on song order. Gonson calls Lash "the money guy," the one "who made everything happen."

So, registering his dissatisfactions with the band's sound, knowing it couldn't represent anything like a long-term occupation, and pushing aside his fears and hesitations, his worries about hurting other people who had been counting on him to advance different collective agendas, Elliott moved ahead, encouraged by Cooper and Swofford. The record never meant to be a record became one despite itself. What is fascinating about the disc that came to be called *Roman Candle*—released July 14, 1994, on Cavity Search—is not only the songs on it but the sound that first made Swofford wince. On one hand it's a smooth continuation of all the recording Elliott had done on his own constantly, in Texas, in high school with Stranger Than Fiction, but it's also an obvious anomaly. The catchy countrified or prog-rock juvenilia of Texas and the virtually orchestral complexity of Stranger Than Fiction gave way to a simplified, audibly tape-hissy aesthetic befitting the cliché "soft is the new loud" that Elliott helped install (although as usual, any cliché drove him bananas).[8] It's not that Elliott set out to define a sound or a style. Such arcane, intellectualized goals were never part of his mind-set. In fact, he didn't like so-called "lo-fi" any more than he liked punk or jazz or flamenco. It was more a matter of expedience, perhaps also a need for secrecy, combined with incredibly honed, refined instinct years in the making. "Sometimes lo-fi is great," he would say later, but "most of the time it's not. I never liked lo-fi bands when I was growing up," he recalls. "I liked the Beatles. I liked George Martin. You have to use your ears, not your head. So, there's no style that's really worth anything, to me anyways."[9]

A nice example of a style-averse song is the record's last number, a sort of throwaway, "Kiwi Maddog 20/20." The tune is a veering drunken instrumental named for the cheap, close to undrinkable wine that broke, incipient hipsters bought at places like Plaid Pantry. It features snare and cymbal by "Kid Tulsa" (aka Pete Krebs of Hazel). At the time Krebs was playing a lot of gigs on snare. "I probably had my kit in the back of my truck," he guesses. "It was a very informal thing." But it worked. And it was easy. The casualness and disinterest in making the whole thing sound perfect, or sound any way at all, runs through the entire record. Elliott's fingers scrape guitar strings as he skids from one chord to another; his S's leap out like he's in your ear, whispering sharply. In all, as critic Barnaby Smith put it, the album evokes a voyeuristic sense of having "walked in on the middle of something." Such was its appeal, its "rough charm."[10] It was a guy jamming with himself (and the very occasional friend) in a basement—literally. But the guy just happened to be a savant, so it lifted to a different height. It soared.

The record is dedicated to Elliott's father Gary, the person who got him one of those first guitars, played him Beatles and Dylan records, jammed with him, sent him recorded radio programs of Dylan's folk roots, and saved him from the swirling agonies of life in Cedar Hill. But it begins darkly with the restless stepdad, the frozen shadow father who wouldn't let him alone, who lurked interminably. In the title track rapidly strummed guitar defines the mood, the sound a swarm of yellow jackets circling nearby. If Elliott at this time was full of fury, as Gonson says he was, those feelings find direct expression. It's a letting out of what was normally walled off. "I want to hurt him," Elliott repeats, "I want to give him pain," spread this "pretty burn." But he backs off a little, suggesting he's "hallucinating." The equivocation implies two different possibilities. Either it's an attempt to distance himself from the song's flammable content—an insinuation that what he's saying is illusory, a figment of his imagination—or it's a reference to the madness Texas engendered, Charlie's crazy-making effects on Elliott as a small boy. At any rate what's in store, the song makes plain, is explosion. It's an inevitability. There is going to be, or there will need to be, at some point, a laying waste to the memory of the anguish or of the relationship itself. The image of the firework Elliott used repeatedly, a bottling up and exploding. *Dead Air*'s "Cannibal" has him on the roof, his head erupting like the Fourth of July. There again he says he's got to get these things "off my head." "Idler," from *Yellow No. 5*, imagines some mysterious stalker pulling up in a car on Independence Day. Then in "Bottle Up and Explode!" with its tell-tale exclamation mark, the habit of keeping "troublemakers" below—a reference to the repression of feeling—fails. It's a short term, non-viable solution. The prescribed explosion always comes, leaving Elliott seeing stars of red, white, and blue.

In these months Chris Cooper spent hours—as everyone close to Elliott did—trying desperately to "talk him out of thinking he wanted to kill himself." The anger went outward, but it also returned to its source. Says Cooper, "I kept telling him that he was a brilliant man, and that life was worth living, and that people loved him."[11] Krebs adds, "In Portland we got the brunt of Elliott's initial depression. Lots of people have their own experiences of staying up with him until five in the morning, holding his hand, telling him not to kill himself . . . I think he always had that kind of [self-destruct] button in there." When the subject of his despair or of its origins surfaced, the most Elliott usually felt comfortable doing was, according to Cooper, "implying abuse."[12] But it was clear to everyone he "battled a lot of inner torment, a lot of stuff that was traumatic." What to do with it all, how to work through and dispatch it, was a daily, urgent, life-and-death question. Songs like "Roman Candle" helped. Just as damaging as the fact that some sort of trauma had occurred was the duty Elliott felt to keep it concealed, at least so far as the details went. The songs were the letting go of blocked feeling, to the degree possible. Elliott read Freud, so the idea of the destructive potential of the suppression of affect was not lost on him. If one could let it out, it might stop banging loudly on the door of consciousness.

Other tunes from *Roman Candle* had looser, sweeter origins. Elliott had seen the Tim Burton animated film *The Nightmare Before Christmas*. In it, as the character Jack flies off in his sleigh, his gal Sally berefly sings her song—"Sally's Song" in the credits. It tells of disconnection, of impending doom, of relationship loss. The last two lines from "Drive All Over Town" exactly sample musically the last two lines from "Sally's Song." She sings: "It's never to become/For I am not the one." Elliott sings, "Until he tracks her down/He'll drive all over town." And in Elliott's tune the basic theme, although opaque as usual, has to do with relationship threat. An unnamed girl drives off at three A.M., much like Jack flew off. He wonders where she's gone; he'll drive all over town until he finds her.

Most of the *Roman Candle* songs, in fact—several missing names in the record version—chart relationship concerns. In "No Name #1" he's at a party, looking "spooky and withdrawn." He sees someone but he leaves alone quietly. He doesn't belong. He tells her not to follow. "No Name #3" pictures some other event he arrives at late. So he just takes off, "home to oblivion." It's a bifurcation Elliott never stopped inscribing dynamically: the risk and fear of getting close. The lure of intimacy, and the safety of numbed isolation.

Two songs are standouts. "Condor Avenue," a recycled tune written when Elliott was 17, and "Last Call," a jarringly electrified stunner, one of Elliott's best. The first is lyrically dense and indecipherable, probably meaningless. A girl takes off for the fairgrounds, rumbling along in an Oldsmobile past Condor Avenue, a Portland street dead-ending at the Terwilliger curves near Oregon Health Sciences University. The sound of the car in the distance leaves Elliott feeling "diseased." He's lying down, blowing smoke from a cigarette, not sure what to do with her clothes or her letters. She will never receive, never understand the meaning of the smoke signals whispering forth. So now he's leaving her alone, "you can do whatever the hell you want to." Na, na, na, na, na, na, he includes as a sort of childish taunt at the end. "Last Call" is a grenade, by far the most musically sophisticated song on the record, singularly intense, its sorrows complex. It fits and it doesn't. It shifts out of under-produced gear, pointing toward a sound more heterogeneous, one to be found on later records, the whispers of the other *Roman Candle* tunes replaced—gradually, as the song progresses—by barely suppressed shouting. Again, Elliott mixes up the point of reference. It's third person at the start, then second person, then finally, in the last section, entirely first person. Possibly parts of the song were written separately then melded together in the end. Elliott channels a cranky, bitter snarl pushed through corrosively. At first he's asleep at home, just plain sick of it all; so the song sets up as a dream, especially since he later wakes to the sound of church bells. Acoustic guitar opens it, but as Elliott harmonizes with himself a sixth above the main melody, electric guitar runs up then down a scale in caustic counterpoint. The section climaxes, then it's back to the verse, and an "endless stream" of sickening reminders he can't escape. "I'm all done," Elliott says, "you can switch me off safely." Last call is a final drink before closing but it's also a last act before the lights go off. He waits at the end for sleep to wash it away, a different version of oblivion. Before that he repeats eight times "I wanted her to tell me that she would never wake me."

As the penultimate tune, the song bookends "Roman Candle," the album's first track. He starts in anger, then ends with a wish that it all stop. In "Roman Candle" he's hallucinating, in "Last Call" he's possibly dreaming, so again there is the question of whether what he's talking about is real or unreal. The fear of Hell that Gonson heard Elliott discuss with genuine terror finds a way in. He promises he'll go to church, he'll go to pray, he'll sing praises to his maker's name, as if performing some kind of obeisance. He will do his best, although he can't seem to join in the celebration, to be as good as his maker made him. "Last Call" includes its own stalker, a "tongueless talker," an icicle, a jaywalker who walks away with a clap of fading shoes. This person may be Elliott himself, his own worst enemy—in terminal "crisis" mode—or someone else. Whatever the case, for what might be the very first time in song, what Elliott seemed to be doing was voicing a passive desire to die. He'd been talking about it with friends, now he was singing about it too, putting it into the music. It was a bold move. It took courage. And it made for a nuanced, gorgeous declaration of blurred melancholic grandeur. Whether it muted any suicidal urges—lessened the intensity of the feelings by letting them out in the public, at least allusively—is hard to say. If it did, the relief was temporary. Like the tongueless talker the feelings returned. They walked away, but they returned.

When the album appeared it featured a cover shot by Gonson taken at a market in New York City. Oddly, especially for a first solo record, Elliott is nowhere to be seen. There appears, instead, a girl named Amy—a friend who had joined them, and whose last name Gonson can't even recall—and

Full Roman Candle *cover shot, later cropped for the record cover. (Photograph by JJ Gonson.)*

behind her, Neil Gust in a stocking cap. "Elliott was throwing a bone to Neil on that," Gonson believes. "As in, 'See? I haven't totally abandoned you.'" It was quite the bone. Because it was Gust on the cover, and not Elliott, *Roman Candle* almost looks to be Gust's record (although there are shots of Elliott inside).

As for sales, it didn't blow up in the first few months, as had Cavity Search's "J. Hell" seven-inch. "It was a sleeper, a slow burn," Swofford says. But critics fell madly in love. Looking back, John Graham calls Elliott an avatar for artistic Portland—literate, stormy, tormented, adored. The record—private and strident—"hit some kind of Portland indie-rock G-spot." It was a "cerebral orgy." The local fanbase "sucked it down greedily."[13]

Rolling Stone put him beyond buzzwords like lo-fi and folk-punk, "ferociously talented" and in his own orbit, the record elegantly despairing, with some of the "loveliest songs about the dissolution of a soul ever written," full of coruscating self-awareness, "hypnotic and terribly, unrelentingly sad." It was—in a comparison Elliott always sniffed at—"Simon and Garfunkel after an idealism bypass."[14]

For Elliott it was a bit much. The last thing he ever foresaw, ever

Pete Krebs, Sean Croghan, Elliott, and Gilly Ann Hanner (L–R), of Calamity Jane, at a group show. (Photograph by JJ Gonson.)

wanted to do, was upstage Heatmiser, or upstage anyone at all—his friend Sean Croghan, his friend Pete Krebs, both of whom also worked solo and would, in time, tour with Elliott as solo acts. Leslie Uppinghouse called him "the shyest performer I've ever met. It was so difficult for him, physically and psychologically, to publicly perform. To get over that fear. He had a lot to say and he found it hard to communicate verbally."[15] Plus, to make matters worse, the music subculture in early-'90s Portland was a cliquey, tight-knit tribe of people and bands and performers, all poor, all working hard. Elliott was "the king of metaphor, symbolism, double-entendre," according to Uppinghouse, but still "everyone knew what the songs were about." That fact increased feelings of awkwardness. "It goes back to this privacy issue," Uppinghouse says, "there was this trust that you didn't talk shit." It wasn't that Elliott violated the trust—he'd never do that. But he was walking a narrow line. The songs were unravelings of inner black knots, but they were also about relationships, attempts to connect, and on those occasions other people appeared—hence the metaphorical elisions, the constant masking.

Leslie Uppinghouse vividly recalls one particular early solo show upstairs at La Luna, in the intimate, dark balcony space with a low stage. Uppinghouse was on sound, as she often was. Usually she and Elliott would talk beforehand, work out the details of what he wanted, make minor adjustments. This time there was no discussion. They were both incredibly spooked. The venue, small to begin with, was jammed. Elliott, Uppinghouse noticed, "was really throw-uppy nervous. I remember thinking he was going to pass out." As he started the first song it was "ten-times slower than average," the opening line a shaky warble. There was, in that moment, no telling what direction the evening might take. "But then," Uppinghouse says, "by literally the second chord, we had them. They did not move a muscle. It was magic." Graham and Baumgarten invoke the same occult ability in Elliott—"he poured himself out into the hushed atmosphere; it was then you realized Elliott Smith could be huge. And not just in Portland. He had a kind of magnetism that quietly worked its black magic ways."[16]

A little-known fact about *Roman Candle*—indeed, about all of Elliott's albums up to and including small sections of 2000's *Figure 8*—is that high school friend Garrick Duckler's lyrics continued to make regular appearances. This may be another reason why Elliott dismissed Cooper's comment about the record having the intimacy of a diary. Sometimes the words weren't even his; if they were anyone's diary, they were Duckler's. One example is "Condor Ave." An original version of the tune, with Duckler's words, shows up on a Stranger Than Fiction cassette (just like "Junk Bond Trader" did, just like "Everybody Cares, Everybody Understands"). "I'm not even sure that Elliott knew where Condor Avenue was in Portland," Duckler says jokingly. When he retooled the song for the record, Elliott patched together old Duckler lyrics with new ones of his own; part of its obscurity, therefore, derives from the intermingling. In this case, the title was Duckler's, as was most of the chorus. "Elliott said more than once he didn't know how to credit me properly," Duckler explains, "but I said that I didn't need any credit and that the intermingling of the lyrics was more a sign of our friendship and influence within each other's minds and lives, and he said that's how he thought of it too."[17] In total, Duckler estimates that somewhere around two to four lines of his resurface in roughly every other song of Elliott's, up to around the year 2000. It is a fascinating detail, one that, to unknowable degrees, scotches attempts at close interpretation because, at any point, one might be dissecting a Duckler line, not an Elliott one. Others in the inner circle were aware of this fact. Tony Lash made the same point, even calling the revelation "explosive." On balance, however, it seems less than that. This was no Bernie Taupin/Elton John–type arrangement. Two to four lines on every other song represents, at most, a minor inclusion; "It really is not something that I care about that much," Duckler adds. He had zero interest in keeping any kind of official tally, nor does he even recollect all the specifics—which words were his, and where. Whatever Elliott wanted to use was fine with Garrick. But what the blending reveals, far more than anything else, was the depth of the friendship, the significance of what the two friends shared. Gonson, who describes an "infinite respect" for Duckler, calls him "really, extremely deep and intelligent." He was, according to Gonson, a "lifelong friend" of Elliott's, and unlike some of the other friendships from earlier days, this one was "not optional" in the least. It was essential.

Relations inside Heatmiser, however, were fraying. *Roman Candle* had not been threatening to the band initially, and Elliott always wrote songs of his own concurrently with Heatmiser tunes. In that way things were status quo. But Heatmiser's vision, where things seemed to be going, was not Elliott's vision. The sound, especially of his voice, struck him as inauthentic. The fit just got poorer and poorer. So in response, Elliott tried exerting more and more artistic control, yet without ever making his frustrations explicit. To Lash it was all "a bit passive-aggressive." Elliott was getting more miserable by the day, but the reasons for the misery were never explored, and this only made everyone more frustrated, more confused. "I'm not passing judgment on his character flaws," Lash says, "It's just that he had a very strong artistic vision. And we could all be fucking difficult sometimes."

There was ire to go around, and Lash tried playing peacemaker as best he could, but the possibility of keeping things intact receded. Something had to change. And whether or not it was fair, or made any sense at the time, all the growing animus crystallized around mercurial Brandt Peterson. Peterson was moody, sarcastic, prone to making flip comments—as he says himself. It was less a matter of degree than of kind. From Peterson's perspective, Elliott had a "really disproportionate sense of personal injury," to make matters worse; "shit that was just shit he'd take as being about him." Also, "once he'd decided you failed him he was unforgiving." To Lash, after Brandt landed in "the bad column" with Elliott, there was no turning that attitude around. And customarily, according to Peterson, "Elliott's default was to decide, 'This person has disappointed me, and the solution is not to talk about it, but for this person to go away.'" Peterson felt targeted, as if he were "this impossibly coarse person"—which he sometimes could be, but usually was not. Peterson was holding back the band, Elliott seemed to have concluded. Even though Lash had his own John Bonham style, to Elliott it was as if Peterson, and Peterson alone, wanted Heatmiser to be some sort of Motörhead, "which was bullshit," Peterson says.

A few incidents magnified, and to some extent justified, any festering resentments. At a show in Seattle R.E.M.'s Peter Buck was in the audience. This was, to be sure, a big deal. As he always did, and to a degree that, he felt, never seriously impaired his bass playing, Peterson dispatched several hefty margaritas before taking the stage. He was drunk, yes, but his performance was hardly "sloppy," he maintains. But Elliott was in a rage, even though what was happening was standard practice. From there it just got more and more petty. At the show's end Elliott would not talk to or even look at Peterson, who was having a hard time locating his car keys. As it turned out, Elliott had grabbed them but wouldn't give them up. There was yelling, and the threat of some pushing and shoving, before Peterson finally erupted, "Give me my fucking keys! I know you have my keys!" A friend finally retrieved them.

Another time, during one of Heatmiser's seemingly endless van tours, Peterson had built a loft in the vehicle to create some additional space for sleeping or just lying around and playing or reading. They had driven straight from Portland to Minneapolis, and everyone's nerves were frazzled. Somewhere in North Dakota wind bent the passenger door, blew it open hard until it buckled. The van was old with no air-conditioning, and inside it got uncomfortably hot. Gonson came along for the ride, and also to photograph; she and Elliott were spending a fair amount of time apart from the others, holding hands, being in love. Throughout all this Elliott refused to speak to Peterson, to the point where it was "almost physically sickening," Peterson says. Jason Mitchell remembers the same chain of events. "That was really fucked up," he says. "A fucking nightmare."

Elliott in the van loft space built by Peterson. (Photograph by JJ Gonson.)

A later gig in front of an A&R guy from Virgin Records upped the tension still more. "Fuck this," was Peterson's feeling. "I am not doing this." In the last minute Gonson stepped in to broker a peace agreement, yet, according to Peterson, "a raw wound remained."

It got to be unfixable. Lash and Elliott had a complicated relationship, but they had been friends since high school, and Lash, apart from his musical accomplishments, was a gifted engineer and producer. Gust and Elliott were almost symbiotically entwined, just as Elliott and Duckler were—the band's two leaders, its creative core. And Elliott was always sensitive about disappointing Neil, who had a way of mostly bringing out his best behavior. Peterson was depressed, drinking to excess, occasionally a loudmouth, so the fit, personality-wise, always teetered on the edge of a deep drop-off. Finally Peterson, not Elliott, called a band meeting. He phoned Elliott up and asked that everyone get together. Although he was very terse about it, and definitely apprehensive—conflict averse to the bitter end—Elliott said okay.

Peterson took the floor. "If it's going to keep being like this," he explained, "I can't do it anymore." Lash was upset; he wanted Peterson in the group. In some ways he and Peterson had become counterplayers to Elliott and Neil. Elliott's response, a distillation of months of frustration, was a cold

In sweltering NYC, where Heatmiser stayed with Josh (on right) and his girl-friend, along with Modest Mouse. (Photograph by JJ Gonson.)

yet honest, "It's going to keep being like this." Peterson was hurt, though not shocked. After all, he had seen this day coming from the moment he and El-liott met, when he told him he'd kick him out of the band eventually, that that's what tended to happen over and over, in several bands leading up to this one. "To be accurate," Peterson says, "I did not get kicked out. I called the meeting and said I was not going to do this anymore unless things change. I felt deeply ostracized. Elliott could be fucking cruel. He could be mean."

Whatever the case, Brandt was out. In a final, well-meaning, but ulti-mately misplaced attempt at consolation, Elliott told Peterson "I want you to know you are a great bass player. It's not about the bass playing." In the mo-ment Brandt took this to be an "asshole" comment, serving to underscore the fact that it was personal, that the problem revolved around *who he was*. It was, to Brandt, a final insult, although Elliott apparently intended the op-posite. Peterson, in fact, never doubted his bass playing. He knew he was good. "My bass lines," he says, "my playing was a key part of the group. It was not incidental or inconsequential." In some small way even Gust tried seeing things from Brandt's side. According to Peterson, Gust told him he wasn't the first person Elliott had frozen out.

Many years later, in one of the last interviews he ever gave, Elliott looked

A Heatmiser tour. Elliott and Gonson in an elevator. (Photograph by JJ Gonson.)

back on this time. Then, from the vantage point of 2003, he called Peterson "very confrontational" and "probably more punk, whatever that means." It came down, he says, to "me kicking Brandt out even though everybody agreed to do it." Brandt, in Elliott's recollection, "started asking everyone personally if they wanted him out. Then it came to me and I said I wanted him out . . . I mean, he was an okay guy and we were friends for a while but he just kind of worked up everybody's nerves. His sense of humor was such that he always had to be making fun of somebody. He was just not a good time . . . That guy was just such an asshole."[18] This was to be Elliott's final take on things; he would not live out the year. Lash felt the comments were "lame." He allowed "that was clearly not Elliott at his most self-aware." To Gonson it was all very sad. On one hand, she says, "Brandt loved Elliott deeply, and he cared a lot about the band." On the other, he was always kept "a little at arm's length." "His input was limited even though he was a phenomenal bass player."[19]

Cop and Speeder, Heatmiser's second record, would be Peterson's swan song with the group. It was released by Lisa Fancher's Frontier in 1994, a few months after Elliott's *Roman Candle* surfaced. This time reception was mixed, although in aggregate the feeling seemed to be that the record improved significantly on *Dead Air*. Vocals were a lot more up front, so what was being said came through discernibly. Friendly local rock writers John Chandler and Scott Wagner, who had followed Heatmiser closely from the get-go, called it more intelligent and well-written "than most card-carrying members of the aggro attack style can muster." Some noted a powerful sense of mood encircling the record, with Elliott integrating his "seething whisper" into the full-tilt sound. The album, wrote *Trouser Press*, lashes out "with vehemence and a dark confessional candor that's not always attractive but undeniably honest." Others got the sense Heatmiser was struggling a bit to play heavy, powerful rock, hampered by their own introversion. The result, wrote Tyler Agnew, was "uneven," with "several gems and more than a few stinkers."[20]

Possibly the most bizarre song on the record, definitely among the most disturbing, although all the songs are disturbing in one way or another, is "Bastard John." It describes a sexual assault by a deceiver who primes his victim with assorted promises sounding like "bullshit." Once the victim played along, but no longer—"I'm not your bastard John . . . I'm not your kid anymore." As mentioned before, in "Roman Candle" Elliott pictured himself hallucinating, in "Last Call" dreaming; here he feels "distorted," but still fighting off the invasions of a seriously messed-up nemesis figure whose "present" keeps on giving every single day. "Bastard John" pops out for its graphicness, but again, it's not incongruous. As with *Dead Air*, lyrics for *Cop and Speeder* describe a world of loss, disconnection, ennui, and dread, that moldy pessimism endemic to dystopian Portland. People lie and feel like fakes; they can't be happy or unhappy, find nothing to stop real pain; lovers sounding like "songs with one fucking note" listen in silence over the phone; true love, whatever that is, blinks on and off "like a bad bulb"; and as Elliott puts it summarily in the oddly titled "Antonio Carlos Jobim"—Jobim wrote "The Girl From Ipanema"—"this is a record full of sour notes." Musically, the album was much more varied than its predecessor; lyrically, it's the same downer dirge. If there's any happiness around, Heatmiser can't find it.

The record was done, Peterson was gone, but Elliott's doubts stayed. It's hardly likely anyone, Elliott most of all, honestly expected Brandt's departure to set things right. In fact, it had little effect on the fundamental conflict,

which was Elliott's. He kept worrying the very same thoughts he'd been circling back to ever since he could barely force himself to listen to *Dead Air*. He
wasn't happy with the lyrical content. He felt disguised, "like a total actor."
He was "in denial" and "could not come out and show where I was coming
from." Even the band's fans started rubbing him the wrong way. "It was kind
of weird that people came to our shows, a majority of them weren't people I
could relate to at all. Why aren't there more people like me coming to the
shows? Well," he decided, "it's because I'm not even playing the kind of music
that I really like."[21] In other words, he was writing and performing for followers he had no interest in reaching. Cobain had faced the same unpleasant
realization with Nirvana. To him, the band's fans represented the same people who had made his life miserable back in Aberdeen, Washington—a horde
of anti-artistic, homophobic, simple-minded yahoos. Elliott knew what the
solution was, but it wouldn't fix Heatmiser: More Elliott Smith.

Jason Mitchell had started his own recording enterprise along with friend
Moira Doogan, the drummer for Trailer Queen. He called it Slo-Mo Records.
He'd brought out a cassette titled *So What Else Do You Do?* featuring songs by
Satan's Pilgrims, Lovebutt, and Boise Courthouse, among others. It also included Elliott's "Roman Candle" before that song even appeared on the *Roman Candle* record. Next came a seven-inch, the path everyone was taking at
the time. The idea, simple at first, was for Elliott and Pete Krebs to do songs
together, writing and arranging on the spot. Elliott didn't get that message, for
whatever reason; instead he recorded a song alone, the title of which Mitchell
can't recall. But he scrapped it and agreed to start from scratch. It was another
low-key affair, a four-track experiment at a friend's house near the Bagdad
Theater on Hawthorne, on a warm mid-August day in 1994. There were goofy
looking animal masks around, which Elliott and Pete slipped on for insert
photographs, one taken in Krebs's Volvo station wagon, the two driver-side
doors flung open. "Masks sum up our relationship," Krebs explained. "To me
and Elliott it was a hilarious, dumb thing to do. Two sensitive songs by guys
wearing dumb masks. He also had this dumb Dracula voice he'd go into. Just
really dry, absurdist humor."[22] The cover for the record (by Chanda Helzer) is
a cartoon drawing of two guys, one in a tie, standing before a red brick wall,
thumbs hooked in pockets, expressions dour, squinting into the sharp sun.
Each casts a hooded shadow. To the right is a driveway filled with cars.

Elliott with Jason Mitchell at the "merch perch." (Photograph by JJ Gonson.)

Krebs's contribution was "Shytown," with Pete on cymbals, the vocals almost spoken more than sung, a creepy, high, jazzy piano intruding atop acoustic guitar. Now and then foggy-sounding moans interject, courtesy of a plastic "freak-out Godzilla" toy on hand. Krebs's lyrics are comical self-mockery. His girlfriend keeps asking him whether he's having a good time. She can't quite tell, apparently. His job, he figures, is to entertain her friends—"I'm someone's boyfriend and a TV set," alone "with the jokes that I forget," crossing his eyes and making faces. Krebs's touch was light; the song's a total charmer.

Elliott took a darker path, in a song written on the spot, to Mitchell's amazement, although it's hard to say whether he might have worked out parts of it beforehand. The tune, "No Confidence Man," reads like an obvious companion to Heatmiser's "Bastard John." Both disentangle the same hairball of abuse, an insistent sameness of theme Elliott found hard to set aside. When something needed to come, this was what announced itself, recommended itself as subject, like some sort of particularly adamant Freudian slip. This time Elliott goes so far as to announce with the very first word who he's talking about. It's "Charlie," with a band in his hand, a rubber loop, spouting the same "bullshit" schemes and stories, with details never spelled out. This is one of the many instances in which others recall different first-draft lyrics. Gonson thinks she remembers "loop" as "stick" originally. The memory seemed to have something to do with a beating by a Ping-Pong paddle, the kind with a rubber surface on it, hence the reference to a "rubber loop" or circle. He "gave me nothing but grief," Elliott sings, "you're on it all the time." At one point he hears bells at nine A.M.—a detail also alluded to in "Last Call." All Elliott wants to do is sleep. Disappear into quiet nothingness, or what he, or Duckler, called "rhythmic quietude" in "Condor Ave." ("Last Call," again, imagines a similar quasi-solution.) Musically the song is a soporific monotone, sung in a stunned daze stripped of feeling. A flurry of Krebs's shushing cymbals ushers the tune in before Elliott counts to four (counting aside, the song is a waltz, as discussed earlier). At points a soft octave harmony tracks the main melody, creating an incongruously pretty effect.

In some ways "No Confidence Man" encapsulates the new direction begun with *Roman Candle*. Now, and from here on out, the harsh, bitter scratching of Heatmiser receded in the rear view, replaced by liltingly pretty songs about ugliness. It was pain made beautiful: stoic, "saintlike" torment. The suffering was the art, an equation Elliott understood perfectly, the mode best suited for his native sense of apartness. He used to point to Kafka's "Hunger Artist" story as a metaphorical self-summation, a portrait of the artist whose very appeal lay in his abject embodiment of tortured erasure, and whose last act was simply to die in a straw cage as crowds of voyeuristic onlookers evaporated. It was hardly a pleasant comparison, but it touched a deep nerve. If fasting is what you do, who you are, then it's the most natural, authentic art—inevitable, genuine, clear. One goes with it, because going with anything else amounts to denial and fabrication, a refusal of individuality.

This question of individuality had been at the root of the label contract disputes Gonson was struggling mightily to resolve with the help of attorney Richard Grabel, the lawyer who had negotiated numerous major grunge deals, a hard-core figure known for tenacity and for getting "big chunks of money" for up-and-coming bands. Elliott—and eventually Neil Gust too—wanted "exclusion from exclusivity" clauses added to all future agreements, a provision heretofore virtually unheard of. The idea, growing more urgent, was to protect the solo work, to keep it separate from proprietary claims that might be made on songs Elliott did for Heatmiser. The solo work he wanted to be his alone, to do with what he pleased. Yet as these entitlements were being hashed out—and as it happened, Elliott would get exactly what he wanted—the feeling was that he ought to record whatever material he currently had, just in case the request for exclusion went up in smoke. So it was back to work, alone as desired, this time at the Mississippi neighborhood home of Leslie Uppinghouse.

This next burst of songcraft was to become the moment when, in the words of Chandler and Wagner, "the shit really began to hit the fan." But in most ways, if possible, it was good shit and a good fan. The work would lead, in its serendipitous way, to the Oscars (along with later work done for the album *Either/Or*). And to a new, larger label, Kill Rock Stars. Also, to a move out of Portland to New York, then to Los Angeles. It would signal, finally, the end of Heatmiser, but not before the appearance of one last album, the best the band would ever make, *Mic City Sons*. It was a fecund time. All the fervid independent recording was about to pay off magnificently.

The choice to record with Uppinghouse was an easy one. Elliott was aware of Leslie's gifts with sound. Plus, the two friends (despite rumors, they were never lovers) shared an inward, shy personality type. Uppinghouse got the fact that Elliott needed a lot of privacy. She never pushed or pried. When the two spoke, it was always as much wordlessly as it was explicit. There was a lot of hemming and hawing, staring at shoes—that casual, relaxed, shared awkwardness one sees in acutely self-conscious teenagers. As Uppinghouse said, Elliott found it hard to communicate verbally. She just let him alone, left him to the task at hand.

Uppinghouse had grown up in the wealthy suburb of Lake Oswego (Lake Ego to outsiders), a bit isolated from Portland, although all her friends, she says, went to Lincoln. She saw a lot of music in the '80s, attended countless crazy Poison Idea shows. She also played bass in "little loud punk-rock bands," her first guitar warped and prone to buzzing annoyingly (like Elliott's Le Domino). There was the art-noise band Mobius Strip, Pavlov's Dogs, and Gopalm with Heidi Hellbender. Along the way she got to know Greg Sage of the legendary Wipers, and started hanging out at his studio, which he built. She calls Sage a "recording demon," a "sort of genius, a real taskmaster." He recorded 24–7. His priority at the time revolved around constructing the "perfect vibe" in the studio, the one most propitious for the creation of truly stellar work. In short order Sage taught Uppinghouse everything she knew about recording. He was her guru, her swami.

In terms of equipment, for the work with Elliott Uppinghouse used two pre-amps made by Sage, one (for vocals) called "the blue knob." With a wide signal it gave massive gain—super-clean, pristine power with very little distortion. When Elliott delivered his already emblematic whispery vocals, "it was just like he was right in your ear."[23] All tracks were laid down on an eight-track reel-to-reel, a Tascam 38 that Uppinghouse bought with her then-partner and quasi-husband Josh Mong, who also played in Mobius Strip. The house in which the recording took place was high-ceilinged with "lots of wood"—a bit like Gonson's home, both contributing promising acoustics.

By this point, what with the thousands of hours of recording, the tours and the sometimes high-stakes performances in front of different eminences, Elliott had finally grown comfortable and confident with his voice, an instrument he took a long time coming to terms with. But still, "he needed a lot of privacy for it." So what Uppinghouse did to get things rolling was to set everything up then step out of the room, leaving Elliott alone to hit play. "It was just something we were doing," she says, "and none of it was important at the time. My relationship with him—we never talked about anything. I didn't bug him. I didn't bother him with anything that wasn't necessary." Neither even quite intended to make a record at all, so in that way the experience resembled *Roman Candle*. There was no sense of goal, no prearranged end point. "He was just putting stuff on tape," as far as Uppinghouse knew or cared. There was urgency connected to the contract situation, a feeling of wanting to make the most of the time together—and Elliott was "super efficient"—but that was about it. They even threw in some goofy stuff. Uppinghouse had an old Italian twelve-string Vox with a cool sound—they tried making use of it. They also featured "a real funny keyboard," one they were mutually enamored with, but it came through too loudly at the end of certain songs and proved to be a problem during mixdown. Another sound making its way onto recordings wasn't exactly a sound at all, or at least not a bona fide instrument. Uppinghouse owned a boxer named Anna who loved Elliott so effusively and was always so excited to see him that it was necessary, before Elliott arrived for the day, to take the dog out for a vigorous walk as a way of settling her down. As Elliott recorded alone in his space, Anna took to lying just outside and whimpering, her nose pressed against the bottom door crack. Uppinghouse swears the dog can be heard on a few of the tracks, although to make out the soft moaning requires very careful listening.

Through all of it what struck Uppinghouse most was a technique Elliott had perfected nearly uniquely and for which he would always be known—his ubiquitous, masterful "double-tracking." For the vocals there tended to be a minimum of two to three tracks in fact, although some songs had even more. Track one comprised the main vocal, track two repeated that vocal identically, then track three added slight harmonies. "He could sing multiple versions of vocals pitch-perfect," Uppinghouse recalls, "each exactly the same, with no deviation at all, entire songs from start to finish." Typically he'd record a guitar track, then a first track of vocals; with those in his headphones he'd then record the third track. "He would mess around and hit harmonies or just hit it straight." These days, according to Uppinghouse, artists try "all sorts of crazy things to get a double-tracked vocal," such as running tracks through a pitch changer then onto a new track. But "Elliott just had a great ear and excellent vocal control so he could nail vocal tracks till the cows came home." In what may be his last interview in June 2003, a transcript of a conversation he had with one of his idols, the Kinks' Ray Davies, Davies asks Elliott about his "nice double-tracking vocals." Elliott describes the sound as "a lot more organic." He liked using it "so much more than delay," which can sometimes achieve a similar effect.[24]

Now and then Elliott shyly asked Uppinghouse to weigh in, to tell him whether something "was stupid"—more dread of cliché, an attention to aesthetic authenticity. But mostly he'd work out parts as he was recording, in between takes. He'd lay down a track, come out from the room he was in, then return to lay down something else. It was a constant back-and-forth. "He spent a lot of time designing, particularly for the song 'Needle in the Hay.' He worked out a lot of that on the fly." It was easy to tell when songs were totally done in his head, says Uppinghouse. "They would go pretty fast and he was more critical about them." Others he'd "monkey around with, work out for a while before recording them." It was these songs, the new ones, he tended to be most enthused about. "I see that a lot in artists," Uppinghouse says. "Once a song is finished in their mind they are looking for something new to inspire them . . . I'm betting the ones that didn't make the cut were the older ones." Those felt staler, less immediately alive.

All this went on over many long days. Elliott's focus was unwavering, a real sight to behold. And though she knew he could be a partier and liked to drink, sometimes to excess, Elliott at this time "was never a drug taker," Uppinghouse says, "never anything like a public nuisance. I've worked with some of the gnarliest people there are, so I know it when I see it." Uppinghouse's sense, being there in intimate contact day after day, watching the songs come to life, watching them find a final form, was that as Elliott made his art he was "isolated from his demons." Demons might have been a slanting force. They might have functioned as a tap root at times. The songs—"peopled with losers, boozers, dreamers, and ghosts that alternately drift and plummet through their existence, looking for the next big fuck up," as Chandler and Wagner mellifluously put it—might have transported listeners into demonic territories, sites of pain and unrest. Yet, allowing for all that, the music was craft. If demons dragged along they were pulled uphill on a chain, beholden to the one real aim: art. They were art's side effect, chiseled raw material, not the other way around. Or so Uppinghouse saw it.

The question of drug use is not incidental. Several of the songs Elliott worked on alluded to drugs—for instance, most obviously, "The White Lady Loves You More." Because of this, people started wondering, whispering. Was Elliott actually on heroin? In Portland? Pete Krebs says no, he was not. To Krebs it was more "shtick," more nominal than real. Heroin was another Texas—a fear repository, one more possibility to dread. Elliott liked to conjure catastrophic outcomes, Krebs says. Things that might, but probably wouldn't, happen. Things beyond his control, things that may befall him. Shooting heroin, Krebs says, was one of these. Elliott himself said much the same thing when the question was put to him directly. He told

Chandler and Wagner, "Everyone read the songs at a very surface level, they wanted to know why there were so many songs about heroin . . . But I used dope as a vehicle to talk about dependency and no self-sufficiency. I could have used love as that vehicle, but that's not where I was." Then he added, obscurely, "I'm just trying to make things so I enjoy being me."[25] This was in fact the more fundamental question—how to enjoy being me. No lasting solution to that question ever seemed to present itself forcefully. And it wasn't that heroin ever stopped being a strong lure even in the Portland days. There were people around, according to Gonson—people who ought to have known better, people whom Elliott trusted—who suggested the drug to him as a method for fighting off, for treating, depression. They said he could use it and not become addicted. He listened, and out of a feeling of desperation actually thought the prospect over carefully. It was seriously tempting. This idea—opiates for mood disorder—had been around since the fifties. Certain depressives, a minority in the scheme of things, responded only to opiates and not to more traditional remedies. So the issue was complicated. There seemed to be legitimate, medicinal reasons for thinking of heroin as an option, especially in light of the utter intractability of Elliott's pain. The notion was preposterous on its face, but Elliott was vulnerable, open to pacifying rationalizations. He did not try heroin in Portland, but it's not that he didn't consider it, didn't want to try it. It was his own tantalizing, secret siren.

As with *Roman Candle*, the set of songs recorded at Uppinghouse's are succinct, deceptively simple, mostly acoustic tunes that showcase Elliott's guitar dexterity, with rapid runs and intricate finger picking, although on occasion other instruments appear, such as soft drums and cymbals, harmonica, or the comically bleating keyboard drawing "Coming Up Roses" to a close. No single song leaps out as exceptionally powerful; there's no "Last Call" in the mix, no obvious showstopper, although "Angel in the Snow" and "The White Lady Loves You More" feature gorgeous lullaby melodies, gentle and sweet, with the kind of captivating appeal Elliott always aspired to ever since finding the Beatles mesmerizing back in Cedar Hill. His songs, as he emphasized, were pop tunes, not monolithic, message-dominated folk. "The only tradition I like," he told Carsten Wohlfeld in 1998, "is the tradition of a pop song being short and melodic. The singer-songwriter thing is kind of irritating because so many of them have made grand statements about what's wrong with the world . . . I just like to describe a situation and how you feel about it. I try to put all the things I like together"—the word-besottedness of people like Dylan and Lou Reed, plus the melodic aspects of the Beatles. What he was after, it seems, most consistently, was just that—melody, not meaningfulness. The latter took a back seat. In fact, one of the things he liked about pop particularly was its ambiguity—it wasn't, in the best of instances, quickly decipherable lyrically, and it might mean several things at once. That's not to say themes don't appear, of course. And this time, unsurprisingly in light of the heroin fascination, the theme is drugs, the quick fix, the cure—as a possibility or an idea, if not an actuality. "Good to Go" features a junkie girl saying "you can do it if you want to." In "St. Ides Heaven" people weigh in warningly about what "you should and shouldn't do, but they don't have a clue." "Alphabet Town," according to JJ Gonson, addresses heroin's temptations directly, Elliott tagging along as a friend makes a buy in New York's "haunted" Alphabet City. "I know what you want and it's what I want," Elliott writes. There's a hand on his arm—as there is in "Needle in the Hay" and in "Single File," where his arm's got a "death in it." "Let's go out, I'm ready to go out," he announces. What the songs document is vacillation, the ambivalence of wanting what part of him knows he needs to avoid. Strung-out people keep grabbing his arms, needles show up—"cold white brothers" in his blood; he throws up whatever gets shot down. It's one scene of temptation after another, and there's dialogue between the characters. Will they judge him, will they say it's okay, will they give him permission, license to do as he wishes. It's as if, in song, he's mulling the subject over, imagining scenarios and future outcomes. But he can't make up his mind; he never arrives anywhere. He tours the junk paradise but he never punches a ticket in. He's still on the outside.

One song epitomizing Elliott's indecipherability, a tune he kept playing even in electric versions over the course of his career, is "Needle in the Hay." (Years later it accompanied a self-cutting scene in Wes Anderson's *The Royal Tenenbaums*, to Elliott's displeasure.) As Uppinghouse noted, he worked hard at it, spent a lot of time getting it just right. There's a drumming relentlessness to the song, Elliott hammering down on strummed and finger-picked half notes as it begins, jumping around the scale; the sense is of someone knocking loudly and persistently at the front door, or of water torture, the drip drip drip getting harder and harder to bear. It's never all that clear what is going on. The narrator's riding Tri-Met. He gets off at 6th and Powell in Portland, pursuing a "downstairs" cure of some kind, one that lets him be quiet whenever he wants. His preference is to be left alone—that's why he's taking the cure to begin with. You ought to be proud, he says, "that I'm getting good marks," dragging the "S" sharply in anger, a human approximation of tape hiss. Like so many other tunes, the song flips confusingly between first and second person. Two different people seem to be involved, the one riding the bus, and another, a doppelganger who wears his clothes, who's head-to-toes "a reaction to you." One striking reference is to a "hay stack charm" around a character's neck. It is an incidental detail not exactly critical to the song's meaning. But at the same time, it may have personal subtext. The so-called "Golden Age of Wrestling" featured a lovably charismatic five- to six-hundred-pound Texan, a barefooted, overalls-wearing, six-foot–four-inch hillbilly by the name of Haystacks Calhoun. His gimmick was a horseshoe charm he wore around the neck for good luck. Haystacks and Elliott almost shared a birthday—he was born August 4, Elliott August 6. Legend has it that Haystacks routinely ate one dozen eggs for breakfast. He also literally, or apocryphally, picked up cows on the farm and moved them across the field as needed. Quite possibly Elliott knew of this Goliath, either by circumstance or through Charlie. So it is Haystacks with a hand on his arm, the gentle-giant wrestler thrown into the plot, a direct reference to long-ago realities. Elliott for some reason makes him "strung out and thin," the opposite of who he was. It's Haystacks turned junkie, a shrinking Leviathan—although, as the first two verses play themselves out, it's not easy tracking who's who, the "he" and the "you" merging into a single figure.[26]

The song could be another blended effort, with a mix of Duckler's and Elliott's lyrics, because by the second section things get clearer. From there it's all first person. The singer's driven almost against his will to locate the man who's going to make everything okay. This mysterious helper—a psychiatrist, a dealer—isn't up to anything good, it seems. "I can't beat myself," Elliott says twice, as if he's after some sort of ass-whooping delivered by a "downstairs" punisher. The bad guy comes up again in "Christian Brothers," which begins with similar half note strumming making it, musically, a companion piece. There he's a bossy "bad dream fucker" blinking on and off, and although Elliott sings "it's sick what I want," he also can't resist it. He won't shake the "motherfucker's" hand, but he wants him all the same—"come here by me." In the end he registers his own self-destructiveness, a sort of self-defining vestigial force, singing "nightmares become me."

Another song from this session is "Clementine." For this Elliott and Uppinghouse called Leslie's mother to get the folk song's original lyrics, including a line Elliott used, "Dreadful sorry, Clementine." It seems like a simple description of drinking in a bar, the bartender flipping around the "open" sign at the end of the night. But although in order to kill time the singer's busy drinking himself into "slow-mo," he can't get "Clementine" out of his mind. The story, about a miner's daughter who drowns accidentally, is surprisingly dark and strange. It's actually the miner's fault that his dearly loved daughter dies—he could not swim, so he could not save her. Thus like Elliott does in his own song, he consoles himself by drinking beer and wine in a tavern. Then he takes his own life.

Finally, and in many ways unsurprisingly, Bunny appears in the song "Southern Belle." He always worried about his mother and what might happen to her without him. In his mind, she was alone and vulnerable ("Nobody talking now/No one's about to shout"). Here the nemesis figure is up to the usual, giving people hell–"it's what they expect from you"–strangely unashamed of who he is or sorry about what he's done. "Killing a Southern belle" is all he knows how to do.

The songs kept coming; it was a virtual explosion of creativity, as Tony Lash would later see it. And what they did, as they added up, was make some sort of major change even more unavoidable than it already was. But there was Heatmiser to deal with still. The contract finally got hammered out after almost two years; Elliott had his exclusion from the exclusivity clause (Neil too, according to Gonson, who had done yeoman's work.) No longer was the band with Frontier; after a confusing sequence of events and much back-and-forth discussion steered ably by Gonson, they signed instead with Andy Factor at Virgin. It was a major, exciting step up. And although he didn't want to agree to terms with Virgin at all—because he knew Heatmiser was not what he aspired to do anymore—Elliott, mostly

Heatmiser visits Disneyland, around the time of the Virgin signing.
Gonson is with purse, Andy Factor is front right, Shelly Shaw far left.
(Photograph courtesy of JJ Gonson.)

out of a sense of obligation to Tony and Neil, finally got on board, albeit dismally. Quasi's Sam Coomes was enlisted to replace Brandt Peterson; it was at Coomes's house that Krebs and Elliott had recorded the songs for Jason Mitchell's "Slo-Mo" enterprise. And thus, for the moment at least, it was half-steam ahead. There was an album to make and there was touring to do, and videos to produce. For Elliott it was as if a second self tagged along wherever he went. There was who he was in the band, and there was who he was alone and apart. Both were promising paths in the present, both also presaged a hopeful future. Superficially, he could not go wrong. But the fact is, one direction required a stultifying amount of compromise or else a collective openness to the prospect of changing band direction, and neither of those options seemed acceptable, for Elliott on one hand and Heatmiser on the other.

At this point Gonson was out. She'd found Heatmiser a booking agent (Shelly Shaw), she'd made the Virgin deal—a stellar accomplishment—but with the end of that negotiation came the end of her service to the band. (As a thank-you, Andy Factor sent her and Elliott a box set of Nick Drake records; an interesting choice, since it dovetailed more with Elliott's solo work than his work with the band who'd just signed the deal.) Also at its end was Gonson's relationship with Elliott. It was never a good idea to begin with, as they both acknowledged. But now the added stressor, one Gonson always felt a little vulnerable to herself, although she never tried it, was heroin. The drug was a new girl with whom Elliott had grown infatuated. He hadn't indulged, but he hadn't put the idea aside either. It was a crush. It was also a way out of pain, or so he had been told, and that made the lure irresistible. It was a new path of self-destruction too, and along with it a means of finding something Elliott always sought in one way or another, and wrote about relentlessly—oblivion. A feeling not only of painlessness, but of nothing, which amounted to the same thing. Gonson had no interest in dealing with the prospect of heroin. In no way did she want to abet it, even as a bystander. Yet by the day Elliott seemed more and more entranced. The danger was imminent. And it wasn't only Gonson he talked with about the drug. The prospect surfaced even with people Elliott hardly knew. "We all had quite a few conversations," Jason Mitchell recalls, about suicide, about depression and drug use. "More than we were even comfortable with." Heroin wasn't life, it was anti-life, it was death. And though everyone energetically warned Elliott against it, they also knew, deep down, the warnings only went so far. He listened, but he didn't listen. As always, part of him wanted to live, part of him wanted to go on making music forever, but part of him also wanted it all to end. Mostly, as he said again and again in songs, he wanted to forget. Gonson's drug years were mercifully behind her. They had to be if she wanted to stay alive. So she got together with a new man, and Elliott got together with the woman who'd broken up with Gonson's new man, Joanna Bolme, who had also lived with Pete Krebs for a time. It was all comically incestuous. Everyone played together—Bolme an outstanding bassist—and everyone was hooking up. It had always been that way. The songs, after all, were secret communications among a very insular set of people, all of whom knew the subtext implicitly. But Bolme? The coincidental link with Gonson struck some as suspicious. Over time her relationship with Elliott grew to be exceptionally meaningful and important; initially, however, the coupling was perceived as a small "fuck you" to JJ, a final cut. The split had not been easy either. Heroin was one

Elliott at AIM Fest. Joanna Bolme is second from left in sunglasses. Sean Croghan is to Elliott's right. (Photograph by JJ Gonson.)

part of it, a partial cause, although Elliott was not using. But James Ewing remembers several long talks between Elliott and JJ on the front porch of the house; it was clear to him something difficult and serious was up. JJ had always been very maternal; she loved to love and take care of people, even feeding them as she came to discover a creative talent for cooking. All this suited Elliott, who needed all the love and support he could get. But for whatever reason he was "very determined" to end things, Ewing recalls. Slowly over many days and weeks the breakup played itself out depressingly.

So Elliott moved to SE 19th, just off Belmont, near a small park and tennis courts, eight blocks or so west of Gonson and not far from the Heatmiser Division house. Gust came along to the duplex-style home with separate kitchens and two entrances at the top of the steps, doors numbered 1 and 2. Jason Mitchell and Gust took the upstairs suite, Elliott and Sean Croghan lived downstairs. Elliott bought an eight-track reel-to-reel, and on the modestly sized front porch they passed time recording Uncle Tupelo tunes, an alt-country band whose first album was titled, coincidentally, "No Depression," a dizzy blend of hardcore punk and Hank Williams. They hung out at Montage, at Dot's on Clinton, at Club 21 on Sandy. Sometimes

Gary Smith stopped by to visit—jamming or talking philosophy or Buddhism—also Shannon Wight, Elliott's high school girlfriend, whom Gonson remembers being around still. While they rented it the house was for sale, and for a brief time Mitchell and the others thought of buying the place, but they could never figure out how to put sufficient money together, and the odds of actually getting a loan were slim at best. It finally did sell, and they moved to a different place near Fremont, a home owned by a black woman named Mrs. White. The new rental had a basement that Elliott liked because it seemed like a space he could possibly record in. Mostly what Elliott did to pass the time was what he always did wherever he was: read, or sit around smoking cigarettes and noodling on guitar, watching Univision and *Xena*, "writing in the glow of the TV static," as he put it in "Junk Bond Trader." "My hands just make songs up without me even being involved in it, because I play guitar a lot during the day," he said in early 1997. "My fingers just do whatever they're doing while I'm watching *General Hospital*. Sometimes I go, 'Oh, good job, fingers! I liked that.'" Other times it was "What was that? Wait, do it again."[27] More writing occurred as Elliott walked the streets at night, when the moon was out—hence the profusion of moon imagery in his work, he says. Friends recall driving alongside Elliott crossing one of Portland's many bridges and asking him if he needed a lift somewhere. More often than not he'd say no. It did not look like it, but he was working. The mechanics of songwriting was a constant line of thought and conversation, the obsession with structures of chords. All afternoon Elliott would play, waiting for magic progressions to erupt accidentally. Lyrics he'd just spit out, rarely attaching intense personal importance to them, although, of course, they sometimes said more than he knew or cared to know. His custom was to write a song and lyrics in one day, then record it that night. And he recorded anywhere and everywhere.

From Virgin, Heatmiser cashed a decent advance to help with the making of the next record. A decision was made to buy equipment and rent a separate space in which to record, a smallish home set back from the street on 19th and SE Ankeny that Gonson initially had scoped out. Sound insulation was pressed up, rooms were blocked out. In all "it seemed at the time to be a pretty elaborate setup for a temporary studio," Jason Mitchell says. It was here, in this nondescript little two-story house, with ample parking in front, that Heatmiser produced *Mic City Sons* ("Mic" pronounced "Mike"). This would also turn out to be the location for the long-postponed demise of the band.

The situation was "fucked up" to begin with, according to Gonson, who was now watching things unfold from afar. The songs Elliott made with Uppinghouse had been culled for 1995's self-titled album, *Elliott Smith*, released by Olympia's Kill Rock Stars. The cover, a picture put together by Gonson, featured two blobby figures falling between bluish buildings, a fitting image, it seems, for a record Elliott later called his darkest by far. Despite his long relationship with Cavity Search, the label Swofford and Cooper had so lovingly constructed, the move to Kill Rock Stars was surprisingly amiable and smooth. As Swofford charitably explained, "It was totally natural that Elliott went to Kill Rock Stars. They had a lot more resources. It was like, 'Elliott, we get it.' Besides, were we in a position to put out his second, third album? That's arguable. We were just fine. It made sense and there were no hard feelings." In terms of their origins, Cavity Search and Kill Rock Stars popped out of the same chaotic murk of tenacity combined with happenstance. Slim Moon was the latter's founder. He'd moved to Olympia in 1986 as a high schooler, then quickly discovered KUPS, University of Puget Sound's radio station featuring songs by the Butthole Surfers and other underground punk outfits. At the time punk was new to Moon. But he started looking for discs, eventually buying a Beat Happening seven-inch put out by K Records. Moon was a spoken-word poet who read over the radio, but he formed bands too—one called Eights and Aces, another (with Donna Dresch) called Nisqually Delta Podunk Nightmare, who shared a bill with Cobain's early Skid Row. Moon's first notion for the Kill Rock Stars label was admirably outrageous—he would devote himself to recording only spoken word, releasing poetry on seven-inch vinyl. In fact he did this several times, carving out a very unusual niche. The label's first release he called "Wordcore: Vol. 1"; it included one of his works, along with "Rockstar," a poem by Kathleen Hanna. She would soon form the band Bikini Kill. Hanna's seven-minute recitation concludes with a woman on her knees "wiping up a boyfriend's vomit after telling him she was raped by her brother": "You sit down to write a song about it," she says. "Fuckin' rock star."[28] Soon such outré poetry gave way to music. With the help of K Records's Calvin Johnson, Moon pieced together a compilation from the International Pop Underground Convention, with songs by the Melvins, Nirvana, and Bikini Kill, among others.

With his punk bona fides obvious, his lyricism—to Cooper and Swofford—Dylanesque, a sort of poetry all its own (with a no-look assist from Garrick Duckler), Elliott easily fit Moon's mind-set. But when the self-titled record appeared, Uppinghouse was stunned. It came as a total surprise, a sort of *Roman Candle* redux. From her perspective Elliott had only been laying down tracks; as far as she knew, it was just more note-taking of the sort Gonson had described, an attempt to catch works in progress on the fly. A record had never been discussed or proposed. But plan or no plan, when the record materialized—with "Needle in the Hay," "Christian Brothers," "Southern Belle," "The White Lady Loves You More"—it was instantly heralded. Critics saw in it a blueprint for all Elliott's later success; it was "his first major artistic statement," deeper, stronger, more complex and more fully realized than *Roman Candle* had managed to be. "Tragically beautiful," they called it. A "masterpiece of minimal folk-pop." These accolades Elliott stiff-armed per usual. "I don't know what to say about that," he replied. "I kind of don't think about attention a whole lot. I don't really deal with it. It exists more in other people's minds. It's surprising, but that's kind of the extent of my feelings about it. Surprising and temporary."[29] He was in the same difficult corner. Here he sat, a promising auteur, on the verge of bigger and better things, but at the same time he'd just inked an important contract with Virgin to make a record with a band he no longer wanted to be a part of.

It didn't make any sense, but for the time being Elliott soldiered on and did what he could to abide by conflicting commitments. He took the path of least resistance, in other words. For the solo work he enlisted the services of manager Margaret Mittleman who, from Long Island originally, got her start in the business working at a record store and record distributor. Her first big break occurred in 1992, when she stumbled upon Beck playing solo at the Sunset Junction street fair in Silver Lake. With her was her husband, Rob Schnapf, a partner in Bong Load Records. "We were walking around," she says, "and we saw Beck playing acoustic guitar and singing under this little tent, right on the street. I just got drawn in; he had a unique sound and look, and his lyrics were hilarious. After the show, I talked to him for a while, and gave him my card."[30] Later the two had a lengthy phone conversation that led to a publishing deal. The big draw was the brilliantly effete nerd rap "Loser," a surreal loop of poststructural self-mockery suggesting "I'm a loser baby, so why don't you kill me?" The tune was released by Bong Load as a twelve-inch single, and it took off, leading to Geffen's *Mellow Gold* album. Mittleman would later sign Built to Spill, the Posies, Lutefisk, Mary Lou Lord (who released several EPs on Kill Rock Stars), The Folk Implosion featuring Lou Barlow, and Neutral Milk Hotel. Her reputation revolved around discovering cutting-edge bands in early stages. She found them, then she helped them develop. It was Slim Moon who first turned Mittleman on to Elliott, suggesting she check him out at L.A.'s Jabberjaw, where he was slated to play as part of a poetry/spoken-word tour. "It felt like the hottest night ever," Mittleman recalls. The cafe's air-conditioning was out, and Elliott performed on a patio in the back. "I just couldn't believe it," says Mittleman. "*Roman Candle* was already out, and he—and I just was blown away."[31] She bought one of his CDs. The two met the next day. "I just offered my services, basically. He didn't want to do a publishing deal. That was the big thing. He wasn't interested. So I just said, you know, that I didn't care about that. [So] we just developed this re-lationship," one that slowly became "more and more official."

For Elliott this new development meant going out on the road—a train tour from city to city, followed by a car tour—in support of *Roman Candle* and *Elliott Smith*. Mittleman says "nobody showed up, just the few die-hards . . . That was very discouraging and disappointing for him, but it was the first time he really did something on his own." He split his time working on *Mic City Sons* and touring on his own behalf, the solo bookings compet-ing with efforts to keep Heatmiser viable. It didn't seem particularly doable, but the minor momentum was there to be seized on. Besides, "there's a part of me," Elliott said, "that wants to go as far as I fucking can with [the solo work]." And although for a while he felt as if it were essential to never get anywhere in a commercial sense in order to feel like what he was doing was worth anything—the whole, "if you make it, you must be a mediocrity" sentiment—he bought in. He got over his self-defeating misgivings. For one tour he went out with headliner Mary Lou Lord, who'd just signed an im-pressive publishing deal. She'd told Elliott he was the next Kurt Cobain, a compliment with terrifying implications; she also "unsuccessfully pursued a romance with him."[32] For another, a one-month jaunt through Georgia, Texas, and California, then back to Portland, Pete Krebs backed him up, pursuing his own solo work, just like Elliott was, after the demise of Hazel (In 1997, Elliott would arrange and produce Krebs's solo album *Western Electric*.) Mittleman had put the two together with a "big black guy" who drove, but was also apparently there to keep Elliott on track, Krebs believed. The money was negligible. Looking out for his own best interests, Krebs said he needed to make a hundred dollars per show. Elliott wasn't so sure, but in the end they came to an agreement, and as Krebs recalled, "it was more than what Elliott was making," a fact that took him by surprise. In the south somewhere near Athens a young girl approached Elliott and Krebs in a bar. She'd been at the show and wanted to say how much she liked it. They struck up a conversation during which she confided she was on the brink of joining the Army. "We spent hours," Krebs says, "trying to talk her out of it. Going over all the possible scenarios." For much of the time Elliott was wrapped up in fear about the prospect of entering Texas, as if simply being within the boundaries of the state was grounds for panic. He was freaked out. Texas meant bad times, and no matter how hard he tried, whether he burned his haunter up in songs like "Roman Candle" or drank him out of his system, the bogeyman flailed, a ghost on the prowl, if not physically present then projected out.

At last Heatmiser's *Mic City Sons* dropped improbably in mid-October 1996, a full year and a half after Elliott's self-titled record. It was nothing like *Dead Air*. Nor was it anything like *Cop and Speeder*. It represented, by leaps and bounds, the best the band could do, or at least the best the band had done to date. Full-blooded, melodic, catchy, hook-infused, it could have pointed in a new direction, one that might very well have added up to something big. But in fact it was, as everyone knew, a last gasp. There was not going to be anything else. As new bassist Sam Coomes told *Magnet Magazine*, "It was a miracle that record made it out into the world. Everyone should just be happy it got that far."[33] The fact of its tortuous emergence was not lost on Virgin, who had in effect signed a band fated to go nowhere. They knew about the deepening conflicts—everyone did—so in a move reflecting the likely absence of any future for the group, they brought the CD out through a subsidiary, Caroline Records. They even passed on a vinyl version. That did eventually appear, but with a Cavity Search imprint. One of the few people not a fan of *Mic City* was Denny Swofford. To him *Dead Air* was the zenith—an obviously contrary judgment. "I'd rather see Heatmiser live any day during the *Dead Air* period," he laughed, "than Elliott alone singing while sitting on a chair." *Mic City*, he added, "is an Elliott Smith album that happened to have a band called Heatmiser playing on it." An acid sentiment, to be sure, but one with a hefty portion of truth. For really the first time, and more glaringly than ever, the Elliott songs leap out sideways. They could just as easily have been included on his self-titled solo album, or saved for future records. Immediately recognizable as paradigmatic Elliott tunes—for instance, the spectacular "Plainclothes Man"—when they appear in the song list their incongruity is plain. They diminish everything alongside them. They advertise Elliott's difference, his gift. He did not and could not fit anymore.

Reviews took note of these disparities, sometimes explicitly underscoring the quality difference between the Smith and Gust songs in a way that probably came as no surprise to Neil but still must have stung. The record was described as "decidedly more pop," Elliott's lead song "Get Lucky"—which Tony Lash dismissed for its clichéd Foreigner bombast—as "swaggering."[34] The verdict seemed to be that these were refreshingly diverse and invigorating tracks and that the record ironically "marked Elliott Smith's maturation into the role of the band's visionary" at the moment when there soon would be no band. As Allmusic.com retrospectively put it, "it's unfortunate that this indie-rock supergroup decided to split up just when they had reached such a creative peak." But the reality was, it was Elliott's peak, and Neil was not peaking along with him.

The softest, most affecting, and by far most Elliott-esque track, strangely "hidden" and not listed at all on the record, is "Half Right," with its mournfully transporting acoustic intro joined by Lash's brushed drumming. It's a song Elliott would keep playing solo, clearly a better fit with the tunes he'd make solo than with Heatmiser. Characteristically ambient on the surface—who is this "you" who shouldn't be "doctoring" herself?—it's another song bent on unpacking the Gonson breakup. When he pictures her

Heatmiser live, Elliott and Peterson. Elliott's shirt reads, "Bloodhound, a Dog Gone Good Chew." (Photograph by JJ Gonson.)

new boyfriend, he doesn't match up. He imagines someone more like him, someone who "looks like what I look like." In alternate versions he asks instead "What's he look like? What's he look like?" In still other alternate versions, those performed live in 1994 at Umbra Penumbra in Portland, he indulges in various bitter predictions: "He's just half-ass, and he won't last." One particular line seems to come out of nowhere. Elliott twice sings nonsensically, "Don't you say hi." The true reference is a real event. At the time Gonson cooked at Dot's, a place everyone gathered across from the Clinton Street Theater with its regular midnight showings of the *Rocky Horror Picture Show*. By this time the relationship was over. The kitchen looked out through a window up front, so that when people passed by on the sidewalk, on their way down the street, Gonson could see them and vice versa. One day out of the corner of her eye she caught Elliott strolling past. Hurt that he didn't at least wave or stop in for a short hello, she rushed out after him, catching him at the intersection, where she blurted out, "Don't you say hi!?" That Elliott wedged this fragment of obvious autobiography into the song makes it a private communication, and not an especially friendly one. He goes on to picture Gonson's dream lover bursting her at the seams. When he calls her up on the phone, he sings, "it's just like being alone."

"Plainclothes Man" is the other standout. Again a dark presence loiters malevolently, scheming to get Elliott alone, working to fuck everything up, "always there when all else fails." The antidote is numbing alcohol—all one ever really needs—or dreaming colorlessly as a way of avoiding more depressing Technicolor details.

Ross Harris directed the "Plainclothes Man" video. He had a history with Elliott. He'd done some photo work for Beck and got to know Mittleman, who gave him a chance to come up with ideas for a "Coming Up Roses" concept, the song from Elliott's self-titled record with the sustained howling electric piano at the end. Others had also pitched, but as Harris saw it, "they wrote some pretty involved things." Before generating his own premise, he'd spoken with Elliott, quickly realizing that "he was not the kind of person who is into some elaborate preplanned scenario."[35] So he landed the gig and met Elliott for the first time at LAX. The two had a meal with Harris's family, plus a "beer and maybe a joint," as Harris laid out his loose treatment—the camera would follow Elliott as he pawned his guitar for food. They shot with a Super-8 camera in the Colonia District of Oxnard, and in Saticoy and Santa Paula, places filled with dive bars and beatup storefronts. Elliott "pretty much went with" what Harris had in mind, but then again "it wasn't like I suggested these high-concept things with an army of Elliotts being attacked by toys and shit." A lot of it, Harris says, "was accidental." As it opens Elliott's in a small room wearing shades and white socks and a white belt, his Ferdinand tattoo visible on his upper right arm. A makeshift band accompanies—Grace Marks on drums, a snare, and a "guy from the neighborhood," Raul, on standing keyboard. Elliott heads out with his guitar in its case, off to the pawn shop. The colors switch from orange to yellow to red to black and white. At one point, not acting in the least, he pitches headlong into the dirt of a country road. A hearse shows up—Harris's friend had just bought it—but it's depicted broken down, getting charged by another car, both hoods open. To Harris the image suggested a cheating of death. No dead soul would be taken today; death was dead, not any person. Finally Elliott gets his cash, shown counted out to him. He buys milk and Jarritos sodas with their neon colors—orange, bright blue, fruit-punch red. As he wanders along a sidewalk kids flow out, some with skateboards, and he passes the soda around, saving one for himself. (The kids were Harris's nephews.) It's an achingly sweet moment; Elliott smiles and laughs as the kids converge on him. The sense is that the jollity is spontaneous. The song then ends, the piano moan erased.

For Heatmiser's "Plainclothes Man" it was a different story. With Virgin tracking the process, Harris filmed with a crew and camera man, the label making things "more difficult." They shot, this time, in Santa Paula. "The idea," Harris explains, "was to have a guy down on his luck and he sees these everyday objects and they cause him to get lost in a daydream." A passing boat on a trailer produces reveries; even the picture on a condom box sends the titular character into a trance visualizing sunset walks on beaches. There's a shot, too, of Elliott inexpertly tackling Gust shoulder-first, a sarcastic comment, Harris felt, "about the supposed tensions within the band at the time," although of course the tensions were a lot more than supposed. Performance shots are interspersed with plot, the white-haired, white-mustachioed man wandering streets asking for cash. He's a benign, feckless presence; nothing like the song makes him out to be—a stalker bent on "fucking up" little boys in blue. In truth, the video easily could have finessed a far darker angle, fabricated a bit more menace. In performance shots Elliott makes zero eye contact, although he's the singer. He looks to the floor, as if reading from a lyric sheet. His lack of affect rhymes better with the lyrical content. He's in a long-sleeved button-down, his hair looking like he showered with lard. Just before Elliott is shown stuffing toilet paper into his jacket in a convenience store, then spiriting out the door, followed by the shop owner. The plainclothes man spies a woman in an upstairs window, shot in overexposed black and white. He is in love, we figure. But a cop materializes by her side, and they wave, smiles pasted on their faces; she's the Law's squeeze, not Plainclothes Man's. The latter spits disgustedly on the sidewalk. No love in his black-and-white world.

Another song, "The Fix Is In," was set early on. It proved, finally, to be a serious shit-stirrer as it came into focus. Elliott had recorded all the music first, Lash explains, and Tony got added in later, layering drums over the instrumentation—"Never," Lash says, "an easy or ideal thing to do." Because it felt wrong, as if it were somehow "rushing the song," Lash kept reworking the drum part, trying hard to get it to a point he felt to be less frenetic and pushy. With each redo Elliott got more and more annoyed, more "bugged." He resented the waste of his time. He wanted to be done, to move on. Lash says, "He really misinterpreted what I was doing as this mindless, unnecessary search for perfection. The perception was that I needed things to be too clean, too precise, too polished." The sense Lash got, the one he always had, in fact, was that if Elliott wanted precision, that was okay; yet if anyone else did, it was a problem. As a group, the *Mic City* songs were looser and quieter, Lash believed. The stylistic shift was obvious and Lash was bored. With Brandt gone, replaced by Sam, who to Peterson was part of the "Elliott Smith fan club" (for the moment, at least), Elliott's animus now worked its way toward Tony. Tony was in the way of what he and Gust wanted. Tony was the problem. There was never any open discussion of how things were going to be different, but still the sound "morphed into something new, something never articulated," says Lash. Elliott was asserting himself, ham-fistedly assuming artistic control. And to abet this, Tom Rothrock and Rob Schnapf, Margaret Mittleman's husband, were brought in to produce just after work began. They were Elliott's allies, more or less, serving Elliott's cause. Lash says now he was "happy to facilitate the recording process," but he chafed at the changes. As he'd explained before, he wanted to rock out, and rocking out was happening less and less.

In the irrepressible "Pop in G," with its contemptuous title and its reference to imaginary Mic City Sons "dumbing everything down," Elliott vented new feelings about Lash. Revealingly, the tune has a mixed-up provenance. Some sources attribute it to Elliott, some to Gust. The sense is that neither felt comfortable owning up to the sentiments inside, references not lost on Tony, who saw the song as a graceless "fuck you." You are as good as they come, but you're "such a fucking trial," sings Elliott. "You make me feel like I'm half my age, and at least twice as nervous." Lash is a "statue" in a bar with feelings to kill. He whistles "Sweet Caroline" cluelessly, not wanting anyone to speak their mind. What he does mostly is bother people on purpose, Elliott (or Gust) writes. The note about feeling nervous and half his age is interesting. The fact is, although he was in the process of overcoming just these hang-ups in 1996, Elliott always felt intimidated by Tony, a tall, quiet, slightly intense presence. Uppinghouse was on hand a year before when Lash helped with the mixing for Elliott's self-titled album. She noticed Elliott's sheepishness around Lash, his deferential attitude. Lash felt, she says, that the product was sloppy, a bit too DIY. He proposed fixing it up, smoothing out annoying elements like the misused electric piano. Uppinghouse disagreed. She felt to do so would destroy the integrity of the songs. She felt they should remain as is, just like *Roman Candle* had before. In the end Uppinghouse's position won out, there was no polishing done, or at least nothing significant. But her sense is that, had she not been there to support Elliott, things might have gone differently. Standing up to Tony was a problem for Elliott, in other words. His impulse had usually been to defer. So with *Mic City Sons* the story was changing. Likely due to his solo success—reviews piling up that confirmed the saliency of his vision—Elliott was newly emboldened. The volume on the self-doubt had been turned slightly down. He knew what he wanted, and people were telling him that what he wanted worked.

Lash also knew what he wanted, though, and it wasn't this. Not only was Elliott dissing him in songs and (less so) in person, he was also announcing indirectly where his true interests were by keeping up a daunting touring schedule at the same time Heatmiser recorded in the Ankeny house. From February to September 1996, Elliott was out performing his own songs, sometimes with a stray Heatmiser tune thrown in, in Tempe, New Orleans, Amherst and Bryn Mawr Colleges, Atlanta, Tempe again, the Knitting Factory in New York City, and Maxwell's in Hoboken. Along the way new songs were being auditioned, to appear on later albums, many among his most arresting—"Angeles," "Between the Bars," and "Say Yes," among them. It was plain Elliott was finished with Heatmiser, and Lash did everyone the courtesy of at last killing the crippled beast. Possessing an above-average talent for crafting angry letters, Lash harnessed it and let rip. In a late 1996 e-mail he told Elliott "screw you." Apart from simply "venting a huge amount of frustration," he accused Elliott of placing no value on his personal relationships in the band, his long friendships; all he cared about was the music, Lash said, and despite what he might believe, music was only part of the picture. Bands were people; the feelings of people needed to be accounted for—their hopes, their commitments, their expectations. "If you don't want to do this anymore," Lash suggested, "let's just call it off, end it." Elliott was nonresponsive. For a long time he was ambivalent about copping to his loss of interest; he felt bad about it, fearful of what it entailed. But he knew he was unhappy; he knew he was not having fun anymore; he knew he had taken over—he and Neil—and that doing so unilaterally and without explanation had destroyed the band. Lash was only saying, then, what everyone else was thinking. So Heatmiser didn't so much die as fade away almost silently. Lash and Elliott did not speak for at least a year, although later, by accident, they made a sort of peace by means of a chance encounter at a coffee shop. This détente was partial, however. Ill feelings never dissipated entirely. And although not exactly deliberately avoidant when it came to Elliott's later career trajectory, not disinterested or dismissive of his later success, including the 1998 Oscar nomination, Lash never listened to Elliott's work, at least not the majority of it. To this day (2013) he has not heard entire albums. They would have been painful to hear, for one. Plus, what brief bits he stumbled on did not appeal to him.

There were, for inexplicable reasons, a few more performances, these with John Moen of the Maroons and Dharma Bums—and later The Decemberists—taking Tony's spot. Jeff Stark reviewed one such 1996 show for *SF Weekly*. Brendan Benson with his occasionally Elliott-esque leanings opened—Stark for some reason found him Pollyannaish, spouting the power of positive thinking. Stark described bassist Coomes as looking at certain points "like he was either fucking or severely drunk." Gust was charming yet "borderline square," his button-down shirt bespeaking "geek chic." Elliott wore an Adam Ant T-shirt. He was "muscular and handsome," says Stark, acting for all the world like "he'd left his depression in rainy Portland." Slim chance of that; Elliott rarely left his depression anywhere. But still there was a lot of goofing off. In a bit of lovable roughhousing, Gust pushed Elliott down in the middle of one song. Coomes at one point announced mockingly, "We've got Soren Kierkegaard on guitar," indicating Elliott, who replied "This one's called 'Fear and Trembling.'"

It sounded like good fun, but it was unsustainable and it was over, a last paroxysm of transient positive vibes. Finally openly avowing what he'd known even from Cedar Hill with Pickle and others, and from high school with Stranger Than Fiction and its later iteration Harum Scarum, Elliott told friends what interested him most was wearing all the hats. He could play bass and think like a bass player. He could play drums and think like a drummer. He could sing, then sing over himself with double-tracking, then harmonize with himself on a fresh track. He could, in short, make a band with chemistry out of how he wanted it to be if it included other real people. As he put it later in the song "Can't Make a Sound," why want any other when you are a world within a world? His approach, which required a Paul McCartney–like jack-of-all-trades virtuosity, left other people out of the equation. They were not necessary. In so many ways, psychologically, artistically, interpersonally, and as a reflection of personality, the solution was perfect. He *was* a band, so why be *in* one? He'd performed his apprenticeship, he'd tried including other players, often generously, self-effacingly; yet from here on out, with occasional minor and usually short-lived flirtations, he'd go it entirely alone, the way he liked to go it. Isolation took him through a tunnel to a bright world "where you could make a place to stay," he sang once, past self-hatred, guilt, and shame. Musically, he *was* a world within a world. Whether he could succeed in being that in life may have been a different matter altogether. Anyway, Elliott Smith was now *Elliott Smith*.

CHAPTER SIX SWEET HIGH NOTES

Wherever one looked, 1997 was a strange, dismal, dysphoric year. Princess Diana died fleeing paparazzi in a Paris tunnel, the world sutured to what Martin Amis and Saul Bellow called the subsequent "event glamour," the drawn-out collective mourning that led, months later, to a new version of an old Elton John song reaching number one on the charts. As if timed to heighten the ritualized despair, Mother Teresa also died, the two figures, both mothers, cemented together in memory, Diana receiving courtesy sainthood. The music world lost The Notorious B.I.G. and INXS's Michael Hutchence, one by gunshot in the rap gang wars, the other by suicide with a belt tied to a doorknob, or, as was later suggested, by erotic auto-asphyxiation (although the coroner disputed this characterization). Sportscaster Marv Albert was charged with biting an unnamed sex partner, Eddie Murphy got stopped by police (though not charged) for picking up a transsexual prostitute. The pop charts were ruled by Mariah Carey and "MMMBop," cotton candy by brothers Hanson. In indie land, Built to Spill, Modest Mouse, Green Day, and Radiohead released records; Bob Dylan, the artist who, according to Denny Swofford, Elliott ranked number one in his pantheon, put out *Time Out of Mind*, which Greil Marcus called a "Western, really, made of ghost towns and bad weather, a complete and uncompromised work of American art."[1] Ghost towns and bad weather describe Elliott's songs too, many of them haunted, many overcast and misty like the Portland in which they came to be made.

For Elliott, the year was a tale of two cities, Portland and New York. It was, in cliché's Platonic form, the best of times and the worst of times. Best in terms of the music, epitomized by the sublime mish-mash record *Either/Or*, released by Kill Rock Stars in early 1997. Worst in terms of the psyche that served it, whirlpooling in drink and depression more and more frightening by the day. It was the same old story under magnification. The music kept rising, the person kept falling.

Like Elliott did, Heatmiser's Neil Gust went his own way too, fronting a new band with the name No. 2, which years later, in 1999, put out *No Memory*, engineered by Bolme, Tony Lash, and another of Elliott's close friends, Larry Crane, with whom he'd helped to start up Jackpot! Recording. Lash also played some electric piano for the No. 2 record, Coomes bass, and for two songs Elliott sang backup, an obvious sign that relationships were not entirely broken. About Elliott's solo work Gust was, at first, enthusiastic. He called the self-titled record "flawlessly executed" and "tremendously inspiring." Later works, however, he had some trouble with. "I start to hear him using music to attack himself and other people," he said, "as his problems become more and more [pronounced]. As it goes on later I do find it hard to listen to."[2] This turned out to be a standard reaction. Lash and Peterson felt the same way. They weren't acolytes, their knowledge of Elliott's catalogue surprisingly spotty.

The pace of Elliott's songwriting from '96 to '97 was a dead sprint, a time when he wrote or recorded the songs that sent him into his own iconoclastic stratosphere. He was in what psychologists of creativity call flow, free from Heatmiser, untethered and generative to a degree new even for him, which is saying something. "Alameda," "Between the Bars," "Say Yes," "Angeles," "Division Day," "Go By," "Going Nowhere," "Abused," "Bottle Up and Explode!" (and covers of "Thirteen" and Bowie's "Rock 'n' Roll Suicide")—all bewilderingly gorgeous tunes, all irresistible, all written in a lightning storm of artistic frenzy. It's mystifying how certain periods in an artist's life come to assume such proportion. Henry Miller liked to refer to the "mysterious X-factor." Norman Mailer emphasized the need for some sort of activating wound demanding documentation, if it didn't eat into you first and kill you. No wound, Mailer asserted, no great art. The wound made the difference. Elliott felt the wound in spades. It dominated his subjective sense of who he was, and his attachment to it would almost end him forever; but he was also enjoying the effects of sustained hard work. All the making of songs was paying off, and in a fashion he most likely recognized, even though he was quick to find fault in what he did. Like most great creators, he'd achieved a fluency that quickened and deepened the process at

once. The larger part of him knew he was very good; he struggled with performance, but he did not lack confidence. The smaller part was a merciless
critic, as if anything coming out of him was axiomatically suspect or flawed.
He found it hard to judge songs. There were times he thought they all
sucked. Unlike Dylan, he struggled to shirk off all the crap piled on top of
him. He worried the music business might grind him up, despite the fact
that, by his own estimation, he didn't sell millions of records nor did most
people have any idea who he was. It wasn't so much that others expected
him to be huge; the conflict was internal, a clash between authentic self-
definition and role playing. Elliott stood here, and right behind him, posturing and murmuring, stood the "Smith Myth." They weren't antithetical, but
they weren't tautological either. As he had said in April 1997: "You gotta get
out there and show what it's like to be a person, that's what I'm gonna do. It
might be good or it might be bad, but I'm gonna show what it's like to be a
person."

In a simple sense what was going on with Elliott was not all that unusual. Self is part story; we script who we are. Everybody has his or her own
personal myth, the master narrative we tell ourselves and others about who
we are. It can be factual, it can be fictionalized. A portion of Elliott's myth
exists in the songs, of course, in lines like the "devil's script" selling him
the "heart of a blackbird," for instance. In that way he was different. Unlike
others not so artistically inclined, he pulled from experience songs that
told stories, and those songs possessed themes implying deep concerns—
the myth in progress, constantly updated and refined. Also, on a large scale,
other people, usually people who did not know him, or knew only the
songs, imposed myths on him—the "troubled troubadour," the death-
obsessed existentialist pop star, the DIY god, the avatar for dreary gray
Portland. These were the notions Neil Gust, among others, felt he was beginning to buy into, the ones that, in some ways, he resented, but in others
found himself living out. Brandt Peterson, whose concept of Elliott is as
nuanced as anyone's, spoke of the "cult of Elliott Smith." To him there were
two main readings. For some people, those not cult members, Elliott wrote
"whiny, narcissistic songs" of failure, weakness, victimhood. For others he
was "insightfully introspective," with a freighted backstory lending "weight"
to the tunes. This is yet another component of every possible myth—the

origin tale. There are torturous beginnings—omitting all the good times with Pickle, Denbow, Kim, and Merritt, with his parents, with Ashley and Darren—but these are overcome by dint of art promising total freedom or even redemption. For a portion of his life this was the space Elliott occupied, the archetypal forked road. One route led to redemption, the other contamination. Everyone in Elliott's life kept urging the redemption direction, waving him forward. Yet Elliott, much of the time and against his own interests, chose the darker side streets.

Recorded in 1996, "Pictures of Me" is an instance of sizing the myth up and refusing to accommodate. Elliott worked on the song for days at Undercover, JJ Gonson's new venture beneath the Morrison bridge on Portland's east side, near where the opening of Gus Van Sant's *Drugstore Cowboy* was filmed. It was part performance space, part compilation/project label. The idea was to produce cover albums (hence "Undercover"). Cat Power did one. Local bands did too, essaying '80s new-wave tunes by the Go-Go's, Gary Numan, and others for an EP called *Tiger Stripes Forever*, put out on yellow and black vinyl. For one of those songs Elliott actually produced (Gonson can't recall which tune this was). The label's most successful record was *Crash Course for the Ravers*, a set of David Bowie covers. Its release coincided with a Bowie anniversary; serendipity led to sales of around eight thousand copies, which set the label up nicely for several additional years of operation. For JJ Elliott recorded Bowie's "Rock 'n' Roll Suicide," a choice suggesting more than slight courting of the Smith Myth. Gonson believes the song was made for the *Crash Course* record, yet, for reasons possibly having to do with timing, it didn't get included. Additional projects included *Fleetwood Mac: Patron Saints of Pop*, on which Jeff Buckley appeared singing backup on a tune recorded by his girlfriend ("That's All for Everyone"), and *Letters to Aliens*, a "totally over-the-top" two-disc set, Gonson says, complete with postcard and sticker inserts.

As Elliott hammered out "Pictures of Me," JJ kept a safe distance. By this point the two weren't speaking, not because they didn't want to, but because it was too hard to try. There was ongoing tension, too, between Gonson and Bolme. "Elliott and I stayed away from each other," JJ says. "If we interacted it ended in drama and tears. One of us would always start crying. It was awful." But from an adjoining room she listened over and over to the pounding of the drums, a track Elliott kept reworking in keeping with the tune's first line, "start, stop, and start." His ambivalence reaches an apex in this song, musically straightforward, lyrically complex. The tune builds slowly, a held synth chord giving way to climbing acoustic runs—as if he's heading straight for the top—then it's all guitar chords pouncing down on the beat, with synth doubling them or departing for harmony. No drums kick in until Elliott works his way through the first few verses. On one hand, the song's a rejection of "all these pictures of me" of which he's sick and tired, external interpretations of identity that keep getting pushed his way, that he can't avoid seeing, even though they strike him as totally wrong. For kicks he flirts with them even as he hides, looking at his feet, frozen in fear every time they appear. He's got himself to "tease and displease," he sings, and in some ways to blame for all of it. He'll end up the victim of his "own dirty tricks"—his desire for fame, for success, and his simultaneous disavowal of the pretense of wanting it in the first place and doing what he can to get it. The song says he knows the game, and he knows he's playing while despising it all the same.

In an unreleased version the plot's simpler. He sees a girl on a blue screen, an image of the one he loves. But another guy appears. "I couldn't compete," he says. "Don't expect to see me begging you please." The finished take obscures the girl, the lover who leaves him, and focuses more on the image, although this "other guy" remains, a jailer wanting Elliott on his "fucking knees." In the first version he's competing with a guy for a girl; in the final version he's competing with himself for the image (that sells "personal hells"). The song thumps to a close and the chorus repeats as if to fade, but its bottom drops out; there's a musical descent like a fall, like sound hitting an elevator shaft. "Everybody's dying just to get the disease," Elliott sings three times. It's a chilling final observation. The disease is the big blue screen of fame—which Elliott predicts with "Pictures of Me," the Oscar performance more than a year off. It may kill him to get it, to find what he wants but doesn't. Reviewing the song, Chandler and Wagner advise, "Don't let the Beatlesesque bounce lull you . . . This candy apple has a razor in it."[3]

The record on which "Pictures of Me" appeared was the anything but declamatory *Either/Or*, its existentialism front and center. The songs,

emerging from different moods and head spaces, employing jarringly different production values, were recorded all over the place, some at Joanna
Bolme's house, some at Elliott's or the Heatmiser house, at Undercover,
Laundry Rules Recording—Larry Crane's home studio from 1994 to 1997—
and The Shop. Elliott saw these tunes as less theory-centered and more
about achieving a sort of poppy irrepressibility—in a word, "catchiness"—
though ideas, befitting the Kierkegaardian title, were not in short supply.
Practically speaking it was an embarrassment of riches, and that fact made
the record almost impossible to get done. They were too many songs,
around thirty or so, and here again, unlike the first two solo albums (criti-
cally adored but not commercially successful), recorded when the background noise of expectation and modest acclaim was easy to mute, the
"little germ," as Elliott said, of what people wanted from him made it harder
not to care, not to tangle himself to the point of paralysis. Creativity was
easier when no one looked forward to a next potential big thing. The songs
were easily the best he'd ever made, yet picking through them, selecting
which to include and which to abandon, was harrowing, an exercise in self-
doubt and second-guessing. In fact, he preferred when other people sang
his songs because then they sounded more real, more like songs. "When I
play them," he said, "they just sound like things I made up and I have no
idea if they are good or bad."[4] As noted, a chief ambient influence was the
Beatles, especially *Magical Mystery Tour* and *The White Album*. (With respect to the former, he says he turned it off after "Penny Lane," skipped
"Hello Goodbye" but really liked "Blue Jay Way.")

The album cover looks like a UPS ad—all browns and oranges—
Elliott smoking in his "Heli-Jet" cap (a helicopter company) and a Hank
Williams Jr./Bocephus T-shirt, behind him a graffiti-strewn mirror filled
with curlicues, and just below it two oxymoronic commands on the wall:
"Fuck you" and "Turn on." The back is a lit chandelier resembling a Ror-
schach inkblot.

The muffled fuzz of "Speed Trials" starts the record off, a tune that
would have been more at home on either of the first two albums. Its hollow
drumbeats echo like a felt stick striking an empty gasoline can. Their snap
grounds the song perfectly, a bee-bee gun day at the rifle range. The lyrics
also describe an echo or ricochet, tracking the same thought paths spelled

out above. "Sweet high notes" of the kind Elliott was known for "echo back to destroy their master." The "little child" thinks he's tough—that's the act, at least—but all the people he feels superior to "know what's the matter." The human pinball follows the path of least resistance. Life's a speed trial—all preparation and qualification, no race.

"Alameda" is song two, and the sound quality, contrasted with "Speed Trials," instantly jolts one out of a late-afternoon half sleep and into bright, sharp morning. Dylan once said that the way *Blonde on Blonde* sounded was exactly how he heard the world. "Alameda's" sound is the way Elliott Smith heard the world. It is dazzling but also slightly overexposed to infinitesimally perceptible harshness. The one song that compares with "Alameda" on the first two albums is the majestic "Last Call," which seems to come from a place no one's ever been or even heard about. But in terms of sound, no song compares. So when listeners got to the second tune on *Either/Or* it was like finding a totally unexpected or possibly uninvited guest at a party who also happened to be the most interesting person there. Pete Krebs was talking about every Elliott Smith song when he said "You had never heard anything in your life that sounded like this," each tune "full of that intangible thing Elliott had." Still, "Alameda" hammers the point in; it's a constellating moment.

The same snapping drum striking the same empty gas can punctuates the opening as guitar introduces the melody. The title is a street in Portland and the song walks it, almost like a march. Background harmonies sigh sleepily as Elliott's voice enters, guitar still tracing the melody alongside. The mood is hypnotic, partly because of the drum slap on every second note—like the clap of the fading-out sound of shoes in "Last Call"—partly because of the high floating harmonies following the walker like thought clouds. Drums stop only as a short bridge appears, a pause in the musical shuffle, a tumble away from the main melodic line. Then it is back to marching again, like there's somewhere he needs to get to. The song is about relationships, but it's got nightmares too, along with an unnamed authority "champion"—Das Man—Elliott gets forced to bow to. As for relationships, they do not work. Beyond everything else, the main thing Elliott's concerned about, he sings, is his own protection. He needed people around him to care—as JJ Gonson put it, "he kept his hook in you all the time then returned every once in a while to check it"—but in the long run, when it came to sustaining connections, his "first mistake" was thinking he "could relate." Nobody ever breaks his heart, the song says, because he beats them to it, he breaks his own: "the fix is in." As themes go, this is the one Elliott returned to, not so much to hash it out or get past it, but as a self-punishing reminder of failures. He had himself on the hook as much as he had anyone else.

As he made the *Either/Or* songs he'd already ended the relationship with Gonson, and started up with Bolme, with whom he was very much in love, in a way that seemed—though he never spoke of it publicly, nor did she—unique, and even potentially lasting, a very good thing that might have made an important long-term difference in his life. So the songs fall in line; they chart feelings of intimacy, connection, hopefulness, but mostly fear, dread, and potential ruination. Whatever was working got broken, the emotional axiom, "Don't count on love, and if by chance you get it, break it before it breaks you" (as he declares explicitly in "Alameda"). The victim, in other words, takes the role of self-protective victimizer. Thus in "No Name No. 5" his fingernails are bitten and his head's "full of the past," as if he's assaying the formula, an inner law to which he's anxiously beholden. Smiles might be sweet, he notes, but they fade fast. "Everybody's gone at last" because that's what they do, they go. He tells himself not to get upset; after all, he's seen it already. There is nothing new wrong that wasn't wrong before. In the end what he gets is a broken heart and a name on his cast.

"No Name No. 5" is a drowsy passive reflection, as if sung at night after several Jamesons and beer chasers. The line that lifts vocally, breaking free into a higher register, is "gone at last," its last two words reflecting a wished-for state alone and away from the hell of other people. There are two other outright love songs on the record, one, "Between the Bars," imagining active intervention, the other, "Say Yes," grounded in surprised hopefulness. "Between the Bars," with its "Rocky Raccoon" opening, pays instant homage to *The White Album* Elliott was listening to as he worked on the tune. It goes back a ways; he actually wrote the song in early 1996—some time before April—while sitting around watching *Xena, the Warrior Princess*. "She's got a killer yell," he tells a Knitting Factory audience. "But I was watching it with the sound off. I think it's better [that way]." The plot, maybe inspired by what he was seeing on the screen, is a rescue, albeit of an emotional kind. The girl is stuck in a state of unrealized potential; she spreads promises she doesn't follow through on. The place he finally kisses her, "between the bars," includes three possible meanings. She's in a cell with her hands in the air; she's between drinking establishments; or he's finding her in the bars of a song, the one he's singing—the girl is in the music. It is one of Elliott's more assertive tunes; he is heroic in it, a sad savior, altering fate rather than getting his ass kicked by it. He and the girl will separate (verb) from the rest, where he likes her the best. It's a rescue and an escape.

"Say Yes" tamps down the feeling of power a little but it's still, as Elliott once said, "insanely optimistic." "It was written about someone particular"—Bolme most likely—"and I almost never do that," he said in 1998.[5] "I was really in love with someone." In fact, as he notes in the song's first line, he wasn't just in love with a girl, but with *the world*, through her eyes. It's a sweet simple melodic line, curving up then down then back up again still higher. Even the mood is uncertain, in other words, but finally, after teasing meanderings, it lifts to the top of a scale. He's high emotionally and vocally. The song, *Either/Or*'s closer, depicts the aftermath of "Between the Bars." He saved her and they separated, but then what? He's not sure, it turns out. He'll be the fool or the exception to the rule. He's standing up, changed around, but his past tells him happy days make you pay and "feel like shit the morning after." One especially brilliant line captures Elliott's emotional checkmate: "Crooked spin can't come to rest/I'm damaged bad at best." It's sung almost happily; there's no bitterness in it, no resentment or anger. The song's otherwise uplifting tone almost masks its meaning. The question is, given who he is, will he ever find true love? What can he love truly? Will love last? She'll decide, he concludes, not him. She's either going to live with and accept the damage, or she's not. It is an open question in the song. But life answered it. The relationship with JJ ended in part because of Elliott's darkness; and as Bolme said, she too found it more and more difficult to be with someone who placed no value on his own life. Years later, around 2000, Elliott told Jennifer Chiba the same thing he'd told quite a few important people in his life: it might not be a very good idea to get close, because he wasn't planning to be alive much longer. Investing, then, was betting on low odds. Love and happiness were sweet in the moment, as on "Say Yes"; but they were temporary. Standing up would soon be falling down.

Other songs stake out similar territories. The underrated "Punch and Judy" is a jazzy two-step pop standard sounding nothing like most anything else Elliott ever wrote. But the main characters keep saying the magic words in the wrong order, and someone's "going to make the same mistake twice." "Angeles" showcases Elliott's guitar virtuosity, with its difficult, rapidly finger-picked opening. Sometimes in live performance even he wasn't up to it. He'd stop and surrender, apologizing, then start in again in response to the crowd's pleas. Then there's the intense dejection of "2:45 AM." He's alone in center circle, the world fading to black.

It was a constant theme in interviews, the only question asked with as much frequency as questions about the Oscar night—why his songs, for instance "2:45 AM," were so depressing, or whether he, like some listeners, found them depressing. The subject is reasonable, less artistically interested than concerned, and genuinely so, about Elliott's state of mind, the viability of his life. What people seemed to want to know was whether his life was as bleak as the songs. Going to the nature of creativity and of creative process and product, the topic was anything but easy to flesh out. To start with, he was clear and insightful about the link between art and creator. He told one interviewer, "Those songs didn't come from nowhere so if [they] seem bleak, then I guess the answer is yes"—the life *is* as bleak as the songs. He told a different interviewer, "Of course the songs have something to do with me." There's this idea—strange and naïve—that art or music stands alone, that it has no connection to the mind that made it, that it tells us nothing about that mind. Refreshingly, Elliott didn't push that line of thought. The songs come from somewhere; he's the one who made them up; so unavoidably and indisputably, the songs are about him, even when they are about other people. But he did not see the songs as bleak. "They have their happy moments," he said. "Maybe that's strictly mine. My own belief." But the perception of darkness in the tunes, relentless darkness—that, he said, "is definitely a problem to me. It's not like I want to carve out a little corner and stay there . . . I'd be really happy if I could write a song as universal and accessible as 'I Second That Emotion.' . . . Happy songs are great when they come along. I mean, they haven't come along a lot . . . It's a big game to play, trying to make something that's mainstream enough and still human." To be mainstream was to erase complexity and darkness, to lie, in other words; to be human in the art was to let everything in, the full range of feeling, and what came, when Elliott did that, was usually sadness—or pain, loss, failure, disconnection.

He was always careful to note that he didn't feel any sadder than anyone else he knew. "I'm happy some of the time," he'd usually say, "and some of the time I'm not." The mood was more harmony than motor anyway, he suggested, even though, like most people, he found it harder to write when happy ("People tend to play better if they're not on a winning team," he said dryly). Anything he was trying to work out or think over—drugs, drinking, women, friendship—anything frustrating him in some way—those were the subjects he turned to. He didn't care whether he understood what he was talking about in the lyrics. As with dreams, he said, "It's good if you can understand what your dream meant. But whether you do or not, it's having an effect on you. And on a certain level, you do understand what it's about," whether you know it or not.

Whatever the case, the songs "are the only important thing," he said. And they did not need to have a point, they did not concern themselves grandly with what was wrong with the world. They were, he believed, descriptive, impressionistic, pictorial—"like a bunch of photographs burned into each other." Before he started, "it's usually a picture. Like describe a picture: Two people are in a room and one person has just insulted the other but the other hasn't realized and the conversation has broken down and one person knows why but the other person doesn't." But pictures have content, they embed stories, capture scenes. Here, in keeping with the kinds of situations explored in *Either/Or*, Elliott singles out relationships. "I'm interested," he explained, "in the way people interact but don't necessarily connect. Or don't connect fully . . . Like dependency and mixed feelings about your attraction or your attachment . . . It's good for you on the one hand, and on the other hand it's not really what you need." He compared human connection/disconnection to atoms, which are "mostly space, there's very little material there. They appear to be mostly material but it's actually just space. It doesn't take much to make something seem real but on closer inspection it's very empty." As a kind of summary, these thoughts—unusual for Elliott since he didn't often get into the origins of the songs' content—serve as artistic statement. When he looked inside to assess and evaluate, to describe the picture, what he saw, the target that popped up, was relationships. At first they seemed real, at first they seemed good for you, necessary, helpful, but as he turned them over in his head what struck him was the empty space between. Like addicts who seek to heighten their natural state—depressives who drink, manics who smoke crack—Elliott sometimes sought isolation. And judged entirely by its effects in and on the life, that strategy backfired. Or, from a different angle, it worked, because he got what he wanted. To say "it's only the songs that matter" is a cliché. But he meant it and lived it, and probably died it.

So what Elliott was after, always, was letting everything in, holding nothing back, the frank fullness of life, what artists are in the business of showing. What that meant, some of the time, was being a hurt, damaged person. This lent poignancy to the words and music, drew similarly vulnerable fans in, but the day-to-day life had to be managed. Now and then he checked to make sure he was "still here," as he said in "Last Call." All he "aspired to do was endure." Embracing only what was would require radical Zen-like self-acceptance, a moment-by-moment nonjudgmental awareness Elliott struggled to enact. This all got hyper-real in 1997. Very strangely, under peculiar circumstances, Elliott ran off a cliff. Without emotion he told interviewers, at least two of them, "Yeah, I jumped off a cliff, but let's talk about something else."[6] It was an invitation to pry and a refusal to enter into the details, strange in light of the explosiveness of the confession. What he seems to be doing is heading the interviewers off at the pass; it's a subject he's not willing to get into. And judging from the quote provided, his statement appears to be a response to a question, less a confession per se. About one year later he was more expansive. He told *Spin*: "I got freaked out and started running, it was totally dark, and I ran off the edge of a cliff. I saw it coming up and I wasn't like, 'I'm gonna throw myself off this cliff and die.'" It was more "who cares," he said.[7]

At this point, although the timeline is sketchy and difficult to track precisely, some time in late '96 or early '97 Elliott relocated to New York, having moved in, more or less, with Dorien Garry and two other roommates, both male—although to say he was "living" in this new space is a bit of an exaggeration. He didn't have his own room. He slept on the living room floor. No one's even sure exactly when he arrived. He was touring incessantly, mostly between cities, working hard to push sales of the solo material. He also tended to keep apartments or rooms in places after he'd actually moved out. It was a peripatetic time; he was out of New York performing as often as he was physically there. Dorien Garry he'd met at Maxwell's, a music club in Hoboken, N.J., across the Hudson River from Manhattan, where she sometimes moonlighted, serving and performing other odd jobs. That night he was playing with The Softies, whose debut record, *It's Love*, had appeared on Calvin Johnson's Olympia-based K Records; they'd also released, in January 1997, a seven-inch titled "The Best Days." Elliott and band members crashed in Garry's flat, a custom that repeated itself several times over ensuing months. When Elliott initially decided to leave Portland and relocate for real, it was Garry he turned to. They had become close; she was someone he could talk to, about things he found hard to share with others. A bit like Jason Mitchell, she was an excellent listener, and most important, she did not judge. Garry's real job at the time was with Girlie Action, a PR/publicity firm hired by Kill Rock Stars to manage Elliott's press. He chatted with her almost daily. It was mildly surprising when Elliott called one day to ask if he could move in, but without much hesitation Dorien said okay. As she recalls—although she can't be sure—Elliott arrived on her birthday, May 27, with a "giant army duffel bag and a guitar."[8]

The cliff jump, although there's legitimate question about whether to call it that, occurred on June 22, 1997. Dorien and Elliott had driven ten hours from New York to Raleigh, North Carolina. The occasion was a tenth-anniversary bash for Tannis Root, a merchandising company specializing in T-shirts. Bands were set to play, including Mudhoney, Red Cross, and Sonic Youth; Garry was friends with Thurston Moore and Kim Gordon, having worked for a time as their child's "touring nanny." The night she and Elliott arrived, worn down by the long drive south, everyone rendezvoused at a bar called the Sting Ray in Chapel Hill. It was "really fun," says Garry, everyone in a festive mood, the vibe distinctly celebratory. Elliott too, for most of that night, seemed to be having a very good time. He was a huge Mudhoney fan, so there was much to look forward to in the days ahead. But then, with a transformation very sudden and, in the moment, startling, "Elliott flipped a switch. He went from fun to none," Garry says. He'd been drinking, as had everyone. The booze, for most of the night, seemed to loosen him up; he was enjoying the buzz, laughing and cracking jokes. Yet, as Garry remembers it, one last drink pushed him past an imperceptible threshold. In an instant he was despairing and tearful, almost as if some chemical process kicked itself on. At the end of this transformation, Garry and Elliott climbed into the back seat of a car in order to give a friend a ride home. The night was very dark; out in the suburbs there were no streetlights, so it was nearly impossible to see much of anything. As they drove Elliott began to cry quietly; it was awkward and very sad, but Garry did her best to console him, asking him what was wrong and whether he was going to be okay, solicitations he didn't much respond to. The friend lived at the end of a cul de sac; it was hard to make out the house, the black night dropping a cape over objects below. As they came to a stop Elliott threw open the back door and bolted. "He was incredibly drunk and embarrassed" by the crying, Garry says, "and I don't think he even realized what he was doing." The impulse was simply to run, to put some distance between himself and the car and the people in it. To be alone, in other words. Garry recalls, "There was a drop-off at the end of the cul de sac that Elliott did not even see, no one could see it." So, without clear intention or any true sense of what he was in for, Elliott ran off the cliff, landing on a tree that stopped his fall and punctured his back badly.

Although in the interviews Elliott sometimes seemed to imply otherwise, Garry's sense is that "by no means was that a suicide attempt. He didn't know there was a cliff there, none of us did. It was just a mistake. I think he thought he was going down some kind of hill where he could be by himself and sit down and get things together." Even so, what seemed obvious to Garry was that "Elliott was not in control anymore, of his emotions or even his physical body, his impulses." She managed to track him down and free him from the tangle he was in, then took him back to their hotel where she tried cleaning his wound in the sink. He refused to go to a hospital, as she knew he would; for hours he apologized, saying all he wanted to do was sleep. "I was extremely shaken," Garry says. "I'd never seen anybody act like that, so emotionally and dangerously. It was really troubling me." When Elliott gave the interview in which he mentioned the cliff episode, he called Garry to let her know it had come up. He "chose to tell that story," Garry feels, chiefly out of what she always understood to be "an instinctual notion that he needed to be honest at all costs," an attitude going back to Texas, where in his family honesty occupied the status of a cardinal virtue. Even when it wasn't in his best interests, truth won out over lies.

There's a minor and superfluous disparity between the two accounts—Elliott's and Garry's more detailed version. Garry says no one saw any cliff; Elliott said he did but didn't care. What happened seems to be this: initially Elliott had no knowledge of a cliff, and only recognized the drop-off moments before he reached it. In the instant he made a snap decision to keep running anyway. As he said, his feeling was "who cares." Anyway, details aside, the "jump" can't be called a suicide attempt. It was more a *fall*. When he tumbled out of the car that night Elliott had no intention of trying to die. As far as he knew, up to the last moment there was no means, the cliff having materialized unexpectedly. Garry called the incident a "mistake." That appears to be what it was—an accident. But although Elliott didn't set out to die, the night exposes the state he now found himself in. For one thing, his drinking was a problem. He'd always drank, as had all his friends, but his use of alcohol was on the rise. He was drunk more often, and according to Garry, he was drinking during the day. This was the main reason for the road trip—to snap Elliott out of a pattern, to get him out of the house. By itself, the drinking might not have become the problem it eventually did had Elliott not also been taking antidepressants. At that time he was on one of the then-newer antidepressants, a selective-serotonin reuptake inhibitor, or SSRI. Garry isn't sure which one, but in the past he'd used both Paxil and Zoloft. Typically patients are told not to mix these drugs with alcohol, something Elliott was doing to excess (an indication of the low regard he had at the time for his psychological well-being). Also, although such reports had not come out yet—chiefly because of repeated drug company denials—SSRIs are now known to cause, in small subsets of patients, a sudden increase in suicidal thoughts. On balance, it's unlikely they did that to Elliott; his suicidal ideas predated his use of SSRIs. On the other hand, the drugs might have exacerbated self-destructive tendencies. They also might have potentiated the effects of the booze. As Dorien recalls, it was as if a switch flipped. One second Elliott was in a happy space, the next he was morose. Part of the reason for the suddenness of the shift, the mood lability, could have been chemically based.

What the cliff mishap also shows is what Dorien says it did—that Elliott was beginning to lose control. He was in a bad way, and he'd stopped caring that he was. In fact, the question about the jump, its suicidal aspects, is minor in the broadest sense. At a July 16 show at the Crocodile in Seattle, Elliott was pointedly telling friends goodbye. He said he'd jumped out of a car; he also said that were he to disappear, he wanted them to know he loved them. The implications of statements like these were not lost on anyone. Suicide appeared dangerously likely, and calls were made to management and others, mostly to apprise them, Margaret Mittleman in particular, of the direness of the situation and to plan, if necessary, some course of swift action should there be a need for it. Things were not improving, clearly; there was no easy end in sight. And the demands made on Elliott weren't helping. In the months leading up to the fall he was locked in a brutal tour schedule. In April there were seventeen shows, in May there were seven. Locations ranged from Boise to Chicago, Philadelphia to Tempe, San Francisco to Ontario. Over the first three weeks of April Elliott had exactly four nights off. Although he did not perform in June, he started up again July 15 in Olympia at Yo Yo a Go-Go, where he played a twenty-five-minute set, mostly of songs from *Either/Or*. Over the next two weeks there were five nights off, with still more dates, densely packed, right up to December.

As Leslie Uppinghouse and others have noted, performing was always a trial; it didn't come without pain of self-confrontation or occasional very strong anxiety that Elliott sometimes lubricated with booze. Plus, the dark, undeniably lovely and accomplished songs he featured, the ones he was touring behind, kept striking him as worthless: "One or two of them sucked," he said. "Then three or four of them sucked. Then they all sucked and everything I did was terrible."[9] He was in a gutter of catastrophic, irrational lines of thought, the kind one expects to find in a person very depressed, an avalanche of negative tunnel vision that to others made little sense in light of objective facts.

The odds are good, then, that Elliott was spent, if not exhausted, by June 1997. But the show beat on, near-death a temporary inconvenience. He'd go forward or burn out trying. Two writers Elliott admired, Kafka and Kierkegaard, addressed the pit he now found himself looking up out of. As Kafka put it, with characteristic precision: "This tremendous world I have inside of me. How to free myself, and this world, without tearing myself to pieces. And rather tear myself to a thousand pieces than be buried with this world within me." Then Kierkegaard: "A little pinch of spice. Here, a man must be sacrificed. He is needed to impart a particular taste to the rest." Rimbaud, too, pursues the same thought train, arriving at the realization that he's a poet, but his fate isn't his fault. "Too bad for the wood that finds itself a violin."[10] There's a price to pay for making art. Not always or inevitably, but often. It goes back to Mailer and the wound. But the cost can be high. On the list of priorities, for Kafka, Kierkegaard, Rimbaud, maybe for Elliott too, life came second. It was sacrificed to the gift, the calling, which felt more alive than life, far more valuable than its diviner.

There were several steps Elliott took away from his own self-interests in 1997. He was in a mode of escape, it seems. Portland was stale, a West Coast Texas where too many emotional bombs had exploded. As Krebs said succinctly, "There was too much shit there." The local rock-god role was tough to take; everywhere he turned he knew someone who looked at him sideways with expectations, assumptions, requests. Early in the year he was of a mixed mind. First he'd just mulled over taking off for New York, but hadn't foreclosed on the possibility. The idea was that, there, he could be just anybody. He craved anonymity, a nowhere man sort of existence. On the other hand, the prospect seemed doubtful. "My problems won't be any different in New York that they are here," he realized initially. Also: "I can't pretend anymore like I could be just anybody. There are things about me that would be present in New York, just the same as here." So the idea had been put on hold for a time. "This is where I'm from," Elliott told Chandler and Wagner in 1997, referring to Portland, "and I'm going to stick with it."

That decision reversed itself, however. The trouble was, although staying in Portland may have saved his life—it was a place that, on balance, checked his more dangerously self-destructive instincts, a place where guilt kept him sequestered from possibly disastrous dalliances, lures such as heroin—it also locked him into various dilemmas. In Portland the "endless stream of reminders" he wrote about in "Last Call," the ones he'd gotten so sick of, kept guard around any corner. But apart from desiring relative anonymity, another reason behind thoughts of taking off somewhere new, about as far as he could get in the U.S., had to do with girlfriend Joanna Bolme. Bolme is an elusive person in Elliott's story. Although the two were very close, and although Bolme knew Elliott intimately for longer than most anyone else in his life and was thus an extraordinarily important person for him, one also deeply connected to the music side of things, she rarely has gone on record to talk about their relationship, or even about Elliott apart from the relationship. An understandably private individual, particularly on this subject, Bolme's friends even mention her reticence, how she kept her feelings close. She always seemed, to some, hard to read, distant, occasionally abrupt, difficult to click with. In short, she was a mystery with what appeared to be a lot going on inside; and just like Elliott himself, she was not the sort of person who ever easily or readily opened up to others. She and Elliott first met in 1991, just after he moved back to Portland from college. A friend introduced them. Elliott "kind of waved and was shy," she says.[11] Still, she did not get to know him well until some time later, when she worked at a bar. "That's when we became friends." It was Neil Gust, in fact, who played matchmaker. "I made him talk to her," he recalls, "I made him do it." At the time he'd been aware of Bolme only from afar, and he didn't come away with a comfortable feeling. Far from it. "She scared the shit out of me," he says, "and I was totally intimidated." According to Gust, Elliott figured Joanna was out of his league. He guessed she wouldn't give him a second look. But Gust says, "I was like, 'She is fucking hot. Don't be afraid. She'll love you.'" In truth he wasn't sure himself that Elliott stood a chance, but Elliott had always encouraged him whenever he had a crush on someone, so Gust returned the favor. "It was his birthday, we were at La Luna [in Portland] where Joanna bartended, and I kept nudging him." They ended up playing pool together. "They had this lovely chemistry," Gust recalls. "He asked her out. It was so lovely."[12]

In agreement with what most everyone says about Elliott, a collective effort to offset all the talk about his crippling depressions, Bolme alludes to how funny he was, his droll, straight-man sense of humor, his aslant take on

Elliott goofing off near Portland's Ladd's Addition neighborhood. (Photograph by JJ Gonson.)

things, especially all things pompous or self-admiring. "He was pretty gregarious once you got to know him," Bolme adds, "[and although] he was always uncomfortable with being human and getting through life, he was still a social person who cooked his own meals, made his own coffee, could wire a studio, that sort of stuff."[13] He was not completely undone by his afflictions, in other words, no "Mr. Misery." He could be, and behave, like anyone else around the scene when he was in a good space, with people he cared about and trusted. Still, at bottom, he had, as Bolme said, that abiding lack of interest in his own life. Some hooked cane from hell kept pulling him down, and as Gonson had also said, when he got dark, he got very, very dark. Elliott loved Joanna deeply, friends say, but the relationship was rocky. Although she obviously really cared about him, he broke up with her several times—part of a compulsion, according to friends, to undo or destroy the good things or people in his life. By 1997 the relationship was off and on, Elliott's interest in drugs the "main culprit," says Bolme. When Krebs dated Bolme "I was a bastard," he says. "And I don't think Elliott improved on my record."

So, overcoming his ambivalences, his doubts about whether it would really improve things, and to get distance, from Bolme and from all that

Portland was starting to signify, Elliott finally did take off, months before the fall from the cliff in North Carolina. And what he said before leaving for New York, the goodbyes he distributed, were deeply alarming, weirdly prescient. Jason Mitchell recalls one conversation in the Space Room on Hawthorne, the night before he left. Elliott said, "Just so you know, if you get a call that something happened to me, don't be surprised . . ." He went on, making sure Mitchell knew it would be no one's fault, telling him not to feel guilty, telling him, again, as he did to more than one person, that there was nothing anyone could have done, nothing particular that could have made any difference in whatever outcome materialized. To Mitchell, New York morphed into a place where Elliott "felt freer to be self-destructive"—a judgment no one close to him would have disagreed with. Looking back, New York seemed, to Mitchell, like the first in a sequence of steps toward catastrophe. At the same time it could be hard to know what to take seriously, and what to dismiss, or what to assume any responsibility for. Over time feelings of resignation set in. As Gust said, "He made his own choices . . . When he bought the myth of being a rock star"—the one emblazoned by Cobain—"it was just unbelievably disappointing." Gust compared the process to the kind of effortful posing people do in photographs: "It's obvious when they are failing at what they are trying to be."[14] Sam Coomes tentatively and very diplomatically suggested the same dynamic. "Part of me is a little bit—this is weird, and I question whether it's sort of petty—but I suspect . . . I mean, Elliott was sort of actively involved in his own sort of myth-making, and I think he was interested in that, and it was something that I kind of frowned on. I always felt like I didn't want to facilitate that much . . . He wanted to be a certain way and be thought of in a certain way, and why not?"[15] Coomes's band Quasi, who toured with Elliott in 1997, went so far to record a song, "The Poisoned Well," that seems to address Elliott's no-win situation. After mentioning an artist's documentation of suicide, Coomes sings, "You won't live long, but you may write the perfect song." Then, in reference to his reluctance to perpetuate Elliott's myth, Coomes concludes, "Please excuse those who choose not to play along." Later Elliott responded to this tune with one of his own, "From a Poison Well"; he accepted the appellation, then sent a message back.

* * *

In its essence, it's hard to see the move to New York as anything but a semi-planned descent into darkness. Not that there weren't good times too; there were plenty of those. But Elliott always courted demons, as Krebs suggested. Only now he was shaking their hands, getting to know them intimately, hoping they might rub off. The fall was alarming, in particular its impulsivity, how Elliott simply bolted from the car bound for who knows where. Yet that was just one of several strange episodes. There were also fights or near-fights in bars, news of which, when it traveled back to Portland, struck friends there as preposterous, bizarrely out of character. On occasion he actively looked for fights. This was definitely new. In Portland the most Elliott did in bars was play video poker or cry; in New York it was fisticuffs.

The one fight, mentioned before, was a reaction. As Garry, who was there, recalls, "Some guy made a shitty comment about a girl and Elliott just lost it."[16] He called the guy out, told him he was an asshole. There was pushing and shoving, Elliott punched the guy, "and then he [Elliott] got pushed down and ended up falling on a pint glass," which cut his back up badly (a photo taken by Autumn de Wilde shows this wound). As he did after the cliff fall, Elliott refused to go to the hospital. He went home with Garry instead and fixed the wounds up himself as best he could.

That altercation occurred at Max Fish on the Lower East Side; there was another run-in there too. Elliott had stepped out for a cigarette, and as it happened, Garry's car was parked out front. Elliott "saw this guy taking a leak on my car. He said something like, 'Go pee somewhere else!' I think he got punched," Dorien says. Later she told him: "That was sweet, and thanks for looking out for your friends and all, but for Christ sakes just let the guy pee on my car. It's not worth getting punched on the street for."[17] Elliott was looking for trouble and finding it.

Another confrontation had a similar vibe. It relates to a woman—Dorien, in fact—but it's also excessive, in some ways comical. Elliott and Dorien were at another bar—it's how they tended to spend most nights, going out and drinking, not always to excess, playing pool, hanging around with friends. Suddenly someone pulled her aside and told her she needed to go to the back—a fight was about to erupt. A "lame" guy she had been dating had entered the place. And without her knowing, while her back was literally turned, "Elliott took it upon himself to go meet the guy . . . and tell him to drink somewhere else." In this instance the guy in question "totally knew who [Elliott] was. He was a big fan of Elliott's and got really embarrassed. It was very sweet and funny, but I was like, 'You're going to get hurt someday.'" Not, Garry meant, by this particular guy, who had the unusual experience of being ambushed by one of his idols, but by someone else, some day, who knew when. "He would pick little fights with people," says Garry, implying that these three events were not exhaustive of every such run-in. "[And] some days Elliott would get hurt when he tried that stuff out." There was something a little "big-brotherly" about it, Garry says. Elliott was super-aware, she adds, guessing that he saw the guy enter and decided he wasn't going to let him bum Dorien out. But a lot of times, and she never knew quite when, Garry says "things would go tits-up and I would have to go pick up the pieces of the mess he had just made."[18]

Not that bars were always sites of unwelcome—or welcome, as the case may be—violence. Elliott hung out in them not just to possibly get beat up—anger was always an issue, a leftover from childhood, but the fights were acts of self-destruction more than anything else—not only to drink, which he was doing at home, and alone, but to listen to music. Sometimes the music was live, but usually it was jukebox stuff. "If you went to a bar with him," Garry says, "you always went to the jukebox, and you put your songs in, and you made sure your songs were coming pretty soon before you settled in somewhere for the night . . . kind of take over the jukebox."[19] On occasion he'd put as much as forty dollars in the machine. Selections might range from George Jones to Hank Williams, Jr., from "schmaltzy '70s soft rock" like Chicago ("If You Leave Me Now") and Seals and Crofts ("Summer Breeze") to the Scorpions or Foreigner or Charlie Rich ("The Most Beautiful Girl"). As always Elliott's affections could be surprising. He liked stuff uncool to like. He respected the expertly crafted tune. Stevie Wonder was another favorite. Garry went to high school with Wonder's kids, and Elliott asked her over and over to tell the story about the blind man *driving a car*. "If I saw Elliott getting really bummed out," Dorien says, "I would say, 'Do you want to hear the Stevie Wonder drives a car around the parking lot story again?'"

Garry recalls one frequent haunt—a little neighborhood fisherman's bar called Harbor Casino in Jersey City, inhospitable to hipsters. It was torn down eventually, replaced by condos. She and Elliott were usually the youngest people in the place. They were gifted with their own nickname, the "Beatles kids," since those were the songs they picked out most often. But they were both also really obsessed with Roy Orbison, the golden-voiced songsmith. One thing Elliott did more than once, touching and faintly sad, was select Orbison's "Running Scared"—a song about rivals anxiously competing for a lover—then immediately leave. Garry recalls, "He would have to physically step out of the bar for it. I was always like, 'Why did you play it if you were going to stand outside?' He's like, 'It's such a beautiful song. I'm waiting for the day I can just sit here and not let it totally destroy me.'"[20] Outside he still got muffled, distant sounds of the music, but not the lyrics. There were plenty of funny times too. Once he and Garry discussed which song, however cheesy, however vile, made them both so upset, so overcome by sadness, that listening to the lyrics was a virtual impossibility. The answer: Phil Collins's "Against All Odds."

A different discussion centered on Joni Mitchell's notoriously dark album *Blue*. One night by chance Elliott stumbled across the record in Garry's collection. Immediately he asked if she'd listened to it. She said no, she hadn't got around to putting it on and checking it out. Funnily, he was relieved. "He made me promise never to touch it. He said it would change me forever." Stay away from it if you know what's good for you, was the basic, partly comical, message. But one night, after drinking half a bottle of red wine, Dorien couldn't help herself. She slid *Blue* out and stuck it on the turntable. Unexpectedly Elliott walked in. "Fuck! You did it!" he said. "You've now taken the irreversible journey of getting real bummed out on Joni's *Blue*."

One relatively unlikely subject was, of all things, clowns. Elliott had a hoax he talked about trying. He pictured driving to the Canadian border, ostensibly to play shows in Montreal or Toronto. As border guards stopped him, he'd step out in a clown outfit, proclaiming a desire to "break into the Canadian clown world." He was prone to wearing squirting flowers, buying rough approximations of clown shoes wherever he could find them. Once he and Sean Croghan, visiting from Portland, rewrote lyrics to the Doors' "The End" so the title character was a clown, his shoes "flopping on down the hall." "I think it's kind of symbolic," says Garry. "I think Elliott had a big inner clown that was dying to get out."

It did get out, more often than most imagined. No one ever underestimated Elliott's enormous talent for humor. It was a saving grace. But just like the stereotypical clown figure, when the face wasn't smiling, it was riven by tears. It's that duality, the clown's hidden dark side, the grimace under the grin, that scares so many kids shitless. As nights at the bars dilated into morning, more times than not Elliott stayed on by himself after Dorien needed to take off. She was around twenty when she met him, and she wasn't a major partier. So when she couldn't extricate him in time for her to get them both home and to bed so she could wake at a reasonable hour in the morning before taking off for work, "he would just stay out until whenever." More than once he was out all night, at Luna Lounge, Bar 88, Blue and Gold. More than once he was "shit-faced." He'd read Jennifer Toth's 1993 book *The Mole People*, an allegedly true account of interviews with tunnel dwellers, homeless people who lived in ordered tribes underground, in subways or abandoned structures. Legend had it that there were hundreds of these groups with cultural traits, formed complex societies, pseudofamilies with codes of conduct siphoning electricity from city grids. Toth took heat for the book. Claims were made that her stories were apocryphal. Attempts to verify met with little success. Still, Elliott was curious. Garry discovered that, on nights he was drunk and out alone, with no one around to keep him in check or look out for his best interests, he'd go down into the subways searching out these communities of people living in hiding. And "he did it shit-faced. It's so dangerous. I can't even fathom," she said. "My worst nightmare is falling off a subway platform, let alone crawling down one and walking through the tunnels." He never did find what he was after; he made no contact with tunnel dwellers. But, as Garry remembers, "there was so much like that, playing with fire, testing his limits, and testing fate down there."[21] The kind of thing, in other words, he'd told Mitchell he went to New York to do. In Garry's view, all the critical attention, the push to sell records—still, at best, only very mildly successful commercially—the fans, the performances, the music itself—none of those things erased the fact that "he had all this stuff he just couldn't . . . deal with. It didn't make it any better; it didn't make it any easier to go through the day. Like, at the end of the day, *just let the people who bummed you out leave your head.*" That is what Elliott was not able to do. The people stayed in his head; they kept bumming him out.

Initially Dorien was Elliott's "first and only friend" in New York. They were never more than friends, but as she says, "I was a little confused on occasion about his feelings for me." Mainly he assumed the role of big-brother protector. He watched out for her, offered advice. He had her back always. At the same time he "hated every boyfriend I ever had," she says, an attitude suggesting he may have felt an attraction of some sort, or else simply distrusted the motives of men. He was an exceptional "people-reader," according to Garry. He had an acute sense of what people were thinking or feeling at any given moment; he sized them up quickly and often unerringly. So the guys trying to get close to Dorien he judged, more often than not, to be suspect. He wanted closeness; he was feeling alone. Perhaps, then, a part of him wondered whether he and Dorien might grow to be more than friends. After all, the breakup with Joanna had been devastating. They'd agreed to separate, Garry recalls, and to seek a distance aimed at guaranteeing the relationship's demise. As Elliott had taken off for New York, Joanna relocated to Chicago. They committed, mutually, to not seeing each other. It was too difficult otherwise. But Elliott "was desperate for love," Dorien says. And at some point while touring in the Northeast he managed to find it, at least temporarily. At a show he met a girl named Amity. Garry never knew her well, and can't remember her last name; she seemed to be from somewhere in New England. One day Elliott phoned to ask whether she could stay for a while in New York, and as she always did, Dorien said "fine."

This new girl was extremely cute, "lovely and adorable," very sweet but also, Garry and most others felt, very "young." She was "bright-eyed" and eager yet obviously unsophisticated, a kind of high-def version of the callow innocent. A virtual Joanna antithesis, Amity's dissimilarity from Bolme instantly struck Dorien as "totally insane." She made no sense; she wasn't the kind of person anyone imagined Elliott being into. Whatever the case, he was smitten. Pete Krebs recalls him flashing around a photograph proudly, almost in disbelief at his good fortune in nabbing her. She'd never been to New York, Garry recalls, so when she arrived she wanted to do all the usual touristy things which Elliott, very uncharacteristically, tried arranging, working hard to put together an itinerary. This wasn't the sort of thing Elliott was good at or ever did; that he put the effort in indicates his degree of devotion. They toured the city, checked out all the obligatory sights and scenes. It was puppy love, cute and surprising to see, but it did not last long, nor did it end at all badly. For one thing Elliott was too busy touring. "His life was still way too up in the air," Garry says. He hadn't yet made serious money, so he scrambled always to make ends meet. He was therefore "hardly in a position to commit to anybody," as Dorien saw it. The flirtation, however exciting and affirming at the time, ran its course. Love came, but in the moment it was impossible to imagine a way of turning it into something viable. What remained, in the end, was what often remained—a song titled, simply, "Amity." In it Elliott notes Amity's "Hello Kitty" cuteness. She catches stars in her arms, and as they walk New York City together she feels "like a lucky charm," her freshness contrasting his own inner "junk" made by God. The lyrics are succinct, hopeful, and rapt. But the song never comes off. In fact, it may be one of Elliott's few failures. As he said, he liked to write when unhappy. Happiness, this time, derailed the music. What he seems to want to do most in the tune is repeat her name, which he does on two separate occasions, a lucky seven times each.

In interviews Elliott laughed the song off, although not without adding an element of pathos. "It's just a big rock song," he told Pamela Chelin, "it's a pretty simple song. It's not so much about the words themselves, but more about how the whole thing sounds." Friends saw through to the tune's true meaning, suggesting "it sounded like I was trying to get something romantic going with someone." Elliott confided "It's a person I know," then added, with a painful honesty characteristic of his approach to even the most superficial interviews, "It was supposed to be—'You're really fun to be with and I really like you a lot because of that, but I am really, really depressed'— but I don't think it came across when I said, 'ready to go,' it was supposed to mean 'tired of living.'" The interviewer stopped short. "Oh," she replied, apparently startled, "like, ready to check out of this world?" "Yeah," Elliott answered, "I was saying, 'I really like you and it's really great to hang out with someone who is happy and easygoing, but I don't feel like that and I can't be that way.'"[22] This was the usual posture. His feeling, one eternally returning, was that he ought not commit to lovers, ought to refuse their love even, no matter how promising or sincere, because his plan was to not be around for long. It was a painful attitude to adopt toward relationships, but at least it was fair and honest, driven by a desire not to cause more hurt than necessary. But it more or less guaranteed isolation.

The hoped-for incantation therefore brought no lasting, revivifying genie from the bottle. Amity was a sweet distraction, an unspoiled partial antidote, but true cure was too much to risk imagining. There would be more Joanna replacements, but these were years off, and marked, as always, by extreme approach/avoidance conflicts. Lacking someone in whom he might locate some small degree of solace, some possibility of comfort, intimacy, and affection, Elliott's mood darkened even more. Without quite knowing it, he was on a track to rock bottom and to a life-altering confrontation. The touring kept taking its toll, different cities every night, different hushed audiences to gauge and win over. And because Dorien was available and sympathetic, willing to listen even if she didn't always quite know what to say, Elliott fell into the habit of calling her almost every night, usually late, from phone booths in whatever city he happened to find himself. These talks could go on for hours, well past the time when Garry needed to be in bed sleeping, resting up for work the next day. Her role, it seemed to Garry, was pseudo-therapist, and it was rarely easy; she felt uncertain, out of her depth. But she did what she could. Elliott was in a tough spot emotionally, and he needed someone in whom he could confide, someone he trusted who would not find fault. The subjects were Joanna, his darkening mood, his drinking, and often, to a degree that was becoming routine, the possibility of suicide. To hear all this was sad and frightening. There were times, no doubt, when Dorien wasn't sure Elliott would survive to see the next day. At last, after many such conversations circling around the same painful nuclei, Elliott sent Dorien an e-mail. He laid out where he was at, saying, in the end, that he could not take it any longer and that he was not sure how much longer he could be in the world. What the message seemed to say was goodbye. There was a conclusiveness to it. Freaked out and feeling as if something needed to be done, feeling, also, that things had progressed to such a point that she could not shoulder the burden on her own, Garry shared the e-mail with her boss at Girlie Action, Felice

Ecker. The immediate question was what to do. Should they take action, or should they hold off for the time being? Ecker panicked, as Garry recalls. Her impulse was to contact Slim Moon at Kill Rock Stars, Elliott's label, and Margaret Mittleman. Dorien wasn't on board. "I knew that wasn't going to sit well with Elliott. He didn't like being told what to do, ever. He was very stubborn. He also was extremely mindful about what he needed." Instantly she regretted showing Ecker the e-mail. "I was conflicted," says Garry. "It seemed like a betrayal of trust. At the time, as far as I knew, he was only talking about these things with me. I worried he'd never confide to anyone again. Plus, I had no faith in what the 'adults' in this situation, those on the music industry side of things, were going to decide to do." Business interests, represented by people who weren't first and foremost Elliott's friends, had one set of concerns; those he was truly close to, who knew him best and understood what kinds of reactions might backfire, had different, competing loyalties. Yet now, although the two groups didn't see eye to eye, they were in league. Garry felt like a kid who had told on a friend to grown-ups.

Moon was "very much on high alert," says Garry. He'd seen other musicians die, so he took the news extremely seriously; he did not want a repeat. The decision, chiefly his, was to stage an intervention, the one occurring four or five months prior to Elliott's Oscar nomination, the storm before the calm. Moon reached out to a Long Island specialist named Lou Cox who had also worked with Aerosmith years before. Pressure was applied to Garry to be there, but at first she was reluctant. She didn't think it would work, for one. She also doubted it was the right thing to do. Still, for Elliott's sake, and despite her fear that he'd see her as a betrayer, she finally relented. Others from the friend faction were also convinced to join in. Sam Coomes's new band Quasi had been playing dates with Elliott, so he and Janet Weiss were approached. Joanna, Neil Gust, and Rebecca Gates, another Portland friend who had sung backup on the song "St. Ides Heaven," all agreed to be present as well. From the business end there was Moon, Felice Ecker, and, as Garry recalls, Ellen Stewart, Elliott's booking agent. The process was typical. Everyone spent two days with Cox prepping. He laid out what he felt needed to happen, the timing, the organization, the requirement to be firm and direct but supportive. In short, the basic intervention algorithm. Per custom there was a strict secrecy element no one felt particularly comfortable with. Elliott would not know in advance what was going on. The event was to be, by its very nature, an ambush. Garry says, "We were supposed to say all the things he had done that had worried us, to share our stories. It was supposed to include stuff he'd done in Portland too, not just in New York. The whole time I was like, 'This is going to fucking backfire colossally.'"

The event, lasting several hours, was staged in the middle of the '97 tour, in Chicago, some time in late July at the home of Rebecca Gates. Everyone assembled in Gates's kitchen, waiting. What Elliott had been told— Garry isn't sure by whom—was that he'd be having lunch there. At no point did he apparently suspect what was in store. Yet as he walked into the room he instantly recognized "what was up," Garry says, "and he was not happy." Cox took the lead as planned. He gave the equivalent of an introductory speech. He told Elliott everyone was there because they loved him. He outlined the format of the proceedings. He gave an overview of the timeline and of the goals for the meeting. And at the end of this no doubt shocking and, for Elliott, infuriating prologue, Elliott decided to stay in the room and listen. The friends present had talked beforehand. They all agreed they were there for support only, not to dogmatically declare Elliott needed to do anything specific, not, in other words, to strong-arm him, because they knew that was a tactic he'd reject categorically. Their message was: "Whatever you choose to do, we love and support you." They also told him, in words that made an impact, Garry felt, since they spoke to a major portion of the conflict, that if he were feeling "shitty"—exhausted emotionally and physically—he didn't need to keep up the tour. "We said he could put the whole thing on hold. He could just stop the train. For now or for forever." This was a sentiment Elliott appreciated, Garry believes. "It made him more responsive and a little more able to listen to the rest."

Then the stories came. Industry people weighed in first, friends at the very end. As people spoke Garry felt unanticipated relief. She realized that what had been happening was not new. Everyone recounted experiences similar to hers. In some vague way that fact made her feel less alone. All of it—the depressions, the suicidal thoughts, the recklessness, the low self-regard—"had been happening off and on for years," she now recognized. It wasn't a New York thing. It wasn't specific to her. The burden was no longer hers uniquely to make sense of and absorb.

It was anything but easy, and Elliott was very angry, incensed at being blindsided, enraged by the various sets of motives in play and the presumptuousness of people thinking they knew what was best for him or what he somehow needed to do, as if he couldn't deal with his own inner torment, something he'd been living with and managing, not always well of course, for nearly a decade. But at the end of the ordeal, as a plan was presented, Elliott agreed to try following it—which shocked Dorien—although he was unwilling to promise complete compliance. Cox had already selected a hospital, a place in Arizona called Sierra Tucson, a residential program founded in the mid-1980s, specializing in what it called "coexisting disorders"— addictions combined with trauma, mood disorders, chronic pain, eating disorders. That angle had seemed appropriate. Sierra Tuscon was not only a detox center. It was, in essence, a glorified psych unit with a less institutionalized veneer. The twin targets would be Elliott's depression and his drinking, a combination usually referred to as dual diagnosis. He was dealing with what clinicians sometimes refer to as the "holy trinity"—addiction, suicidal thinking, and mood disorder. Length of stay at the facility varied according to individual circumstance, but the minimum required commitment was thirty days, which might stretch to ninety or more in rare cases. Most rooms were doubles. There was breakfast at the ungodly hour of six forty-five (earlier for eating disorder patients), then lectures, groups (crafts, relaxation, twelve-step, and so on), community meetings, one-to-ones, and family work, if necessary, followed by dinner at five and the end of programming at nine or nine thirty. Everyone knew, except maybe Cox, that this was precisely the sort of top-down, imposed structure Elliott detested. It was foreign to his nature. He almost never did anything "on schedule." The odds he'd shift the experience into a turning point, a personal epiphany, were slim at best. As Garry said, and she was hardly alone, "I didn't think it would work to begin with." But he agreed to go, he agreed to try. The deal was that he'd play a handful of additional dates, up to a Knitting Factory gig in New York, then fly to Arizona along with Joanna some time in early September 1997. It was unusual—typically interventions conclude with the patient flying to treatment immediately, leaving no opportunity for backsliding—but it had to do. It beat the alternative—doing nothing, extending the status quo.

At the designated time Elliott got on the plane, he checked into the glorified hospital, he started the program, but he did not stay. He bailed. By this time booze had become his primary mood stabilizer, his mood defeater. It was the one reliable path to his most cherished state—painless oblivion. As he'd put it in Heatmiser's "Plainclothes Man," alcohol was the only thing he "really needed," "something that will treat me okay, and wouldn't say the things you'd say." Drink was a faithful friend. The booze abided, always, and it didn't talk back, it was kind, dependable.

On a hot September day in New York Garry had gone to the beach with a friend. As she returned home and opened the door to the apartment, there, to her partial surprise, was Elliott, sitting in the living room. "Hey, I'm home," he said. "I decided I couldn't do it." Garry's response was disappointment mixed with fear about what might happen next, how the pattern might reinstate itself—that entrenched "holy trinity"—but as she'd insisted all along, from the plan's inception, "I never had any belief that it was going to work." He gave the "typical Elliott reasons" for discharging. He didn't like the staff or patients. There was no rapport. And he found the group therapies, crafts and so on, occupational therapy–type interventions, "annoying." Making collages from magazine pictures cut out with safety scissors, constructing "welcome mats" to take home for later use, building tiny painted jewelry boxes—all of it struck him as time wasting and ridiculous. He didn't see the point. His natural bent was skeptical, and there was plenty to be skeptical about at Sierra Tucson. Nonetheless, Dorien sought whatever silver lining she could in the experience. "Maybe he knew now the jig is up," she concluded hopefully. He'd gotten the message that people believed he was in trouble, so perhaps that would translate into internally executed change. It seemed like the most anyone could hope for, given how things had turned out. The plan that evening had been to meet Janet Weiss for drinks. Elliott asked to tag along, Weiss naturally surprised to see him. But the two had a long talk. "Elliott wanted to go and tell her what had happened," Garry says, to try explaining the change of course.

As days went on Elliott was anything but contrite. His mode was not apologetic. He expressed little guilt. What he was, for weeks and months thereafter, was angry. "What I had to do now," Garry says, "was deal with his anger. He wasn't angry at me at all, for some reason. But basically he felt like the whole response was too reactionary. Mostly he was angry at Slim. He wasn't nearly as mad at anyone else. He needed to direct his anger somewhere, and Slim got it." He would keep getting it too. That particular relationship never healed. Others would, without great difficulty, but from here on out Elliott cut Moon off. And in time his deal with Kill Rock Stars would also go by the wayside.

What, exactly, Elliott was into besides alcohol proved, in mid-1997, hard to figure out. Everyone smoked dope, of course, but in New York Elliott's tendency was to abstain. Weed made him too paranoid, Garry recalls. As for harder drugs—speed, cocaine, meth, heroin—the ones he'd implied he might try upon leaving Portland, Garry wasn't directly aware of those being any kind of issue. Vaguely she recalled Elliott mentioning sampling heroin even in college, but that was all he'd said. Never did she find him in a state suggesting more than drunkenness. Yet, as she explains, "I was really young, and I had no reference point for when things were getting out of control." His attitude toward her wavered, too. On one hand he was comfortable in the friendship, inclined to confide freely. On the other he was protective, especially "as far as me knowing too much." So he could have been using, for all Dorien knew, but keeping it secret. He wasn't around a lot and she didn't know all of his acquaintances, so what he was up to in the middle of the night as Garry slept was a bit of a mystery. Any drug use, she says, "he may have kept compartmentalized." At any rate, he did not go to Sierra Tuscon for anything like heroin addiction. It was the drinking and the expression of suicidal ideas that led to the intervention, not a concern relating to harder drugs. Those would come soon enough. But in New York, he wasn't a junkie.

As far as years in a short life go, 1997 may have been Elliott's most eventful. He had signed with a new label (although that situation would quickly change). *Either/Or* was an artistic triumph—but no commercial juggernaut. He was back on the East Coast, heartbroken over ending a uniquely significant relationship. There had been the cliff fall, the intervention, the stint at Sierra Tuscon. It was a bewildering mixture of very good and very bad. But more good was imminent. Soon it would be Oscar time. As he stepped onto that worldwide stage, in his white suit, holding nothing but his guitar for protection, almost undone by the sight of rotund Jack Nicholson feet away, it could only have seemed, as it did to friends around the nation, like a moon landing. How did he get there? What did it mean? The crowd took in the nervous kid next door—someone they'd babysat, someone they'd coached on a soccer team. The lyrics might have been a tip-off, if anyone paid attention. But chances are no one inferred the "troublemaker below," the inner demon whose taste in suits was anything but white.

CHAPTER SEVEN ROBOT HAND

The intervention's failure was not, obviously, a hopeful sign. Had he stuck with it, had he found some way of overlooking the deadening tedium of the inpatient routine, had he come to see the depression, the suicidal thinking, the drinking as a trio of enemies, the attitude shift might have saved Elliott. What it seems to come down to, for most people in a similar predicament, is a commitment to placing supreme value on one's life and regarding all anti-life forces as egodystonic, in clinical terms—in other words, *not me*. Psychologically, the failure suggested a refusal to relinquish devices that weren't working. Or, from a different angle, they *were* working, they *were* effective, but they guaranteed a larger, deeper, long-term failure. There was the alcohol. There was the longing for non-being, that fantasized escape from chronic feelings of worthlessness. But more important, there was the depression, Kierkegaard's "faithful mistress," which as Gonson had said, Elliott was in love with. He had a hard time imagining life without it, and he'd come to connect it with his creativity. Far from seeing it as an enemy, he clung to it as indispensable. He was a ghostwriter, he said, "for an ocean in a shell, from a poison well." It was the poison he dipped into. What remained when the poison was gone? He knew the poison; what he didn't know was what life might feel like without it. Fans, too, wanted the "sad song symphony." The sadness was the act. They came to feel it, to mutely observe, to find themselves vicariously redeemed, just like Kafka's hunger artist's groupies. They weren't there for new songs or happy songs. They wanted Elliott to "go down." They were there for the torment saint. It was his job to deliver them from evil, to share his vulnerability genius.

The intervention had another negative side effect. In its aftermath different long-term friendships began eroding slightly. It was difficult to stick by a person with so little interest in self-preservation. There was scant faith he'd get any better. He'd asked in songs why anyone kept faith "with this disaster." Friends started wondering the same thing. Most stuck it out, but with a building feeling of hopelessness and dread. Happy endings were hard to visualize.

So after leaving Arizona, bailing out on Sierra Tucson and dropping back down almost magically on Dorien's couch, Elliott's existence got even more peripatetic, not unlike the days in Portland when he lived, unofficially, at JJ's while he kept a room in the Heatmiser house. His habit, in fact, had always been to keep spaces as he relocated. He was usually spread out all over, in a state of metaphysical homelessness. Eventually the arrangement with Dorien came to a natural end. The entire time he was there he kept insisting he needed to find his own place soon. "He was hyperaware he was in somebody's space," Dorien says. And although her two male roommates "really liked him in the beginning," after many months "they were like, 'How long is he staying?'" One roommate was a merch guy, on tour a lot, "so that bought Elliott more time." Still, it was not a setup built to last. At some point, then, he moved to Park Slope in Brooklyn, to a flat including his own room (something he did not have at Garry's), with a very sweet couple, Shawna and Pierre, who were friends with Ellen Stewart. Soon the couple moved to a different apartment in Park Slope, and Elliott tagged along. Later he'd also live for a time with artist and college friend Marc Swanson, and with a woman, Jackie Ferry, whom no one knew well but who had some sort of job in the music industry, according to friends of Elliott's.

In New York Elliott's sister Ashley reentered his life on a semi-regular basis, although there had never been any real estrangement to speak of. She'd started college at University of Southern California, so she was on the other side of the country. But they made a mutual promise to always be together on Thanksgiving. It was their special holiday. She would travel to wherever he was to spend the week with him, wherever he happened to wind up on the holiday, Park Slope, Jersey City, or Hoboken. For the first time she got to know his newer friends, including Dorien and others. "He opened up this whole new world to me," she says. "I was pretty rigid and math-minded"—this was the primary subject she studied in college, although later she also developed a strong interest in primate, specifically chimpanzee, research. "I had blinders on," she adds, "it was an awakening for me . . . He was totally different than all my friends and how I'd grown up. He was open-minded and really compassionate . . . just the open-mindedness and the artistic side, his activist mentality, his fairness, he totally turned that on in me." The meals put together always made for happy, positive, festive occasions, everyone chipping in with entrées or side dishes. Often the combination of people present was slapdash, more or less accidental. Once Elliott was in charge of carving the turkey, which they'd named Tom. On another occasion the turkey seemed to be undercooked. Everyone started panicking, calling mothers for advice. "So it took hours," Ashley says. "There was me, his little sister, like a little dork visiting from California, but I had such a blast!" After finally getting the turkey figured out, essentially slow-cooking it, Ashley, Elliott, and Kazu Makino from Blonde Redhead took off for the video store, at last deciding on *Austin Powers*. Ashley recalls, "We got back and put in the movie, and within half an hour all of us were just like snoring, asleep."[1]

Ashley and Elliott also toured the art museums, despite the fact that Bunny, the average concerned mom, kept telling her "Be careful in New York!" (Venturing out, even to museums, was apparently some slight cause for concern.) It was actually more pleasant than usual to be there with her brother. Outside New York he'd get stared at a lot—"He looked kind of grimy and, you know, well, unkempt." Store personnel targeted him for a thief sometimes. But in New York, Ashley says, "he was just another guy. He said he never felt scared in New York because if you walk around and you don't look like you have anything, no one bothers you." In the museums his knowledge of art and artists—their culture, the period, their place in art history—astounded her. He read a huge amount, she says, and as they looked at various paintings he provided a kind of running tutorial. Once he gave her a Rothko book—an interesting choice, since like Elliott, Rothko also attended Lincoln High School in Portland (as had poet Gary Snyder and *Simpsons* creator Matt Groening). The two did their share of dumb, goofy things too. In bars Elliott liked to play Ms. Pac Man, for instance. "He was so good," Ashley remembers. "He looked up the highest scores online one time and his score was way higher than the highest-scoring Ms. Pac Man champion."

Having Ashley back around, involved in his life, watching out for him as best she could, was a major gain for Elliott. She was someone to trust implicitly. He knew he could turn to her; he knew she loved him enormously and wanted the best for him always. She was a little sister first and foremost, so his relationship with her had always been similar to the one he'd formed with Dorien, also several years younger. But more and more she also assumed the role of default caregiver, especially after the New York years ended and Elliott moved to L.A., where Ashley would also eventually live in order to provide much-needed support. She had not been present at the intervention, according to Garry. But she knew of it, and she was keenly aware of the nature and the depth of his struggles.

It was, despite Elliott's travails, a hugely exciting time. *Good Will Hunting* premiered in Westwood on December 2, 1997, then played again two days later in New York, a screening Elliott attended along with Garry and others. Wide release of the film occurred January 9, 1998. The lead-up to Oscar night included numerous performances, some low-key, some high profile. Elliott played Largo twice in L.A., with Jon Brion sitting in. This was a collaboration that would deepen over the years, yet end unhappily. He also played Spaceland in Silver Lake, a gig including the first live performance of the JJ Gonson–inspired song "Pitseleh," with its gorgeously tasteful, dancing piano interlude trailing the line "no one deserves this." It wasn't the first time, nor the last, that Elliott employed piano brilliantly as embellishment, a stately guest in songs consisting mostly of finger-picked acoustic guitar. On March 4, 1998, Elliott appeared on Conan O'Brien. He would not be allowed to sit down for the Oscars, but this night he did, in a T-shirt emblazoned with the state of Texas—a rich symbol if ever there was one—and a light blue stocking cap that would become, over the next several months, a trademark accent. Sounding a little hoarser than usual, he sang the expected tune, "Miss Misery." It is a soulful performance, with little trace of nerves. At the song's conclusion the audience erupts spontaneously, Elliott's softness and subtlety having apparently won them over, as it tended to do in the small clubs, where he had that ability to render everyone instantly, expectantly silent. It's easy to see his coiled power.

The next day it was MTV Live with Carson Daly, in a glass studio over Times Square. Here it was pure showbiz glibness in the face of raw authenticity, the chasm between the two widening as a prefatory interview proceeds, although Elliott clearly does his best to sound polite and appreciative. He wears the same outfit as the night before, an attempt by handlers, no doubt, to present a consistent "indie" image. Daly begins oddly, asking Elliott "You feeling alright?," a strange question to put to a "star" supposed to be born alright, always at the ready. Most likely Daly sensed nervousness, and Elliott definitely appears uptight, his eye contact sporadic at best. Immediately Daly asks about the Ferdinand tattoo, which Elliott obligingly, and revealingly, interprets as a "bull who doesn't want to go to the bullfight but he does"—a clear reference to his present situation. "That's awesome," Daly replies lamely. Later Elliott can be heard to say, softly, "whoops," as his fidgeting leads him to slide off the stool he's sitting on. The interview gives way to yet another performance of "Miss Misery." There's brief discussion of Elliott recording with an eighty-piece orchestra alongside Danny Elfman, who scored the film. The song then was "Between the Bars," and Elliott recalls the experience as "really fun." It was done live, and "the whole thing only took five minutes," he says. "It was really easy."

Perhaps the biggest change of all to Elliott's life coming out of the suddenly oversized attention had to do with his label situation. There had arisen, as Barney Hoskyns put it in a radio interview with Elliott, a potentially "fairytale" development. Elliott transitioned from Kill Rock Stars to the impossibly gaudy DreamWorks, developed in 1994 by Steven Spielberg, Jeffrey Katzenberg, and David Geffen. DreamWorks Records was the music arm of the enterprise, its initial project George Michael's *Older* album. The first band signed was Eels, who recorded *Beautiful Freak* under the imprint in 1997. Elliott's take on the switch was circumspect, omitting deeper specifics relating to Slim Moon and the deterioration of that relationship in the wake of the intervention just months before. "I was happy on Kill Rock Stars," Elliott tells Hoskyns, "but I couldn't stay . . . I sort of had to be on a major label because of contractual things."[2] In other words, someone with the necessary resources needed to buy him out of the old Virgin deal he'd signed years back as a member of Heatmiser. But he'd already been recording with Kill Rock Stars. He could have chosen to stay on, or he could simply have spoken with Virgin about his desire to end their relationship. Instead he took a different tack, succumbing to the interest

DreamWorks had been expressing even before the big Oscars-driven push. As he explained, the deal "had been getting wrapped up when the Oscars came along." He was not signed because of the Oscars. The move was in motion months prior. At any rate, whatever exactly went down, whatever convoluted financial and contractual chaos needed sorting out, Elliott was, at least initially, happy in his new home. "I like DreamWorks," he said simply. "They are very nice." For one thing, they didn't seem particularly concerned with generating hits. He didn't feel as if he were getting groomed for some sort of improbable stardom. Also, for the very first time, he had mind-bending resources at his disposal. Now he'd record "in a real studio," with no limit on the number of tracks available. The days of forced austerity, by-products of make-do recording situations in friends' homes or basements, were over forever. Anything was possible. And as Elliott explained, this opened up his process. He could try any and all instruments, even the "vibes" his grandfather played, to see what worked and what didn't. "For me," he said, "it's always better to try the most preposterous thing because—who knows?—happy accident."[3] It all might sound more polished, or maybe not, maybe much the same as before. But the possibilities were endless—strings perhaps, piano for sure, even suspended orchestral bass drums. As he'd slept those months on Dorien's floor and stayed home alone all day while everyone else went to work—sometimes drinking, sometimes not—he wrote songs continuously, his usual method of unconscious noodling. Many new tunes already existed in at least nascent form. In the studio environment made possible by DreamWorks, they'd take on texture.

As expected, DreamWorks wanted a video. Elliott was, of course, no stranger to the medium. He'd done "Coming Up Roses," as well as the small number of Heatmiser videos. And as far back as October 1996, he'd worked with independent filmmaker Jem Cohen on *Lucky Three*. For that, a roughly twelve-minute film featuring three complete songs, one a cover ("Thirteen," which Cohen had specifically suggested), it was just Jem and Elliott, no crew. The two sought out locations in Portland important to Elliott, several near Gonson's Undercover studio/work space. Cohen recalls the three-day process as simple and pleasant, never difficult, never convoluted or in any way troubled. He had very little in the way of resources but somehow, despite that fact, the project came together fabulously. The entire enterprise was adamantly independent. Then the idea had been simply to depict a musician doing what he naturally did in an unpretentious, unmediated way. *Lucky Three* was decidedly not a video project, not a label-sponsored or label-driven product, but more a reaction against music videos with their often formulaic artificiality.[4]

Lucky Three was the result of a one-time-only partnership. So this time Elliott wound up working with Ross Spears again, who told him his preference was to not intersperse shots from *Good Will Hunting*—"which in the entertainment industry is close to impossible," Spears maintained—but Elliott agreed, "and that was that," Spears said. "I *thought*."

Immediately people from DreamWorks and from *Good Will Hunting* checked out Spears's other Elliott videos and found them to be "pretty lo-fi." What they wanted, predictably, was more production value, more gloss and sheen. Spears's response was that "if they gave us some decent money it would look good and everyone would be happy."[5] They did not, however, go for the notion of omitting clips. That idea was shot down, and according to Spears, Elliott didn't really mind.

The movie's producer told Spears to go out and watch the film, which he did, at a midnight showing he somehow managed to walk into for free. As he returned the next morning the same producer had a TV set up in his office. He began to play the film but Spears stopped him, saying "I saw it just a few hours ago in a theater." "Sure you did," the producer replied, and walked out, leaving Spears with the feeling he was back in high school in the principal's office. They talked later about which segments of the movie might be useable; Spears felt the romantic scenes between Matt Damon and Minnie Driver could work, but he wasn't so sure about "the stuff with Robin Williams because he's always hugging Matt Damon and stuff and that might come out a bit homoerotic." It was mostly a joke, Spears's aside, but sure enough no clips of Damon and Williams were made available in the editing room.

For the outdoor shoot that followed Elliott as he walked through a Silver Lake neighborhood, in sunglasses, in his white suit with pink carnation, Spears recalls him "in good spirits," his confidence "pretty high" on the heels of the nomination. A motorcycle cop happened to be on set controlling traffic. He looked so "typically cop" that Spears and Elliott both started laughing. On the spot they decided to put him in the shoot; the idea, initially, was to have him follow Elliott down the sidewalk on his bike. He said that was impossible; to do so would be illegal. So the motorcycle was set aside, but the cop stalked Elliott on foot, still wearing his shades and helmet. "I would tell Elliott to look over his shoulder from time to time," which he did, with decent acting chops. Spears said, "He nailed that look of annoyance and paranoia. Maybe from experience." It's true, cops unnerved him. And though, in the video, the lurking policeman comes off as comically feckless, watching bemusedly as Elliott sticks coins in expired parking meters, in reality the paranoia was all too real. As he told an interviewer for MuchMusic his habit was to steer clear of authorities at all times and to deliberately try not doing anything to draw their attention. Also, years later, toward the end of his life, in fact, the fear of being followed would reach extreme proportions. It wasn't anything to laugh about. Other shots put Elliott at a bus stop with backup singers mouthing "Ahhh," along with close-ups in the doorway of the Smog Cutter, a famous L.A. dive bar.

In editing Spears was ambushed. Another editor had done his own cut, full of fast edits and much jumping back and forth between locations, the kind of ADHD aesthetic that prevailed at the time. He said he didn't like it; the second editor asked where they ought to start, then. Spears answered, "By erasing everything." In the end two edits were made, one with film clips and one—a director's version—without (both can be seen online at YouTube.com). But before finishing up Spears was made to contend with tedious, self-canceling lists of notes from *Good Will Hunting* people, Capitol Records (which put out the soundtrack), DreamWorks people, Elliott's management, and so on. His response was that he was only taking Elliott's suggestions, "and that pretty much ended that." Elliott himself was not totally pleased. He didn't like the super close-ups. "I told him he was a handsome stud and to just deal with it," Spears recalls.[6]

To Spears, who had worked with Elliott closely on several very different projects and over several very different vibes of years, from anonymity to relative fame, he was "a real down-to-earth person" who liked, very dryly, and with no tip-off flavor of sarcasm, to poke fun at pretentious behavior of every stripe. There would always be absurd incongruities. He'd be recording in an expensive studio then slip outside for a "spastic skateboard session," everyone wearing wigs all day. Once Elliott stayed with Spears, at a time when Spears's neighbor was living behind a big bush. Apparently his parents had insisted he move out; he did, but only so far as the front yard. Later Spears ran into Elliott, who told him to say hi to his family, and also to the guy "who lives in the bush." For Spears, the remark epitomized Elliott's brand of humor; "he would say things without a hint of irony." Such remarks were often outrageously funny yet no one could explain exactly why.

The scrutiny of press wouldn't alter Elliott's more entrenched and charming tendencies. He felt "pretty much the same," he said, which was both good and bad, "in that I think a lot about the same things." At the time he was working his way through Proust's *Remembrance of Things Past* a few pages at a time. Before that he'd taken on Beckett's fictional trilogy *Molloy, Malone Dies*, and *The Unnamable*. These were minimalist tales of vagrancy, death, inertia, and institutionalization made up, in some instances, of lengthy inner monologues. No doubt they spoke to Elliott's sense of dread and of ennui. At the same time he did admit some differences in his life and world, mainly because "there's quite a fuss made over people who are on TV for some reason," adding: "Personally, I watch TV with the sound off."

The other challenge, a sort of side effect of the general fuss—the new label and the demands made as industry types sought to capitalize on the potential of the new platform—was that time for making up songs, the leisure to settle in and let the sounds emerge, was getting harder and harder to find. It was all about serving the brouhaha. So, despite the fact that, pre-Oscar nomination, Elliott had been steadily at work on handfuls of new tunes, those written in Garry's living room in New York when time was seemingly endlessly in supply, they lived in a state of incipience. They waited like impatient friends, understanding but eager. Meanwhile Elliott found himself dealing with the likes of *People* magazine, which had run a dismissive piece calling him a Beck impersonator for wearing, like Beck did once, a white suit. It was hard for him to ignore such opinion. A new thing to absorb, it tended to bum him out. So he decided, self-protectively, to stop reading press. It was easier, he figured, than having to deal with the insecurities unkind stories might provoke.

In time the pro and con judgments did at last slow to a trickle, the night came and went, Elliott survived, and he lost to the kind Dion, as expected—the dogs barked and the caravan moved on, in other words, as Truman Capote once put it. Then, with relief, it was back to the music. Many of the new songs he was trying out, in various degrees of completion, as early as 1997, but others emerged in 1998. Sometimes he'd play them as straight instrumentals before lyrics were written. This was the case for what would be called "Waltz #1." Others were sung with first-draft lyrics that later would be jettisoned almost entirely. His habit was to ask the crowd whether they wanted to hear an old song or a new song. Usually they would call out some old number, something they knew and loved. But other times a request for something new broke through the din, and then he'd oblige, often apologetically, saying "This one isn't finished yet, but . . ." One regular haunt which he played several times before Oscar night was L.A.'s Largo, a hive of accomplished, experimental musicianship and songwriting run like a cabaret. He was there twice in January 1998, then again in late March, four days after the Academy Awards ceremony. The place was bought in 1992 by Mark Flanagan, a "burly Belfast native," and his wife, Aimee.[7] Regular performers included Aimee Mann, her husband, Michael Penn, Fiona Apple, Rickie Lee Jones, Neil Finn, Mr. E of the Eels, Jakob Dylan, and Ben Folds, among others. But it was known for the regular Friday night residency of savant Jon Brion, who championed what he charmingly called "unpopular pop." Brion's father was a band director at Yale, his mother a singer. At seventeen he'd dropped out of school, teaching himself to play several instruments and studying the "rudiments of orchestration." At age seven or eight he recalls an epiphany. He had asked himself, What if I can't spend my life making music? "And I remember rationally thinking, with no drama whatever, that I'd just have to commit suicide if it didn't happen. I've never not known what I was going to do from that moment on."[8] He formed a band, the Bats, which put out an album, *How Pop Can You Get*, in 1982. Another band, World's Fair, followed but fizzled out quickly. He then toured with 'Til Tuesday, Aimee Mann's new-wave outfit, whose song "Voices Carry" was an MTV staple. He went on from there to produce Mann's first two solo albums, *Whatever* and *I'm With Stupid*, full of thoughtful, finely crafted, lyrically complex pop. He also worked on Fiona Apple's

Extraordinary Machine album, and Sean Lennon's *Friendly Fire*. Lennon compared Brion to Prince. Working with him, he said, was like "having a weird alien prodigy in your room."

The Friday night events at Largo were Brion's "private playground." He'd conduct pop song chemistry experiments, building layered compositions from the ground up. According to a *Chicago Tribune* article titled "Who is Jon Brion (and is there anything he can't do)?," he'd begin "with a groove on drums, then shift to keyboards, then bass and guitar, all the while taping and looping each segment until a complete song appeared." Even covers could be inspired beyond belief. He'd take something like Captain and Tennille's "Love Will Keep Us Together" and fashion it lovingly, if not entirely unironically, into something lush and surprising. As Flanagan recalled, "Word got around, and it went from being a fun, casual thing to becoming an event . . . First people started turning up to see who would get on stage with Jon, but after a while it turned out that they didn't care who would or wouldn't get up; they were just into him."[9] Another novelty element was the "armada" of instruments he used night after night, either on his own or when sitting in with others. He picked them up at flea markets and garage sales, Optigans, Marxophones, Chamberlins, old Wurlitzers bought for fifty dollars. "Sometimes I keep broken stuff just because it makes this one great weird sound. And I'm not going to get rid of it until I can find a place where that one weird sound is going to have a happy home. Most of the stuff I do," he explained, "is a coloring job. The hard part is finding human beings who know what they want to convey in a song. Unfortunately, there aren't that many people who have a real individualistic stance."[10]

Mann, of course, was one such person. The two talked frequently and with "militant" intensity about the components of a truly good pop song. He had similar discussions with any number of intelligent, adventurous musicians out to undercut and challenge pop structures, including, eventually, Elliott. The two were introduced by Mary Lou Lord. At a gig she'd played an old Heatmiser tune Brion had never heard before, the JJ breakup number "Half Right." "I absolutely loved it," he said. He asked, "Does he have any other songs that are that good?" "All his songs are that good," Lord replied.[11] This sent Brion on a "mad hunt" for old Elliott albums. As he listened he "flipped out . . . Within two songs I was absolutely sold for life."

At Lord's suggestion Brion showed up at one of Elliott's gigs armed with a vibraphone and a Chamberlin, saying "Hey, Mary Lou sent me down." He offered to sit in at sound check, playing as little or as much as Elliott desired. By this point Brion knew Elliott's entire catalogue, sometimes even better than Elliott did. If Elliott struggled to recall chords, Brion jumped in, "and Elliott would look over at me in absolute shock."[12] For Elliott, the attention must have been immensely flattering, a deep knowledge of his tunes in someone so gifted, along with a deep respect for what he was crafting. From that second on, Brion recalls, "we were pretty much close." They would sit together after hours at the piano, working on or playing songs they both adored, like Elvis Costello's "Blood and Chocolate" or "Saturday in the Park," or tunes from Elton John's *Goodbye Yellow Brick Road*. For what may have been the first time, Elliott, to a degree that went far beyond previous partnerships and collaborations, found himself face to face with a genuine peer, someone who understood songcraft just as well as he did and who heard in tunes the same magical changes. In fact, having studied it carefully, Brion became one of the most insightful interpreters of Elliott's canon, aware to an amazingly subtle degree of what set it apart so decisively from the sorts of things others were attempting. "We had never met anybody else who had harmonically heard things in the same way," Brion recalled. "It was actually downright strange at times." If they happened to be listening to someone else's music, they'd shoot each other glances at the same moments. Much of it had to do with harmonic invention, the "harmonic turn of phrase," which in Elliott's case was without peer, Brion believed. "His chord changes," he said, "the internal motion of the chords, were always logical in a very beautiful way . . . He really loved the emotions that were generated by chord changes. He understood it better than anyone I ever met, quite honestly, by a long shot."[13] At the same time, Brion felt, Elliott was no borrower. He had little interest in making his songs sound like older music he liked. What he was after was "new beauty," an unmistakable modernity with "natural motion." Some songs might sound Beatles-y, but they usually included changes that "never happened on a Beatles record." That, Brion said, "was one of his many copious gifts." On occasion the motion was contrary, an anomalous harmony giving rise to feeling. Brion noticed even Stevie Wonder DNA in tunes like "Independence Day," the way chords drifted down appealingly.

Songs came together strangely at times, products of bizarre circum-stance, not that it really mattered much. A song was a song. It worked or it didn't, regardless of how it materialized. "Waltz #1" is a case in point. Apparently Elliott constructed its moody, eerie piano, overlaid with sleepy, sighing vocal harmonies, after listening for eighteen hours straight, high on mushrooms, to the song "Goodbye Yellow Brick Road." Flanagan recalled him sitting and playing it on Brion's Casio, telling the story of how it came to be. Again, the waltz affection ran deep, ferrying feelings whose begin-nings tracked back to the Texas years with Pickle, the difficulties with Charlie. As Elliott told Barney Hoskyns in April 1998: "For a while I made up nothing but waltzes. It was really weird. I wasn't planning on that. But everything was, like, ¾." As Hoskyns pointed out, there was art, on one hand, and chaos on the other. "You can't fall apart totally if what you want to do is create," he added. "You have to be able to function. You can't just dive into the chaos." Elliott agreed, in part, saying, "Even with that, it's hard to represent chaos or an absence of something. It's much easier to represent the presence of something, or a situation. People can be chaos, but it's hard to fit it into some creative piece. People try to do it over and over, and it's good that they do, but it's hard."[14] "Waltz #1" was anything but chaos. It came from a chaotic space, an altered state of consciousness, but what it achieved, as allusive, appositely ambiguous lyrics got added in, was an au-gust, chaos-defeating form, a magisterial beauty ill-befitting its origins. It was, in other words, art. Manifest chaos would come for Elliott many years later, when in 2000 and up to the last weeks of his life he worked on the songs for the album he never completed, *From a Basement on the Hill*. For now, he was in beauty mode. His inclination was to leave things pretty, not ugly them up with discordant soundscapes or "experiments in sonic tex-ture," as he put it to Hoskyns in late April.

Elliott's January Largo gig included Brion on several newer tunes—waltz numbers 1 and 2, "Bottle Up and Explode!," "I Didn't Understand," also a cover of "Walk Away Renée" by The Left Banke. Alone Elliott played "Between the Bars," "Bled White," and more. "Miss Misery" made its obliga-tory appearance, as did the guaranteed crowd-pleaser, "Say Yes." Less than one week later the two covered the Beatles song "Rain," a John Lennon B-side on the "Paperback Writer" single. The album Elliott would finish in mid-April—it was mastered and complete on April 29—was to be called, initially, *Grand Mal*. Later that title was abandoned—a band by the name objected—and replaced by *XO*, a decision Elliott was marginally happy with, although he worried the phrase, its emotional connotation, might be "overly dramatic." A song "Grand Mal" was recorded, with an opening similar to an earlier tune "Georgia Georgia," but with the title going by the wayside, the song did too. A released version concludes with Elliott saying, "Forget it, now it's too fast," frustration clearly present in his voice. Apparently he could not get the tune into a shape he found acceptable.

Many of the *XO* songs were written in 1997, during a portion of that year Elliott called a bummer and a "drag," referring to the cliff fall and the intervention that followed, plus his time, shortened, at Sierra Tucson. Friends felt *XO* was at least partly a response to those events, a sort of reaction, as one put it, to feeling really betrayed by a lot of people around him. The fact that the title suggests composed letters makes sense, each song its own missive, each targeting a different person or group, a collage of regrets, losses, and disappointments, sometimes pointedly delivered. Musically, it was a tried and true formula. With a camouflage of lyrics decipherable only by those in the know, Elliott expressed a rage he always disavowed if questioned directly. It was a way of having his cake and eating it too. Less autobiographically, the songs, as certain reviewers suggested, amounted to a Dylanesque moment. With the increased potential for polish, the virtually unlimited number of tracks available, and the use of unexpected instrumentation brought in, mainly, by Jon Brion, all of a sudden it seemed as if Elliott, like Dylan with "Like a Rolling Stone," was forsaking his roots. Lo-fi simplicity had seen its day, never to reappear. The unhappily labeled folkie was now a glittering pop star. Would he prosper in that role, the question seemed to be, or would the label jump undermine the focused, quiet complexity of the earlier, mostly homemade recordings?

These apprehensions proved short lived, and in some ways fatuous. What happened was what always seemed to happen with Elliott. The new album was better than anything that had come before. Improbably he kept improving on what had seemed unimprovable, his art a linear, incremental triumph. As a group, the songs were "more rock," he reflected, "but they just turned out that way. They didn't have to be rock songs."[15] But then, as always, the notion of preset categories—"shorthand ways of saying nothing"—held no interest. Folk he called a "ghetto of rampant sentimentality"—he knew that wasn't him, from the moment he began recording in Texas. Nor was anything else, really. "The less I think about how I fit in the happier I am," he told *Triple J* in a 1998 interview. "I don't really care where I fit into anything or if there's anything to fit into. It's just that I like music. It's not complicated."

And in most ways, it wasn't. What emerged was more of the same. The record recycled old and seemingly irrepressible lyrical themes, the ones at the center of all Elliott's work because they were at the center of his emotional life. Love and hate battle each other as Elliott imagines burning history backward in the first song, "Sweet Adeline," a nod to his mother's musical side of the family, his grandmother in particular and her Sweet Adeline choral group. In "Pitseleh" the devil drives him to give up the thing he loves (here that "thing" is JJ Gonson). In "I Didn't Understand" he admits "there's nothing here that you'll miss," comparing himself to a "cloud of smoke." "Waltz #1" circles the same dynamic, the same repetition. Because he never leaves his "zone" he goes home alone, wishing he'd never seen the girl's face. "Amity" takes the formula to its extreme. God made him junk and he's ready not to love, but "to go," by which he meant stop living. The album's second song—the breathtaking "Tomorrow Tomorrow"—spells out in the very first line Elliott's own "eternal return," as Nietzsche once called it: "Everybody knows which way you go/Straight to over." Trauma gives rise to fixed, petrified sentiments that repeat compulsively to no emotional benefit. The past-focused songs keep predicting the same bleak future to the point where sedation alone, being "fully loaded," stands any chance of disconnecting his head. He says twice in the first two songs he's "deaf and dumb and done." He's heard "the hammer at the lock," and there's no way out of the space he's in. Or there is, potentially, but when he tries following the "reflected sound of everything," the noise coming out unstoppably—the music, in other words—even it does not lead to anything. He hears it, he makes it, but by doing so he is no less "done."

Once again, the content of the songs makes for anything but an antidepressant. Yet just the same, and just as before and always, the songs are undeniably, inexpressibly beautiful, practically Kafkaesque in their baroque suffering. The most attacking songs, the ones aimed at sanctimony and self-righteousness, at people who seem to think they know what he needs, he groups together toward the end of the record. In "A Question Mark" he gives back hatred to the world that treated him badly, sickened by all the people who seem to know what's up. Mockingly he repeats the words "you know" nine times, as if to call out all the people who tried setting him straight, who imposed their judgments on his life. The target is the delusion of misguided helpers; he tells them they can give him a call if they ever want to say sorry. But it's with "Everybody Cares, Everybody Understands" that Elliott really bears down scathingly. This is the remade tune going back to college years, the one first recorded by Harum Scarum in 1989 for the cassette *Trick of the Paris Season*. Musically it is relatively unchanged in basic structure, but Elliott wrote new lyrics reflecting current thoughts and feelings. He first performed the reshaped version just around the start of the year, in January 1998, with the intervention still fresh. Here understanding amounts to a kick in the head, it's fake, a "quiet lie." It makes him want to scream and shout, but instead he lies dreaming, he retreats to the solitude of private inner experience, just as he does, too, in "A Question Mark." There are two responses available, it seems—fury or isolation. Either satisfies, but the longer-term solution, the one he kept resorting to, was isolation. People think they mean well, he sings. They say they care, they say they sympathize, they say they want the best for him. But it is all bullshit. "Fucking ought to stay the hell away from things you know nothing about," he snarls at the song's end. It's clear from the start something heavy is up. Elliott strums a single chord over and over, an ominous tolling of dark sentiment. At its close the song erupts with unexpected smart piano and layered instrumentation as it builds to a climbing crescendo, with Jon Brion on Chamberlin and vibraphone. It's yet another example of Elliott expertly crafting a tune, as simple guitar chords give way in the end to a musical cacophony recalling Lennon's "A Day in the Life."

The song setting these two tunes up is older, first performed in spring of 1996. "Bottle Up and Explode!" is one of the several firecracker tunes, a cousin of sorts to "Roman Candle." It's an expression of dual identity. The "troublemaker," a buried second self, proliferates below, gathering strength. Although he's always been aware of his presence Elliott looks at him like he's unrecognizable. But he's coming through anyway, he can "make it outside."

"I'll get through," he warns, "becoming you." It is a canny song ordering. The bottled-up devil inside explodes, followed by "A Question Mark" and "Everybody Cares, Everybody Understands," the songs written in the devil's voice.

But the fire and brimstone is only part of the record, its own compartmentalized closet of rage. "Baby Britain" is a sublime pop confection with a slight nod to the Beatles' "Getting Better," about drinking with a girl who floats over a "sea of vodka." The Beatles even get an explicit mention as the two listen to "Revolver." A minor theme in the record is drink, and everyone seems to be getting hammered. "Bled White" has Elliott wasted in order to take away the curse (although all it does it make him feel worse). "Sweet Adeline" extols the feeling of sedation already mentioned. Happiness arrives only when the bottle's broken, it appears. And although it's hard to imagine any real solution, Elliott still musters a kind of half-baked hopefulness, deciding, at the end of "Bled White," "I'm not fucked, not quite."

Then there's "Independence Day," one of Elliott's most hopeful songs by far about a "future butterfly" biding his time until finally he soars brilliantly. The temptation is to connect the tune to Elliott, to see it as a moment of positive feeling. In fact, it was written about his New York friend Josh. Dorien Garry is certain of this, since it was one of the few occasions Elliott told her explicitly what a song was about (he mentioned the same connection in an interview, as well, calling the song "optimistic," its message being "you have everything you need to be happy but you've just got to wait a bit"). Garry knew Josh and had introduced him to Elliott. The two became close during the roving East Coast year. Finding the good in others was always a lot easier than finding it in himself, although it was there, of course, just constantly getting snuffed out.

The record's crowning moment, Elliott's crowning moment in fact, comes with song number three. "Waltz #2 (XO)," the album's single, is a pop masterpiece from inception to close, cited even by one of Elliott's heroes, Elvis Costello. The song went through a number of iterations, as Elliott, out of fear of what it might reveal, revised to disguise. The opening is inexpressibly ominous, a perfect distillation of dark intent, creating a mood of foreboding, as drums give way to repeated guitar chords much like those in "Everybody Cares." Guitar lead then tracks a melody down as piano comes in to duplicate the same run. There's a momentary pause, followed by a skipped drum beat, and the first verse begins. In a weird way the song sounds like nothing else in Elliott's corpus of work. It is a strange singularity—everything led up to it, but nothing resembles it. It's utterly *sui generis*. The basic plot was described earlier. The setting is a karaoke bar, like the ones Elliott frequented in Portland, such as Chopsticks Express on East Burnside. Bunny sings a tune, as does Charlie. Her song, "Cathy's Clown," calls Charlie out; his, "You're No Good," summarizes his feelings about Elliott as a young man. As for Bunny there is ambivalence. She blunts her feelings, she pretends she does not see, and he actually reassures her, saying "it's alright, nothing's wrong," although occasionally in live performances he replaced that line with "it's alright, it's all wrong." His final conclusion is simple and heartbreaking. He'll never really know her now—he's left Texas behind for Portland—but all the same, he's going to love her always.

The record was released August 25, 1998, with a collage cover of splashed black-and-white Polaroids and two oblique shots of Elliott crouched over with eyes closed in one, and tuning a guitar in the other. As usual Elliott is not the cover's focus. His name appears at the bottom, but to make out the two images of him takes some doing. *Spin* noted the "sweetly inescapable catchiness" of the tunes, which hung around in your head "like stray dogs shown kindness for the first time." Not self-pitying, not raging against the pain, in the suspect words of the *Spin* reviewer, Elliott is "just sad, and he understands his ache to make it sweet." Others noted the increased amount of sounds at Elliott's disposal, finding these to be a welcome expansion of what had sometimes been a "samey blandness." To *Sputnikmusic* Elliott's "imagery and allusions" were "beyond comparison," and though he is said to "speak of suicide in an almost prophetic way," *XO* "seems like the perfect record, almost too perfect." The BBC observed an "expert maintenance of atmosphere." The lyrics, they say, depict "clear emotional unrest," and despite the fact that "situations get the better of Smith, resolution rarely presents itself." *Treblezine* called the lyrics "heartbreakingly tender and true." When the dust cleared many years later after Elliott's death, *Spin* placed *XO* at number ninety on their list of best albums of the last twenty-five years (this was in February 2012), *Pitchfork* at number twenty-three of records from the 1990s.

One of the more madcap and apparently enormously enjoyable offshoots of *XO* was *Strange Parallel*, a roughly twenty-minute bizarro film made with Elliott by Steve Hanft, an independent film director responsible for Beck's hilarious "Loser" video (filmed on a three hundred-dollar budget). In one short cut the cinephile filmmaker chain smokes in a darkened theater, observing in a French accent something along the lines of, "This has style but no continuity." It's an adroit description, a sort of built-in getting ahead of the story. As a kid Hanft had commandeered three records from his parents that he wore out listening to: *Yellow Submarine*, the Monkees' *Greatest Hits*, and Dylan's *John Wesley Harding*. He went through a hardcore Devo phase, "then all of a sudden I was punk." He sported spiky hair and started turning up at Black Flag and Bad Brains shows. Yet like Elliott his tastes were democratic. He liked George Jones, Fleetwood Mac, Leonard Cohen, and the Velvet Underground too. As he said by way of summary, "I can't like music that is overproduced in a crummy way or has no spirit."[16] Hanft also played in bands, one with Beck called Loser before the "Loser" single appeared. (Later the band name was changed to Liquor Cabinet.) His stage persona amounted to "screaming a lot in the mic wearing only underwear and a stupid wig." Elliott came to some of these shows; his typical request was for a tune called "Beeper City." As for filmmaking Hanft was always drawn, he explained, to "losers who are original." He did not know exactly why except for the fact that "I love them."

The film begins with Elliott scurrying across a road comically in order to exhume a guitar buried in the woods. A film crew of two keep wandering around Portland asking, "Have you seen Elliott Smith?" It's established that no one knows where he is, he's the archetypal nomadic free spirit. It is our fourth day here, they add, and although they keep checking out different bars in the hope of meeting up with Elliott, "he keeps giving us almost the right address," they realize. Freeing the guitar from its underground hole, Elliott then sits and sings "Waltz #2 (XO)." At different points a bartender enters the narrative to say things like "Elliott is a real gentleman" or "He's really quiet" or "He's a lovely person." In fact it is this bartender who provides the film's title. He notes a strange parallel with Elliott in that he too is a writer, and what Elliott did in the bar was write. One scene features "Miss Misery" lyrics sitting face up on the bar as a toy robot shoots fire at them. It seems to be an acerbic comment on fame and on the tiresomeness of the song in the wake of the Oscars. In a very nice touch Elliott lights a cigarette on the robot flame.

Scenes drop in desultorily, creating a collage effect to mirror, most likely accidentally, the XO cover. Elliott is shown recording "Brand New Game." He's filmed as an interviewer queries him, inaccurately, about performing at the Grammys. He's shown smoking, with Joanna Bolme in the room too, in a white lab jacket. Larry Crane of Jackpot! recording, with whom Elliott recorded "Baby Britain" and "Amity," which in its original version included Pete Krebs on vox, is heard to say, "It's hard to find Elliott."

But then the plot finds itself as Elliott sits in a hotel room watching a ridiculous Spanish infomercial for a mechanical hand. It promises to "expand your guitar virtuosity immediately" for three payments of 5,999 dollars. Elliott buys one from a guy on the street calling out "Get your robot hand! Robot hand is the future!" This is followed by a cut to a boardroom in which a man in a suit and headphones who's been lurking throughout the film urges Elliott, along with several others, to "get the robot hand." (He's actually already gotten it, so the scene is a little nonsensical.) The absurd demands from "the suit" in the meeting pokes still more fun at the industry side of things, it seems clear. Elliott plays a small section of the gorgeous George Harrison tune "Isn't It a Pity," then says, with hilarious deadpan, "I think the music business will eventually crush me. But I'm ready."

Things wind down goofily with a shot of Quasi, Sam Coomes in a skeleton outfit, Janet Weiss dressed as Cleopatra, sitting in a backyard talking about Elliott's dark lyricism. Elliott then has a "good old daydream" on a plane, which leads to a blood-spattered scene of his arm being hacksawed off by a Jamaican surgeon, then later tossed on a bar where Sean Croghan appears as a drill sergeant, screaming at Elliott: "I can't help you till you admit you have a problem!"—a loaded statement if ever there was one, under the circumstances. And: "You have to admit your future is uncertain!" Toward the end Elliott plays ZZ Top, followed by Rachmaninoff. The filmmaker intones, "Even though we worked on the film for a few months, Elliott was still a mystery to us. He lends a hand to all the lovely ones"—a robot hand, as it were, but still a hand, broadly speaking.

Constituting anything but mainstream MTV-type fare, and with its length, hardly a commercially viable vehicle for positioning Elliott as a tender, sensitive artist type à la "Miss Misery," the film illustrates both Elliott's willingness to make light of his persona as well as his artistically experimental mind-set, how he wanted, to the very end, to leapfrog convention, usually sardonically. It also speaks well of DreamWorks, for that matter, since they officially produced it. There was no music video made for the record's single, "Waltz #2 (XO)," but there was for "Baby Britain," also directed by Hanft. It recycles shots of Elliott in the robot hand, but focuses on him in the studio with Bolme—for several years the relationship was on again, off again—as he plays every instrument in sight. A few live shots also get thrown in, two with Quasi's Janet Weiss on drums. Bolme's presence is especially effectively conveyed. It is always in passing, the camera never lingers on her, nor does it linger much at all throughout. But it's clear, somehow, that she and Elliott are exceptionally close. She keeps popping up in the studio, hovering lovingly and supportively. Although it does not present itself in this way at all, the video comes across as a sort of love poem.

By October 17 it was back, forcefully, to the big time, as Elliott played "Waltz #2 (XO)" on *Saturday Night Live*. That Xena's Lucy Lawless hosted makes for amusing serendipity given Elliott's Xena love (at least with the sound off). Rumor has it that producers asked him to play "Miss Misery," an idea he rejected. Jon Brion, it turns out, was part of the backing band that night, as he had been on the record version of the tune. Then it was off to Europe in the first part of November, Elliott playing Brussels, Paris, Norway, London, then returning to Seattle for the Deck the Hall Ball on December 9, 1998, an event also featuring Courtney Love's and Eric Erlandson's band Hole. Newer tunes kept entering the set lists: "Stupidity Tries" (the clever Oscars bash) and "Ballad of Big Nothing." Two cover tunes made consistent appearances, too. "Thirteen" (already featured in Jem Cohen's film *Lucky Three*) was a sweet Big Star number written by Alex Chilton after watching a Beatles performance. His band was British invasion–inspired, influenced heavily by the Beatles and the Kinks, just like Elliott was. *Rolling Stone* called "Thirteen" "one of rock's most beautiful celebrations of adolescence." (Elliott's recorded version was later used, posthumously, in the 2005 film *Thumbsucker*.) Another cover, George Harrison's "Give Me Love (Give Me Peace on Earth)," often closed this set of shows. Friends and fans alike often debated which Beatle Elliott most resembled musically. Melodically, it is easy to see the McCartney influence in songs like "Baby Britain," and Elliott sometimes stood up for Paul when others bashed his brainless poppiness. Elliott clearly adored Lennon. He covered "Jealous Guy" regularly during 1998, and some suggest "A Day in the Life" was his all-time favorite Beatles tune. Harrison is sometimes left out of these comparisons, although he shouldn't be. In some ways Elliott's songs are unmistakably Harrisonesque with their jangly swirling atmospheres, their way of sounding slightly off, slightly disarming while also listenable. Years later, according to Elliott's friend Nelson Gary, Elliott even "started intentionally looking like George Harrison circa "All Things Must Pass,'" growing his hair longer, dressing like a hobo hippie.[17]

The merciless touring, the interviews, the grinding fame-shot—Elliott seemed to handle it all passably well. It's not as if he collapsed in a pool of panic at the Oscars. As he said so many times, to the point, in fact, where the remark begins to sound suspicious, the night was too bizarre for any real nervousness. Antidepressants might have helped to take the edge off, although in the long run they never seemed like a workable solution. No doubt his confidence was growing, the accolades shoring up feelings of self-assurance. He was very good, the world kept telling him, and even if large parts of him doubted that proclamation, some portion of the message must have started to snake through, to alter his always shaky self-perceptions. Still, he grappled with guilt. He told himself "What I do is no better than anyone else," so why this success, and why for me? He was embarrassed signing autographs, being recognized. He made music because it was in him, not to please anyone. The latter was a constantly surprising side effect. There were stomach problems, brought on by nerves or drinking, or the combination of the two. He'd sometimes stop in the middle of performances to use the bathroom. But the wheels were in motion, fame had him spinning, holding on to the wheel for dear life. He loved hair-raising carnival rides, the ones no one else dared trying, and fame was a Scrambler like no other. Yet as 1998 faded into 1999, the XO touring chewed him up to the point where he got sick of playing his own songs. In March, for instance, as he worked his way from the Fillmore in San Francisco to L.A., New Orleans, Austin, Orlando, Nashville, New York, and Boston, he had exactly six nights off. In April it was much the same—roughly ten nights off, with a second trip to Europe beginning on April 17.

A gig at The Trees in the Deep Ellum area of Dallas on March 9, 1999, was an especially interesting evening. Pickle got word of the performance (not from Elliott; the two had long ago fallen out of touch); he'd been tracking Elliott's success with a mix of pride and amazement. That night he, Denbow, Mark Merritt, Elliott's old girlfriend Kim, and Denbow's younger brother Kyle all took in the show, as did "Zott," the older girl Elliott once made out with in the back of the high school band bus. Kim screwed up the nerve to ask a security guard to deliver a message to Elliott backstage, and he invited them all in. (A picture shows Elliott in an "88" T-shirt surrounded by his Cedar Hill bandmates, Kim blond and to his right in a fetching red dress.) Yet another friend on hand, Mark Pittman, recalled the night. "All of us who knew him back when were beaming uncontrollably, probably looking like idiots to the man on stage. Kevin Denbow was standing next to me, a few feet from the front of the stage, enthusiastically singing every word to every song back at Elliott."[18] Pickle says Elliott "spoke to us all for about an hour, which was very nice." He was gracious, kind, open to reminiscing a bit about the better parts of the Texas years, including the time he beat Pittman in a talent contest by playing an eighth-grade love song. Pittman suggested he should have won; Elliott happily agreed with him. All the same, to Pickle Elliott appeared "socially ill at ease." He "didn't seem comfortable," most likely because the very idea of Texas always left him worked up. By this time, Pickle observed, Elliott had "fully adopted this thing, a permanent part of his personality later in life. When he didn't want to talk about something, he'd just stop, and evaporate." Whatever the case, it was a thrilling evening for the old gang. One of them, the person they'd sung with on "Outward Bound," jammed with on "Inspector Detector," rocked out with on "Carry On Wayward Son" and "Stairway to Heaven," had made it big. It was impossible, but it was true. And they had been there when it all began. Their Steve Smith was now Elliott, a bona fide star in the making. The eight hundred or so kids in piercings and "unnaturally dyed hair" merely fantasized closeness to the shy guy on stage. Pickle and the others *knew* him. He was their *friend*. That night he proved what they always suspected—that Elliott was different, that for him the sky was the limit.

CHAPTER EIGHT A SYMBOL MEANING INFINITY

Around 1999, once the touring trailed off and there was time to breathe again, to take stock and start imagining several possible futures, a signal event occurred that, retrospectively, many would point to as the start of a long train ride to Hell, the most recent beginning of a dreadfully antici-pated end. Elliott moved to L.A. It was where he would die, four years later, and for some, it was *why* he would die, as though grimy, smoggy, shallow Los Angeles bore down on a fragile target. Crackerbash's Sean Croghan, for instance, took this position at first. The feeling was that, had Elliott instead returned to Portland, his life might have been spared. Now even Croghan isn't so sure. "I kind of call bullshit on [that] now. I don't know anything. All I know is that I loved him very much, and there are people [in Portland] and obviously in L.A. who [loved] him a lot."[1]

At first the relocation was meant to be temporary, a short-term neces-sity. Dorien Garry had moved into a four-bedroom apartment in New York with her boyfriend, and she took quite a bit of Elliott's stuff to the new place. Elliott asked if he could rent one of the rooms. He helped with the security deposit, he paid several months' fees, but he was almost never there. Finally Garry told him what he was doing made no sense. He was wasting money. New York was where he wanted to be, but as Dorien figured out, "he kept needing to stay in L.A." for industry-driven reasons. At last, mostly out of inertia, he wound up living there. The decision was made pas-sively. In New York, as he often said, and as others like Ashley noticed, "there's just more people that look like I do. Not that . . . I don't look any particular way, I don't think. But I'm not the . . . People don't stare at me. I don't look outrageous at all. There's always much bigger freaks than me in New York, on every block." L.A. was different. At first he didn't "feel quite right there." It was full of "falsely tan people with great abs, that wear impossible clothes, and I'm always the scrappiest person walking down the street, and it makes me uncomfortable."[2] Famous people had always left him feeling "a little edgy." He avoided places where up-and-comers networked, talked about their careers incessantly, perpetually on the make. He mostly sidestepped Hollywood, he said. But the L.A. cartoon intrigued him. As he told CNN, "that seemed like a good reason to check it out. 'Let's get the cartoon out of the way and see what it's really like there.'"

Some of the impetus for the move came from manager Margaret Mittleman. She "really, really wanted him to live in L.A.," believing that being close to her, and to husband/producer Rob Schnapf, might be good for Elliott, a change of scenery, a possible change of mood. She looked forward to him getting to know her young assistant, Alyssa Siegel, to whom Elliott would grow close. Mittleman figured Siegel and others, including photographer Autumn de Wilde, who later produced a sort of oral biography of Elliott, replete with hundreds of photographs, "would be a good influence in his life."[3] Yet as she and others quickly realized, though L.A. did seem to help for a bit, manufacturing, for Elliott, a host of salutary music-focused distractions, the effect was temporary. Elliott "was always going to be drawn to a dark crowd," says de Wilde, and "that was always going to be frustrating for the people who were looking out for him." The crepuscular red-walled Roost was one typical hangout. Elliott spent hours there alone drinking beer and writing, bartenders protecting his privacy, just as they had done in New York. Schnapf recalls one exchange, a night he told Elliott he needed either to deal with his shit, accept the fact that it wasn't working—the drinking, the habitually gloomy frame of mind—or go down "that other path." On one hand, Elliott's people radar helped him pinpoint the good souls he needed in his life. On the other, he sometimes felt as if he could not live up to his own expectations, a mind-set encouraging self- and relationship sabotage. "Everybody's got a story," de Wilde said. There was the funny point with Elliott, usually just after meeting him—he was very good with strangers, said de Wilde. There was the inspiring point, the dawning recognition of his uniqueness, his giftedness. Then there was the disappointing point, the moment he disappeared, flaked, failed to stick to the straight and narrow, made the destructive rather than the healthy choice. To Schnapf, the goal of steering Elliott toward the right path was almost hopeless. He so often seemed, at root, to be dealing with "irreversible damage." The damage might be momentarily muted, but that was about it. It came back. It fought through demonically. Some of this was Elliott himself, who he was, the strategies he had evolved for dealing with negative emotion—booze, psych meds, self-erasure. Some was the people crowding in on him, drawn like humming insects to the fame flame. Polymath Nelson Gary, a whirlwind of esoteric literary and philosophical knowledge, a writer and painter and rock aficionado, crossed paths with Elliott accidentally during these years, and later got to know him fairly well, even appearing in one of his songs ("Coast to Coast"). Gary was acutely aware of what he called the "sycophant, madding crowd of banditos" following Elliott around, yes men and women, self-obsessed enablers, one of whom, Gary says, "looked like Chico Marx." When Elliott wanted to go dark, they were there, dimming the flashlight. When Elliott wanted to hear only what he wanted to hear, they said the right words.

In early 1999 Elliott responded to a set of questions for *NME* in a piece titled "Elliott Smith on the Couch." His answers read like a mini-life review, touching on many of the experiences of the prior few years, along with their emotional sequelae. "Posh restaurants full of winners, I hate winners," was his answer to the question "What is Hell?" The song he felt "described him best"—another question posed to him—was Quasi's "Success Can Only Fail Me Now," a reply italicizing his attitude toward mainstream acceptance and the constant ambivalence attending his pursuit of recognition for his music. Like the earliest memories recalled by most people who fight depression, his was less than positive, albeit comical. He remembered finding a turtle in Dallas that peed on his hand. At first it was cool, then it wasn't. As for the worst trouble he had been in, he tracked back to the week he spent on the psychiatric unit in Arizona. Then, asked on whom he would most like to "extract revenge," he named one of the doctors there, someone he'd "like to have incarcerated for a week," a sentence fitting the one meted out to him, a turning of the tables. A year and a half later the intervention betrayal still stung. He wasn't over it, nor would he really ever be.

By mid-May 1999 the arduous *XO* tour was concluding, the experience of "living out of an eight-wheel steel tube" near its end.[4] For some of these gigs—for instance, an appearance in Minneapolis at the 1st Avenue Club, where Prince's *Purple Rain* concert footage was filmed—Joanna Bolme was on hand, the on-again, off-again relationship temporarily back on apparently (although an article describes her as a "traveling companion"). In fact, it was never entirely off. For the next several years he would fly to Portland intermittently in order to see her. He felt, he told friends, that she was the woman he was "supposed to marry." He wanted the relationship to work, but at the same time he doubted his ability to carry it off. Committing meant getting better—drinking less, primarily, and making positive life choices—for the sake of his partner if not for himself. It meant living, pushing self-harm stirrings decisively aside. But that was the rub. He was never convinced he had it in him to effect the necessary changes.

Throughout 1999 the older *XO* songs were slowly replaced by newer tunes during performance, many of which found spots on the next record, the one that would be Elliott's last. The "couple killer" single "Son of Sam" entered the set list in Tokyo in January. One month later it was "Everything Reminds Me of Her" and "Easy Way Out." (Even the comparatively old "Flowers for Charlie" showed up in late March.) The next night Elliott announced, understandably, that he was sick of playing his songs. Night after night it had mainly been the same old stuff, and it was getting exhaustingly formulaic. He abandoned the set list and took requests. But still more new tunes came to the rescue. There was "Wouldn't Mama Be Proud" in July in Olympia, the devastating "Can't Make a Sound" and even more devastating "King's Crossing" on the same October night in Portland at Satyricon. *XO* had been a definite game changer, but he was in the process of moving on, bringing in still more instrumentation, growing more lyrically adventurous, more imagistic and elliptical.

The songs, at any rate, always took care of themselves. They rolled on like a semi, headlights tearing through the night. They came out of their own sequestered life force, impervious to tumult, swimming in the flood and "counting the waves," just like the female character in the song "Baby Britain." Summer of 1999 brought with it a new main character, one who would play a key role in Elliott's final moments. At Spaceland he first met Jennifer Chiba. He had wandered in just as she'd finished a gig—Chiba played bass in a band called The Warlocks. Mutual friend Steve Hanft was there too, and Elliott asked for an introduction. He and Jennifer talked some, about compassion and Russian literature, about the Ferdinand story, one of Chiba's favorites from childhood too, both staring at their shoes, both smiling shyly. To Chiba Elliott seemed "really uncomfortable," his usual transient awkwardness showing.[5] He had just moved to L.A.—he didn't even know his phone number—so he asked for hers, then gave her the number of Mittleman's assistant. Chiba's first instinct was to tell him to call her when he dropped out of the music industry. She'd recently ended a ten-year relationship with Weezer's Rivers Cuomo, and in the moment she didn't feel she could "deal with being in the public eye" again. She knew who Elliott was. She had seen him on the Oscars in his white suit, and she'd been blown away, finding his songs "amazing" and "breathtaking."

Weeks later Elliott showed up at her next gig. There they talked more, discovering surprising commonalities. Chiba had grown up in Africa, but moved to Texas, graduating high school in Houston, where she was a stand-out student, and attending college at Trinity in San Antonio, finishing up in 1989. Her father was a NASA scientist in Zimbabwe. He remarried at seventy, Chiba's mother having died in 1993. Like Elliott, Chiba had pushed through her share of emotional storms. She had been hospitalized for depression and suicidal thinking, and she shared with Elliott "all the medication cocktails I was on," adding that "most made me feel worse." In what she later understood to be a "fugal/medicated state," an episode of altered consciousness, she had tried taking her own life, and Elliott "seemed extremely interested in the details." She found she could talk with him without shame, and he told her of his own experience at Sierra Tucson. They agreed that hospitalization sucked; confinement, they felt, made things worse, not better. As for the drugs they spent hours comparing notes. Both concluded meds seemed at best fractionally helpful, their idiopathic nature a source of frustration. Even when they worked, no one knew why, or whether they'd keep working, or for how long. They also believed "that we had the right to live or not live, as we saw fit." That was the problem with confinement. The freedom it limited included the freedom to die. It prevented the ultimate escape. In forcing life upon patients it seemed like a form of death, a curtailment of limitless possibility, suicide included. Moved by her candid descriptions of what she'd been through, sympathizing with her pain, Elliott told Chiba, "I hope you don't try to hurt yourself again, because I'd like to get to know you better." For her, this was an "astounding" thing to hear, coming as it did from someone she so admired and respected, someone she instantly adored. On the spot they reached a provisional agreement: "Neither of us would hurt ourselves." This came as a relief to Chiba, however fragile the pact turned out to be. At that time she felt she needed external motivation; she could not rely on herself "to provide the will to live" or even to take care of herself. She had no interest in bringing Elliott down with her, so the fact that he "had been there," that he'd "spent a good amount of time feeling similarly" and therefore understood, provided "much-needed hope." Here was someone who got it, someone who knew what it was like, someone in daily search of a reason to keep fighting.

But like always, it was touch and go, the agreement more fragile than ironclad. They liked each other, that much was clear. It was possible to envision a future, maybe not always a rosy one, maybe not one bereft of all pain, but a future nonetheless, a way of possibly being together. So Chiba immediately asked, "What do you propose we do about it?" Elliott's answer was unexpected but characteristic: "I'm too depressed for a serious girlfriend." Chiba, of course, was depressed too; she didn't see why shared mood problems ought to disqualify the positive feelings they seemed to have. But Elliott held back. He wasn't sure he had it in him to stay alive, agreements notwithstanding. In fact, as he told Chiba, he'd been entertaining the possibility of dying "accidentally" so as not to hurt those who loved him, using drinking and drugs as instruments of self-cessation. Plus, there was Joanna. How could he like Chiba, he wondered, if he was supposed to be with Joanna? Chiba says Elliott felt as if he had "ruined her life," and sometimes when he returned from Portland he'd be "super depressed." All the same he loved Joanna; in many ways she was the one constant in his life, apart from the music, which she was indirectly a part of, at least in terms of the recording process. It was all very frustrating, confusing, a mixed bag of hopefulness and clear-headed self-doubt, but in the end Chiba came away impressed, if not undeterred. Elliott seemed unwilling, admirably so, to "allow his demons to destroy a relationship with someone else." He said he wished they had met at a different time. For her part Chiba knew what they shared wouldn't evaporate; she told him she'd always be there, yet privately wondered whether she could wait "for him to go through whatever it was he had to go through." This turned out to be a prescient question. What Elliott was about to go through flung him into an abyss.

For now, that abyss was still one year off. And there was plenty to take his thoughts away from inner checkmates. For one thing his grandmother died, and after taping a Jon Brion show at the Santa Monica pier he had to fly out the next morning. This turned out to be the first time Elliott hung out with Alyssa Siegel. He was worried about getting to the funeral on time, so she wound up volunteering to stay with him at his hotel. "That's how stressed out he would get," Siegel says. "He didn't ask me to stay, I offered. It was clear he couldn't deal with the idea of doing it by himself."[6] He slept as Siegel finished a crossword puzzle. When she got him to the airport, Iggy Pop was also on the flight, a strangely reassuring coincidence. Back from the funeral, he recorded later in 1999 the Lennon tune "Because" for the *American Beauty* soundtrack, the film released in September. It was note-perfect, as George Martin proclaimed, a slow build of texture, all soaring multiple falsetto harmonies that, at first, Elliott did not think he was up to. When the film came out he hesitantly made his way to the afterparty, its location marked by strewn rose petals. As Autumn de Wilde recalled jokingly, "He was miserable." Showbiz stuff was never his thing; he was more at home in dive bars like Club Tee Gee or the Roost, at least on nights when they weren't overrun by frat boys from local colleges. But it was a triumph. Here he was in yet another film. His star kept rising, whether he liked the attention or not.

Siegel recalls another moment that inspired, in an indirect fashion, the concept for the next album. She and Elliott were driving around L.A. (like in high school with Garrick Duckler, he drove around all the time, and when he did, there was always music playing, his own or someone else's) and she slid into the car stereo a tape with songs from the kids' TV show *Schoolhouse Rock!* Jazz singer and pianist Blossom Dearie had lent her bright, childlike voice to three of the tunes, "Mother Necessity," "Unpack Your Adjectives," and "Figure 8." On the latter, Dearie's sharp-edged vocal punctures the unspeakably eerie, saturnine roll of the piano. The effect is transporting, the song in its first and final portions seeming to issue from some gloomy, vestigial portion of an infantile unconscious, like a dream one wakes to partly recall. The middle portion of the song gets a lot more bouncy, with Dearie singing multiplication tables. She concludes with a high vocal run—"place it on its side and it's a symbol meaning infinity." As Siegel remembers, the two listened to the tape several times, its atmospherics registering strongly. When Elliott got back to his house he sat down at the piano and worked "Figure 8" out. Then some time in July or August at Capitol Studios in L.A. he recorded it along with numerous other songs, including the piano piece "Bye," "Junk Bond Trader," "Color Bars," and "Everything Reminds Me of Her."[7] Elliott's version of the "Figure 8" piece models itself on Dearie's (although he recorded just the first section, and with less instrumentation). There's the same juxtaposition of crisp vocals with muffled, faraway piano. The song's theme of a circle turning around upon itself struck a nerve. It's a picture, inescapably, of infinite repetition. To Elliott it suggested the dead-endedness of flawlessness, a kind of going nowhere and going somewhere at the same time.

This idea of endlessly skating the very symbol of infinity, a Beckett-like stasis in the midst of apparent motion, stuck. It appealed to Elliott's Kierkegaardian leanings, the nausea and pointlessness and absurdity of existence, suggesting, as he explained, "a self-contained pursuit that potentially could be kind of beautiful and has no destination." One "can't get out of it," he added, "without ruining it. I kind of like that."[8] The song itself, "Figure 8," never made it on to a record. It was "there until the last minute when it was replaced by 'Easy Way Out,'" he explained. The song got dropped, but not its sentiment. Elliott elected to name the album after the Dearie *Schoolhouse Rock!* tune. "Figure 8" captured where he was at, where he was always at, the majesty of, in his way of thinking, going nowhere.

In interviews leading up to the record release, the usual probings came, this time made more piquant by a perception of inchoate stardom. Sitting for these was its own figure eight; at times it appeared no one ever came up with anything new to ask, the questions recycling themselves, tracing identical arcs forever. Was he a loner? Were his songs autobiographical? Why were his songs so sad? What did he expect people to feel when listening to the record? Does his music have a healing effect? At times he was obviously annoyed by the sameness. For VH1 he sat with tightly crossed legs and tapping toes, far crankier than usual, determined to say as little as

Elliott at piano in 1999, around the time of the making of Figure 8. *(Marina Chavez/Corbis.)*

possible, a blonde female interviewer growing more flummoxed by the second. But sometimes he rose to the occasion. John Mulvey singled out his maddening inconsistency, telling him "come on, check your script," to which Elliott shouted, "Everybody's [inconsistent]. Everybody pretends like they are more coherent so that other people can pretend that they understand them better. That's what you have to do. If everybody really acted like how they felt all the time, it would be total madness."[9] There is an interesting exchange on the subject of autobiographical source material, a topic Elliott always tried finessing as best he could, saying, for the record, "I will do anything I can within my power to prevent myself becoming just another cartoon rock star with all manner of dysfunctions," while at the same time, occasionally, in ways not within his power, doing anything but. His songs, he emphasized, are dreams, little movies; "you can watch if you want," he noted, but the aim wasn't to make people feel like he did. Interpretations focused on personal secrets he found "insulting." "True songs for me are about mystery. Their charm is that they are open-ended." The notion that he just has a "bunch of issues" he unloads on strangers? "Not the case," he maintained. Still, when questioned specifically, when asked in detail about what sound like cogent hypothetical readings of lyrics, he allowed, "Maybe," as he "blows cigarette smoke towards the window, from which he'd presumably like to make his getaway."[10] The difference seems to be between what the songs are often truly about and the myth Elliott would prefer to represent. He admits that certain songs on the new record did have something to do with, for instance, the lingering resentments about Sierra Tuscon, then quickly adds, "I don't want to perpetuate the notion that if somebody plays music, they must be fucked up or crazy."

As with *Magical Mystery Tour* and earlier records, at the time Elliott was obsessed with what might be, by critical consensus, one of the most "fucked-up and crazy" albums ever made, Nico's *The Marble Index*. He called it the perfect antidote to L.A. He liked how it put him in a trance. Nothing moved except the vocals, he said, monotonously wavering over static music. The record came out in 1969, the year of Elliott's birth. Nico wrote the songs and played her signature harmonium; avant-garde composer (and former Velvet Underground member) John Cale arranged, adding glockenspiel, electric viola, bells, mouth organ, and bosun's pipe. Nico's musical pedigree is dense. At Warhol's suggestion she appeared on The Velvet Underground's debut album, as, in keeping with Warhol's stylings, chanteuse. Dylan wrote a song for her, and the Stones' Brian Jones recorded her first single, produced by Jimmy Page, no less. Assorted efforts to come to terms with *The Marble Index* read like reluctant, frankly terrified night terrors. *Trouser Press* called it "one of the scariest records ever made." The *Guardian* found it "remarkable," possessing the "annihilating beauty of a later Mark Rothko painting"—Elliott's favorite artist—then added forewarningly, "if you're ever in the perfect mood to play *The Marble Index*, then it's probably the last thing you should be playing." Even Lester Bangs weighed in, in a piece titled "Your Shadow Is Scared of You: An Attempt Not to Be Frightened by Nico." The vocals, to Bangs, call to mind "twisted pterodactyl shrieks," the harpsichord jabs like "murderous hailstones," Nico herself lying "interred in the endless wastes of the arctic night." The record, in short, is a brief reactive psychosis, a sort of schizophrenic apophany. Musically, there is zero affinity between the songs Elliott was recording at the time and the songs Nico made. What thrilled him more than the sound was the record's absolute apartness, its originality and uncategorizability. His goal, if there was one, was to make *Figure 8* "indescribable." In other words, to make it a little like *The Marble Index*, or like Rothko.

Thankfully, life in its zanier moments punted Elliott out of the Nico daze. On New Year's Eve 1999 he was back in New York, playing the Knitting Factory, a gig he closed with the song "Last Call." Afterwards Rye Coalition's Dave Leto, whose band featured a "brashy Jesus-Lizardy mix with Led Zeppelin and AC/DC," threw what he called an "epic" Y2K party with Dorien Garry (Leto lived next door). Elliott dropped in after the show in a hooded full-length red robe and slippers.[11] By the time he arrived everyone was totally wasted. They had gotten their hands on a smoke machine. Elliott set it off over and over until it triggered the fire alarm, then ran off screaming and dancing. You could not see the person in front of you, the smoke was so thick. He and Leto tore through Garry's record collection in search of the Stones' *Performance* album, which, once located, they played on repeat for ten hours. "He was obsessed with that album too," Leto notes. Leto in fact spent a lot of time hanging out with Elliott in the New York days, "back when he was just a dude at Dorien's." Then "it was all jokes, seeing if you could push the limit to the most vulgar thing you could think of, cross-the-line-type stuff." On occasions when Elliott was asked to DJ in Brooklyn, Leto came along. "Mobs of Brooklyn kids would crowd around," he remembers, "saying, 'Hey! I'm a huge fan.'" Strangers were always "trying to get a piece of him, make a connection. They felt like they knew him. He was always so courteous with everyone but after a certain point we felt like we needed to make an escape." For Leto, these exchanges epitomized Elliott's attitude toward fan worship. "He had zero care for money, fame, adulation. All he wanted to do was make music." When Dave and Dorien came upon some of the stuff he'd left behind in the move to L.A., they found "sizable checks he didn't bother to cash" as if the money meant nothing. The songs brought the money, but the money wasn't the reason for the songs.

By 2000 Elliott had around twenty-five songs in his pocket, all solid, all promising, the embarrassment of riches he faced routinely. He thought, at first, about making a double record, something he had contemplated even back in the *Either/Or* days. "If I could put out a record every six months I would," he said. "People used to, but it's not how the monster is meant to operate."[12] The feel of the tunes—more dense, more edgy and biting— recalled "someone who isn't in a band emulating one." At the same time the point wasn't "to make anything more complicated," Elliott explained. "Actually, there wasn't any point. I just started adding instruments because I could," as he had done with *XO*.[13] The precise number of songs actually became an issue, according to producer Rob Schnapf. One idea was to keep the set at eleven or twelve, but then, when two or three songs got nixed, or the tune "Figure 8" set aside, the collection "had this humpback . . . it became overly weighted in one way or another."[14] For the label—"the wrong people making all the judgments," as Mittleman put it—less was more. Schnapf disagreed. He told people, "We can't abide by this twelve-song rule. We need to make [the next record] as long as it's going to take to make sense . . . I thought it was going to tie everything together." In the end, "people didn't get it. It didn't do it." Then it was all about culling material, making impossible choices that, no matter what anyone did, never felt satisfying. Elliott's instinct at the time was to go grand; he wanted a bigger sound, big production, not the "stripped-down, right-in-your-ear" intimacy of early years. But Schnapf kept after him, steering him toward more acoustic stuff, telling him they needed to make sure they got that side of him. At first Elliott resisted, but he slowly came around, the fugitive pleasures of simplicity coming back to him as he blew through one new song after another.

There were thrilling developments. The main one had to do with location. Elliott had casually mentioned the possibility of recording at Abbey Road studios, the historic home of the Beatles. It wasn't a serious idea at first, more a lark. But "for some bizarre reason" his label took the notion seriously, they picked it up and organized it. A week or so later, Elliott found himself there, with Joanna Bolme and others, including Sam Coomes, who had played on the final Heatmiser record. "Just walking in the place was amazing," he said. "I made up a song on the same piano they used for 'Penny Lane.'" Most of the time, he says, he was busy thinking only about the songs, not about the fact that he was standing where the Beatles stood. Though it was certainly a very big deal, he liked to "play it down."[15] Bolme was more forthcoming in a piece she wrote for *Tape Op: Book II*. "You name it, they got it," she said. Steinway grand and tack pianos, a Hammond C3 organ with two Leslies to choose from, electric harmonium, vintage Ludwig drum kits, even a pub in the basement with beers on tap. Studio one was thirty-nine feet high; it's where orchestras and film scores got recorded. Studio three gave Bolme a weird vibe. She learned it was where *Dark Side of the Moon* was recorded; the Spice Girls, Morrissey, and Phil Collins also used it. Certain songs included orchestration—violins, violas, basses, and French horns. Elliott's process was to play out what he had in mind on the piano, then give it to an arranger. If he happened to hear anything that did not sound quite right, he'd get on the talkback right away. The players found it to be an easy day's work, repairing afterward to the pub. They were used to orchestral music and to working with temperamental conductors. Last-second changes, the sort Elliott introduced, were no issue at all. "It's their job," said Elliott. Even some "little smart-ass rock 'n' roller" failed to rub them the wrong way.

In all something like five songs were recorded in various versions at Abbey Road, including "Stupidity Tries," an alternate take of "Junk Bond Trader," and an acoustic "Pretty Mary K," along with others that did not make the cut, "Brand New Game," for instance, and "Tiny Time Machine." (Draft lyrics for that tune feature Elliott dressed in black, a knife in his back, people crowding up his path to the future. A girl with a place in the sun sells people shade.)

Apart from the turn-taking between large-sound songs like those recorded at Abbey Road and more familiar acoustic numbers, there are aspects of the record that came to be called *Figure 8* (finally released in April 2000) that make it yet another departure. The album features a cast of characters straight out of "Desolation Row," including stick men, Sergeant

Rock, invisible men changing clothes, statues, clowns, heroes, hitchhikers, police, Son of Sam, junk bond traders, songbirds, generals, a gentleman in green, a girl named Angelina, and even some guy appearing out of nowhere, Bruno S. As it turns out, Bruno S. is Bruno Schleinstein, an actor in several '70s Werner Herzog films, including *Stroszek*. He didn't so much act; he played himself, more or less, and some scenes were actually shot in his flat. As the *New York Times* explained, "he occupied the roles of damaged characters so completely and genuinely, so uncannily, that it was never quite clear how much he understood about what use was being made of him by the director. His performances were riveting, but he was obviously not well mentally."[16] Bruno's personal history resonated for Elliott. He was beaten as a child. Nazis performed experiments on him. Music "gave him a measure of solace and a way to escape his loneliness." Shuffling between institutions, he first picked up the accordion, then grew adept at piano, bells, and glockenspiel. For Elliott, Bruno S. was a "real man," a sort of existential model of being, an actor who did not know he was acting. In draft lyrics for the song "Color Bars" he also calls him a mirror mind, dancing in disease. Wedging Bruno into the song makes for a shot of covert autobiography. He had no interest in being a film star. And music was his way out. No other record includes this sort of parade of characters, this congress of selves. Metaphorically Elliott tossed out a range of secret identities, the sum total of which signifies, cacophonously, who he might be: stickman songbird.

Figure 8 also unpacks a conspicuous army-related theme, the generals, sergeants, and noncommissioned officers all showing up at different junctures. A sergeant, for instance, breaks the key off in a lock in "Color Bars," pinning Elliott in the place he comes from. Veiled suicide references appear as everyone wants Elliott to ride into the sunset, but he battles back, for the moment, declaring "I ain't gonna go down," a phrase he was drawn to as a symbol of giving up and losing all hope. "Pretty Mary K," most likely about his mother, whose name was Bunny Kay, pictures a soldier in bed with a "wound to the head." Again he has run into the sun; he calls out to the woman, but a man in a soldier's uniform waves her away. One of Elliott's most powerful images occurs in "I Better Be Quiet Now." He says he has a long way to go, but no matter what he does, he seems to be getting farther away. It's two steps up, three steps back. He recalls a dream. He's an army man, ordered to march where he stands, as a "dead enemy" springs and wails in his face. It's a picture of torture, Elliott in the role of castle guard who's expected to stand stolidly and imperviously as any manner of torment works to alter his features. The record externalizes the internal war.

One other feature is a litany of absolutes, a prison of superlatives. The word "everything" shows up at least twenty times, along with numerous nevers, nothings, everyones, nobodies, nowheres, and alwayses. The song "Everything Means Nothing to Me," which Elliott once called his favorite, appears just after "Everything Reminds Me of Her," as if to dismiss the prior sentiment. In other words, even she means nothing. Initially it was meant to just be piano but in the studio the ending morphed into something a lot more bombastic, with drums and strings sweeping over the title Elliott keeps repeating in a stepwise upward scale. Finally drums and strings fade, and what's left is the lonely piano, chords now falling down the scale in counterpoint, as if to signify the dropping mood. Elliott told an interviewer the song was, for him, uplifting. It was good to get to the point where it all meant nothing. It suggested the possibility of radical equanimity. Just like XO's "Waltz #1," the tune was written in L.A. during a two-day mushroom bender. As he told NME in April 2000, "I've made some things up in different states, but that was pretty new for me." Mushroom-abetted or not, the land of absolutes is a land of raised emotional stakes. If not always, never. Theorists of depression call it "all-or-none" thinking. He's stuck on a side he never chose ("Easy Way Out"), he's got nowhere to go ("Son of Sam"), nothing could have been done ("Happiness"), he'd prefer to say nothing ("Better Be Quiet Now"), and as he notes on the record's penultimate tune, just before the closer "Bye," a piano piece with a sound identical to that on "Figure 8": "the monologue means nothing to me." There's a ghost in every town, the hero killed the clown, yet he can't make a sound.

Despite all this several reviewers went out of their way to label the record Elliott's happiest. The verdict seems like wishful thinking. Even people who did not know him felt an instinct to wish him well, to picture him rising above it all. He declares he's a "silent movie," they declare him "high on the sound."

As it happened, the song receiving the most attention—he played it on the Conan show in late April 2000, with Sam Coomes supplying sweetly high harmonies—was the uninvitingly titled lead track, "Son of Sam." In interviews Elliott took care to note that, grisly title aside, it wasn't about any actual historical figure. What he meant to convey was the image of a destructive, repetitive person, or as he also said, two destructive figures. He might have had anyone in mind; at the same time, he might have been thinking of himself, his circling tendency for sabotage, especially when it came to love relationships. He was, as noted before, his own "couple killer." When things got good, he got suspicious, doubting that he could count on them staying good for long. On the surface, however, it's one of his more obscure numbers, a mash-up of ellipses. A boss shows up, as do doctors and nurses. Even Shiva opens her arms "to make sure I don't get too far."

A proper music video was made that the label distributed to outlets like MTV, among others. Elliott per usual didn't want some "hot-shit Hollywood guy to make God knows what."[17] He'd got to be friends with Autumn de Wilde, who lived just up the hill from Elliott in L.A.'s Echo Park, on Sutherland Street (Elliott's place was a 1920s bungalow, with Alyssa Siegel next door). She'd taken *Figure 8's* cover shot, and although she'd never made a video, she was interested, and Elliott liked and respected her photographs. The result was a comment, it seems, on fame's deflations. In a mix of still pictures and live action, Elliott follows a red-orange balloon along city streets, in a brown suit jacket and a T-shirt matching the balloon's color. He grabs its string, but releases it again, only to recommence the chase. It deflates in front of the Sunset wall featured on the record's cover. Elliott picks up the forlorn rubber heap, then walks through the wall's door. The balloon appears to have led him there; it's as if he's walking into his own album, a very nice effect. De Wilde's record cover shot includes a comical element. Shadow apparently rendered Elliott's hair invisible; his bowl cut, therefore, is a computer simulation. As de Wilde explained, "I gave him the choice of three hairstyles."[18] For the video itself, his hair is atypically washed and nicely combed. He almost does not look like himself; he's a sunny honor student out for a city stroll.

Figure 8 was met with the usual ethereal accolades, its top chart position ninety-nine in the U.S., thirty-seven in the U.K. "Shows the artist at the peak of his powers," gushed *Rolling Stone*, a "haunted high-water mark,"

Elliott's perpetual bummer expressed with "exquisite purity" and "ruthless, sad-eyed insight." The magazine ranked the record number forty-two in its list of the hundred best albums of the 2000s. *NME* agreed, calling the record "Smith's finest effort to date," "awash with pretty ambiguities and difficult twists." "Everything comes together with nary a wasted note," said *Sputnikmusic*, the album "timeless" and "universal." *Pitchfork* marveled at the effortlessness with which Elliott seemed capable of "crafting albums of instantly accessible pop," an ability his musician friends recognized early on. Every song was good. He almost never misfired. There were rarely any simple duds.

The summer 2000 tour introduced a few new wrinkles. To this point Elliott had been mostly backed by Portland band Quasi, in his words the best rock 'n' roll outfit in the world, Coomes on bass and Sleater-Kinney's Janet Weiss on drums. Coomes remained, but Scott McPherson took over drumming duties, and cowboy-hatted multi-instrumentalist Shon Sullivan, whom Elliott nicknamed Goldenboy, was brought on for guitars, piano, and occasional cello. Sullivan had seen Elliott before at the Troubadour, when he strode out in a hunter's cap, carrying his guitar in a case. He played songs from the self-titled record, and Shon was "blown away. He was so spot on." Yet again, what registered most with Sullivan at the time, what registered with everyone, was the fact that "all the songs were good. Every single one!" Later he watched *Good Will Hunting* and realized, "Hey! This is that guy."[19]

The two first met at McPherson's home in the Fairfax District in L.A., just after *Figure 8* appeared. They played through a number of tunes to see how things might work out, Sullivan essentially auditioning. Piano parts, he felt, "were tricky," full of "crazy chromatic runs" as in "Everything Means Nothing To Me," and unique ways of "fingering chords and triads." The piece Elliott liked to call "Honky Bach" struck Sullivan as especially "foreign" in terms of its phrasings, a result, most likely, of Elliott's mainly self-taught piano. In all they rehearsed just three days—"Elliott wasn't a big rehearsal guy," Shon adds—then it was off to the U.K. and a "huge, huge show" at the Reading Festival. Sullivan sensed "it was a relief for Elliott to be away from the U.S." He'd always felt "really, really stressed out" when family or friends were in attendance, so playing for relative strangers was an easier experience, less fraught with emotion. On the tour bus they kept a battery-operated keyboard everyone messed around on, and after shows Elliott enjoyed cranking up The Stooges' *Raw Power* record. As was his habit, he'd play it over and over. Another tune he was "obsessed with" at the time was Lennon's jaunty "No Reply," about a girl who lies. Its A-minor, A-major shifts inspired a new song Elliott was then calling "Somebody's Baby." He tried it out for Sullivan, asking "You think I say *baby* too many times?" That very night the band played it in a musty civic hall.

One thing no one anticipated, a series of events, in fact, that weirdly duplicated Dylan's electric rejection of folk, was crowd displeasure. It was hardly the norm, not a terribly big deal, but now and again people started calling out "do acoustic!" They wanted the old Elliott, not the new one with the fuller sound. They wanted "Roman Candle," not "Junk Bond Trader." At times amateur music historians in the crowd cleverly shouted "Judas," the same accusation leveled at Dylan. And copying Dylan's reply exactly, Elliott said "I don't believe you. You're a liar!"[20] The new songs "caught people off guard," Sullivan recalls. They weren't getting what they thought they'd paid for. All the same, "it was the direction Elliott wanted to go in," Sullivan says. "He didn't want to do more acoustic tours." He'd been there, he'd been the lonely tortured troubadour, and he was restless for new modes, new forms of expression. The older stuff bored him, and if he played it now, which he still did on occasion, he electrified it, in the process amping the songs up with gloriously unexpected energy, breathing heavy, almost grungy life into them, as in a truly spectacular September 2000 performance in Seattle at Bumbershoot.[21] What is fascinating about these electrified revisions of the acoustic material is how well the songs came off. They had always seemed intrinsically acoustic, ill-suited by definition for any other treatment. But they weren't at all. They could actually rock, as with "Needle in the Hay," the Bumbershoot opener. It was almost as if, with some of these later performances, Elliott returned to a Heatmiser mode. He demonstrated what many had sensed all along, what JJ Gonson, for one, had argued back in the early '90s: Elliott's solo material could have, with the right finessing, fit into the Heatmiser vibe.

* * *

This 2000 tour included one other fresh development, less musical, more personal. In the long run it would alter Elliott's life, not always for the better. His tour manager was a man named Miles, Shon Sullivan recalls; but also working the cause was a woman named Valerie Deerin, who chipped in with all manner of tasks, doing "a little PA stuff" and managing sales of merchandise, a "merch girl." Deerin was Scottish. Sullivan recalls her as a "really nice girl, kind of fun, definitely outgoing, and very un-L.A." The last bit might have appealed to Elliott; she wasn't L.A., far from it, but she'd done a decent amount of work in the music business. She knew bands and band members. She was connected and in the scene. Whatever the case, she and Elliott started going out, yet not, according to Sullivan, "really heavily or seriously." In fact, for Elliott it was no more than a tour hook-up at first. In most ways he and Deerin had very little in common. Unlike JJ and Joanna, unlike Chiba, with whom Elliott was still only "friends," she was not artistically inclined. She also lacked the sort of inner chaos Elliott was usually attracted to. She wasn't troubled, at least not in the beginning, and she was no introspective brooder. She was, as Sullivan said, upbeat, high energy, apparently well put together, the product of an idyllic childhood that could not have been more different from Elliott's. As it was, the last thing Elliott wanted was a relationship—he had already told Chiba he was too depressed for it—or all the baggage and responsibilities sure to follow. Yet Deerin pursued him, she wanted badly to be his girlfriend. She wanted, as many people around him did, to save him, to somehow buffer him against his demons. This was yet another psychological function of Elliott's depression and suicidality. It mobilized support. It made people care. It drew people to him, people, usually women, who believed, usually erroneously, that their love could turn him around, heal him once and for all.

Before Elliott, Deerin dated Flaming Lips drummer Steven Drozd, according to Dorien Garry. Drozd himself first met Elliott in 1996. "We hit it off," he said, "but he was always in his own world." By 2000, Drozd says, "I got to know him really well. I knew he was struggling just to get through the day. For me," he adds, "my fondest and most disturbing memory of him was when we did ecstasy together one night . . . That song 'Goodbye Yellow Brick Road' came on and he started bawling his eyes out."[22] To this point numbing alcohol remained Elliott's drug of choice, although like most everyone else, he experimented now and then recreationally. Drozd, however, was notorious for serious addiction problems, including heroin. In an intense, candid six-minute clip from a Flaming Lips documentary, he actually shoots up on camera, describing the entire process, how the drug fills his body slowly. He talks, also, about his addiction history, how he started with alcohol, speed, Ecstasy, and how he finally turned to heroin in London during a tour with the Red Hot Chili Peppers. In the end, he says, as the addiction deepened and took him over entirely, he lost all his money, all his equipment, even his car. His expectation, then, was that he'd either kick somehow or the drug would kill him.[23] It's a frank assessment. It's not pretty to watch although, at the same time, Drozd's honesty is admirable. The segment morphs into a sort of anti-addiction commentary. The feeling some people got from Deerin, more a sixth sense than anything else, an intuition, was that she may have been drawn to drug takers like Drozd. The role she perfected was helper and healer.

It's not as if Deerin was evil. She adored Elliott, she says, and would have loved him no less had he worked as a plumber.[24] The music, to her, was secondary. It's also not the case that she, or anyone for that matter, was to blame for Elliott's crash, which began, in a kind of slow-motion fashion, before the European gigs concluded. He had made a so-called "heroin record," the self-titled album, when he wasn't even on heroin, employing the idea of the drug intellectually, metaphorically, as a symbol for dependency. Back in the Portland days, when heroin was in the scene and easily available, he had mused about the prospect of trying it out, to the dismay of people like JJ Gonson. There was also that idea, suggested to him by others, that it might qualify as unorthodox treatment for intractable depression, a notion he did not dismiss. But now, in fall of 2000, what finally happened was what seemed, always, to be in the process of happening—a *fait accompli*, a delayed enticing inevitability. Whether out of boredom, hopelessness, exhaustion, defeat, self-hatred, or because, in the back of his mind, it had been the plan all along, a way of stopping pain once and for all, and in some respects stopping life itself, Elliott signed up with evil, as he wrote in the song "Angeles." As if turning to look in the face of someone perpetually standing directly behind him, he caved in, he tried heroin, the "devil's script." He did, in effect, exactly what Drozd had done—graduated from party-atmosphere drug use to drugs as full-time occupation. He was now, and for the rest of his life, an addict. He became, in a way that must have felt, in a sense, like a relief, the junkie everyone had erroneously assumed him to be before. He would never be the same. He would never crawl back out. Whoever he was, he was irreversibly someone else, a diminished, degraded version of an original identity. This was to be *the* turning point— very real, and in the long run, very catastrophic.

What he told select friends—and he wasn't bragging about it, or the least bit proud of it, or romanticizing it in line with the rock star mythos— was that he had picked the habit up on tour, while far away. Rumors circulated as to who was to blame. Some contended, without clear evidence, that Chiba was the culprit (she denies this, and in fact, she wasn't even there; she was back in L.A., merely a friend). Others floated different names. In any case, the fault-finding made no sense. Heroin had always been a lure, a sort of waving siren, a last-ditch option, and whoever made it available, El-liott took it. He was a grown man; he made his choices. He alone elected to succumb. And once he did, an effect was the solidifying of Deerin's position in his life. From here on out he needed her just as much as she needed him. Being alone was always difficult, and now more than ever. So when he finally returned to L.A., to the cottage complex on Sutherland Street, not far from where the *Figure 8* cover shot had been taken, Deerin tagged along. The idea was to kick, with Deerin's help. There was urgency, he had to do it, chiefly because of a string of dates in Japan in early December. He needed to be clean before taking that trip. The flight itself was long, and the prospect of dealing with addiction so far away seemed impossible to contemplate. Where would he get drugs? He couldn't take any with him, obviously. At first he tried managing the process at home, a do-it-yourself detox. He was extremely ill—vomiting, his bowels giving out—in the throes of his very first massive withdrawal. It didn't go well. It wasn't working. In the end, against what he had hoped might happen, against his initial plan, he sought medical treatment, and got on methadone. Slowly, then, he dug his way out over the last week of November and the first few days of December. Throughout the agonizing several-week ordeal, Deerin to her credit was completely sober. She was not, herself, a drug user. She took her role as nursemaid seriously. It was a 24–7 engagement—as it would be years later for Jennifer Chiba—and she was there for all of it, a true asset, Elliott coming to realize that, whatever his misgivings, he could count on her. She proved instrumental in getting him past the worst of it.

Morbidly, as the closer for many of the fall shows, Elliott sampled "Don't Fear the Reaper," a secret admission of the road he was on, a coded message to himself. Heroin equaled escape, but it also equaled death, the escape of death, and as he declared back on *Figure 8*, "I don't feel afraid to die." The reaper, he was prepared to face. Far from fearing death, it sometimes seemed, as it virtually always had, like long-awaited relief. He made it to Japan, where he played on December 3, 4, 6, 7, and 8, a grueling string in light of his condition, but he stopped a number of songs, finding he could not get through them. This had always happened. He'd always stopped songs, just cut them off when they weren't flowing the way he wanted them to, or when he'd forgotten lyrics. But from here on out it was to become a regular occurrence. On any given night, with a set list of, say, fifteen tunes, he might abort six or more. Crowds never seemed to mind. They called out encouragement. They marshaled supportive and understanding patience, telling him to try again, telling him he could do it. Sometimes he listened, sometimes not. Shows turned into tests of endurance. Was he going to make it through?

If there was a point at which, after numerous intimations, life became slow dying, this was it. Everything collapsed into addiction, the dreadful grind of days dealing with the realization that his life didn't belong to him, that he was chained to a chattering monster. He'd made it through Japan, but when he returned, it was back to zero. He'd been getting by on methadone, managing passably well, but he'd started sharing his supply with a friend, also addicted, so he wound up in withdrawal, then, in no time at all, back on heroin. In the moment there seemed to be no other way of controlling the situation. Friends pleaded with him, urged him to stop, saying they loved him and wanted him in their life, but his answer, now, always seemed to be the same. He did not want to do drugs, he said. But his feeling, one that never seemed far off, was that the world had a gun to his head. Heroin was the only way he could stand it. To stay around, to keep living, as everyone seemed to want him to do, even if he did not, he needed to be high. Otherwise, he'd kill himself. It was that simple. It was one or the other. Death or drugs.

With that sort of self-justification firmly established in his mind, it was full steam ahead, complete surrender. At this point, several people self-enlisted to devote nearly every waking minute to the job of keeping Elliott alive. It was exhausting, a nonstop anxiety attack, but the alternative was losing him, and nobody wanted that. Deerin took the lead. She was, as usual, bright and cheerful, a natural extravert, clean and sober, and most important, utterly devoted. Elliott accepted her care more passively than anything else. Privately he kept telling friends he was not into her, that he wasn't sure he loved her, but he didn't want to hurt her, he didn't want to ruin her life by sending her away, and he fell into the habit of introducing her as his girlfriend, making their pairing more or less official. Besides, he couldn't manage without her. She bought his food, ran his errands, cooked for him, nursed him, fawned over him, and although she insisted she wanted him off drugs, she kept striking many as a "quintessential enabler." She accepted Elliott's state, and by not pointedly confronting him, avoiding ultimatums, she abetted it. Taking care of every last task of daily living, she freed Elliott up to stay addicted. It was, as most everyone agreed, a messed up situation, a textbook instance of codependence. But she wasn't alone. A confederacy of helpers was on call, including Alyssa Siegel, who was close to the situation, Jennifer Chiba, who at this point mainly watched from afar, Autumn de Wilde, Margaret Mittleman, and Ashley too, who made the decision around 2001 to move to L.A. to be close to Elliott, understanding all too clearly the dire condition he was in. She'd remain there through to the end, doing her best, like all involved, to prevent him from throwing his life away.

Elliott, however, was not on board. He wasn't in a recovery mode. He had not made any true commitment to getting clean. In fact, his habit was about to extend itself in ways that, even under the circumstances, no one anticipated. But first there were practical matters to deal with, some quotidian, some relating to new and surprisingly powerful music. Strangely, when just on heroin Elliott could seem marginally functional. He smoked it, he never shot up—he was petrified of needles, and once after pricking himself accidentally, he completely freaked out—so the threat of death by overdose was not as pronounced. He still went out, he still performed, although less frequently. There was, for instance, a February acoustic show at the Silver

Lake Lounge in L.A., where he played a set of seven songs, including "Strung Out Again," "Fond Farewell," and "True Love," all newer tunes, all preoccupied, directly or indirectly, with heroin or death or both. The first, "Strung Out Again," is a dark, crashing meditation with guitars banging in forebodingly, full of disturbing imagery befitting his mind-set. He spies an "evil emperor" wearing his clothes, the new person he had become, in charge of him, in control. He hates the look of his own face. The tide's coming in, he says, he's strung out again, a floating body, face down.

"True Love" fashions heroin a lover. On the surface, in fact, the song seems to be about a destructive relationship. It's a companion piece to "Say Yes"—the same ambivalences, the same unpredictability. Will "she" stay or will she go? Will she love him as he needs to be loved, or will she screw him over? Far from accidentally damaged, his heart's been "attacked," shattered by "tough love, bad love."[25] Real love, true love, lives behind glass, locked and kept closed. So he finds it on the street instead, marries himself to "heavenly bodies above." With his new love he steals away to some hideout. He finds she's either madly in love or else mean, it's always one or the other; he can't make any sort of stand. She's got him where she wants him and there's nothing he can do about it, he "has to cause harm." To get back on his own somehow, he must go to rehab. Doctors write him new prescriptions as he swallows his sword. The song concludes with some of the most depressing sentiment Elliott ever mustered, an impressive feat considering the melancholy infusing so many of his tunes. In soft, dreamy, high vocals while wishing he were "no one," he asks his "lover" to take him home, to take him out of this place, to take him up with her today. What he seems to be requesting is a sort of silvery, astral death, an ethereal ascent into nothingness. He felt like a liar telling this "girl" he loved her—a possible reference to Deerin—but he can't say no, he can't resist, and he wishes she'd free him at last, a final intervention by the same "Miss Misery" who had once transported him to a very different ether. The song is a death fantasy; the job is assigned, wishfully, to heroin, the last love available to him.

Also on the set list was the gorgeous "Let's Get Lost," another love dirge. This time he's invited in, but he goes missing, burns bridges, pursues "some beautiful place" to get lost, his lifelong default setting. True love, when it comes, he makes die. She says please stay, he pushes her away. It's interesting, because in an earlier version of the song he's a bit more hopeful. Rather than getting lost, he imagines sticking around at all costs, coming forward again. "Let's Get Lost" unpacks a core script. He wants to belong but can't. He wants love but the price is steep. He's too sad to be all there, he says.

There was vanishing little life left, its force leaking out, but still it had to be lived, or the pretense of living, the pretense of caring whether he lived or died, had to be sustained, for now at least, because that's what those around him wanted, and the better part of what he wanted too. Some time in 2001 Elliott moved from Sutherland Street, with the dedicated Deerin in tow. Not far away in Los Feliz, although some called it Silver Lake, there was a cluster of eight dwellings named the Snow White cottages or Seven Dwarfs cottages by locals, purchased by Sylvia Helfert in 1976. Elliott took the first one on the right, in the 2900 block of Griffith Park Boulevard, before moving later to a different unit. Ben Sherwood had designed the properties in the early 1930s; they were used by Disney animators, the studios just around the corner, and they likely served as the inspiration for the seven dwarf dwellings in the Disney film. The roofs seemed built by "drunken elves." Workers deliberately broke the shingles, singed the edges, and placed them in random patterns. Inside, each unit ran to around seven hundred square feet, with one bedroom; some, like Elliott's, featured wood-burning fireplaces, others faux fireplaces with gas burners. At one point Helfert cut a hole in the unit Elliott occupied, installed circular stairs and finishing the attic, "replete with toilet, pedestal sink, and monstrous claw-foot bathtub."[26] Apparently Elliott wrote a lot of songs in that upper space, according to a tenant who replaced him. By all appearances it was a charming, almost literally storybook setup. Elliott settled in and did what he could to approximate a regular existence. Deerin was not able to stay continuously; because of visa requirements she needed, now and again, to return to Europe for months at a time before being allowed re-entry into the U.S. So for stretches Elliott was on his own, although Ashley was around too (later, in 2001), and also Chiba, whom Elliott would reconnect with whenever Deerin took off, much to Deerin's displeasure. When he spoke to Chiba about Deerin, he described her as someone who had more or less "barged into" his life. Chiba naturally wondered why he didn't simply break up with her, if that's how he felt. But he believed if he did, it would destroy her. She was too into him; in some ways, he felt, her existence depended on being into him. He therefore took the path of least resistance, the easy way out, his life a disorganized, noncommittal back-and-forth between Deerin, Chiba, and Joanna, whom he still secretly hoped he'd get back with, although with the move to L.A., her presence became scarcer, as did the presence of most of his Portland friends, and others from the New York days. On this point Dorien Garry is adamant. "When Val and Elliott were dating, the days at the Disney cottages, that was the only time I had no contact with him. He wouldn't answer an e-mail, he wouldn't return calls. I feel like Valerie was 100 percent responsible for that." She seemed to have figured that the only way to keep him was to keep him from others who might take him away or in some fashion undermine the exclusivity of their bond. Then again, Deerin wasn't always around, her control occasional, intermittent. When she was gone, Elliott was free to do as he pleased, to see whom he pleased.

Another ten-year resident of the cottages was Barb Martinez, whom Elliott slowly grew close to. She had worked as a personal assistant for Henry Rollins and Taj Mahal, her partner a film editor. She and Elliott called him her "imaginary husband"—a bit like Deerin, he was gone as much as he was around. Just after Elliott moved in Martinez threw a brunch in the courtyard area and invited all the residents to come. Elliott was hesitant but he did finally show up. To smooth the way for conversation, Martinez asked everyone to wear name tags, which Elliott found amusing. "He wasn't a celebrity to us," Martinez explains. "He had to wear a name tag just like everyone else!" Early in the proceedings a friend came to pick him up, Elliott declaring with mock outrage, "But I've got a name tag!"[27]

Martinez owned an old saloon-style upright piano, always slightly out of tune, which Elliott dropped by to noodle with after the two had become more familiar. Occasionally impromptu jam sessions erupted with Russell Pollard, who played with Sebadoh and the Folk Implosion. They took to calling these events "unexpected parties," everyone drinking and hammering out Flying Burrito Brothers tunes, Martinez pitching in with guitar and harp. Together they sometimes planned excursions to McCabe's guitar shop

*One of the Disney cottages
Elliott lived in, first on the
right in a set of units.
(Photograph by Henry Love.)*

in Santa Monica, where Elliott purchased a harmonium. He also borrowed
a celeste from one of Martinez's friends, intrigued by the bell sound it emit-
ted. It looked just like an upright piano, but with a tone resembling a glockenspiel. Silver Lake Guitar was another hangout. Once while there they
came across a Paul Williams poster—the diminutive '70s singer/songwriter.
Someone had ostentatiously signed it—not, apparently, Williams himself—
and they laughed long and hard. Something about its fake grandiosity
struck them both as insanely funny. As always Elliott now and then spent
entire days listening to a single tune, for instance "Guitar Man" by Bread.
But he had his musical pet peeves too. "If you wanted to piss him off," Martinez said, "you played 'Sound of Silence.'"[28] What Martinez gradually became was a sort of surrogate parent; she played that role with a lot of
people. Even Elliott's true parents called her to check in when they could
not reach him (at this point, indications are that they knew nothing about
his addiction). In person she met Gary Smith and Bunny, finding them
"nice" and "sweet," respectively.

For food Barb and Elliott favored a nearby Trader Joe's. To carry their
stuff she brought along a red wagon that Elliott liked to pull down the sidewalk, joking that it was like commandeering a parade float. "It looked pretty
stupid on the way there," she recalled, "because it was empty." Elliott's
prized item at the time was dulce le leche caramel ice cream. It's the one
thing he always bought. "He was big on that," Martinez remembered.

Having spent her life working with stars, Martinez knew better than to pry. She stayed well away from difficult subjects, an attitude Elliott no doubt appreciated. She never asked probing questions, feeling more comfortable "talking about mundane things." What she was struck by, however, especially in retrospect, was that Elliott "never seemed compromised." He was not "running back and forth doing drugs," so far as she knew, although she adds, "I could have been in complete denial." "I loved him very much, and I never noticed anything and I'm not that easily fooled." She figures she "would have seen it" had there been any serious heroin usage; on the other hand, "if he was doing that," she says, "he was pretty skilled at concealing it from me." Given Elliott's predilections at the time, the latter possibility seems most likely. As mentioned, he could function passably well on heroin; he did not present like the textbook junkie. He held it together admirably, at least in its initial stages, before it began destroying him.

If the life force was slowly leaking out over the span of the year, the songs were too, in their always relentless fashion. Heroin was temporary (or so Elliott thought). It could be beaten. It could be left behind. As it came, it could go, given the necessary commitment to getting clean. But the music was permanent. It couldn't be beaten. It was inherent from day one. Scattered songs kept making their way out, some from back in the *Figure 8* years, some totally fresh. There was always a question of the next album, addiction aside, and Elliott's initial instinct, a very good one, was to work with Jon Brion again. Brion was on a roll. In 1999 he had composed the score for the film *Magnolia* (he was nominated for a Grammy). He'd produced the three stellar Aimee Mann records, *Whatever*, *I'm With Stupid*, and 2000's *Bachelor #2*. Mann had become a critical darling. The new-wave chanteuse for 'Til Tuesday transmogrified, with Brion's assistance, into a bona fide pop star, her songwriting chops undeniable. It could have been, had things gone smoothly, an incredibly satisfying, productive collaboration, two virtuosos working side by side, bringing out the best in each other, crafting first-class pop. And at first it worked, or it seemed to. They managed, even in Elliott's beat-up state, to get through a number of tunes: "True Love," "Twilight"—the "Somebody's Baby" song Elliott had played for Shon Sullivan—"Fond Farewell, "Passing Feeling," "Don't Go Down," "Confusion," and "Shooting Star." By April Elliott was playing tracks from these

Brion sessions for friends. Things were coming together. "Don't Go Down" and "Confusion," in particular, were subject to many long lyrical revisions. The first, a sort of plea, explores the dangers of succumbing, a lure Elliott knew too well. Initially the words were "don't *look* down"—don't descend, avert the eyes, resist. When evil talks to you, Elliott wrote, just keep good and quiet; you can't get out once you're in. There is a strength to the words, refusal still possible. Look at me, he says, I'm going to stay. "Confusion" is the most post-Beatles John Lennon song Elliott ever wrote. It sails along winningly, happy and poppy. It's a bit "Crippled Inside," a bit "Oh Yoko!" In draft lyrics he pictures himself in a cave, dying looking up, living looking down, always looking down. As early as May 2000 he played the song in Austin.

As for the process of recording these new tunes, the Brion sessions were not the first. As far back as 2000 Elliott had laid down acoustic versions on his own. He sent cassettes to friends, including Dorien Garry and Ashley. In the car he played early versions of "Strung Out Again," "Passing Feeling," even "King's Crossing," which itself went through countless lyrical revisions, just like "Don't Go Down." To some degree Elliott had gone into the work with Brion reluctantly. He didn't exactly want help. It wasn't something he felt he needed; he was perfectly capable on his own. Some feel Elliott believed he was doing Brion a favor—Brion wanted to work with him, Elliott let it happen. The songs themselves were a different matter, however. About them Elliott was adamant. With acute presentiment he took to telling friends, "If I die, make sure this record comes out. I don't care how." The songs weren't dismissable. He wanted them to be heard, no matter what. He also, as Shon Sullivan recalled, "wanted one name and one name only on the record." From the beginning it was to be all him, Elliott Smith, a kind of emphatic self-redefinition, real, uncompromising, utterly authentic.

Perhaps predictably in light of Elliott's condition and his uncertainty about whether he really wanted help, the Brion experiment ended badly. Unlike others in Elliott's life, the "sycophant banditos"—as friend Nelson Gary, the poet and writer, called them—Brion rejected addiction. He was confrontational. He called Elliott out. Unaccustomed to such directness, never a fan of open conflict, Elliott blanched. Brion had problems with the drug use; Elliott had problems with Brion's honesty. Brion had seen both sides, and he wanted no part in encouraging the self-destructive one. "Any of us who knew him when he was on, long before he sunk," Brion said, "had a kind of love for him that you reserve for very few people in your life. He generated that kind of feeling . . . It was usually spontaneous and heavy. And it didn't take some bad events." On the other hand, the sense shared by many, especially from 2001 on, was: If you are going to care about this person, prepare yourself for the strong possibility that he may not make it. "We all knew it was a possibility," Brion noted.[29] There came a point, Brion says, "where I knew. I remember the conversation. I remember his inability to speak coherently. I remember realizing he had gone too far . . . It felt like the person I loved wasn't home anymore. And the filter that normally exists between the soul and the rest of the world was so mangled." To Brion, Elliott was living "a nightmarish life with ghosts in the closet coming to get him."

"The friendship kind of fell apart all of a sudden one day," Elliott told *Under the Radar.* "Those weren't happy days." He found himself so depressed he couldn't even hear the songs. "It just made it kind of awkward being alone in the car listening." Money also entered the picture. Brion sent DreamWorks a bill, claiming Elliott owed him cash. To Elliott he had merely been helping him "record some stuff"; there had never been any sort of pay arrangement. Meetings were held, but they proved fruitless. Nothing definite got accomplished. It was back to square one. The work hadn't come to nothing, but it left in its wake dispiriting feelings, a patina of failure. The label, of course, was concerned, about the music and about the client. In a state of desperation, Elliott resorted to disturbed strategies, telling Dream-Works to release him or else. Or else what? Or else, Elliott apparently suggested to label overseers, he might kill himself. He'd always talked about suicide; in fact, increasingly so. Now he was using the possibility as a threat. This was a relatively new gambit—anguish as a manipulative tool.

All of the worst in Elliott, a clear representation of the suicidal rut he'd wedged into, was on ghastly display in August, when he attempted, terribly unwisely, a performance at Sunset Junction. He wore braided pigtails and a pink hat, in full George Harrison mode. He could hardly string sentences together, talking or singing, his speech slurred and garbled. Several songs he aborted, or managed to get through in a truncated fashion, cutting them off in random spots. His delicate finger-picking abandoned him; mostly he strummed, almost amateurishly. He tried "Southern Belle," dropped it, then segued into "Last Call." On "Alameda," as if talking to himself, he got to the point in the song where he sang "you can't finish what you start," then shut it down, smiling at the coincidence. Obviously, he was high and sedated, listing on a wave of legal and illegal drugs. "I'm sorry," he offered, miserably. "I can't remember the words. I'm so fucked up." At this time it wasn't just the heroin. In fact, to some, the heroin was the least of it. He'd taken to carting around thirty-odd prescription bottles in a toiletry travel bag he sometimes called his "man purse," which he dipped into precariously. He had "zero objectivity" about what he was doing, his goal to "get high or to destroy himself."[30] A preferred defense was intellectualization, "he'd get obsessed with the action of meds in his body even if they damaged him," studying putative mechanisms of action, interaction effects that were purely speculative. The crowd, on hand to witness catastrophe, chimed in with encouragement, egging him on, calling out songs, begging him to finish whichever number he'd started. It was the kind of performance almost never seen. Essentially it wasn't a performance at all, nothing was held back, nothing concealed. This was life blowing up live. There was no end, no encore. When the music stopped Elliot wouldn't step off stage and return, out of view, to who he really was. This was who he really was. Yet what people started to realize, not the least bit happily or reassuringly, was that Elliott actually could stay this way indefinitely. He had built up, shaped like a muscle-bound athlete, an ironclad constitution. Nothing took him down. He kept coming back. In the old days what he came back from was alcohol. He'd get hammered, then record the next morning, impervious to hangovers. Now it was everything, all the time, and he kept somehow living, even if it mattered little to him to do so, as if the fact that he stayed alive justified, or countered, the damage of the path he found himself on. If he wasn't dead by now, why stop? Maybe this was, actually, the one way he could marginally exist. High, dazed, incapable of feeling.

So he did what was second nature. He went back into the studio. What else was there? Besides, the songs were waiting; they did not forget him, they did not abandon or judge. Shon Sullivan had a buddy and sometime bandmate, Dave McConnell, with a studio, Satellite Park, on a cliff in Malibu. Sullivan was there as Elliott got down, yet again, to business. In fact, he was working on his own record with McConnell, *Blue Swan Orchestra*, which would appear in 2002, a set of tunes strongly influenced and inspired by Elliott, who had always championed Sullivan's songwriting. He had written quite a few of the numbers while on the *Figure 8* tour, in spare moments on the bus or whenever he had a few hours to himself. Sullivan's song "Summertime" features a diminished seventh chord first introduced to him by Elliott, in fact. While at Satellite Park Elliott, essentially on his own, tinkered some with "Summertime," layering over Sullivan's vocals a total of thirty-six overdubbed high falsetto harmonies. "He did it just because he wanted to do it," says Sullivan. "Like, 'Oh yeah. I did this vocal part. See what you think of it. If it works for you, great.'" Sullivan was touched. He loved it. With Elliott's stealth assistance, the song soared.

"The hours were intense," Sullivan remembers. "He'd want to work at night," a detail jibing with the witchy three A.M. vibe many of the tunes possessed. At the same time, according to Sullivan, it was clearly a "very dark period. All the usual vices kicked back in." It looked grim, Sullivan felt. Elliott was "very thin." There were evenings Shon "hardly recognized him." He was bored with the attitude everyone seemed to have, this sense that he needed to be rescued. He wanted none of it. To Sullivan, "that's definitely what happened with Valerie, for instance. She was in way over her head."

The studio's location encouraged anything but lifelessness. Visually, the place was a revelation—angled into a hill, with an expansive view of the rich blue Pacific flattening out into infinity like a massive pastel plate. It was a kind of nirvana. But the feeling as Elliott and McConnell worked ran in an antithetical direction. Elliott, it quickly became clear, was a complete mess. The afternoons with Pickle laying down "Inspector Detector" on his father's four-track, or with JJ in her Portland basement, or with Uppinghouse and her boxer Annie whimpering at the door—all this receded to a dot on the horizon. They were someone else's life by now. They belonged to a history that seemed to have no connection to the present. Now, through fall of 2001 and on into 2002, it wasn't just heroin taking Elliott away. He was smoking crack. He was abusing benzos like Klonopin. He was, to get some energy back, relying on Adderall, an ADHD med. He had become a living drug cocktail, a human pharmacy, spending, on average, fifteen hundred dollars per day on his habits, according to some rough estimates. There was no way to help him, McConnell recalled. "He would have killed himself before he let anyone intervene."[31]

McConnell says he had Elliott on a sort of suicide watch (whatever that means exactly). "At least ten times" he tried OD'ing, apparently.[32] "He would say things like, 'The other day I popped fifteen Klonopin, thinking it would help me die and it didn't.'" Or, "Fuck man! I just did eight hundred dollars' worth of drugs in an hour. What's wrong? What the fuck!" No one had seen anything like it. Nothing fazed him. He absorbed any blow then stumbled back for more, begging to get hit, begging for the TKO that never came. In his mind it was all very scientific, his body and brain a carefully conducted experiment. "He knew more about drugs than most therapists," says McConnell. "He talked about it like a scholar. He had medical books"—the Physician's Desk References he bought at thrift shops, out of date but still usable, Band-Aids serving as bookmarks.[33] McConnell recalls one drunken night in which the two posed for pictures in front of prescription bottles, stacked like a pyramid. It was crazy, he says. Besides, the regimen made no sense, each drug canceling the effects of another. In addition to the Klonopin and Adderall, the crack and heroin, there were antidepressants, antipsychotics, Elliott's brain a chemical soup.

At one point he referenced a possible psychotic episode while making *Figure 8*. This wasn't something anyone else seemed to know about. It's contestable whether it happened at all. But Elliott said he'd carved the word "Now" into his arm with a knife, sick of everyone foisting possible futures upon him. He claimed he had written "Everything Means Nothing to Me" with blood dripping out of him, congealing viscously. The more common story was that he'd been on mushrooms at the time. Perhaps he was actually referencing that; perhaps there was more going on, it's impossible to say.

But high or sober, unhinged or clearheaded, music got made, of a kind utterly new. McConnell set up mics all over the house—a virtual nerve spaghetti—so that when inspiration struck, he'd get it on tape. In keeping with what was going on internally, the inner discord, Elliott's aim was fierceness. The sound had to be raw, uncooked. The sound had to be nasty, "sonically twisted and lyrically abstract." He had spoken before about the impossibility of capturing chaos, how it was worth trying but hard to bring off. Now he gave it a shot, the songs like drip paintings splashed across canvas, nearly unrecognizable as art. In the back of his mind the model was the *White Album*, a disjointed, free-form mix of styles, some tunes sweetly melodic, some snarling and screeching, like Lennon's "Yer Blues." On purpose he'd detune guitars. He waved aside concerns about pitch. If anything sounded pretty or traditional, he'd efface it, wanting the music to "make your stomach churn." In short, the songs were a mirror. They were a way in, not a way out. They advertised dysfunction, a portrait of the artist as perfected, frank, brutal mess.

The way McConnell saw it was simplified. It seemed, to him, like catharsis. "He was getting shit out," McConnell felt. "Lyrically," he said, "this was the most profound record I've ever heard in my life, from any artist. I'd hear the words and I'd just start crying. He was really speaking to his oppressors . . . Saying a lot of things he just had to get off his chest." Yet catharsis implies relief. And there was none of that. If Elliott got things off his chest, they didn't dissipate. They were lethal. They came out and stayed, pointing fingers, jabbing him in the chest. And the songs weren't just about oppressors. More than attacking real and imagined enemies, Elliott attacked himself. He was the target. The weapon might have been jammed, but the ammo was live.

In all, the sessions resulted in nearly a dozen songs, including, in various versions, finished or unfinished, "Stickman," "See You in Heaven," "Little One," "Mr. Goodmorning," and others. The vibe was "My Bloody Valentine," a band Elliott was into then, injected with melody—a swirling, looping metal machine music not unlike Velvet Underground's "The Murder Mystery."

One tune epitomizes the new direction better than any other, the searching, merciless "King's Crossing." It stands alone. Along with "Waltz #2 (XO)," or possibly "Last Call" from *Roman Candle*, it's Elliott's unquestionable masterpiece, drug-addled and suicidal, as if through dark magic he dragged it out by the hair, kicking and screaming. It had been around for a while. He'd recorded acoustic versions; it was on cassettes he'd sent to friends. In that form it was sweet and sad, no major departure from the songs he'd been making since first going solo. With the new treatment it grew fangs, snapping at empty air like a cornered dog. The lyrics went through several revisions, some just as effective as the finished version. The picture he presents is pitiless. He's a scraping subject bowing low; he can't go any farther down. He's the "singing scream of a failing fake." Judges, appointed for life, reach harrowing conclusions—everyone needs to die in their prime. He said he wouldn't pay attention; he finds he already has, however. Someone tells him to grab his gun; if he doesn't, the world below will destroy him. You're a hero, he decides, "once you've become no one." Beverly Hills fat cats show up. Skinny Santas with slurred speech say something, but he only understands "every other word." The song starts with aimless electric guitar, chattering voices discussing someone falling out of a tree, Elliott singing a high "ahhh." Then, smoothly and seamlessly, piano chords appear, on Philip Glass–like repeat, as if they could go on forever, as if they could be the song in its entirety. When vocals kick in, the piano drops out, music tumbling choppily, like it's falling down the stairs. As Elliott reaches the line, "I can't prepare for death any more than I already have," drums stumble in, as if to drive the sentiment, pounding the message. He's "seen the movie," he says. He knows what happens. "It's a hell of a role, if you can keep it alive." Whether he "fucks up" or not makes no difference. He's got a date with a rich white lady, a heroin anima. "Give me one good reason not to do it," he shouts. But he doesn't really want an answer; the question's rhetorical. In any case, when he played the song live, Ashley—and later, Jennifer Chiba—fell into the habit of calling out, "Because we love you." Love was the reason. People cared, people wanted him alive—that's why not to do it. But Elliott serenely answered back, "So do it." Do it *because* he was loved. Do it to set others free from him. Do it as a gift. The song ends with a twin plea, part directed at himself, part at others. "Don't let me get carried away" and "don't let me be carried away." The prescience of these lines is terrifying and uncanny. Interestingly, they arrived as a last revision. Initially in the song, pretty nurses and instruments on a tray were meant to "take the sickness away." In final form hope has faded. It's not sickness coming to an end. It's Elliott.

* * *

By December 20, 2001, Elliott was back home, temporarily, in Portland, at the Crystal Ballroom downtown. The crowd was deliriously energized, Elliott less so, his speech slurred, his guitar playing knuckly, his ability to remember chords and lyrics always in question. The silence was thick as he sang, alone, all acoustic. But as songs concluded everyone erupted, screaming out requests, telling him he looked great, telling him they love him. At one point someone said "Come back to Portland." "I'm gonna come back to Portland," he replied, then added, "I think. I'm gonna move out of L.A., that's for sure . . . It sucks." A girl near the front informed him it was her birthday; she asked for "Miss Misery." He wasn't sure he could bring it off but he tried, then aborted it. "I put that one way out of my mind. It was too much," he explained. "Division Day," a tune possibly referencing the street he lived paces away from back in the Heatmiser days, ended similarly. He did not get through it, saying, "I don't know this anymore. There has to be a major fuck-up somewhere." As he finished "True Love," his heroin sweetheart tune, he told everyone "that's a true story. An epic." It's a confession of his mental state. As was his custom at the time, he carried with him his bag of pills, his man purse. Sadly, he showed it to friends, as if almost proudly providing evidence of how messed up he was, as if to say, "I know I'm hurting you all. I'm sorry"—but not, they felt, sorry enough to stop. Stopping was not in the plan. Drugs in all forms had become, friends realized—this time more forcefully than ever—his new self-identity. The voice was the pills. They were a veil over everything. The person they saw in front of them was a shell. He said he wasn't capable of feeling. He seemed like a zombie, he seemed lobotomized. For many who knew him this was to be a final image; some never saw him again. The holidays came and went, and he was back, not to Portland, but to L.A. Impossibly, there was more trouble awaiting him. It would get worse, then better, then worse again.

CHAPTER NINE CAN'T MAKE A SOUND

What led at last to some slight shift in the direction of better health was a Google search. At wit's end, Elliott tapped in the word "heroin."[1] That took him to a *Heroin Times* essay on Lou Reed, about Reed studying poetry with mentor Delmore Schwartz, an "alcoholic speed-addict" for whom he wrote two songs ("Our House" and "European Son"). Sections described Reed shooting up on stage, acting as a sort of "poster boy for heroin chic." Others noted his "fine blend of street wisdom and book knowledge," the way he gave voice to the "downtrodden and repressed," how he kicked his habit through the help of Alcoholics Anonymous: "The Velvet Underground may have started Reed's adulthood, but AA saved it."[2] "It's my wife, it's my life" Reed had written, tersely summing up what heroin had become for him; Elliott captures the same sentiment in "King's Crossing—"All I want to do now is inject my ex-wife"—the "ex" adjective more wish than reality, in all likelihood. (Also, by all accounts, Elliott never shot up.)

Reed, the essay continues, dons his blue mask to simultaneously reveal the "raw vulnerability and live-wire sensitivity beneath it." The theme of compassion emerges, its necessity for true healing, especially in a form directed toward the self. In the end Elliott's beloved Nico even appears, saying "I find it hard to believe you don't know the beauty you are."[3]

Elliott read on with building interest, even a sense of hope. Here was, first of all, a writer who seemed to know what he was talking about, someone who had been there and crawled out. Here, also, was the prototypical addict, heroin's New York hero. If Reed could do it, if Reed had found something useful in AA, of all places, then why not him? After all, Elliott was decidedly minor league compared to Reed. Reed *was* heroin, a kind of living symbol. On the other hand, maybe it was all bullshit, Elliott figured, hyperbole, wishful thinking. Did Reed really do this? Was he really clean?

So with Valerie along for the ride Elliott showed up at the *Heroin Times* offices in Malibu. He wanted to know who had written the article, who had made these claims. He was on a kind of fact-checking mission. As it happened, Nelson Gary sat at the front desk. He was the author, he said, and all of it was true. At first Elliott was skeptical. But Gary knew people who knew Reed; he wasn't making anything up. He'd done his homework. It was all fact. Besides, Gary wondered, why doubt it. Why the incredulity?

When Elliott arrived he was pissed off. Gary had no clue who he was. He looked homeless, and to Gary he seemed, at first, delusional. Sounding like some two-bit wannabe with nothing to show for himself, a faux artiste, a faux songwriter, he railed against the radio and why he wasn't on it more, he complained about the need to tour. As for fame, "he wanted it"; it made him sick but at the same time "he felt he had been overlooked." "I don't think he was coming from a narcissistic place," Gary said. "He just heard people on the radio sounding like him and making lots of money. He was interested in acknowledgement in the broadest possible sense."[4] As the two talked Elliott finally cooled down some. At one point someone whispered in Gary's ear, clueing him in on whom he was speaking with. It caught Gary off guard, but he quickly realized that one of the reasons Elliott listened, maybe the only reason, was that Gary hadn't recognized him. He wasn't some sort of star fucker. He was, for all he knew, talking to a complete nobody. Elliott found something instantly endearing about that.

"We hit it off," Gary says. "But it was an edgy relationship. He was cerebral and I'd be contrary for the hell of it." Elliott adored the Beatles, Gary figured out, so he dissed them cajolingly, telling Elliott he was living a much more Rolling Stones life. They argued about who was better, and Elliott "was a scrapper, he was a junkyard dog. I wouldn't say he was mean, but he could defend himself. He had all the intellectual subject matter but he was doing stuff too," not just talking about it. "He wasn't an encyclopedia with shoes," Gary recognized.

Over time they met about once or twice per month—as friends, not as therapist/patient. Gary was a painter, writer, poet, and exuberant, inventive spoken-word performer, his lexicon impressively large; he quoted easily from Kierkegaard to Hinduism, Nietzsche to Coltrane. His mother, Jan Fuller, was a feminist who'd appeared on numerous talk shows, and his wife worked in the music industry, so he knew his artists inside and out, a major Dylan, Bowie, and Stones fan. His job revolved around addiction treatment; he counseled at Malibu Ranch and then transitioned to program director at the Malibu Coast Treatment Center. He was well versed in the vicissitudes of detox, and he understood intimately the complications of dual diagnosis, Elliott's struggle. Depression engendered drug use, drug use magnified depression. The former had to be treated just as aggressively as the latter. It was a multipronged attack or it was nothing.

Although he's not sure what kind of direct impact it had, one idea Gary introduced to Elliott was Tamil Siddha, or tantric twilight language, also called "intentional language." At the time Gary was "mesmerized" by it— the idea of expanding the mind by deliberate use of opposites, a dialectical synthesis achieved through paradoxical juxtaposition. Gary isn't certain it had anything strictly to do with him, but Elliott wound up retitling the song "Somebody's Baby" "Twilight," and it does, in the recorded version, include several Siddha-like antitheses—laughing so hard he cries, being with some-one only to disappoint her in the process, and loving two dissimilar women at once. But if the idea ever reached an apex, it was with the song "Coast to Coast." What Elliott was after, Gary believes, was a specific, complex heal-ing, "catharsis without resolution," or as Elliott himself put it in the song's two opening lines, confused resolution. He told Gary his character was a preacher, a circuit rider, traveling from town to town, in love with two women, one stable and boring, one signifying chaos, the final detail dupli-cating the theme of "Twilight." Gary goes on: "Elliott sings repeatedly about doing something for a certain 'you,' feeling that he has already done things for this 'you' a number of times and he has nothing new for them. Every reviewer I've read misinterpreted this. They were too focused on the artist, not the art. They wrote things such as 'I've got nothing new for you' is a joke; it's silly. That's true. But as an artist he was attempting to get people to pay attention to the art, not him ultimately. The 'you' he is addressing is one fictionalized romantic love interest (the road girl), a second romantic fiction-alized love interest (the stay-at-home girl or wife), God, and to some degree, the general audiences he seduces going from revival tent to revival tent. It shows the speaker's disillusionment about what has life has brought him in terms of relationships . . ." Elliott was at a crossroads, Gary suggested, of the sacred and profane. He often told him "the intermingling of the two is the only place true holiness can exist." The "lowness of the high, the low in the high, the profound, even potentially holy relationship between them. That's one of the major things Elliott was investigating."

For the song Gary was brought in to provide a "waterfall of words" or "John Coltrane sheets of sound." They recorded on Good Friday in Hollywood. Steven Drozd was on drums; so was Autumn de Wilde's husband, Aaron Sperske of Beachwood Sparks. Gary had a poem in hand. He recorded it in voice-over numerous times, take after take. Elliott wanted a range of personas, different accents, different attitudes. He would say "miss it, but be late" or "miss it, but be early." His intent was for the words to sound obliquely off, never managing to find any sort of groove or rhythm. "I went by the lower notes of his guitar playing," says Gary.

But the song begins with machine whining, industrial mine-shaft scraping. Drums awake fumblingly at first, hibernating large animals resentful at having their slumber interrupted, then crash in obligingly aside electric guitar. Elliott says two words—*preachy* and *pushy*—as piano chords tumble. There's nothing new, Elliott says, no new act to amuse, no desire to use. Anything he does would not be good enough anyway. He figures he'll just forget it; it's really easy to do. "If you can't help it, just leave it alone." He introduces the circuit rider, who comes "every fifth Sunday." And Gary, in two different studio-altered voices, appears over a tinkling piano tracing a high, haunting melody, in some ways the most powerful moment in the song. For reasons Gary never understood, Elliott recorded himself saying "that's why" as the piano fades. He seemed to mean it as a reaction to some line in the poetry, but it's hard to say. It may be more randomness, more meaningless noise.

Everything done, the subject of money arose, awkwardly. Gary had assumed he'd be compensated, and he was, a total of fifteen hundred dollars. Elliott said, initially, "I thought we were doing this as two artists." Gary's impulsive reply: "Tell that to David Geffen." It wasn't a serious disagreement, however. Things ended on very good terms.

Besides, there was a lot more to talk about, namely emotional pain and drugs, and what to do about each, how to move past them somehow, if possible. Gary's sense, based on hashing the subject out with Elliott in detail, was that childhood trauma had permanently changed him, that there was little chance of reversing its effects. He had tried "being okay with himself," being "accepting," but radical acceptance only went so far. It didn't change the facts, obviously; and more important, Elliott continued to feel angry. Although he tried, his attitude was not always one of equanimity. There was shame too, self-hatred, confusion, loss. The two discussed how drugs functioned as an extension of trauma, a form of self-abuse, of "administering the torture on yourself." One becomes his own destroyer, in other words. Gary was also aware of cutting incidents, occasions on which Elliott harmed himself superficially. It was another piece of it, more marks of self-loathing. None of this was new to Elliott. He knew what was going on. The question was, did he really want to change it. Did he want to take it on, or did he want to let it slowly destroy him?

The answer, currently, though tentatively, was no. Then it was back to Lou Reed, AA, the best path to take. Gary put Elliott in touch with Jerry Schoenkopf, an addictions specialist with a history of working with rockstar junkies. Schoenkopf's memory is that he first met Elliott in 1996, under unclear circumstances. At any rate, the connection was made, and it deepened. Jerry and Elliott never went more than one month without talking.[5] They met consistently, although somewhat sporadically. To Schoenkopf, Elliott was smart, a true intellectual, and very sweet, but also "very depressed," and using drugs "to get more depressed"; as he saw it, "just like depressed people do, he used alcohol, heroin, any downer. To deepen the depression." The two reviewed Elliott's abuse and detox history, how he'd get better, stop getting better, then get worse. There was a sense that he was fragmenting, that he was tired, that the drugs for depression weren't cutting it. In fact, as Schoenkopf examined Elliott's drug regimen, he began to feel "this is not the right stuff." "Psych drugs can be a problem," he said. "We had long talks about psychiatry. Psych drugs can only take you so far. I don't want to say it was wrong, what Elliott was on, but it didn't work"—a hardly uncommon reality, with anywhere from one third to one half of depressed patients treatment refractory (i.e., drugs don't help them at all).

What Schoenkopf counseled was complete abstinence—"it's playing with matches, heroin, and you're a baby." Elliott's "center was fragile," Schoenkopf felt, "and he couldn't afford to wobble. It's not like he could try to become a weekend heroin user. His core was too unstable." You can't compete with these drugs, he'd say, and Elliott agreed. He was "obsessively interested" in them, on one hand, but he also "knew he was losing his capacity to be creative." Elliott had said something similar to Jennifer Chiba, once telling her "I think I've destroyed that part of me that can make music. I feel like I'm already dead." This was, in many ways, a do-or-die realization. Destroying any other part wouldn't have mattered in the least. It was what Elliott was busily doing, tempting fate with overdoses, with murderous drug combos. He placed little value on his life. He was sick of it. But the music was something else. It was the one thing, maybe the only thing, he did not want to disappear. Losing it was losing the last bit of hope he had, his one reason for trying. If, in some crazy, magical reality, he could die and the music could go on—that would be fine. He'd be good with that. Yet there was no magical reality. As he'd figured out long ago, to keep making music he needed to sacrifice; he needed, that is, to give up death, his attraction to ending everything, to numbness, emptiness, isolation; he needed to choose life, whether he wanted it or not. This was the perpetual struggle. Why not kill yourself? The question rarely left him. And the answer, the only answer ever, was music. For now at least, he could not lose it. He wasn't ready to let it go too.

There was something else at work, something that made daily life a living hell. The drugs had fomented a fierce paranoia, in some respects more destructive than the substances themselves. Some days Elliott believed in these fears, others he saw them for what they were—side effects of continuously damaged chemistry. The one way out, he realized during saner moments, was to stop using. Shon Sullivan recalls a late night-trip to a Burger King drive-through. The truck behind was revving its engine, and Elliott latched onto the idea that it was following him. "He began to see all these coincidences," Sullivan says. "It was standard, textbook stuff." He thought his car was bugged. He thought DreamWorks was tracking him, breaking into his home and stealing songs. Once he decided scores of people were hiding in the grass outside his home, invisibly spying. At four A.M. he headed to an all-night Home Depot, his plan to buy a machete and cut the grass back. But the main fixation was white vans. He saw them everywhere, and white cars. As he drove around L.A. he took pictures—of license plates, of suspicious vehicles—then uploaded them into his computer as evidence, scores and scores of arbitrary images. He also recorded a running monologue, documenting what he was seeing, making imaginary connections in his head. Clearly fear was rendering him psychotic. Everyone around him knew he was out of his mind, the paranoia erupting over and over, hard to predict. Most of the time it was fruitless to talk with him about it. It pissed him off to be questioned, and he sometimes folded the questioner into the delusional mind-set, saying, "You are part of it too?" Deep down, however, he held on to slipping insight. He'd say to friends, "I sound like I'm totally batshit crazy, don't I?" Schoenkopf discussed with him the chemical aspects. First off, crack caused delusions. This was amphetamine psychosis, a dopamine-driven paranoia. To stop it, he'd need to stop the drugs. It was simple. But there was more too, an additional difficulty. "If you take these drugs long enough," Schoenkopf explained, "and then you stop, the paranoia stays, and finds a home in your brain." So there were chemical elements, and psychological ones. Combating the fears required a multidimensional approach—no more drugs combined with psychological insight into their sequelae. Nelson Gary chimed in too, his sense of things a bit more nuanced, more emotional than clinical. "He certainly had depression—that's for sure," said Gary. "In terms of the paranoia, Elliott was a cutter—you become very raw. What happens is you can get into a very sort of oceanic experience and a lot of uncertainty, and it's scary. He opened himself up to a lot of stuff in the music, in songs like 'Coast to Coast' and 'King's Crossing,' and it ripped him apart. His strengths were also his weakness. He was stepping out and taking a chance as an artist. The new songs were different and his fans weren't prepared for it. That fear, with drugs, with abuse, with depression, led to the paranoia." In the end, "Elliott's sensitivity was his undoing; paranoia is really just hypersensitivity."

Whatever the proximate causes—and depression alone is another, its mood-congruent delusions—the question was how to stop the fear, how to *not* stop the music. Elliott couldn't do AA. He could not honestly take the first step, which required admitting he was at the mercy of a higher power. Power was an idea he had always rejected totally. So in August 2002 he latched on to a biological remedy, a decidedly fringe medical solution called Neurotransmitter Restoration, developed initially by William Hitt. It was

fast, it promised a ten-day detox. It claimed to produce substantially re-
duced withdrawal, decreased cravings, restored mental clarity. NTR, as
practitioners called it, intravenously saturated the body with nutrients, naturally occurring amino acids, minerals, and buffers, stimulating, the theory
said, a cell shift into repair mode, with drug-damaged neurons returning to
normal functioning, brain receptor sites coated with a cool, wet blanket.
Detox from crystal meth might require one amino acid and mineral solution, heroin and alcohol another. The tonic was determined by the specific
case.

Elliott described the process to an interviewer, clearly, at this point, a
believer. "What they do is an IV treatment where they put a catheter in your
arm, and you're on a drip bag, but the only thing that's in the drip bag is
amino acids and saline solution. I was coming off of a lot of psych meds and
other things. I was even on an antipsychotic, although I'm not psychotic. It
was really difficult . . . It's usually a ten-day process, but for me it took a lot
longer . . . It just bombards your system with amino acids that kick all the
shit out of your nerve receptors."[6] He continued, "There's such a taboo of
even talking about drug use, and then there is the added problem if you play
music. Then there's this sort of melodrama that surrounds it, which wouldn't
necessarily surround someone who doesn't play music. So, it's kind of an
off-limits subject. Actually, I thought I would just try to avoid it, but I'm
not different from other people with drug problems. So, given the opportunity to speak, then I guess I will."

Schoenkopf wasn't a fan, nor was most anyone with an appropriately
critical mind-set. "I think little of it," he said. "They look at your history,
then come up with a soup of amino acids." His belief was that it was "essentially garbage," at a cost of a thousand dollars per day, a minimum ten
thousand dollars total. "Once you take the IV out, it's bullshit. It doesn't
work." Schoenkopf knew of Hitt. He was a big, good-looking, charismatic
guy who spoke with confidence, employing soothingly scientific language
that seemed, in his mouth, legit. He was persuasive; but questions dogged
him. New Zealand's *Listener* checked into his background in an investiga-
tive piece. They found a total absence of undergraduate or medical degrees,
a fact Hitt admitted to in sworn documents filed with a court. He'd claimed,
audaciously, to have won a Nobel Prize. That, too, was false, as was his claim

of an Eli Lilly award. There were also contentions that Hitt, now deceased, "doctored test results."[7]

Elliott never questioned Hitt or his credentials. And despite the inherent illogic of the treatment, its flimsy conceptual foundations, he believed, strongly, that it had helped. It was grueling, for a time it left him reeling, but he did feel restored, rejuvenated, as if something deep had shifted in him. Did it cure the paranoia? No. The fears lingered, although they became less consuming. And his hope, now that he'd made an honest stab at getting clean, was that slowly, as the fog cleared, the creative capacity might return with fresh force. But something unexpected happened. In the midst of all this change, the effort to turn things in a promising direction, one consistent with life, a new conflict emerged.

Nelson Gary always felt "Coast to Coast" was a metaphor for Deerin and Chiba, for stability, which Elliott needed, and disorder, which he also needed. The two were vying for Elliott's affections. When Deerin left—which she needed to do with some regularity—returning home to sign visa papers, Chiba and Elliott hung out (just friends with a mutual sense of growing affection). When she returned, she did so with understandable jealousy. Who was this woman, and what were Elliott's intentions toward her? Deerin was mild mannered, sweet, kind, and helpful; she did everything she could for Elliott, the two even making efforts to start a foundation for abused children, an enterprise Schoenkopf was also peripherally involved with. But whenever the name "Chiba" came up, she'd turn suddenly irate. Occasions when they ran into each other, at shows or bars, devolved into drama. Once, according to Chiba, Deerin called her a "fucking whore," and accused her of addicting Elliott to heroin. It was an ugly, contentious triangle. Even Elliott's neighbor, Barb Martinez, told Valerie, "You've got to move on." She struck Martinez as "a little young." The sense was that she was in over her head. She encouraged Elliott, she "kept him from being lazy and reclusive," Martinez says, but at the same time it was clear things were not working. Something had to give.

It's more evidence of the effects of Elliott's early relationships—the abandonment by his father, the idyllic interlude when he had his mother to himself for a period of four years—when, in his mind, they needed no one else to be happy—his mother's eventual abandonment, of sorts, as she remarried, and the damaging relationship with Charlie. What evolved for Elliott was a mix of strategies. There was self-sabotage—he ended relationships even when they were good. As he wrote in "Go By," he'd "leave you even if" things were promising. In other words, he preempted relationship failures; he expected them to fail, so he torpedoed them, he cut them off before they reached their inevitable—in his mind—end. Nobody broke your heart, he sang in "Alameda"; "you broke your own." But he also needed love; he hated to be alone. So he sought intimacy as he doubted its viability. In short, he resisted breaking up with anyone—as in the relationship with Bolme, which kept dragging on—and he didn't want to risk being with anyone either, especially in the sense of needing them, coming to depend on them, tying his feelings up with them and in the process making himself vulnerable to painful disappointment. Yet finally, through a process not entirely clear (Deerin decided, after many invitations and one e-mail exchange, not to be interviewed for this book), Elliott ended things with Valerie. As Chiba put it, "he sent her back to Scotland." Martinez recalls her leaving quickly, but in fact, she stayed around L.A. for at least a matter of weeks, if not months. Or, she left, then quickly returned. And as several people have described, in close detail, she seemed to fall apart. She was thrown into what appeared to be some sort of emotional tailspin—very sad, very unexpected, and very hard to watch. Elliott's feeling—perfectly understandable in light of his own history—was that she did not deserve to be abandoned. But he found he couldn't stay with her either, apparently. She quickly went from being, at baseline, extremely neat and tidy and well put together, to not bathing, not changing her clothes for days at a time, according to several people who were there to see the regression. More than once she allegedly, and vaguely, threatened Elliott's life, saying, in effect, that something drastic was going to happen, and that she wasn't talking about herself. Elliott, wisely, holed up in a studio he'd recently built, with the name "New Monkey," in an office complex in the San Fernando Valley.

Calls were placed on Elliott's behalf to his psychiatrist, Dr. Schloss— the "brain boss" with whom Gary Smith had set him up. At times he and Valerie had met with Schloss together—as had Bunny and Ashley and Jennifer Chiba, even Dave McConnell. Clearly his parents knew he was in some degree of trouble emotionally; they also were learning, piece by piece, the extent and seriousness of his addiction history. At some point Schloss was told of Deerin's condition and asked for advice about what to do. She obviously needed help badly; it was far from clear how things might turn out. Schloss, however, was apparently dismissive. He said he knew Valerie, and she couldn't hurt a fly.

By this time she was telling people she was going to win her man back. She was on a mission, driven by a monomaniacal mind-set, now at a point—some believed—where she'd overstayed her visa. She slipped into shows in strange disguises, wearing white wigs. Those who knew her saw who she was; the fear, always, was that she might do something desperate. In late January 2003, several months after the breakup, the "get a backbone" episode occurred. This was the message she called out to Elliott in the middle of a performance—another rocky one—right after he finished the song "Pretty (Ugly Before)." She may have believed she would have gone undetected, unidentified—she was in disguise. Yet several people who were there that night positively indentified her, and although Elliott did not know, at first, that Deerin had made the remark, he did the next night, when he played the same venue again.

What everyone understood was that Valerie needed help, Schloss's demurrals aside. They were sympathetic; they didn't demonize her. It was understandable what she was going through. She had devoted her life to Elliott; she'd done all she could to support him, to the degree she knew how; she'd been there when he was at his worst, beset by nightmares in which he beat himself up, in which he "kicked [his] own ass for treating me badly," and recognized he needed to "separate drug use from escaping my past and/ or stupid 'I don't remember what happened' saddened self."[8] The struggle had exhausted her, unhinged her; the result was some form of emotional breakdown. Elliott had deserted her; he'd rejected her perfect love. And it was a decision she simply could not and would not accept.

Still reeling mentally and physically from the ghastly Neurotransmitter Restoration, and deciding, reasonably, that it might not be a good idea to go home—he'd taken to sleeping in a drum isolation chamber in New Monkey—Elliott turned to Chiba. At the time he was weakened, she says, to the point where he found it hard even to get up. Still, he asked her to meet him at the Roost. He told her he'd sent Valerie home, that he had finished up the ten-day treatment, and that he needed somewhere to stay because he could not take care of himself. The two had a natural bond. Their histories lined up—depression, thoughts of suicide, drug use, both legal and illegal. Chiba played music, and knew Elliott's catalogue inside and out. She was a trained art therapist too, a counselor, with an MA from Loyola Marymount, so she had the requisite skills. She was in a position to understand Elliott's psychology, and to apprehend the connection between his art and his moods, the role played by imagination in his overall well-being. At first there was little thought of becoming romantic. They were obviously attracted to each other, but that took a back seat to the main objective—getting well, trying to find some sort of mental clarity away from drugs, especially crack. As it would be to the last day of his life, paranoia was still present. It kept materializing just as Schoenkopf predicted it might—it found a foothold in Elliott's brain, a residue of dopamine hyperactivity. The obsession with DreamWorks was an ongoing consternation, impossible to dismantle. He would tell Chiba, "Someone's trying to kill me, you know." While living with Valerie back at the Disney cottages, and even when recording with McConnell in Malibu, all Elliott ever seemed to want to eat was ice cream—Double Rainbow. It was the same with Chiba; he kept a healthy stock in the freezer. At times he refused to leave the house to buy it. He pleaded with others to do it for him. Once, deprived of food, he passed out and turned blue at the Greek Amphitheater. As always, if anyone tried questioning him, attacking, however gently, the irrationality of his beliefs, he'd reply with, "What?! Even my friends don't believe me now?!?" His ideas were deeply entrenched; cutting them out through any sort of disputing process seemed mostly hopeless. Other possibly paranoia-related odd behaviors materialized too. Chiba says "he started taking computers and telephones apart and putting the pieces in the refrigerator."[9]

As he moved with Chiba to a small home on a hill, at the end of a long drive behind another house out front, and next door to Roger and Mary Steffens (Roger Steffens was a world-renowned reggae expert who maintained a reggae museum), her feeling, one that others around Elliott shared, was that he "was already gone. It was just a shell of him then." It was as if a part of his personality had been removed. He was dulled, mentally mud-

Elliott in 2003. (Wendy Redfern/Getty Images.)

dled, tired, internally besieged. Even his compassion, his vivacity, his concern for others had leaked out invisibly. Naively, but just like most everyone else in Elliott's life, especially women, Chiba thought she could save him. "I loved him," she says, "but at the same time I wasn't sure I had what it took to stay with someone so fucked up." She did her best; she stuck with it, feeling as if she were doing the world a favor. But it was like three full-time jobs at once. Day and night she was on call, in the back of her mind realizing "people are going to do what they are going to do."

Her belief, no doubt correct, was that Elliott was "definitely insecurely attached." Admirably, "he exposed his vulnerability immediately," he was "very clear and open about how he felt," yet when it came to relationships he tended to be "guarded and unsure," or ambivalent, resistant. He told her succinctly "my childhood made me feel like I didn't exist. I was nothing." What Chiba focused on, apart from managing day-to-day needs for nutrition, getting Elliott back to some approximation of physical well-being, was the music, encouraging him to work when he felt up to it. New Monkey was set up; he had begun renting the Van Nuys space back when he lived in the Disney cottages. For a time, he kept equipment in the cottage loft, reachable via the circular stairway. It had functioned as his home studio. But he moved all he had to the new space, eventually, its name a hopeful inspiration, music a "new monkey," a replacement addiction. Once he got it up and running he spent days at a time there, sometimes sleeping in the same drum isolation room, buying new gear, taking it apart when necessary and doing what he could to fix it. At first it was a total mess, but Elliott and Chiba got it organized. They put inspirational quotes on the board, tapestries on the wall (partly to dampen sound). Drawers and cabinets were painstakingly labeled.

Apart from a Fairchild compressor, which Elliott also really loved, his overriding fixation, one that dominated the last year of his life and became, indeed, a new monkey, was a Trident A-Range mixing board, one of eleven made, the same sort of range the Beatles had used at Abbey Road. Initially the board was a piece of shit, according to Nelson Gary. When it arrived it failed to function properly, and Elliott concluded he'd been ripped off. But he tore into it with total absorption, dedicating every free moment to getting it up and running again. Gary calls the board Elliott's "second most impairing obsession," the first being DreamWorks. He still was not able to shake the notion that the company was bugging his home, tapping his phone, hiding listening devices in plants in his lawyer's offices. As a sort of accidental treatment, he trained all his attentions on the Trident. In Gary's estimation, "it was the place he would go as an escape from mad thoughts about DreamWorks," yet it led to "circular ruins of despair." There was nothing Elliott failed to comprehend about the board in terms of how it could or could not function. But he wasn't exactly a techie, so no matter how hard he worked to get it repaired, it remained unyielding. The board, Gary believed, was Elliott's new "speedball." In his fantasies he'd picture it by his side as he took a stand "against the evil leviathan of the corporate record label." In short, the device made him crazier, he couldn't get his mind off it, but as a symptom it more or less worked. He'd stopped heroin for good, crack too, and their place in his psyche was taken by the Trident. He lived and breathed the maddening thing, but it was a better drug, less destructive if still bizarrely consuming.

The Trident was a means to an end, even if Elliott sometimes treated it as an end in itself. The truer focus was the music he'd make with it, the activity it was supposed to serve. Handfuls of songs were scattered about, some old, rejects from prior efforts, some relatively new, performed but previously unrecorded. It's not clear how much actual recording Elliott got around to at New Monkey. Most people feel very little was laid down on tape there. Not exactly nothing, but not a lot. Yet despite the condition he was in—still physically ravaged, paranoid, now and then secretly abusing Schloss's prescription drugs, intensely fearful of imaginary spying by DreamWorks—he got to the point where he envisioned a double album, a sort of concept album, looser than, say, *The Wall*, more like *Sergeant Pepper's* or the Beatles' *White Album*. By now he'd cut off McConnell, possibly out of more paranoia, but his intent was unchanged. He wanted something adventurous, edgy, dirty, with songs spiraling off in many directions at once, messy but with an underlying unity, a whole exceeding the sum of its parts. Chiba hired Fritz Michaud as a studio assistant, the person heard at the start of "King's Crossing." And like a well-meaning taskmaster, she sent Elliott and Fritz off to work; she pushed and prodded. Some days Elliott got almost nothing done; other days he'd return with tapes and play back what he'd come up with. It was decidedly slow going, but it seemed to be working. In between trips to the studio Elliott and Chiba indulged in what she called "retail therapy." They headed off to Home Depot, Fry's Electronics, the Bodhi Tree Bookstore where they bought baskets full of self-help titles. Now and then, on rare occasions, Elliott donned "the green goggles," slang for getting stoned. He smoked, Chiba says, to combat Adderall addiction (the stimulant ADHD drug), a remedy he felt worked. She didn't like it, but it seemed at the time like a harmless enough irregularity, and it never led to anything harder.

In terms of the music, a total of something like fifty-eight songs awaited refinishing, Chiba recalls. Of those, twenty-eight to thirty were to be culled. Some were frankly experimental, "Melodic Noise," "Blind Alley," and "Yay"; some were layered, wall of sound concoctions like "Stickman" and "Coast to Coast"; some were meant to slowly explode after gentle beginnings, like "Abused"; some featured "insane amounts of guitar tracks," Chiba says, along with Motown vocals and drums arrived at by happy accident, such as "Shooting Star," a song Chiba says Elliott wanted as an opening track. To be expected, certain numbers were also acoustic—"Let's Get Lost" and the comparatively old "Memory Lane," about Elliott's Sierra Tucson experience. It was all slowly coalescing. This was to be Elliott's epic, a Homeric statement to exceed all others. The list of tunes expanded almost daily— there were, in addition to those named above, the instrumental "See You in Heaven," "Mr. Goodmorning," "From a Poison Well," "Here If You Want Me," with lyrics added to an instrumental riff from *Figure 8*, "True Love," "Taking a Fall," "Go By," "Talking to Mary," "Sons and Daughters," "Going Nowhere," and the insouciant but ominous sounding "Suicide Machine" (once titled "Tiny Time Machine"), the tune in which Elliott imagines making a "happy home out of hellish things" (in draft lyrics). He rides a pony on a neon night, saying everything will be all right. Chiba says Elliott "worked tirelessly on the mixes to get them just the way he wanted"; he pushed the limits of the recording equipment, using unorthodox setups. He "ran the sonic gamut," intrigued by any potential new direction. Even Neil Gust re-materialized, showing up for a short visit at a time when Elliott's paranoia was on the increase, Chiba recalls. The two recorded a song, just like back in the Heatmiser days in Portland. "I spent a week and a half with him," Gust says. Elliott brought up the band's demise again, apologizing once more for what had happened. "He said he wanted to make another Heatmiser record, go on tour. Kind of crazy. But he was a mess. I was like, You need to get healthy first."[10] As for the recorded song, Chiba can't remember its title, or if it ever had one; she later gave the master to Gust.

What is indisputable is that the record was set to explode a brand-new

Elliott Smith with a brand-new game. It was to be a colossal artistic departure. All the inimitably nuanced beauty of the prior efforts was retained, in songs like "Let's Get Lost" and "Going Nowhere," the lyrical weight and density, the intricacy, but the range of sound roamed heedlessly, numbers dropping like deliberately amateurish homemade explosives, creating a corrosiveness never before seen on any other of Elliott's records. Gary believes some of the strain Elliott felt at the time had to do with this change of direction. He knew it wasn't going to jibe; he knew it might unnerve or confuse fans to whom he always felt a degree of devotion. He understood that, on its face, it was a bit of a disorganized tangle, a lot like the *White Album*, in fact, with its jarring incongruities, from "Dear Prudence" to "Revolution 9." But so be it. It was Elliott's *Finnegans Wake*, his electrified Beckett. And if DreamWorks detested it, all the better. He was up for a total sonic rebuke, all paranoia aside.

The sad question, of course, was whether he could bring it off, did he still have it in him. His plan was to gather up the demons then throw them against the wall where they'd burst in messy melody, curlicues of scraping sound. But the demons had their own designs, as always. It's not as if they were primed to cooperate; they never had been before. Projections onto DreamWorks notwithstanding, Elliott always understood the enemy was within. It went where he went, everywhere from Home Depot to New Monkey. With tenacity, and with every last iota of self-preservative feeling he could muster, he'd defeated heroin and crack. The struggle, now, was with legal drugs, with psychiatry, his father's profession. Chiba recalls ninety-minute sessions with Schloss, sometimes as frequently as three times per week. They worked away at his issues, but they also got sidetracked, discussing abstract math theories, among other recondite topics. What came to alarm Chiba, she says, was that nearly every day Elliott emerged with new prescriptions, even for laughably dubious diagnoses like restless leg syndrome. Chiba wound up purchasing "the most complicated pill case you've ever seen," about the size of a human arm, with extra-large compartments. Once, when Chiba came along for a session, she asked Schloss pointedly, "Why do you prescribe like this for someone with a drug habit?" By this time Elliott was spending upward of seven thousand dollars per month, Chiba estimates, just on medication. Gary Smith had seen Elliott's man purse of drugs, and it shocked him too, Chiba recalls. Some nights she called Elliott's father in desperation. In many ways, as close friends had begun to realize over the span of several years, the psych meds were just as ruinous as the street variety. Elliott was chronically oversedated, his thinking soupy, his speech garbled. Several of his final 2003 performances were iffy affairs. He still seemed out of it. He was wobbly, his voice undependable, his playing imprecise. People speculated he was still on heroin, still a junkie. He wasn't. It was the psychiatric drugs. They were making him look like someone chronically mentally ill—slowed, sluggish, emotionally deadened, carelessly medicated.

There were scant few performances in 2001 and 2002, the addiction years. They just weren't very possible. As he took to telling crowds, "I'm too fucked up." In 2003 his pace picked up some as he tried to power through, to get back on his feet. He played New York's Bowery Ballroom in late January, again stopping a few tunes; there were the two consecutive gigs at Henry Ford Theatre in L.A., when Deerin showed up in disguise. In June he appeared at the Field Day Festival held in New York's Giants' Stadium. Dave Leto was there and spent time with Elliott backstage. As Leto recalls it, his mystique was still uniquely powerful. All the big stars and big bands, from Radiohead to Beck to Bright Eyes, watched him speechlessly from the wings, as if studying a master. The day poured rain; it was Portland weather, of a sort Elliott felt at home with. But to Leto, although Elliott soldiered through the set, he was not exactly on his game. He looked different, for one. More ravaged than usual, more blurry. Parts appeared to be missing somehow, as if his personality had been turned off. After the show Leto, Dorien, Chiba, and Elliott met up in his trailer. With Jennifer Elliott was "very touchy-feely, very PDA-ish." They seemed close; they seemed clearly bonded. Chiba and Dorien left, and Elliott told Leto he wanted to play him a song, a Kinks tune called "Days." Leto says, "It was really cool. I felt pretty special. It was like a concert for one." This was a song Elliott had played many times for Chiba, telling her, "You can listen to this when I'm gone." It's a sort of summing up, a melancholic thank-you. "I'm not frightened of this world," Davies writes. "I won't forget a single day," even though the night is dark and brings more sorrow.

As the year dragged on, the psych meds continued their destructive arc. There were far too many, for one, at least six or seven—a newer anti-psychotic, Zyprexa, now known to cause metabolic disorders, the Adderall, the Klonopin, Serzone, a serotonin reuptake inhibitor that worsens, in rare instances, suicidal thinking. There were days when Elliott took the proper dosages, abiding by his doctor's orders. Other times he manipulated the system, taking more than he should, hoping to disconnect himself, dampen the always intense emotional pain, hiding information from different prescribers, some he would see on his own at all hours of the night, on mysterious errands.

Back in 2002 he'd told McConnell about overdosing, how he'd been deliberately reckless, not caring what the effect might be. One night in 2003 he tried it again. This was to be the first in a handful of crisis evenings. Chiba discovered Elliott had taken twenty-two Klonopin. His frighteningly blithe attitude seemed to be, "Let's just see if I die." Jennifer immediately called Ashley, who raced over, Chiba says, to find Elliott still conscious and propped up, but looking very slowed and sedated. The idea, reasonably, was to call 911. But Elliott was adamantly opposed; they knew if they made the call, he'd find it unforgivable, more a betrayal than an honest attempt to get him the help he needed. Again, he feared cops, and in his paranoia expected the worst from any contact with authorities, even ambulance personnel. Essentially, his stance was to "prevent us from preventing him from dying," Chiba recalls. So no call was made. But Elliott rose up awkwardly, with the intent of getting his car keys and driving away. Chiba and Ashley ordered him to lie back down, yet he kept totteringly trying to escape, insisting he was taking off. Chiba finally needed to physically block his path, and the two crashed to the floor on top of each other. Elliott was not trying to hurt her, but Chiba was hurt—she had hit her head—and Elliott bolted to the door. At this point he had his car keys, and Ashley chased after him, determined not to let him get behind the wheel, apparently. As Chiba recalls it, Elliott finally agreed, after much discussion, to hand the keys over. Ashley wound up driving, the two staying in the car for several hours until, slowly, Elliott calmed down, became more lucid, the sedation clearing. Chiba was traumatized, concerned about possible injury. What remained was a feeling of helplessness. No one wanted to guess how much longer this could go on, or what the final result might be. Once more Chiba wondered whether she could take it. How was she going to make it through months, years, even, of virtually uninterrupted emergency? Suicide had become a daily topic. "Like the boy who cried wolf," Chiba says, "it was almost a joke." Elliott might tell her, for instance, "Today is the day they are going to put me down," using, almost comically, a veterinary analogy. Chiba took it all in, feeling alone and spent, as did Ashley, who was nearby and on constant call. In one way, at least, all the suicide talk seemed geared to "take the charge out of the subject," Chiba believed. She felt it was better, in a sense, for Elliott to be open about it, although the openness hardly diminished the fear everyone had.

By August 2003, several developments merged, adding layers of complication to an already vexing situation. Around his thirty-fourth birthday, on August 6, Elliott came to a monumental decision. He elected, impulsively, and not entirely advisedly, from a medical or detox perspective, to go off everything, to try an immediate, total cold turkey. He stopped the psychiatric drugs, including a newer one, Strattera, for ADHD (it had been prescribed as an alternative to the more "speedy" Adderall). He also stopped smoking, drinking, caffeine—all of it. There was no tapering, no slow cessation of usage. He just plain hit the brakes. Therapeutically, he began pounding kava, a drink with sedative properties, and a green concoction Chiba prepared, a foul-tasting nutritional elixir. This seemed like a direction no one could argue with. He was getting clean, purging his system of every last toxin. But there was fallout, especially from the psychiatric drugs. His brain had become sensitized from years of usage; sudden cessation therefore came with added anxiety, moodiness, irritability, agitation. And the paranoia lingered around the edges, a renegade variable he now confronted with zero chemical assistance. He and Chiba took long walks in a canyon, to promote activity and mindfulness. Elliott kept at the music, recording the Cat Stevens tune "Trouble" in their bedroom on a twenty-four-track—it left him weeping—and the Bob Marley song "Concrete Jungle." He was ragged, his nerves shot, walking on a wire, but he kept fighting.

In this precariously drug-free state, his mind, both more lucid and more discombobulated, latched on to a terrifying, depressing circuit. It was a subject he'd actually been circling for some time, never sure what to make of it, never sure how much to believe, at once certain, at once thoroughly mystified. With Chiba he had bought a book on the sexual abuse of young boys. He read it closely, underlining pages, making notes in the margins. Broadly, it matched his sense of his own history—of emotional pain, hypersensitivity, disconnection, fear. He'd lived in the same atmosphere of torment and anger. He decided—or suspected, or intuited, it's impossible to say—that he, too, might have been sexually abused. The realization hit him like a hammer blow. The implications were horrifying, there was the question of what to do about them, but suddenly, in light of this revelation, his agony found clarity. He figured, correctly or not, he might have some kind of answer now. The depression, the suicidal feelings, the self-abuse—it all made provisional sense at last. Everything he was in the process of uncovering he shared instantly with Chiba. He even disclosed it to others, in her view indiscriminately. It became all-consuming, something he needed to get out whenever and wherever he could. In his mind, as he dug through dim recollections, he seized on some sort of event in an attic. There was another that seemed to have occurred in a shower. "He told me," Chiba says, "as he got sober, all these horrible, shameful memories." But he also doubted their accuracy. He couldn't ever be sure. He'd speak, in one moment, with absolute certainty; then he'd take it all back, saying "actually I don't think that happened at all." Chiba had worked with sexually abused kids. "He asked me," she recalls, "'You've got to help me through this.'" Back in Portland he'd made similar intimations. Then he'd identified someone outside his immediate family, a person with whom he'd only had sporadic contact.

In any case, there seemed to be little way of knowing, with certainty, whether this was a false or a true memory. It was—no doubt—psychologically and emotionally real, its effects monumental, but what really happened, and who had been the abuser? On that subject Elliott wavered. He was reluctant to name anyone. He was confused. He didn't trust his own memory. Yet finally, over days and weeks, and never without some trace of uncertainty, he seemed to settle on the likeliest possibility. The abuser, he now suspected—rightly or wrongly—had been Charlie.

It wasn't Elliott's plan at first to take this up directly. There was too much uncertainty, and the last thing he wanted was a confrontation. But as he did now and then, he called his mother, Bunny. She may have been in her classroom at the time, where she taught, or she may have been at home. She mentioned, in passing, that Charlie had been to school. She told Elliott the kids there had come to view him as one of the teachers—he'd been doing a lot of volunteering. On occasion they ran to him to tattle on peers, a fact Bunny found funny, since he wasn't, technically, a school employee. Hearing this, Elliott was alarmed. Two different ideas came to him suddenly. First, Chiba remembers, he had the paranoid sense that Charlie was planning to kill his mother. He felt he had to warn her. He had to protect her. Second, he insisted Charlie should not be around the kids. He wasn't to be trusted. By that, Bunny knew what Elliott meant. The connotation was sexual. He had asked her once before, "Do you think Charlie ever sexually abused me?" He'd told her he wasn't sure; he was trying to figure things out. Still, she was shocked. He'd never before made specific allegations, yet for the moment he seemed convinced. He was angry and adamant. And over the course of the conversation, he divulged everything, all the memories (veridical or reconstructed) he had withheld before, of abuse generally, and also of sexual abuse. Bunny's response was that she'd never observed anything, never seen anything suspicious. Elliott, however, insisted he needed to protect the children, to which Bunny suggested that perhaps he wasn't thinking straight, perhaps his mind was playing tricks on him. He'd gone off all drugs, after all, and he clearly wasn't in the best condition to accurately reach such conclusions. What she proposed was a meeting, a chance, she hoped, to set things straight. She and Charlie could come for Thanksgiving, to spend the holiday with Ashley and him, and the three of them could talk. This Elliott found "terrifying," Chiba says. Not only was his mother skeptical, albeit possibly reasonably, in the circumstances, but he'd be put in the position of facing Charlie, a person he viewed with a mix of abject fear and contempt.

In this swirl of emotional chaos, everything spinning off in several directions at once, Elliott fearful, guilty, uncertain, angry, and still intermittently paranoid, as always, there occurred still another frightening act of self-abuse. He and Chiba had planned to attend the film *Lost in Translation* (released on August 29). At the time Elliott had been listening to My Bloody Valentine, the band's aesthetic, its crawling noise, an inspiration for the music he was working on. Five tunes by Kevin Shields, My Bloody Valentine's vocalist and guitarist, were featured in the film; plus, Brian Reitzell, former drummer for the punk band Redd Kross, had supervised the soundtrack, and Elliott was set to work with him on the movie *Thumbsucker*, for which he'd recorded "Trouble." But at the last minute Elliott decided not to go. He wanted to stay home and record. So after some discussion, Chiba went alone. She thought it was odd, but there was no convincing Elliott otherwise.

When she returned the house was suspiciously dark, Elliott nowhere to be seen. She called but there was no answer. At first she assumed he wasn't home. Yet as she wandered, anxiously, room to room, she finally located him under the covers in bed, "cowering and crying." She noticed a knife, then she saw blood in spots across the sheets. There were cuts, she saw, superficial ones, at various points on his body. It was too much to take. Instantly she thought, "I can't do this anymore. I can't live with him. I need to break up with him." The ordeal of managing his day-to-day needs was seriously undermining her own mental stability. Again she moved to call 911; again Elliott begged her not to. She asked, "Why Elliott?" It was a question everyone had been asking him nearly all his life. His answer was, "I don't know." Chiba quickly contacted Ashley, and like always, she drove over immediately. For the next several days Elliott wound up staying at Ashley's place, partly to give Chiba a break, partly to pull himself together. But this was the beginning of the end. His life was lived moment to moment.

Chiba kept trying. She loved him, and she wanted him alive. But in the last month everything seemed to pick up pace. Despite all that had been going on, Chiba says, they were actually working to get pregnant. They had even tossed around possible names, "Tuesday" if it was a girl, "Harmony" if it was a boy. On September 19 Elliott played Redfest in Salt Lake City. It was his final performance. The songs spanned the years. There was "Plainclothes Man" from the Heatmiser days, "Needle in the Hay," "Between the Bars." He closed with George Harrison's "Long Long Long," something he did often. "I love you," the last line in Harrison's song, were Elliott's last words to a live audience.

In early October Dorien was in L.A. With Valerie gone her contacts with Elliott had become less sporadic. She was no longer cut off. She stopped by the house, and the two talked about Elliott's decision to go cold turkey, how he'd done it essentially overnight. She told him she didn't think it was a good idea. She said it made more sense to taper gradually, that doing so would be better for his body and his mind. But he wanted to have a child, he said. His plan was to "conceive with no drugs in his system." He also felt that "having a kid might help him get his shit together."[11] Garry was happy for him, sympathetic, but once more she warned him, "You need proper medical guidance to get off this shit," referring, at this point, to the psychiatric medicines, the benzos, the antipsychotic, the antidepressants.

By mid-October Elliott felt well enough to plan future performances. Fellow Lincoln High School grad Matt Groening was curating the All Tomorrow's Parties festival in Long Beach, set for the first week of November. He had chosen Elliott to play, along with the Shins, Built to Spill, Mission of Burma, Modest Mouse, Sonic Youth, and others. "We rehearsed for about two weeks," Shon Sullivan recalls. "And Elliott was doing so well. He wasn't drinking, or doing anything. He put on weight. He looked healthy and strong." He seemed, Sullivan felt, to be in a very "good spot" in his life. "I remember thinking this is going to be good for all the people who care about him." They could see he was back. They could see he'd come out of the living hell alive, purged and rejuvenated.

Yet around the same time, Elliott had driven to Malibu Ranch to check in with Schoenkopf. Schoenkopf remembers thinking "he was not well." Apparently, then, there were good days and bad days. Also, because of the nature of his relationship with Schoenkopf, Elliott may have felt freer to disclose. Clearly, according to Schoenkopf, Elliott "was interested in the dark side." Yet: "I don't remember any obsession with death," he said. "I don't know that he had a death wish."[12]

On October 17, Charlie typed out a letter. In fact, he typed out two: one to Chiba, and enclosed within it, another, longer one, to Elliott.[13] He told Chiba he hoped all was well with her, and said he enjoyed meeting her when he and Bunny had come to L.A. over the summer. He felt, he said, that she was a good person for Elliott, and a good influence in his life. He asked her to read over what he'd said to Elliott, and to give it to him if she felt it wouldn't upset him. He also asked her to let him know whether Elliott had read the letter, because he and Bunny were planning to arrive for Thanksgiving. He included his phone number and e-mail address, thanking Chiba for her help.

The letter to Elliott is in some ways a brave, self-aware statement. He had written at least one other letter like this, several years before, also addressed to Elliott; now he was more direct, focused on Elliott's intuitions of sex abuse, which he had heard about from Bunny. He starts by admitting, again, that Elliott's early life in the family was not happy. Again he connects this to his deficiencies as a father, saying he lacked experience, that he was too demanding, quick to anger, judgmental, and downright mean at times. But he says he's changed. He's a different person now. He had made efforts, he adds, to see Elliott when possible, but notes Elliott's unwillingness to let either him or Bunny into his life. The sexual abuse he denies thoroughly. He admits it sometimes occurs in families, in the U.S. and elsewhere around the world. He calls it immoral and depressing. Then he asserts pointedly that he's never had any urges to sexually abuse anyone, ever. Charlie does not say "I never sexually abused you, Elliott." Instead he denies even the slightest thought of such behavior. It is a global rejection of a concept, almost; it is not personalized to the specific situation. He closes by saying he'd like to talk the matter over, along with many other subjects. The letter's final paragraph is two sentences. He asks Elliott to take care of himself. Then he says, heartbreakingly, I love you.

Elliott never saw the letter.[14]

October 21 was a Tuesday. It was to be taken up with errands for Jennifer. In the morning she had a medical appointment; her blood was being monitored for possible leukemia. Weeks before she'd had a suspicious lymph node removed. Elliott drove her in her Saab (he had to do it; she'd gotten a DUI). Test results looked good, they were told. There would be no need for additional monitoring. The two left with a feeling of relief. Chiba was going to be okay.

As they got home again they reviewed the plan for the afternoon. Chiba had a therapist appointment; again, Elliott would need to drive her. The doctor was Abigail Stanton. As it turns out, Elliott was planning to see Stanton too. He'd ended things with Schloss, the plan being to make a fresh start. Stanton, then, would be taking over his care, managing his meds in the event he decided to start them back up again, this time more thoughtfully. Based on what Stanton knew already, she had concerns. In her view Elliott's decision to go cold turkey from the psych meds was perilous, Chiba says. She intended to speak with him about it. Her idea was to evaluate and reassess.

All this was up for discussion as Chiba laid out the day's remaining agenda. But suddenly Elliott interjected: "Don't talk out loud in the house. You know it's bugged." Chiba tried laughing the comment off, thinking she might neutralize it. She answered, "I'm not paranoid like you are." Elliott now was on the computer. He called out, "Are you working for somebody? To sabotage this record? Are you working against me too?" Overwhelmed by the emotion of the day, feeling hyped up and anxious from the earlier medical appointment, Chiba locked herself in the bathroom. It was something she'd done before. It was her way of getting some distance, a temporary respite. On other occasions like this Elliott had called Ashley, who came by to mediate, to talk Chiba out. This time, in the moment, he did not. He knocked on the bathroom door. He told Chiba he was sorry. He asked her to come out. He told her he knew he was crazy. He apologized for what he had said. But Chiba wasn't ready yet. Impulsively, as she'd said before, she told him to leave her the fuck alone. She was sick of the paranoia.

For several long seconds there was quiet, only the usual sounds of the ticking house. Then came an awful noise, a scream Chiba vaguely recognized, both familiar somehow and utterly alien. A few nights prior she and Elliott had stayed up sharpening a new set of knives. As she flung herself out of the bathroom and ran to the kitchen, where the scream seemed to come from, she found Elliott at the sink. He had his back to her, but as he turned, she saw a knife in his chest. In milliseconds her mind raced over scenarios. Was this a dream? Was it some kind of joke? Was the knife even real? What, exactly, was happening? Looking in Elliott's eyes his expression was "apologetic" but also hard to read. He seemed "half panicked." Not thinking, her hands did what seemed to make immediate sense. She pulled out the knife. Elliott then crashed onto the balcony, as if, she believed, he were trying to jump off it somehow. She tackled him there, then quickly climbed off him to call 911, seconds later performing citizen CPR. For a split second, seeing the knife on the floor, she thought of using it on herself.

The call was made at 12:18 hours. LAFD paramedics arrived on the scene, quickly transporting Elliott to a hospital emergency room. In the chaos Ashley got a message from one of Chiba's friends. As she reached the house, two police officers were stationed out front, she later told Chiba. They said Elliott had been taken away; they told her Chiba was still inside, but they refused to allow any contact. In fact, at this point, Chiba was being questioned. She says the police forced her to describe the sequence of events over and over, "as if to trip me up." Then what seemed to be a suicide note was discovered. Chiba had been in the habit of sticking Post-Its around the house, each with a little encouraging message. As detectives questioned her at the kitchen table, her eyes passed over one. On it Elliott had apparently written, "I'm so sorry—love Elliott God forgive me."[15] There was no date.

At 13:36 hours, after having what turned out to be two lacerations to the heart surgically repaired, Elliott was pronounced dead. Chiba wasn't there. She arrived one hour later, having changed into an Elliott Smith T-shirt. She found Ashley, sitting beside a tiny, angelic, female African American security guard. The two hugged, sobbing. It was impossible to believe. He'd always seemed bizarrely resilient, somehow indestructible. But now it was over. He was gone.

The next day Chiba found Charlie's letters in the mailbox. Ghoulishly, a package also arrived. It was from the record label Suicide Squeeze, which had brought out "Pretty (Ugly Before)" and "A Distorted Reality Is Now a Necessity to Be Free." Chiba took the discs to Sunset where, in front of the *Figure 8* wall, fans had gathered in mourning. She passed copies out to the people there, vinyl from heaven.

Running through Chiba's mind was "an endless barrage of woulda, shoulda, coulda." "I was going crazy," she says. "I lost it." In the moments before Elliott died she had been thinking, "This will never end. I can't do anything right." Yet as he had told others on different occasions, Elliott said to Chiba, "As soon as I am gone, I will unburden you." He was gone, but as events unfolded, she would be anything but unburdened, for reasons no one anticipated.

* * *

Elliott was cremated, this being what everyone concluded he would have wanted. The ashes were divided three ways—one third to Ashley, one third to Bunny and Charlie, one third to the Smiths. At first the plan was to hold a funeral at the home of Neil Gust and Joanna Bolme, who were roommates at the time in Portland. For some reason that didn't happen. The service occurred instead at the Smiths'. The ashes weren't on hand because the coroner would not release them. Chiba was there, having made the trip from L.A. For the first time she met Gary Smith in person. Sean Croghan, Pete Krebs, and Jason Mitchell were also present. Krebs in particular made a point of talking with Chiba. He wanted to know the story. He wasn't suspicious, no one was, no one had serious doubts at the time as to what had occurred; he just felt a need to get the facts from the one person who possessed them. For several hours everyone milled about, talking in small groups inside and outside, in the backyard. There wasn't a lot of demonstrative grieving. No one recalls any memorial speeches being made. The mood was one of resignation, of deep, gnawing regret.

In his cover of Cat Stevens's "Trouble" Elliott had sung of "death's disguise" hanging on him. He'd asked it to be fair, to be kind, to leave him in his misery. He didn't want a fight, he sang. "I haven't got a lot of time."

CODA **THE HERO KILLED THE CLOWN**

From a standpoint of parsimoniousness, the philosophical principle that simple explanations stand the best chance of being correct, few causes of death could seem less questionable than Elliott's. He had been depressed and suicidal for much of his life. He had written songs declaring suicide's lure, if not its inevitability. As Pete Krebs said, his finger never stopped circling an inner self-destruct button; he was on it all the time. He frequently told people he wanted to die; every new day dawned as if by accident, especially in his final few years. There had been several apparent prior attempts, deliberate overdoses. He was a cutter. Toward the end of his life he'd taken to scrawling the words "Kali the Destroyer" across his arm in indelible marker, to hide visible scars. He was paranoid, believing his record label was trying to kill him. And he'd impulsively stopped most if not all meds, his brain chemistry in gnarled flux. Plus, there was a note, along with a set of statements provided by Chiba.

All this qualified itself irreversibly on January 6, 2004, when forensic pathologist and Deputy Medical Examiner Lisa Scheinin released her signed findings.[1] Each of the two stab wounds entered the chest cavity, Scheinin found. Only one of these, stab wound number two—not necessarily the second in terms of order inflicted—perforated the heart. This wound, therefore, was the likely fatal one. Toxicology tests revealed no illicit substances. But Scheinin writes, "All medications were therapeutic or subtherapeutic," suggesting psychiatric drugs *were* in fact present in Elliott's system. He was not entirely drug free at time of death. But he was not abusing his legal drugs, either; nothing was untoward vis-à-vis their levels in the body. In fact, one or some—Scheinin does not provide names because they were already in the toxicology report, and also "noncontributory to death"—were subtherapeutic.

It's Scheinin's second paragraph that leaps off the page. With it, and to this day still, Elliott's posthumous life was altered, along with Jennifer Chiba's and everyone else's who loved him or cared about him or counted themselves a fan. Scheinin called the mode of death "undetermined at this time." Chiba was hurt and alarmed. She'd spent one year of her life caring for someone she adored, someone with whom she was trying to have a child. Now the insinuation was that she, or less likely, someone else, could be a killer. It was monstrously, inconceivably depressing. And not just for Chiba. No one, it seems, had seriously considered a possibility other than suicide. If anything, suicide was predetermined, overdetermined, not "undetermined." Yet with Scheinin's ruling a new avenue opened up, especially for fervid fans who felt abandoned by their Virgil. Elliott was murdered, some of them declared. Chiba stabbed him twice in the chest.

Scheinin based her conclusion on five factors; she kindly and very helpfully answered detailed questions about each, along with a number of additional questions on peripheral aspects of the case, for a total of four pages of information.[2] (She also read several drafts of this section of the book, in order to check for accuracy.) The "atypical aspects of the case" Scheinin documents in her report are these: (1) the absence of hesitation wounds, (2) stabbing through clothing, (3) the presence of small incised wounds on the right arm and left hand ("possible defensive wounds"), (4) Chiba's removal of the knife, and (5) her "subsequent" refusal to speak with detectives. Before getting into these, there is a broader question. Nelson Gary explained, "As far as the possible murder, I know nothing, really"; but he went on to say, "in existentialism, there is no valuable meaning in existence. But Elliott didn't live that way. He was a fucking perfectionist, always trying to tweak things and make things better." He added, "Stabbing himself twice—there is just something wrong with that. It doesn't seem physically possible." When asked about this, Scheinin replied simply, "Your friend is wrong. It is indeed possible to stab oneself in the chest (and other places) more than once," especially in cases where nerve connections are spared. "If the first stab wound does not hit a vital organ," Scheinin said— and wound number one did not—"there is nothing to prevent additional self-inflicted wounds." David Campbell, official spokesman for the office of coroner, told journalist Liam Gowing the same thing. In fact, he referenced a specific case, one involving an LAPD detective shot through the heart, who stood up, drew his weapon, returned fire, and killed a suspect. "We've had other stories," he added, "where people have had injuries to the heart and they continued running and collapsed thirty yards away. So it is indeed a fact that a person can sustain heart trauma and not be suddenly incapacitated."[3]

So what, then, of the first atypical element, the apparent absence of hesitation wounds at the site of entry? Scheinin says these are "less often seen with stab wounds," more common with slash wounds of the neck or wrist. But with stab wounds particularly, the person might simply "obliterate the mark," stabbing himself clear through any small hesitation puncture. A lack of visible hesitation marks, therefore, "doesn't mean the person didn't hesitate," Scheinin explains.

As for stabbing through clothing, Scheinin's reply is matter-of-fact: "People usually do not stab themselves through clothing, but that does not mean it never happens—it does." Elliott disliked showing his unclothed body; it made him extremely uncomfortable, according to numerous friends. The last thing he would ever do—and Scheinin is not suggesting he *did* do this—is parade about the house shirtless. The notion, then, that in a moment of suddenly agonized impulse he'd think to remove his shirt is nearly untenable. Not only was doing so out of character; it also fails to jibe with the suddenness of the decision. He spied the knife sitting nearby, and he grabbed it. On this point, Scheinin clarified her meaning: "People do not necessarily take their shirts off if they are going to stab themselves, but they usually do lift them up, move them aside or unbutton them, primarily to see exactly where they are going to put the knife and secondarily to have nothing extra between the skin and the blade." This can be done relatively quickly, Scheinin adds. So, most typically, clothing will be moved aside in one way or another, and Elliott did not do that; he stabbed himself through his shirt. On the other hand, as Scheinin allows, people do sometimes stab through clothing anyway. The action is not unique.

Of all the questionable elements, the presence of "possible defensive wounds" appears on its face most compelling. Yet these were "very small," Scheinin revealed. Plus, alongside the tiny incised wounds and "quite easy to tell apart," Scheinin noted what she called "round scars consistent with cigarette burns." Elliott, in other words, had been putting lit cigarettes out on his skin—another commonly encountered self-harm habit, among many. Gowing says Elliott habitually worked a knife on top of scars left from these burns; he claims to have received this information from credible sources unwilling to go on record. That aside, the very small wounds were located on the left hand and right arm. Another, on the bicep, "is in an odd location," Scheinin remarks, "for a defensive wound." At any rate, there are, Scheinin says, "other explanations." Perhaps Elliott mishandled the knife, she says. Perhaps he first "tested the point." Beyond these reasonable possibilities, there's a larger, more obvious anomaly. If Elliott was indeed stabbed—not once, but twice—unless he submitted to the act, essentially opening his arms and allowing it to happen, defensive wounds would be anything but "very small." They would be plentiful. Even in his anguished state, he would have fought instinctively to live, to protect himself. There is no evidence that happened, no indication of a fight. In cases of struggle, Scheinin says, "we often see long incised wounds on the palmar surface of the hands as the person attempts to block or grab the knife." These are missing. But what if Elliott had been blindsided, with no time to defend himself? Here again, it seems extraordinarily unlikely that a small woman could enter a kitchen, grab a knife, and stab a person not once, but twice, with zero evidence of any struggle. Parsimony dictates a different explanation. As Scheinin explains, summarily: "I don't think we can know with 100 percent certainty whether the incised wounds were intentional self-injury, testing the point of the blade, or defensive."

Chiba says she pulled the knife out in a moment of thoughtless impulse. That fact also seems unsurprising. As spokesman David Campbell told Gowing, "If you saw someone who was still alive and they have a knife in their chest, what would you do? The first thing you'd want to do is stop the bleeding, and you can't do that if the knife is still there."[4] Scheinin adds, "I realize that it's a very human thing to pull out a knife, but that can also turn out to be the wrong thing to do, since the knife would act as a plug or partial plug limiting blood flow." (As a small consolation in the circumstances, Chiba says hospital personnel told her that pulling out the knife did not kill Elliott; he would have died anyway from massive internal bleeding.) As for Chiba's subsequent refusal to speak with investigators, she claims she was interviewed three times at the scene. She told them everything she knew. There was nothing new to add. She had more than cooperated.

Gowing says Scheinin told him her "gut feeling" was that "it was actually a suicide," and that she ruled as she did to assist police who might pursue a homicide angle. "He got me wrong," Scheinin claims, "but just by a bit. I said it certainly could have been [a suicide] for various reasons. That statement remains true," even though, at the time she compiled her report, "several details of Elliott's life"—some strongly suggestive of the possibility of suicide—"were not available to me." She adds that the undetermined mode was, for her, the "only viable option." "If Mr. Smith had been completely alone when he died, it would have been much easier to call it a suicide, but there was another person present, and unfortunately this muddies the water." Moreover: "We have to do the best with what we know at the time. It is important not to rush to call something a suicide, since the designation can be very difficult for surviving family to deal with on personal, religious, and sociological levels . . . I do not call anything a suicide unless I am absolutely certain . . . If there is anything irregular, I am constrained to be cautious. While I do listen to what police have to say about cases, I do not assign manners of death to help out investigators or to force them to do an investigation—that would be totally inappropriate."

Finally, as for Chiba specifically and her possible role in Elliott's death, Scheinin said emphatically, "The Undetermined mode is NOT an indictment of the girlfriend" (caps in original).

Of course, that has been precisely the unintentional effect of the ruling. Chiba was never charged, but in the minds of a minority of vociferous fans, she's guilty, or at least under very serious suspicion. It's an attitude she still confronts almost daily. (As did Scheinin herself once, when a "completely dishonest" fan saying she was "clearing things up for a friend," in effect misrepresenting herself—to Scheinin's "great irritation" when she later found out about it—asked for an interview the results of which she posted on a website, in the process "misquoting" Scheinin and getting various things she said "completely wrong.")

As an aside, it is worth noting that after decades of scientific research into precursors of violence, one variable reliably surfaces: history of violence.

Jennifer Chiba in her home, Los Angeles, May 2008. (© Samuel Kirszenbaum/ Modds.)

Recent violent acts predict—albeit not especially powerfully—future violent acts. Chiba had no history of violence. Alternatively, some fans have proposed, on message boards and blogs, an intruder theory, based on a hackneyed "drug deal gone bad" scenario. Scheinin finds that possibility unlikely for a host of interconnected reasons. There would have been signs of a struggle in the home, as well as clear defensive wounds. Also, even though she had locked herself in a bathroom, Chiba would have heard something and told the police about it later. Finally, any hypothetically ticked off drug dealer would have brought his or her own weapon—a gun, for instance—rather than making random use of a nearby kitchen knife.

As for Chiba, when Elliott died she had every reason to believe she might be pregnant. She was in love, and she had no reliable means of support. Elliott was everything to her. She'd devoted her life to keeping him alive. As Shon Sullivan put it, "She was solely committed to him. She got him to doctor's appointments. She kept him going. She'd drive him from rehearsal in his little black Passat. If it was not for Jen, it would have happened two years before it did." Plenty of people told Chiba the same thing, she says. For Sullivan, the idea that Jennifer Chiba murdered Elliott Smith is "totally retarded."

Others, very few in number, and including not a single person interviewed for this book, with the sole exception of Jerry Schoenkopf,[5] felt inclined, at least initially, to imagine otherwise. Chiba says Gary Smith made a call to her therapist, Abigail Stanton. He asked her, "Do you think Jennifer could have killed my son?" She said no, absolutely not, Chiba maintains. "The only person Jennifer is capable of killing is herself."

If Chiba made any mistake, it was understandable and hardly murderous. She locked herself in the bathroom. She wasn't available in that moment; she wasn't responsive. "Elliott was afraid of losing me on several different levels," she says. "He had formed this almost unhealthy attachment to me. He'd say, 'Chiba, you're the only reason I'm alive. If you leave me, I'm killing myself.'" The breakup with Deerin had been traumatizing. He could not endure any similar ordeal. It was too much to contemplate. Suicide therefore equaled pain cessation. It was a kind of preemptive strike, a world killer, leaving preferable to being left. And as Elliott always liked to imagine, it was, paradoxically, in the fractured logic of hopelessness, a gift. "I can't prepare for death any more than I already have," he sang in "King's Crossing." It's true. He'd practiced. He'd come close. He possessed the requisite courage. He was, in this way, fearless. But he was also scared of being alone. He couldn't make it on his own; he'd burned too many bridges. Friends did not know him anymore, they said. They felt stupid for trying to help. They just wanted everything to be normal. "We should have left all his records playing on his doorstep," Autumn de Wilde says. "He wrote all the right lyrics for our complaints."[6]

Death was the final unburdening, a formula Elliott always espoused. There was no good reason not to do it. There never really had been.

In Elliott's car a CD was found after his death, with fifteen different versions of the song "Stickman." It's a buoyant, upbeat number, beginning with guitar that almost seems out of tune, like his life by this time. He sings over and around a constantly repeating, bending single chord. He shoots blanks at emptiness, he says, the ammo dead, the world dead. He reloads to make a silent sound, killing nothing but time, spinning the world on its flipside, listening backward for meaning. In one version the song's a dirge for a depth that dropped even lower. Remember that when you hear some sad song, he suggests. It's a print he shot in reversal, a reverse shot, as in film technique, when two people appear to be reacting to each another, one onstage, one off. The frames, he sings, go one by one. But if you speed them up, it's clear he's on the run, "from some monster off-screen killing sons." This is the fear that never left him, revisited in slow-mo in a movie he draws from memory.

"Mental pain," he concludes, "is the sharpest knife." It's the one he always carried. It sharpened itself. And in the end, by a means far more plausible, far more clear, far more unavoidable than any other, and far less open to any serious question, it killed him. There were two knives. One, the sharpest, was always in his heart. The second was almost a redundancy.

ACKNOWLEDGEMENTS

I've been very deeply touched by the kindness of Elliott's friends, many of whom devoted more than twenty hours to my questions, and helped out in ways far too numerous to try listing. This book has changed my life. The reason why has largely to do with the people in its pages—smart, talented, compassionate, creative, sweet, protective, and real. One never enjoys finishing a book. The process, so magical, ends. But here there is an added element of mourning. I will miss my interlocutors.

Some people I want to thank with special emphasis, for a generosity of time and spirit that was truly extravagant: JJ Gonson, Denny Swofford, Steven Pickering, Jennifer Chiba, Dorien Garry, and Jason Mitchell. In a sense these six people span the years of Elliott's life, in a chain from beginning to end, from Texas to Portland to New York to L.A.

My deepest thanks also to Pete Krebs, Tony Lash, Brandt Peterson, Garrick Duckler (for kindly fact-checking assorted details), Sean Croghan, Christopher Cooper, Scott Wagner, John Chandler, Sluggo, Mark Baumgarten, Luke Strahota, Tom Johnson, Leslie Uppinghouse, Matt Schulte, James Ewing, Mark Merritt, Kim (who asked that I not use her last name), Kevin Denbow, Dave Leto, Neil Karras, Barb Martinez, Dan Eklov, Ethan Lewis, Nelson Gary, Lisa Scheinin (M.D.), Jerry Schoenkopf, Shon Sullivan, Roger and Mary Steffens, Jimi Jones (archivist at Hampshire College), and Lewis and Clark College Library.

Over the years I've worked with students on a number of Elliott Smith–related projects. For helping me sharpen my thinking, I thank Sarah Marker, Kerry Roche, Josh Pruden, Katie Castillo, Mariellen Thomas, Peter Safran, Christian Demko, Maria McLaughlin, Nick Kelly, and Denea Reopelle. Thanks also to Pacific University for two travel grants to Los Angeles.

Laura Eckstein was a resourceful on-call research assistant.

Julia Speicher was helpful in securing Lincoln High School yearbooks for me.

Bobbi Baker, Andrew King, and Julie McNamara, all Elliott Smith fans, all unknown to me personally, reached out with kind support and interesting ideas to share, some about song interpretation.

At points along the way, I discussed the book with quite a few people who weighed in here and there enlighteningly: Andrew McCarron, Yishai Seidman, Don Cohen, David Morrison, Josh Shenk, Abby Gross, and Lori Stone.

Shar Deisch was on hand for almost every single word.

Whatever I've managed to accomplish in the world of writing and publishing I owe to my magnificent agent, Betsy Lerner. I extend to her a warm-water tsunami of thanks. I've been lucky, too, to work with Kathy Belden at Bloomsbury USA. I am grateful for her support, patience, and astute counsel on countless details related to the refinement of the manuscript. I also appreciate Nick Humphrey's encouragement from across the sea at Bloomsbury UK.

Sweet Adrienne: Thanks for unintentionally pointing out the path. This book is for you.

Sweet Henry: I appreciate your love and patience, and from now on may you only ever hear "Angeles" or "Everything Means Nothing to Me."

Theresa: With endless love, thanks for everything, all the time.

I never knew Elliott Smith, though I'm guessing we silently crossed paths more than once at Django's, the Space Room, or 1201. It is presumptuous and faintly delusional to say, but for the past several years he has been my best friend, thoroughly alive in my mind. As I suppose all properly obsessed biographers do, I dreamed about him more than a dozen times.

I set out to make a book as beautiful as the music. That goal was impossible, of course. But I've done everything in my power to come as close as I could.

NOTES

Introduction: The Smith Myth

1. There were two stab wounds, but as I explain more fully in the final chapter, just one of these was likely to be fatal, according to L.A. coroner Lisa Scheinin.

2. McConnell makes this statement in the Gil Reyes documentary *Searching for Elliott Smith*.

3. See "I Think I Was There: An Oral History of Satyricon," *Willamette Week*, accessed June 6, 2011, http://wweek.com/portland/article-12560-i_think_i_was_there.html.

4. For an immensely informative history of Portland rock, see SP Clarke, "History of Portland Rock," http://www.spclarke.com/?page_id=22.

5. Ibid.

6. Ibid.

7. Ibid.

8. SP Clarke, "History of Portland Rock," http://www.spclarke.com/?page_id=22.

9. Ibid.

10. Smith interview, accessed June 7, 2011, on *YouTube.com*: http://http://www.youtube.com/watch?v=lDm588bHCxA.

11. Accessed June 7, 2011, from http://www.youtube.com/watch?v=XnqjZzMscFo.

12. Jeff Giles, "Everybody Hurts Sometime," *Newsweek*, accessed June 7, 2011, http://www.newsweek.com/1994/09/25/everybody-hurts-sometime.html.

13. "I Think I Was There: An Oral History of Satyricon," http://wweek.com/portland/article-12560-i_think_i_was_there.html.

14. Ibid.

15. On the other hand, Drake's music was at times far more orchestral than Smith's.

16. I once talked to a psychiatric patient who tried, mainly out of curiosity, to remove her own appendix. She explained that it was an "unnecessary organ." I mentioned that she could have died. She told me something I will never forget: "You don't understand. I don't care whether I live or die."

17. In terms of intelligence, lyrical complexity and depth, and melodicism, the closest comparison would be Aimee Mann. Like Elliott, she was an "Oscar loser" (her own description on Twitter, as of August, 2011). Phil Collins took the statue over Mann's truly stunning work for the equally stunning film *Magnolia*. Mann and Smith were friends. They played at Largo for the Acoustic Vaudeville nights, overseen usually by Jon Brion, who also worked with Elliott on the album *From a Basement on a Hill*. Here's Mann on the Oscar disappointment, from http://www.avclub.com/articles/aimee-mann,13687: "I was playing a show in New York with Michael Penn. It was part of the Acoustic Vaudeville tour, and we had a comedian come with us to do our banter. So it was that show, and at some point somebody yells out, 'What's your Oscar speech going to be?' And I said, 'Here's my Oscar speech: Phil Collins sucks. How about that?' It was just a gag. And then I said, 'Wouldn't it be funny if he wins and I boo him?' I thought it would be so funny, not that anyone would do it, but I'm always waiting for someone to be a sore loser. That would be so hilarious. Anyway, some jackass from *Newsweek* takes that quote—'I'm going to be the first

person to boo one of the winners; when [Phil Collins] wins, I'm going to boo him'—totally minus the sarcasm and irony, and reports it as straight reportage. Like I'm announcing that I'm going to boo this guy and that he sucks. Of course, it was like, 'Well, that sucks, because I'm not a Phil Collins fan, but he does what he does and I don't want him to think that I think he's some kind of asshole. How creepy is that?' So I sent him a fax that said I was just joking, and that *Newsweek* is a bunch of morons. So I ran into him backstage, and he was really nice. They had a little meeting—him and his people—and decided I was joking."

18. This is not a judgment Smith would agree with. To take just one example, during a break in one performance he called the song "Pitseleh" "long and boring."

19. Comment made by David McConnell in the documentary *Searching for Elliott Smith* by Gil Reyes.

20. See William Todd Schultz, *An Emergency in Slow Motion: The Inner Life of Diane Arbus* (New York: Bloomsbury, 2011).

21. In "Furry Sings the Blues" Mitchell cops to this quality, writing, "WC Handy I'm rich and I'm fey, and I'm not familiar with what you play, but I get such strong impressions of your heyday, looking up and down old Beale Street."

22. Fans debate this particular lyric. Some believe Smith wrote "sonnet fuck you." I think "sonic" is more likely, and makes more sense in the song's context.

23. Scott Wagner interview, August 1, 2011.

24. John Chandler interview, September 6, 2011.

25. This remark is taken verbatim from an online bootleg recording of the January 31, 2003, concert at the Henry Fonda Theater. The concert has been uploaded in its entirety to YouTube.com as of August 11, 2011.

26. Ibid.

27. Anonymous interview, September 14, 2011.

28. Andrew Watson, "Beck+The Flaming Lips," accessed September 15, 2011, http://www .popmatters.com/pm/review/beck-021021.

29. See "Friends, Peers Mourn Elliott Smith," accessed September 21, 2011, http://www.billboard .com/news/friends-peers-mourn-elliott-smith-2008549.story#/news/friends-peers-mourn-elliott -smith-2008549.story.

30. Ibid.

Chapter One: Hey Mister, That's Me Up On the Jukebox

1. John Chandler interview, September 6, 2011.

2. John Chandler and Scott Wagner, *The Rocket*, April 9, 1997. The article can be accessed at http://www.sweetadeline.net/rocket49.html. Accessed April 7, 2013.

3. Scott Wagner interview, August 1, 2011.

4. *The Rocket*, April 9, 1997, by John Chandler and Scott Wagner. See: http://www.sweetadeline .net/rocket49.html.

5. Jonathan Valania, "Elliott Smith: Emotional Rescue," accessed September 20, 2011, http://www .magnetmagazine.com/2001/01/02/elliott-smith-emotional-rescue.

6. R. J. Smith, "No Way Out," *SPIN*, January 1999.

7. Valania, "Elliott Smith: Emotional Rescue.".

8. See Elliott Smith official website, accessed September 20, 2011, http://www.sweetadeline.net /bio9.html.

9. *LA Weekly*, November 6, 2003. See: http://www.laweekly.com/2003-11-06/columns/elliott-smith -1969-2003/. Accessed April 7, 2013.

10. "Smith's Songs Have Optimistic Moments," *Boston Globe*, June 4, 1998.

11. Matt Dornan, "Elliott Smith," accessed September 20, 2011, http://cwas.hinah.com/interview /?id=11.

12. In the alternate version Smith refers to a TV comedy from the '70s, with a lead no one recalls, who vanished into oblivion, an "easy" thing to do. It's an intriguing, mysterious line. Since the song is about depression, and since vanishing can connote suicide, it may be that Smith is referring to Freddie Prinze, and the show *Chico and the Man*. Prinze shot himself in 1977 after talking with his estranged wife. The death was ruled a suicide, although a later civil case found it to be accidental.

13. *Q Magazine*, January 2011. An interview with several of Elliott's friends that appears on pages 102–04.

14. Valania, "Elliott Smith: Emotional Rescue."

15. "Smith's Songs Have Optimistic Moments," *Boston Globe*, June 4, 1998.

16. Dornan, "Elliott Smith."

17. *Q Magazine*, January 2011. See pages 102–04.

18. The shot of Elliott Smith standing behind Madonna is here: http://www.youtube.com/watch ?v=2X-GOXPMq5M. Accessed October 3, 2011.

19. *Q Magazine*, January 2011. Coomes watched the performance in the video store where he worked. See page 103 of the original article.

20. See Marcus Kagler, "Elliott Smith: Better Off Than Dead," *Under the Radar*, accessed May 2, 2012, http://web.archive.org/web/20060615125926/http://undertheradarmag.com/issue4 /elliottsmith.html.

21. Jennifer Chiba interview, October 9, 2010.

22. This is a comment by Smith from a live performance at La Luna in Portland, May 16, 1998.

23. See http://www.youtube.com/watch?v=wTt_TggXr9M. Accessed October 4, 2011.

24. Kagler, "Elliott Smith: Better Off Than Dead."

25. Ibid.

26. Anonymous interview, August 18, 2011.

27. See http://www.youtube.com/watch?v=wTt_TggXr9M. Accessed October 4, 2011.

28. John Chandler interview, September 6, 2011.

29. See http://www.youtube.com/watch?v=Br2j_lQqF_Q&feature=related. Accessed October 6, 2011.

30. Valania, "Elliott Smith: Emotional Rescue."

31. The NCO is the primary link between enlistees with zero power and commissioned officers with true authority. That fact suggests some autobiographical meaning: Smith is the enlistee, his stepfather Charlie the commissioned officer whom his mother, Bunny, links him to as NCO.

32. There's debate about these lyrics. Some say the line is "torment saint," others "torment sail." Consensus opinion is "torn main sail."

Chapter Two: Center Circle

1. In what follows I simply refer to Elliott as Elliott, since calling him Steve would, I feel, make for slightly confusing reading.

2. See http://www.theseniorvoice.com/pdffiles/SV0612.pdf. Accessed October 20, 2011. *The Senior Voice* is a Dallas, Texas, publication "devoted to the heart of the senior community." Berryman's profile appears in the free December 2006 issue, on page 4.

3. Valania, "Elliott Smith: Emotional Rescue."

4. Letter from Garrick Duckler, *The Real Estate*. This is an untitled, four-page memoir by Duckler, not currently publicly available online.

5. *Plum Creek Press* 6, no. 3 (2006). A publication of the Plum Creek Homeowner's Association, Kyle, Texas. The interview with Bunny and Charlie lists no author. It appears on page 2.

6. Kagler, "Elliott Smith: Better Off Than Dead."

7. Valania, "Elliott Smith: Emotional Rescue."

8. Interview Tony Lash, October 28, 2011.

9. Interview Shon Sullivan, December 31, 2010.

10. Interview Jennifer Chiba, October 16, 2010.

11. Ibid.

12. Interview Jennifer Chiba, December 2, 2010.

13. Interview Jennifer Chiba, October 2, 2010.

14. Interview Steven Pickering, November 10, 2011.

15. Ibid.

16. Interview Kevin Denbow, November 12, 2011.

17. Interview Mark Merritt, February 15, 2012.

18. Interview with Kevin Denbow, November 12, 2011.

19. Kagler, "Elliott Smith: Better Off Than Dead."

20. See Elliott Smith official website, http://www.sweetadeline.net/melodymoo.html. Accessed November 5, 2011.

21. Interview Kim, April 20, 2012. In the text I refer to Kim only by her first name, at her request.

22. The interview can be viewed online at http://www.youtube.com/watch?v=t_XNghTKvq8& feature=related. Accessed November 20, 2011.

23. Interview Kevin Denbow, November 12, 2011.

24. For the record, this track was laid down when Smith visited Texas in the summer, after he had moved to his father's home in Portland, Oregon.

25. Interview Brandt Peterson, December 4, 2011.

26. Interview Jennifer Chiba, October 9, 2010.

27. Interview Denny Swofford, November 25, 2011.

Chapter Three: Raining Violins

1. Interview Tony Lash, October 28, 2011.

2. Ibid.

3. See Elliott Smith official website, http://www.sweetadeline.net/frenchart.html. Accessed January 4, 2012.

4. Kagler, "Elliott Smith: Better Off Than Dead."

5. See Elliott Smith official website, http://www.sweetadeline.net/bio4.html. Accessed January 4, 2012.

6. Duckler essay, on the subject of the song "The Real Estate." Quoted with Garrick Duckler's permission. This is a four-page essay by Duckler not currently available online.

7. See *Alphabet Town* message board, http://alphabettown.freeforums.org/1985-stranger-than -fiction-any-kind-of-mudhen-t128.html.

8. Some websites give this title as "Mudher" rather than "Mud Hen." From what I can gather, that title—"Mudher"—is erroneous.

9. Side one is: "halfway to forever (autumn signs)," "looking at my watch," "the machine," "joy to the world," "uncertainty," and "another letter." Side two is: "it was a sunny day," "wind through my life," "pbida," "chemistry," "nothing to do with you," "pull me through," and "to build a home."

10. Duckler, essay on the making of "The Real Estate," quoted by permission.

11. Ibid.

12. Ibid.

13. The cassette clocks in at more than more than sixty minutes of music. Side one includes "Wandering," "Song to the Great Serpent," "Living in Rotational," "The Crystal Ball," "Freedom of Expression," "Instinctual Disjunction," and "The Vatican Rock." Side two songs are: "Jump Across the Mountain," "Tunnel Vision," "Nothing to do With You," "Sound to Me," "In the Light," "Great Serpent Reprise," and "Laughter." Tony Lash produced, engineered, and mixed. Elliott plays bass on "Laughter." Sally Tapanen provides the tap dance on "The Vatican Rock."

14. Duckler recalls *Menagerie* as the first cassette recorded at Woofbark. In fact, liner notes for *Still Waters*, the preceding album, also reference Woofbark.

15. "Elliott Smith (1969–2003)," *Willamette Week*, October 29, 2003. http://wweek.com/editorial /2952/4489.

16. Kagler, "Elliott Smith: Better Off Than Dead."

17. Steve Pickering recorded this jam session and very kindly made the recording available to me.

18. All these quotes are derived from Lincoln High School yearbooks during the years Elliott attended.

19. See *Taking Root*, a 1985 Hampshire guide sponsored by the Advising and Alumni Relations offices, by Mark Tuchman and Barbara Kann.

20. Ibid.

21. This student was Ethan Lewis.

22. Interview Neil Karras, June 22, 2012.

23. Tracks were as follows: A side—"Expectation," "Small Talk," "Key Biscayne," "This Bed," "Catholic." B side—"Fifteen Minutes," "The Real Thing," "Slapstick," "Clark Bar," "Bald Faced Lie." Engineering was by both Lash and Karras, all songs written by Garrick Duckler and Elliott Smith, except for "Small Talk," credited to the entire band. Date of release is 1989.

24. Autumn de Wilde, *Elliott Smith* (San Francisco: Chronicle Books, 2007).

25. Ibid.

Chapter Four: Some Reverse Pyromaniac

1. SP Clarke, "History of Portland Rock," http://www.spclarke.com/?page_id=20.

2. Ibid.

3. Ibid.

4. Interview Tony Lash, October 28, 2011.

5. Interview Pete Krebs, January 24, 2012.

6. Interview Jason Mitchell, January 7, 2012.

7. The B side was "Day-Glo" (or "Joe Louis Punchout"). The record was produced by Mike Lastra and Hazel in July 1992. The cover has Hazel at the top in orange, above swirling flames obscuring some naked background bacchanalia. The vinyl itself is also orange.

8. For the record, there was one prior release, but under a subsidiary label called Wahini Records. This was, officially and nominally, pre–Cavity Search. The first seven-inch was by Jerry Joseph. Swofford calls it a "guinea pig" effort, a sort of testing of the waters to see whether they could actually do what they set out to do.

9. Kagler, "Elliott Smith: Better Off Than Dead."

10. Interview Brandt Peterson, December 4, 2011.

11. Neil Gust interview, "Five Years Later," Oregon Public Broadcasting, "Think Out Loud" series, October, 2008.

12. Interview Jason Mitchell, January 7, 2012.

13. See Elaine Beebe, "Punked Out: Half of Heatmiser's Songs Are Straight," *The Tribune*, May 5, 1994.

14. Abernathy, William "Yellow Heat," *The Rocket*, May 25–June 8, 1994, Issue #182.

15. See Elaine Beebe, "Punked Out: Half of Heatmiser's Songs Are Straight," *The Tribune*, May 5, 1994.

16. Ibid.

17. Abernathy, "Yellow Heat," *The Rocket*, May 25–June 8, 1994, Issue #182.

18. See Elaine Beebe, "Punked Out: Half of Heatmiser's Songs Are Straight," *The Tribune*, May 5, 1994.

19. Interview Brandt Peterson, December 4, 2011.

20. Brendan Joel Kelley, "XO, Elliott," *Phoenix New Times*, October 30, 2003.

21. Interview Jason Mitchell, January 7, 2012.

22. Interview JJ Gonson, May 15, 2012.

23. See http://www.daggerzine.com/interviews_lisafancher.html.

24. See "Interview With Lisa Fancher," http://punkmusic.about.com/od/recordlabels/a/An-Interview -With-Lisa-Fancher-Of-Frontier-Records.htm. Accessed April 7, 2013.

25. Interview with Jeff Scharlau, titled "Come on Feel the Warmth, Heatmiser," 1993.

26. Ibid.

27. Interview Leslie Uppinghouse, April 20, 2012.

28. See piece Abernathy, *The Rocket*, May 25–June 8, 1994.

29. Interview Brandt Peterson, December 4, 2011.

30. Interview JJ Gonson, February 14, 2002.

31. Interview James Ewing, June 25, 2012.

32. de Wilde, *Elliott Smith*, 60–61.

33. Interview JJ Gonson, February 14, 2002.

Chapter Five: Yesteryear Soon

1. See, for descriptions of Elliott's genius, http://louderthanwar.com. January 8, 2011, Rob Haynes.

2. Interview Christopher Cooper, October 12, 2001.

3. *Sunk Music* interview, June 1995.

4. Ibid.

5. "Misery Has Company," *Los Angeles Times*, April 19, 1998. See: http://articles.latimes.com/1998 /apr/19/entertainment/ca-40637. Accessed April 7, 2013.

6. Kagler, "Elliott Smith: Better Off Than Dead."

7. Interview Tony Lash, October 28, 2011.

8. See, for a close and thoughtful analysis of Smith's musical aesthetic, Elizabeth Newton, "Between the Bars: The Early Musical Language of Elliott Smith," Summer Research, Paper 53 (2010). Accessible at http://soundideas.pugetsound.edu/summer_research/53.

9. See M. Bates, "Walkin' After Midnight," http://jimzine.tripod.com/no1/elliott.html. Accessed April 7, 2013.

10. See Barnaby Smith, *Roman Candle* review, *The Quietus*, http://thequietus.com/articles/04066 -elliott-smith-roman-candle-reissue-review. Accessed April 7, 2013.

11. See "Elliott Smith: One of Us Is on the Moon," http://www.mtv.com/bands/s/smith_elliott/news _feature_102903/index3.jhtml. Accessed April 7, 2013.

12. Interview Christopher Cooper, October 10, 2011.

13. See "Elliott Smith (1969–2003)," at http://wweek.com/popup/print.php?index=4489.

14. See "Elliott Smith Album Guide," *Rolling Stone*, http://www.rollingstone.com/music/artists /elliott-smith/albumguide. Accessed April 7, 2013.

15. Interview Leslie Uppinghouse, April 17, 2012.

16. John Graham and Mark Baumgarten, "Elliott Smith: Errant Son," *Willamette Week*, http://www .wweek.com/portland/article-4196-1997.html. Accessed April 7, 2013.

17. Communication with Garrick Duckler, May 25, 2012.

18. Kagler, "Elliott Smith: Better Off Than Dead," in the "bonus material" section.

19. Interview JJ Gonson, January 31, 2012.

20. Tyler Agnew, "Precluded Predecessors, Vol. 1: Heatmiser," *Treble*, http://treblezine.com/columns /112.html. Accessed April 7, 2013.

21. See Elliott Smith official website, http://www.sweetadeline.net/rocket49.html.

22. Interview Pete Krebs, January 24, 2012.

23. Interview Leslie Uppinghouse, April 17, 2012.

24. "Back Where They Started," *Filter Magazine*, May/June 2003.

25. See Elliott Smith official website, http://www.sweetadeline.net/rocket49.html.

26. The Haystack Calhoun connection was suggested to me by an Elliott Smith fan, Julie McNamara.

27. Bates, "Walkin' After Midnight."

28. For more on this episode as well as Kill Rock Stars and K Records, see Mark Baumgarten's excellent history of that era, *Love Rock Revolution* (Seattle: Sasquatch Books, 2012).

29. See http://www.well-rounded.com/music/reviews/elliottsmith_intv.html.

30. Dale Kawashima, "Top Success Story: Cutting-Edge Music Publisher and Manager Margaret Mittleman," *SongwriterUniverse*, http://www.songwriteruniverse.com/mittleman.html. Accessed April 7, 2013.

31. de Wilde, *Elliott Smith*, 215.

32. Kelley, "XO, Elliott."

33. See "The Over/Under: Elliott Smith," *Magnet Magazine*, March 31, 2009, http://www .magnetmagazine.com/2009/03/31/the-overunder-elliott-smith. Accessed April 7, 2013.

34. See, for instance, Allmusic.com. See: http://www.allmusic.com/search/all/elliott+smith. Accessed April 7, 2013.

35. See Elliott Smith official website, http://www.sweetadeline.net/ross.html.

Chapter Six: Sweet High Notes

1. Greil Marcus, *Like a Rolling Stone: Bob Dylan at the Crossroads* (New York: PublicAffairs, 2005).

2. See OPB radio show interview, "Five Years Later," October 21, 2008.

3. See Chandler and Wagner, *The Rocket*, April 9, 1997.

4. Interview with Carsten Wohlfeld, 1998. See: http://www.lunakafe.com/moon44/usor44.php. Accessed April 7, 2013.

5. Dornan, "Elliott Smith."

6. Kelley, "XO, Elliott."

7. RJ Smith, "Elliott Smith: He's Mr. Dyingly Sad, and You're Mystifyingly Glad," *SPIN*, http:// www.spin.com/articles/no-easy-way-out. Accessed April 7, 2013.

8. Interview Dorien Garry, August 7, 2012.

9. See *Under the Radar* interview, 2003.

10. These quotes are from Alex Stein and Yahia Lababidi, *The Artist as Mystic* (Victoria, Australia: Onesuch Press, 2012).

11. *Q Magazine*, January 2011, 102–04.

12. de Wilde, *Elliott Smith*.

13. Ibid.

14. Ibid.

15. Ibid.

16. Ibid., 66.

17. Ibid.

18. Ibid.

19. Ibid., 69.

20. Ibid., 70.

21. Ibid., 69.

22. See Elliott Smith official website, http://www.sweetadeline.net/pamart.html.

Chapter Seven: Robot Hand

1. de Wilde, *Elliott Smith*, 154.

2. Interview Barney Hoskyns, April 30, 1998.

3. Ibid.

4. Jem Cohen chose not to do an interview for this book but he was willing to corroborate certain facts about his film *Lucky Three*.

5. See Ross Spears interview, sweetadeline.net. See: http://www.sweetadeline.net/ross.html. Accessed April 7, 2013.

6. Ibid.

7. Greg Kot, "Who Is John Brion (and is there anything he can't do?)," *Chicago Tribune*, http://articles.chicagotribune.com/2003-02-12/features/0302120057_1_jon-brion-instruments-aimee -mann. Accessed April 7, 2013.

8. Ibid.

9. Ibid.

10. Ibid.

11. de Wilde, *Elliott Smith*.

12. Ibid.

13. Ibid.

14. Interview Barney Hoskyns, April 30, 1998.

15. Ibid.

16. See "Music by Day" interview, November 20, 2007. See: http://www.musicbyday.com/steve-hanft -interview/16/. Accessed April 7, 2013.

17. Interview Nelson Gary, March 27, 2012.

18. Mark Pittman, "Memory Lane: Remembering Elliott Smith," *Being There*, http://beingtheremag .com/archives/content/0502/smith.html. Accessed April 7, 2013.

Chapter Eight: A Symbol Meaning Infinity

1. Casey Jarman, "Missing Misery," *Willamette Week*, http://wweek.com/portland/article-18112 -missing_misery.html. Accessed April 7, 2013.

2. Bates, "Walkin' After Midnight."

3. de Wilde, *Elliott Smith*, 218.

4. Keith Cameron, "Pretty Barfly," *NME*, reproduced on http://www.sweetadeline.net/barfly.html.

5. Interview Jennifer Chiba, October 9, 2010.

6. de Wilde, *Elliott Smith*, 79.

7. See recording sessions link at http://alphabettown.freeforums.org.

8. John Mulvey, "Brood on the Tracks, *NME*, April 8, 2000. Reproduced at http://wwwsweetadeline .net/nme00.html.

9. Ibid.

10. Nick Duerden, *Q Magazine*, August 2000. See: http://www.sweetadeline.net/q00.html. Accessed April 7, 2013.

11. Interview Dave Leto, September 27, 2012.

12. *NME* chat, March 28, 2000. See http://www.sweetadeline.net/3280ochat.html.

13. Paige La Grone, "Go Figure," *Mean*, May/June 2000.

14. de Wilde, *Elliott Smith*, 219.

15. Alex Steininger, "Interview: Elliott Smith," *In Music We Trust*, http://www.inmusicwetrust.com /articles/34h03.html. Accessed April 7, 2013.

16. Michael Kimmelman, "From Berlin's Hole of Forgottenness, a Spell of Songs," New York Times, http://www.nytimes.com/2008/12/25/arts/design/25abroad.html?_r=1&. Accessed April 7, 2013.

17. Ibid.

18. Valania, "Elliott Smith: Emotional Rescue."

19. Interview Shon Sullivan, December 31, 2010.

20. Ibid.

21. As of October 2012, this entire show can be seen on YouTube.com at http://www.youtube.com /watch?v=O_ZpXFoO3I8.

22. "Flaming Lips Star Remembers Elliott Smith," *NME*, http://www.nme.com/news/elliott-smith /15386. Accessed April 7, 2013.

23. The clip can be seen here: http://www.youtube.com/watch?v=-hLVl7Asp3k.
24. E-mail exchange, Valerie Deerin.
25. These lyrics are from the final version of the tune, its finished form. At Silver Lake Lounge he was less direct. There he simply noted true love's cost, how it required more than anybody could earn.
26. R. Daniel Foster, "Curiosity for Rent: Snow White cottages in Los Feliz," *Los Angeles Times*, http://latimesblogs.latimes.com/home_blog/2011/11/snow-white-cottages-silver-lake.html.
27. Interview Barb Martinez, July 2012.
28. Ibid.
29. de Wilde, *Elliott Smith*, 211.
30. Interview Jennifer Chiba, December 2, 2010.
31. See *SPIN*, October 2004, Liam Gowing, "Mr. Misery."
32. Jonathan Valania, "All Things Must Pass," *Magnet Magazine*, http://www.magnetmagazine.com /2005/01/28/elliott-smith-all-things-must-pass/. Accessed April 7, 2013.[AU: date of retrieval?]
33. See *SPIN*, October 2004, Gowing.

Chapter Nine: Can't Make a Sound

1. Interview with Nelson Gary, April 16, 2011.
2. The essay is by Nelson Gary. It's titled "I'll be Your Mirror: Blue Mask," and it appeared in the online publication Heroin Times, date unknown. Provided to author by Nelson Gary.
3. Ibid.
4. Interview Nelson Gary, April 16, 2011.
5. Interview Jerry Schoenkopf, March 27, 2012.
6. Kagler, "Elliott Smith: Better Off Than Dead."
7. See, for a review of these charges, http://www.listener.co.nz/uncategorized/back-to-earth/print.
8. See, for this nightmare and one other, Valania, "All Things Must Pass."
9. Interview Jennifer Chiba, October 25, 2010.
10. de Wilde, *Elliott Smith*, 61.
11. Interview Dorien Garry, August 22, 2012.
12. Interview Jerry Schoenkopf, March 27, 2012.
13. I have seen these two letters, and read each closely, taking written notes on them.
14. It arrived in the mail the day he died.
15. An initial police report erroneously gave the name on the note as "Elliot," as if it had been misspelled. That was a simple recording error. The note in fact was signed "Elliott."

CODA: The Hero Killed the Clown

1. The L.A. County Coroner's report is available online, in partial form, including the autopsy report. See: http://www.thesmokinggun.com/documents/crime/rockers-autopsy-doesnt-rule-out -homicide. Accessed April 7, 2013.
2. Interview Lisa Scheinin, May 2011. This was an e-mail correspondence spanning one full week. Scheinin was interviewed again in early 2013 on two separate occasions.
3. For this and more from a letter Gowing wrote to an Elliott Smith fan who had questioned his initial article in *SPIN* magazine, see http://www.myspace.com/justiceforelliottsmith/blog /537716700.
4. Ibid.
5. Schoenkopf told me that, in his view, if Elliott had wanted to commit suicide, he would have done it by heroin overdose, not stabbing.
6. de Wilde, *Elliott Smith*, 221.

INDEX

A NOTE ON THE AUTHOR

William Todd Schultz is a professor at Pacific University in Oregon. He edited and contributed to the groundbreaking *Handbook of Psychobiography*, and curates the book series Inner Lives, analyses of significant artists and political figures. His own book in the series, *Tiny Terror*, examines the writings of Truman Capote. He is also the author of *An Emergency in Slow Motion*, a study of the art and personality of Diane Arbus. He blogs for *Psychology Today*. His personal website is williamtoddschultz.com. Follow him on Twitter at @WTSchultz.